NETWORKS

In the last 20 years interest in network phenomena has grown immensely among anthropologists, psychologists, political scientists, economists and lawyers. Empirical observation shows that network arrangements can be found in many branches of business. This is often linked to rapid changes in today's markets and technologies, but it is not the only reason. Legal institutions have been at the centre of private law since the industrial revolution but today contracts and corporations cannot cope with the risks and opportunities posed by networks. Legal practice needs solutions which go beyond the classical traditions of thinking in the dichotomy of contract and corporation. This volume is the outcome of a conference held in Fribourg, Switzerland, which focused on the legal treatment of contractual networks, in particular questions of network expectations, the fragility of network institutions, and the question of how law can minimise network specific risks towards third parties. The contributors, among them many of the world's leading scholars in this field, include Roger Brownsword, Simon Deakin, Gunther Teubner, Hugh Collins and Marc Amstutz. The book will be of interest to scholars of contract, corporate law, and legal theory.

International Studies in the Theory of Private Law: Volume 6

International Studies in the Theory of Private Law

This series of books edited by a distinguished international team of legal scholars aims to investigate the normative and theoretical foundations of the law governing relations between citizens. The context for such investigations of private law systems is set by important modern tendencies in systems of governance. The advent of the regulatory state marks the withdrawal of the state from direct control and management of social and economic activity, and the adoption instead of procedural regulation and co-regulatory strategies that promote the use of private law techniques of ordering and self-regulation in social and economic interactions between citizens. The tendency known as globalisation and the corresponding increases in cross-border trade produce the responses of transnational regulation of commerce and private governance regimes, and these new systems of governance challenge the hegemony of traditional national private law systems. Furthermore, these tendencies towards transnational governance regimes compel an interaction between different national legal traditions, with their differences in culture and philosophy as well as their differences based upon variations in market systems, which provokes questions not only about competing policy frameworks but also about the nature and adequacy of different kinds of legal reasoning.

The series encompasses a diverse range of theoretical approaches in the examination of these issues including approaches using socio-legal methods, economics, critical theory, systems theory, regulation theory, and moral and political theory. With the aim of stimulating an international discussion of these issues, volumes will be published in Germany, France, and the United Kingdom in one of the three languages.

Editors

Hugh Collins, *London School of Economics*
Christian Joerges, *European University Institute Florence*
Antoine Lyon-Caen, *Université de Paris X-Nanterre*
Horatia Muir Watt, *Université de Paris I*
Gunther Teubner, *Frankfurt University*
James Q Whitman, *Yale Law School, New Haven CA*

Volumes published with Hart Publishing, Oxford

1. David Campbell, Hugh Collins und John Wightman (eds), *Implicit Dimensions of Contract: Discrete, Relational and Network Contracts* (2003)
2. Christian Joerges, Inger-Johanne Sand and Gunther Teubner (eds), *Transnational Governance and Constitutionalism* (2004)
3. Oren Perez, *Ecological Sensitivity and Global Legal Pluralism: Rethinking the Trade and Environment Debate* (2004)
4. Harm Schepel, *The Constitution of Private Governance* (2004).
5. Nili Cohen and Ewan McKendrick, *Comparative Remedies for Breach of Contract* (2005)

Volumes published in German by Nomos Verlagsgesellschaft, Baden-Baden

1. Peer Zumbansen, *Ordnungsmuster im modern Wohlfahrtsstaat: Lernerfahrungen zwischen Staat, Geseelschaft und Vertrag* (2000).
2. Dan Wielsch, *Freiheit und Funktion: Zur Struktur- und Theoriegeschichte des Rechts der Wirtschaftsgesellschaft* (2001).
3. Marc Amstutz, *Evolutorisches Wirtschaftsrecht: Vorstudien zum Recht und seiner Methode in den Diskurskollisionen der Marktgesellschaft* (2001).
4. Christian Joerges and Gunther Teubner, Gunther (eds), *Rechtsverfassungsrecht: Recht-Fertigungen zwischen Sozialtheorie und Privatrechtsdogmatik* (2003).
5. Gunther Teubner, *Netzwerk als Vertragsverbund: Virtuelle Unternehmen, Franchising, Just in Time in sozialwissenschaftlicher und juristischer Sicht* (2004)
6. Daniel Dédeyan, *Macht durch Zeichen: Rechtsprobleme der Kennzeichnung und Zertifikation* (2004)
7. Dietrich Claus Becker, *Von Namen und Nummern: Kollisionen unverträglicher Rechtsmassen in Internet* (2005)
8. Vagias Karavas, *Digitale Grundrechte: Elemente einer Verfassung des Informationsflusses im Internet* (2007)

Networks

Legal Issues of Multilateral Co-operation

Edited by Marc Amstutz and Gunther Teubner

·HART·
PUBLISHING

OXFORD AND PORTLAND, OREGON
2009

Published in North America (US and Canada) by
Hart Publishing
c/o International Specialized Book Services
920 NE 58th Avenue, Suite 300
Portland, OR 97213–3786
USA
Tel: +1 503 287 3093 or toll-free: (1) 800 944 6190
Fax: +1 503 280 8832
E-mail: orders@isbs.com
Website: http://www.isbs.com

Hart Publishing, 16C Worcester Place, OX1 2JW
Telephone: +44 (0)1865 517530 Fax: +44 (0)1865 510710
E-mail: mail@hartpub.co.uk
Website: http://www.hartpub.co.uk

British Library Cataloguing in Publication Data
Data Available

ISBN: 978-184113-945-6

Typeset by Columns Design Ltd, Reading
Printed and bound in Great Britain by
Lightning Source UK Ltd

Preface

What is Legal Analysis of Contractual Networks?

In the past 20 years, interest in network analyses in the humanities and social sciences has grown immensely. Not only sociology, anthropology and psychology, but also political science, economics and—last but not least—the law have been directing their attention to network phenomena to an increasing extent. What are the reasons for this increasing interest in networks?

First, there is the empirical observation that numerous indications for a hitherto unknown spreading of network arrangements between organisations can be detected in many branches of business.[1] Often, this observation is linked to swift changes in today's markets and technologies: industry has responded with radical re-organisation which aims at more disaggregate and more flexible production arrangements. But perhaps the fascination which the network phenomenon causes must be explained on a more profound basis. It is not the empirical frequency of the network phenomenon, but rather the circumstance that this phenomenon goes beyond the scope of the forms of action established in both the economy and in society that should be considered as crucial: the network can neither be subsumed under the category of market, nor under the organisation category.[2]

This also indicates the difficulties with which the network phenomenon confronts the law. The legal institutions which have been at the centre of private law since the industrial revolution—contract and association—cannot cope with the risks and opportunities posed by networks. Numerous cases brought before the courts show that these institutions are not able to deal with the co-ordination and liability problems which are generated by networks. Legal practice needs solutions which go beyond the classical traditions of thinking in the dichotomy of contract and association—without being able to count on veritable support from legal doctrine in doing so. This provides the motive to invite legal scholarship to develop solutions that are held to be adequate for the network phenomenon.

This volume is the outcome of a conference held between 6 and 9 October 2005 in Fribourg, Switzerland. In this conference, an invitation

[1] See, generally, WW Powell, 'Neither Market nor Hierarchy: Network Forms of Organisation' (1990) 12 *Research in Organisational Behaviour* 295–336.

[2] See, generally, G Teubner, *Coincidentia Oppositorum*: Hybrid Networks beyond Contract and Organisation' (ch 1), in this volume.

was addressed to legal scholars with different legal and cultural backgrounds in order to engage in an international discussion on the legal treatment of contractual networks. The results of this discussion are presented here along the lines of three different questions, which are crucial for the legal treatment of contractual networks.

The first question concerns the issue of the emergence of contractual networks in law. We have already referred to the overstraining of law caused by the emergence of contractual networks, since the two modern institutions of law, contract and organisation, are ill-suited to deal with this new social phenomenon. Contractual networks defy a clear-cut subsumption under one of these institutions, thus bringing the law into confusion. So, what kind of cognitive and normative resources does the legal system have to mobilise in order to grasp this new phenomenon?

The second question refers to the internal network perspectives. Contractual networks are fragile institutions, which are always in danger of dissolving. People enter contractual networks because they rely on specific trust relations. But trust is always endangered by opportunism, which is subsequently the result of 'capture' of the network parties in a so-called 'double bind' situation. Due to certain economic developments, network parties are exposed to two different and, at the same time, contradictory demands. On the one hand, they are forced to co-operate with each other, and, on the other, they are forced to act competitively. How can law untangle such a paradoxical situation? What can law's institutional contribution to the stabilisation of these fragile institutions be?

The third question deals with the external network perspective. For all their flexibility and productivity, networks have acquired a bad reputation for their 'organised irresponsibility'. Contractual networks generate risks towards third parties because of their chameleon-like character. When it comes to issues of liability towards third parties, the parties of a contractual network are involved in another kind of opportunistic behaviour: this time, they point to the internal structure of the contractual network as a mere bundle of bilateral contracts, thus suppressing certain 'organisational' elements of the contractual network in order to avoid liability. This kind of opportunism has to be dealt with by law. Accordingly, the question is: How can law minimise these network-specific risks for third parties?

I. NETWORK EXPECTATIONS AND THEIR LEGAL EMBODIMENT: A MERE QUESTION OF LEGAL TRANSLATION?

'Network is not a legal concept'.[3] Although Richard Buxbaum is right on this, his statement can, nevertheless, only be the starting point for our enquiry into law's capacity to reflect upon the network phenomenon. This is, indeed, a question of an epistemological character, as it refers to law's capacity to quasi 'transcend' its own borders and 'reach' its own environment. In systems-theoretical terms, we can even argue that this is a question of justice, if we actually understand justice—as it has been defined by Niklas Luhmann—namely, as 'adequately complex internal consistency of legal decisions'.[4] But how can law do justice towards the network expectations that arise outside of its own '*forum proprium*'? To put it more clearly: How can law show responsiveness towards the network expectations that arise from bilateral contracts, linking a certain number of actors beyond the explicit contractual substance of these bilateral contracts? As we stated before, traditional contract law is blind to these kinds of expectations because of the dominance of the principle of privity, which forbids any reference to external expectations other than those of the parties of the bilateral contract. But the help that the law of organisations offers here also proves to be insufficient, as it is not sensitive enough towards such flexible arrangements as contractual networks that consist of a number of bilateral contracts. Quo vadis, then?

Gunther Teubner abandons, from the outset, the hope that empirical results or theoretical insights from the social sciences can guide law in a direct manner. As he points out in his introductory essay,

> the decisive legal irritations are not supplied by inter-disciplinary contact with social science disciplines *stricto sensu*, but with normatively-loaded reflexive practices in various social fields.

In other words, 'network expectations', as mapped by social scientists, cannot be translated directly into law. A transfer of reflexive social practices into legal doctrine is impossible. The only way out of this impasse of mutual exclusion of legal doctrine and social sciences is, instead, the irritation of legal doctrine towards the development of conceptual innovations by its own, internal, path-dependent evolutionary logic. Teubner also takes as his starting point Buxbaum's statement that 'network is not a legal concept', but he goes one step further, as his analysis tries to discover legal complements for what legal sociologists call a 'contractual network'. It is in the legal figure of the so-called

[3] RM Buxbaum, 'Is "Network" a Legal Concept?' (1993) 149 *Journal of Institutional and Theoretical Economics* 698 at 704.

[4] N Luhmann, *Das Recht der Gesellschaft* (Frankfurt aM, Suhrkamp, 1993) 214 *et seq*.

'connected contracts' ('*Vertragsverbund*') that Teubner identifies a potential doctrinal basis for developing a legal constitution of contractual networks from within the law.

Although he does not follow a systems-theoretical perspective in his essay, Jean Nicolas Druey still shares with Teubner the same opinion about law's exclusion of the world of facts, as he calls it. But he is, at the same time, quite sceptical about the law's ability to be irritated by network concepts; this scepticism is also shared by other contributors of this volume, such as Hugh Collins, to give one example. The reason for his concern lies mainly in the general 'hype' around the term 'network'. It is true that the term 'network' has been used and celebrated in the relevant literature in a rather hypertrophic way. For Druey, the discussions about this concept have not contributed to its further clarification; the network concept remains, instead, a very ambiguous one that is in need of further differentiation. For example, many characteristics which have been attributed to the network concept so far, such as—in the words of Druey—the *mixture formula,* which describes networks as a combination of market and hierarchy, are also typical in other contexts, such as that of an organisation. As long as the term 'network' remains so vague and undifferentiated, it can hardly be absorbed by law because of law's 'natural' resistance to such vagueness. Druey draws our attention here to the evolution of the concept of *societas*, which also had to wait a long time till it could be established as a well-defined legal concept. It only remains to be seen if the network concept will also have the same destiny.

Marc Amstutz's concluding essay in this volume is positioned somewhere in between these two approaches. On the one hand, he shares Druey's reservations, on the other, he acknowledges Teubner's plea for a legal re-construction of network expectations mainly because of the risks that they generate. However, he does not share Teubner's optimism towards legal scholarship's ability to create a new constitution of the network on the basis of the concept of 'connected contracts'. He therefore argues for a (from a doctrinal perspective) different approach, which he calls a 'contract collision' approach. His suggestion is that, in cases of network conflicts, one has to use the rules applicable to the individual contracts of the network as quasi conflict-of-laws norms, and thus try to build the blocks of a legal constitution for the entire contractual network. The crucial question is, of course, under which rules of a contract out of the whole contractual nexus should a network conflict be subsumed? Inspired by the conflicts-of-law[?] scholarship, Amstutz formulates the following criterion: conflicts in a contractual network come under the contract whose rules in the specific case ensure the functionality of the network as such. He then illuminates his approach by analysing relevant decisions of the Swiss Supreme Court.

Amstutz's approach to the complete issue is, in this regard, in line with Roger Brownword's proposal, which encourages us to work with a 'general network principle', according to which the fact that bilateral contracts are part of a network should be taken into account in legal analysis. In his essay, Brownsword succeeds in demonstrating that contractual networks are not as exotic as many might think. Instead, they are—in numerous instances—typical paradigms of self-imposed governance structures, as in the case of bilateral contracts. Consequently, by importing the network argument into legal doctrine, we enable ourselves to solve doctrinal puzzles that have bothered the courts and academia for a long time now (because of our obsession with the privity of contract), such as, for example, the puzzle with the spill-over effects from one bilateral contract to another. In this context, Brownsword makes a very insightful distinction when it comes to contractual networks: he distinguishes between voluntary, versus imposed networks in contracts. In the case of the voluntary networks, we are actually dealing with 'true' contractual regimes, whose justification lies in the genuine will of the parties. In the case of the imposed networks (Brownsword speaks here of imposed governance structures), the justification for the imposition of the network concept is, instead, based upon substantive goals, such as fairness or efficiency. The network argument is, however, legally relevant in both cases, as the general principle always remains the same: in both cases, bipolar contracts are superseded by a unifying objective.

While Brownsword argues, for the above-mentioned reasons, against consigning networks to history, it is to history that Simon Deakin turns in order to assess the network phenomenon today. For Deakin, network forms are not a manifestation of the 'post-industrial society' of the late-twentieth century, but rather a very old phenomenon, successfully suppressed by the emergence of the industrial society. It is, concretely, the medieval guild, in which Deakin recognises a predecessor of the various network forms today. By studying how the medieval guild declined on the eve of the industrial society, thus paving the way for the emergence of the integrated business enterprise, we can—according to Deakin—learn a lot about the legal policies which we have to deploy if we do not want present-day network forms to share the same fate as their predecessors.

Poul Kjaer challenges this view of the network phenomenon as the return of the medieval guild. By deploying the systems-theoretical distinction between *stratificatory* and *functional differentiation*, he argues that the function of networks in late modernity, characterised by a radical functional differentiation, is fundamentally different from the function of the guilds in the medieval societies, namely, societies with 'a strong differentiation between the centre and the periphery as well as a high level of stratification'. While guilds in the medieval societies handled—

among other things—the exchange between centre and periphery, contemporary networks act instead 'as integrative measures under the condition of radical functional differentiation'. Accordingly, one has to be cautious when using old concepts in order to assess modern ones.

One of the main goals of this first theoretical section is not to reach an agreement, but to advance polyphony. Admittedly, this polyphony suits the nature of the network phenomenon best because of its multi-faceted character, but it also promotes a better understanding of the legal problems that arise with the emergence of contractual networks. As mentioned above, these problems mainly concern issues of solidarity among network participants, as well as issues of liability towards third parties. Thus, we come to the next section of the volume, in which the internal relationships among the network participants and the duties deriving from them will be closely explored.

II. INTERNAL PERSPECTIVES OF CONTRACTUAL NETWORKS: THE VIEW FROM WITHIN

One of the most interesting questions regarding contractual networks is that of whether network advantages are granted to the initiator of the network, for his or her organisational work, or to the network partners. This is a question which is frequently raised in franchise networks and one which has so far been dealt with by courts in a number of cases, especially in Germany.[5] Hence, the question is of great interest, since we can, at this micro-level, clearly observe the nature of contractual networks, as well as the legal doctrine's difficulties in dealing with the network phenomenon in general. In franchise-systems, the suppliers of the network are, indeed, entering into isolated bilateral contracts with the initiator of the network. The latter can, in turn, negotiate certain advantages with these suppliers, such as purchase rebates from a relative power position, from which he makes capital out of his bilateral contracts with the franchisees. Taking this picture as a starting point, one certainly misses the quasi-vertical integration of the franchise system if one only stresses the fact that the various actors are only related by isolated bilateral contracts. In such cases, the franchisor indeed seems to be free to decide as to whether he will pass on the network advantages or not. But is this, indeed, the case? Does not the multilateral interconnection in the franchise system produce network effects that would justify a duty to pass on network advantages? This is the topic of Reinhard Böhner's interesting essay. The author discusses the various cases that have been

[5] See R Böhner, 'Asset-sharing in Franchise Network. The Obligation to Pass on Network Benefits' (ch 9), in this volume.

decided by German courts, in which he was also personally involved as the attorney on the franchisee-side. The aforementioned question has been answered by the German Federal Court of Justice in the affirmative in three leading cases, but, as Böhner criticises, on shaky doctrinal grounds. The obligation to pass on network advantages in these cases was subject to standard contract clauses, which had to be interpreted, and thus the court decided the cases as a question of the correct interpretation of standard contract terms. But, as Böhner argues, for the future we have to decide this question upon more stable doctrinal grounds, as it is possible that, following this jurisprudence, the franchisors will delete from their contracts with the franchisees such provisions, thus leaving the issue open once more for adjudication. Thus, Böhner explores from a German *lex lata* perspective, with much detail, on which doctrinal grounds this question should be solved in the future. Even more interesting, though, is his analysis of law's contribution to the stabilisation of these fragile social institutions, as they are always inclined to self-destruction because of the opportunism of their actors.

Peter W Heermann deals in his essay not only with the problem of profit sharing, but also with issues such as the division of risk, piercing legal liability within the network and external network liability. At the same time, however, his inquiry seems to be narrowly framed, as he only explores so-called (mini-) networks, such as credit card transactions and bank transfers. The synallagmatic structure of this kind of network, which is analysed on the basis of his concept of the so-called trilateral (or rather multilateral) synallagma, might serve though as *landmarks* for legally assessing broader contractual networks. In a dogmatically elaborate essay, Heermann analyses the points at which his concept diverges from that of Teubner. These differences mainly pertain to the legal consequences that he draws out of his concept of the trilateral synallagma, as well as the general question of the legal constitution of connected contracts. By making the distinction between connected contracts *with* synallagmatic structures and connected contracts *without* synallagmatic structures, he argues that the legal consequences for the former primarily derive from the principles of the trilateral or multilateral synallagma—in other words, from the performance obligations stemming from the various bilateral connected contracts—whereas, in the case of the latter, the legal consequences have to be defined either on the basis of a further development of his concept of a trilateral (or rather multilateral) synallagma, or according to the law of contractual associations, depending on the degree of legal interdependence of the various bilateral connected contracts. In his analysis, Heermann shows reluctance towards Teubner's sociologically-charged concept, although he acknowledges many of the virtues of Teubner's sociological observations. He nevertheless seems to trust more in positive law and what it provides.

With respect to this, Marina Wellenhofer's approach is in line with Heermann's approach. To the fundamental question of whether the network phenomenon, the affirmation of the network purpose and the specific structure of interests within networks really necessitate new legal constructions, her answer is negative. Though she acknowledges the legal relevance of network effects, she is, at the same time, quite sceptical about the necessity of developing new legal concepts. In a critical assessment of various legal concepts developed for contractual networks, she tries to show the doctrinal deficiencies of all these concepts. She argues, instead, for a tort law approach to the legal problems that are posed by contractual networks. Her plea for a tort law approach is, indeed, very interesting. Tort law with its reference to *boni mores*, good manners, and customs of trade is closely linked to social practices, social norms and social institutions, and—as a legal concept—it might indeed show a greater responsiveness towards contractual networks, which are also social institutions. However, one has to consider that the nature of the *boni mores* rules is a transitory one and that the question is whether we should hence try to develop a more stable doctrinal basis for dealing with the network phenomenon and its effects, or rather learn to live with these anomalies and their situational interception by tort law?

Cordula Heldt definitely argues for the first alternative in her essay, in which she compares two prima facie entirely different contractual networks, namely, franchising and construction contracts. Her studies focus especially on the internal relationships within these networks. These are the legal relationships of the participants in a construction co-operation (networks of construction contracts) or in a franchise system, which are contractually unconnected. The interesting twist in Heldt's essay is that she is deploying Friedrich August von Hayek's theory of spontaneous orders in order to explore the structures of these contractual networks. According to her view, both types of contract network indicate a structure of semi-spontaneous orders, which is legally reproduced as a multilateral special relationship ('*Sonderverbindung*'). She then goes on to apply this theoretical concept in order to deduce concrete legal consequences concerning the internal relationships of the various participants of both network forms.

III. EXTERNAL PERSPECTIVES OF CONTRACTUAL NETWORKS

Patronage relations, clientelism, '*amici degli amici degli amici*', quasi-feudal trust relations, collusion, restraint of competition, and mafia-like structures are just some of the characteristics that have been attributed to modern networks and that have contributed to their reputation as new institutional forms of 'organised irresponsibility'. Consequently, the law has so far oscillated in its treatment of these new forms of action in modern societies between two extreme positions, namely, between total indifference or strict forbiddance. It is, indeed, a fact that these designations are not ungrounded. In particular, the risks that networks generate towards third parties have certainly contributed a great deal to their bad reputation as quasi-parasitic social institutions. At the same time, these risks also constitute one of the most difficult problems that the law has to tackle today. Therefore, if the stabilisation of these fragile institutions is one of our main goals, then one also has to pose the difficult question of the legal organisation of their relationships within their environment. However, this does not preclude the issue of protection against interference by third parties. The following essays mainly deal with these issues, arguing, in many cases, also for alternatives to legal regulation.

Hugh Collins begins his essay with two stories, both concerning supply chains in the grocery market, in order to illustrate his argument. The first story refers to the imposition, on the part of the supermarkets, of retrospective price variations on suppliers in breach of contract. The second story considers the legal status of consumers in supply chains, as well as their legal rights deriving from it, especially in cases of stock-outs, ie, when the legitimate expectations of the consumers for supply have been frustrated. Collins asks, accordingly, how the network analysis might change our perception of these two cases? And, in broader terms, what is the value of the network argument for legal analysis? In this sense, the questions posed by Collins bring us back to the first section of this volume, where the issue of the legal embodiment of network expectations has been thoroughly analysed. Collins's analysis of the architecture of supply chains highlights many aspects of these contractual arrangements, which remain unseen by the traditional approach, which observes them mainly through the lenses of the private law of sales. The author, nevertheless, doubts if this conceptual analysis of the network architecture of modern supply chains can, indeed, help to develop a normative reorientation of private law, thus sharing the scepticism of many previous authors such as Druey and Wellenhofer. Although he ascertains the fact that the network architecture of supply chains constitutes a distinctive form of business organisation, he nevertheless believes that, instead of trying to develop new legal constructs in order to deal with the results of conflicts arising within the network or with issues of external liability of the network,

> non-legal sanctions may serve sufficiently to protect the network from the disintegrative pressures which arise from opportunism, without the need for the law to re-allocate liability risks.

In other words, Collins argues for a self-regulation of the various participants in such contractual arrangements—a self-regulation that might be more efficient than any legal intervention.

In his commentary of Collins's paper, Stefanos Mouzas offers a detailed empirical analysis of the networks analysed by Collins, as well as a well-founded critique of one of Collins's main assumptions, namely, the one regarding the need for a legal recognition of these networks. The main problem lies, according to Mouzas's view, not so much in the inadequacy of legal concepts for such kinds of contractual networks, as in the encounter of issues such as the external liability of networks. Here, he agrees with Collins that non-legal interventions might be proved to be more efficient than legal ones. However, his distrust towards legal interventions in such cases is based upon the assumption that such interventions might jeopardise the efficiency of one of the most important pillars of our private law system, namely, freedom of contract, which consists—in his words—in leaving parties free to negotiate their own contracts. He therefore argues in favour of a mixture of self-regulation and governmental intervention.

Not only are issues of external liability of contractual networks crucial and in need of legal solutions, but also issues concerning the problem of the protection of networks against interference by third parties. This is the subject of Manfred Wolf's interesting essay. By analysing two cases decided by German Federal Courts—the first, the so-called 'product test case', decided by the Federal Court of Justice (*Bundesgerichtshof* (*BGH*)) and the second, the so-called 'strike case', decided by the Federal Labour Court (*Bundesarbeitsgericht* (*BAG*))[6]—the author tries to develop a stable doctrinal base for encountering the damages that third parties may cause on networks. In a doctrinally elaborate analysis of the German *lex lata*, the author recognises such a legal basis in 'the right on established and ongoing business'. As he mentions in his concluding remarks,

> Network contract systems and, possibly, also—albeit to a lesser extent—chain contract systems should be protected against interference by third parties under the right of the established and ongoing business if they are organised as fixed-supply models, ie, their internal structure is organised in a way that the members of the system are constantly tied together by their contractual relationships and are therefore dependent upon each other.

Wolf's analysis is exemplary in this sense, because it clearly shows how old doctrinal institutions, such as the one analysed in his essay, can be further developed in a very productive way, in order to encounter new challenges posed by contractual networks.

In this sense, Gralf-Peter Calliess's analysis lies not far away from Wolf's productive re-examination of old doctrinal institutions. By using

[6] See M Wolf, 'The Protection of Contractual Networks against Interference by Third Parties' (ch 12), in this volume.

as a case study consumer contracts in fitness clubs, Calliess also highlights the need for thinking productively when dealing with novel issues. Accordingly, the author criticises the traditional view that defines the formal legal structure of fitness clubs as consisting out of a multitude of parallel, but separate, bilateral consumer contracts. This view is—according to the author—distorting, and even leads to inefficient results when it comes to issues of consumer protection in cases of breach of contract. The author argues instead for using the network concept as an argument in order to disclose the real nature of fitness clubs. According to his view,

> [t]he fitness club is specific in creating a club-like structure of mutual subsidies between its members, thus loosening the tight 'do ut des'-synallagma of the typical bilateral business-to-consumer contract.

In this regard, Calliess is in line with Brownsword's argument that we should work with a 'general network principle', as he also shares the belief that the deployment of the network principle will enable us to see the hitherto hidden dimensions of this bundle of bilateral and parallel contracts of which a fitness club consists, and thus regulate them in a more fair and efficient way.

Contractual networks are not the prerogative of private actors alone. In the last decade, we have instead experienced the emergence of such arrangements both among public and private actors, not only at the supra-national level of the European Union, but also within the various nation states. These intensified forms of 'co-operationism' between public and private actors have plunged the law into deep crisis, as Andreas Abegg argues in his essay. This crisis is the product of two explosive implications of these new 'constellations' for the legal system, first, the freeing of the public administration from the rule of the bindingness of statute, and, secondly, the transfer of the duty to provide public goods to the hands of private actors—a duty that has so far been the only prerogative of public actors. Well-defined legal distinctions, such as the one between private and public law, have subsequently been criticised for being totally inadequate to capture the nature of these new arrangements; hence, the term 'hybrid networks' in the relevant literature. But, under these circumstances, what is most feared is the loss of the ability to bring these hybrid networks under legal and democratic control. Abegg develops his argument on the basis of an illustrative case decided by the Swiss Federal Court regarding the third-party effects of an agreement on a code of conduct between the Swiss National Bank and the Swiss Banks. It can be summarised as follows: by using evolutionary systems theory, he suggests viewing this kind of arrangement as effective structural couplings between the political and economic systems, and accordingly, tries to propose appropriate legal rules to protect and reinforce such couplings, and thereby provide the conditions for a process of co-evolution of the relevant systems, so that public interest demands can be satisfactorily harmonised with the demands of the economy. This may involve—according to the author—using the kinds of contractual networks which are the main concern of this volume in order to frame these relationships and provide these couplings.

In his thoughtful comments on Abegg's paper, Terence Daintith challenges this view. As he states,

> [w]hat, for him [Abegg], is a contractual network with a high capacity for structurally-coupling different social systems (politics and economics) with positive results, looks to me like an ingenious, though essentially artificial, use of contract as a formal vehicle for command-and-control regulation, under a scheme whose lack of legitimacy could not be cured without depriving the structure of the very advantages which Abegg attributes to it.

Subsequently, the author criticises the deployment of such a concept for achieving certain regulatory purposes.

The exploration of all these aspects of the network phenomenon forces us at the same time, though, to realise the limits of legal analysis. As one of the authors of this volume put it, the world of facts is far more complex than the law, which relies on a rather simplifying function when it is confronted with the former. This condemns legal analysis not to paralysis, but to an eternal struggle to understand the world outside and to try to develop legal rules that are socially adequate. And this, again, is an issue of 'justice' which cannot be dismissed light-heartedly.

Marc Amstutz, Vaios Karavas,** Gunther Teubner****

* Professor of Commercial and Economic Law, University of Freiburg, Switzerland.

** Associate Professor of Legal Sociology, University of Lucerne, Switzerland.

*** Professor of Private Law and Legal Sociology, Johann Wolfgang Goethe University, Frankfurt, and Centennial Visiting Professor, London School of Economics.

Contents

Part I.

The Emergence of Networks in the Law

1

Coincidentia Oppositorum: *Hybrid Networks Beyond Contract and Organisation*

GUNTHER TEUBNER*

I. THE IMPOSSIBLE NECESSITY OF SOCIOLOGICAL JURISPRUDENCE

'NETWORK IS NOT a legal concept'.[1] If Richard Buxbaum's apodictic judgement is true, then lawyers can have little to say about networks. Should they wish to make appropriate judgements when business networks, franchising arrangements, just-in-time-systems, or virtual enterprises do cross their paths, then they must consult social scientists, such as economists, organisational theorists and sociologists. For better or for worse, they must engage in sociological jurisprudence. Yet, 'sociological jurisprudence' is a pipe-dream. After a heated debate for almost a century, lawyers know that, logically speaking, it is an oxymoron—like a white raven. Practically speaking, it necessarily falters in the face of the normative closure of the legal system. This is a lesson that we are correctly taught, not only by traditional doctrine and by Max Weber's theory of formal legal rationality, but also by advanced systems theory.[2]

I seek to support—and simultaneously to undermine—this claim through concrete examples. My concrete observations are about new network phenomena, how they irritate the courts and provoke the judges to juridical adventures. I will raise the question of whether restrictions in

* Professor of Private Law and Legal Sociology, Johann Wolfgang Goethe University, Frankfurt and Centennial Visiting Professor, London School of Economics.

[1] RM Buxbaum, 'Is "Network" a Legal Concept?' (1993) 149 *Journal of Institutional and Theoretical Economics* 698 at 704.

[2] For legal doctrine, for example, H-M Pawlowski, *Methodenlehre für Juristen: Theorie der Norm und des Gesetzes. Ein Lehrbuch* (Heidelberg, CF Müller, 1999) 74 *et seq*; for formal legal rationality, M Weber (1978) *Economy and Society* (Berkeley CA, University of California Press, 1978) 85 *et seq*; for contemporary systems theory, see N Luhmann, *Law as a Social System* (Oxford, Oxford University Press, 2004) ch 2.

the two common ways in which the law observes its social environment—judicial and legislative reality reconstructions—systematically preclude an adequate treatment of such new social phenomena. Does the law actually need a third mode of observing the so-called 'social reality'? Business co-operation networks provide an example for the observation that this third approach cannot simply be secured through the social sciences, but is instead wholly dependent upon a unique combination of legal doctrine and reflexive social practices. I describe this 'third way' as an effort to irritate the legal system selectively with particular demands from its social environment. I still call it sociological jurisprudence, although, and even because, this is the same form of necessary pipe-dream that 'legal policy analysis' or 'legal economics' represent. Attempting to take a couple of steps along this impossible, but necessary, third way, I shall demonstrate how the legal qualification of networks, and in particular, their legal conditions and their legal consequences, can be tackled through confrontation with non-legal social reality constructs.

***Thesis 1*:** It is a scientistic misconception of the law to believe that empirical results or theoretical insights from the social sciences can guide law to any significant degree. The decisive legal irritations are not supplied by interdisciplinary contact with social science disciplines *stricto sensu*, but with normatively-loaded 'reflexive practices' in various social fields. My example, the dramatic extension of liability throughout network systems, is a judicial reaction to social perceptions of the risks posed by economic networks.

***Thesis 2*:** The 'translation' of reflexive social practices into legal doctrine is not a direct knowledge transfer from the social to the legal field. Private law doctrine can only be persuaded to develop conceptual innovations by its own, internal, path-dependent evolutionary logic. My example is that 'network' is not a legal concept. It is a social construct and its legal complement can only be reconstructed within the law, possibly by developing 'relational contracts' into 'connected contracts' (*Vertragsverbund*).

***Thesis 3*:** One of the most important achievements of sociological jurisprudence is that it has been able to support law's contribution to the problem of how to deal with the paradoxes within social practice. My example is that networks emerge when actors are confronted by paradoxical demands in their environment. The law reacts to such network paradoxes with a new legal concept of 'double-attribution'.

II. PIERCING THE CONTRACTUAL VEIL IN DISTRIBUTION NETWORKS: THREE LEVELS OF LEGAL REALITY CONSTRUCTION

A Japanese car importer built up a dealer distribution system in Germany. The importer had only succeeded in gaining German market entry relatively late in the day and had difficulties in finding responsible dealers. As a consequence, the importer's marketing efforts were reliant upon working relationships with dealers whose business credentials and solvency were not immediately apparent. The contracts stipulated that the vehicles would remain the property of the importer until full payment of the sales price had taken place. A customer took possession of a vehicle from a dealer, paying an initial instalment on the sales price. The customer was given the vehicle, the keys and a road licence, but not the ownership papers since, according to the distribution contracts, these remained in trust until the full payment of the sales price. Under pressure from the dealer and his incorrect claim that full payment was necessary for the internal sales completion, the customer paid the remainder of the sales price, without, however, receiving the ownership papers of the vehicle. On the insolvency of the dealer, the importer demanded the return of the vehicle from the customer. The customer then claimed that the importer, as the central actor within the distribution system, was liable for the failure of the direct dealer to fulfill his legal obligations.

In a courageous judgment, the Karlsruhe Court of Appeal (*Oberlandesgericht*), departed radically from contractual privity, a fundamental principle of German private law.[3] By 'piercing the contractual veil', the Court made the network centre directly liable, although there was no contractual link between the customer and the centre whatsoever. The Court first confirmed the importer's demand for the return of his property[4] and then rejected the customer's claim to having received the property in good faith on the basis that the customer's naïveté constituted gross negligence.[5] Employing a daring sleight of hand, however, they then allowed a compensation claim against the importer. The Court finally decided in favour of direct liability of the central distribution node, and held the importer responsible for the dealer's breach of legal obligations, notwithstanding the independence of the latter.

The grounds for this decision, however, are extremely unconvincing. The judgment is an explosive mixture of German law's principles of organisational responsibility, of directors' liability and of *respondeat superior* for the acts of individual agents. However, the quality of the judgment still fails to improve, even if we make a clear distinction

[3] OLG Karlsruhe (1989) 2 *Neue Zeitschrift für Verkehrsrecht* 434.

[4] § 985 of the German Civil Code (*Bürgerliches Gesetzbuch* (*BGB*)).

[5] § 932(II) BGB and § 366 of the German Commercial Code (*Handelsgesetzbuch* (*HGB*)).

between the various grounds for liability. Either the Court should have fundamentally changed at least one of these principles, explicitly distinguishing it from the previous precedent, or it should have refused to pierce the contractual veil. Currently, precedent in German law would refute the Court's finding that the construction of a business network with dealers of a dubious character gives rise to an organisational liability.[6] To date, organisational liability has only been applicable to authentic legal persons. Its extension to other group phenomena remains in any case anchored in the law of associations, and thus organisational liability has no application to simple contractual relationships.[7] By the same token, the breach of directors' liability, in such a case, is precluded by the conditions of the delictual general clause.[8] Equally, the escape hatch of *respondeat superior* is closed, since independent enterprises simply do not qualify as 'agents' in tort law.[9] In view of these problems, it is little wonder that the Court of Appeal cooked up a strange mixture of these three liability forms and thus neatly avoided the question of whether and, if so, how it wished to overrule the precedent by piercing the contractual veil of a business network which is made up by bipolar contracts.

'The soundest judgment with the dullest opinion'—is the judgment best summed up by this cruel phrase? Certainly, the result is plausible and the justification weak. However, the judgment is not just wrong. This is because the Court was called upon to tackle a phenomenon that cannot be addressed within the concepts of contract and tort—the network phenomenon. In the last few decades, a massive increase in contractual networks has confronted the law with the troublesome implications of an evolutionary trend, which it cannot—in its entirety—decode using its own analytical tools. Independent business units commit themselves to closely interconnected co-operation networks and thus undermine both the distinction between market and hierarchy, and the distinction between contract, torts and corporation. If distribution systems were organised under the law of corporations and labour law, we would still be confronted by the problem of liability, but this would no longer be an issue of 'veil-piercing' liability, nor would it violate the principle of

[6] § 31 *BGB*. See H Heinrichs in O Palandt, *Bürgerliches Gesetzbuch*, 62nd edn (Munich, CH Beck, 2003) § 31, at 3.

[7] H Roth, 'Anmerkung zu OLG Karlsruhe' (1998) 2 *Neue Zeitschrift für Verkehrsrecht* 435–6.

[8] § 823(I) *BGB*.

[9] § 831 *BGB*. See Thomas in O Palandt, *Bürgerliches Gesetzbuch* (n 6 above) § 831, at 8. Several authors urge the courts to overrule this old principle, Roth, 'Anmerkung zu OLG Karlsruhe' (n 7 above); P Bräutigam, *Deliktische Außenhaftung im Franchising* (Baden-Baden, Nomos, 1994) 130 *et seqet seq*; E Pasderski, *Die Außenhaftung des Franchisegebers* (Aachen, Mainz, 1998) 174.

contractual privity. The dealer's behaviour would simply be imputed to the manufacturer/primary dealer, according to established rules of principal/agent law,[10] on the basis of the contractual obligations of the corporation. In contrast, if the distribution were organised between independent business units in a competitive market, then relationships with the external partners of the distribution system could not give rise to 'veil-piercing' liability. Thus, in conclusion, establishing a network between independent enterprises causes judicial irritation. An integrated distribution system which, on the one hand, entails more than simple market relationships, but, on the other, does not create any true organisational relationships, forces the judges to pierce the contractual veil, but, at the same time, causes them huge difficulties when they attempt to justify this decision.

'Judicial irritation' has a double significance.[11] Judges are irritated by networks, and are provoked to respond to anomalies with piercing techniques that contradict the logic of their own system. In turn, judicial precedent on piercing irritates doctrine, which regards such seemingly equity-oriented, ad hoc exceptions to privity of contract as a challenge to the workability of doctrinal concepts.[12] Is traditional doctrine in a position to qualify network phenomena to the extent that simple equitable exceptions can be transformed into conceptually precise legal network rules? Or, is the only source of help here 'sociological jurisprudence'?

II.1 Approach 1: Casuistry

Even the most detailed case law analysis has little, if any, help to offer. The blinkered reality perspectives of courtroom proceedings prevent an appropriate recognition of the trend toward networking. Since the courts' reality construction is founded in two-party proceedings, it necessarily dissects the complex relationships that multilateral networking establishes, into bilateral claims and counter-claims. Working from the viewpoint of plaintiff or defendant, this reality construction can only take limited note of the overarching conflicts and risks that networks entail. In this perspective, any doctrinal approach seeking to generalise from case

[10] § 278 *BGB*.

[11] For a concise analysis of judicial irritation in franchise law, C Joerges, 'Status and Contract in Franchising Law' in H Joerges (ed), *Franchising and the Law: Theoretical and Comparative Approaches in Europe and the United States* (Baden-Baden, Nomos, 1991) 11 *et seq*, and 21 *et seq*.

[12] For comprehensive discussion of piercing the corporate veil, see E Rehbinder, *Konzernaußenrecht und allgemeines Privatrecht: Eine rechtsvergleichende Untersuchung nach deutschem und amerikanischem Recht* (Bad Homburg, Gehlen, 1969) 69 *et seq*; E Rehbinder, 'Neues zum Durchgriff unter besonderer Berücksichtigung der höchstrichterlichen Rechtsprechung' in *Festschrift für Friedrich Kübler* (Heidelberg, Müller, 1997) 493 *et seq*, and 496 *et seq*.

law can only reproduce the claim and counterclaim culture and conclude by just balancing out the interests of the two parties.

As a consequence, then, doctrine should decisively free itself from systematically limited judicial models that can only react to the irritations of networks with individual equitable corrections. These models are not to be criticised for the manner in which they demarcate conflict:

> instead, the reality construction entails the recognition of only two contrasting spheres of influence, represented either by the plaintiff or by the defendant. In this manner, courtroom proceedings are projected into the social order such that points of legal reference are in turn identified within the social order.[13]

With regard to networks, such proceedings are fatal precisely because the networks are distinguished by their extra-positional effects.

II.2 Approach 2: Political Law-Making

Similarly, following policy-oriented trends within legal doctrine, it is not enough simply to adopt the reality constructs that emerge from the legislative process. Such a perspective entails too ready an acceptance of the world-views of practitioners who prepare and pre-structure legislation. This can only implicate law within the uncontrolled balancing of interests that takes place in opportunistic reaction to transient social pressures and political preferences. Similarly, it is not enough to adopt a perspective of 'legislative policies', since this means accepting the reality constructs of political parties and national and European political institutions, which, likewise, alienate 'real' social conflicts through the filtering processes of power and consensus politics.[14] In network matters, legislative interventions are paradigmatic examples of political tunnel-vision. European initiatives to free franchising from the strictures of competition law were selective responses to the highly effective lobbying activities of interest groups.[15] Similarly, in Germany, purchase money loans have been regulated, from the exclusive perspective of consumer protection, even though they also raise comparable regulatory problems in other contexts.[16] Were doctrine nothing but a systematic reproduction of the

[13] N Luhmann, *Grundrechte als Institution: Ein Beitrag zur politischen Soziologie* (Berlin, Duncker & Humblot, 1965) 206.

[14] Here, one is drawn into the dilemmatic juridification of 'legislative policies'; see E Steindorff, 'Politik des Gesetzes als Auslegungsmasstab im Wirtschaftsrecht', in *Festschrift für Karl Larenz* (Munich, CH Beck, 1973) 217 *et seq*.

[15] M Shapiro 'Globalization and Freedom of Contract' in HN Scheiber (ed), *The State and Freedom of Contract* (Stanford: Stanford University Press, 1998) 269 at 285 *et seq*.

[16] For an extensive analysis, see PW Heermann, *Drittfinanzierte Erwerbsgeschäfte: Entwicklung der Rechtsfigur des trilateralen Synallagmas auf der Grundlage deutscher und U.S.-amerikanischer Rechtsentwicklungen* (Tübingen: Mohr & Siebeck, 1998) 92 *et seq*.

policies of interest groups and legislators, then, it would only intensify the existing inadequacies within the political reality constructs.

II.3 Approach 3: Reflexive Social Practices

Legal doctrine will only make a genuine contribution to the law of networks if and when it establishes—as opposed to case law and legislation—a 'third way' of approaching the reality of change in economic organisation. Today, this is no longer possible through the 'silent power' of autonomous legal conceptualisation. Instead, what is needed is an explicit 'structural coupling' of law with reflexive practices in different fields of society. All intensive co-operation notwithstanding, structural coupling does not merge social and legal practices: it ensures the autonomy of law.[17] At all costs, however, one must avoid the scientistic misconception, current within sociological jurisprudence and legal economics, that the law simply adopts the conclusions of social sciences.[18] This misconception is fed by the notion that the social sciences supply the empirical facts and the theoretical generalisations from which follow the law's normative perspectives. Notwithstanding the significant role that scientific analysis may play in identifying the workings of networks, law needs to be far more concerned with the normative orientations in society that neutral sciences are simply not in a position to provide. Such orientations can only be found in the normatively-loaded dogma within society; in other words, in discourses in which social practices reflect upon their own self-perceptions. Legal doctrine itself, and the mother of all dogmas, theology, are both organised as academic disciplines, but are, of course, not social sciences in the strictest sense. They represent social practices of law and religion which reflect upon themselves. The same holds true for other academic disciplines, such as business management, economics and political science (or, at least, for some of their sub-disciplines), which do not, as such, form a part of the disinterested, value-neutral social-scientific search for truth. Instead, they are the manifestation of the reflexive practices that take place in different social sectors. They make part of what David Sciulli calls 'collegial formations', that is, the specific organisational forms of the professions and other norm-producing and deliberative institutions within society.[19] It is social practices in the worlds of business, economy and politics that each create

[17] See, on the structural coupling of legal theory and social sciences, Luhmann, *Law as a Social System* (n 2 above) chs II and VII.

[18] RA Posner, 'The Decline of Law as an Autonomous Discipline: 1982–1987' (1987) 100 *Harvard Law Review* 761–80.

[19] D Sciulli, *Theory of Societal Constitutionalism* (Cambridge, Cambridge University Press, 1992); D Sciulli, *Corporate Power in Civil Society: An Application of Societal Constitutionalism* (New York, New York University Press, 2001).

their own self-descriptions, which, in turn, inform and guide the underlying social practices. In each discipline, an internal distinction must be made, at least, between scientific discourse and reflexive social practice. In the case of law, legal theory as a reflexive counterpart to legal practice needs to be distinguished from legal sociology as a social-scientific observation of law.[20] Similarly, in the other social sciences, we need to distinguish between discourses taking part in social practices, and discourses taking part in the scientific observation of these social practices.

What we are looking for, then, is an autonomous legal reconstruction of normative social orientations; orientations that law can glean in its interchange with reflexive social practices. How do they perceive the opportunities and risks of the network revolution? This gives us two advantages above the common misconception of the scientist. Reflexive social practice, in enjoyable contrast to the normative poverty of scientific analysis in its narrow sense, provides us with a plethora of normative perspectives—the famous *idées directrices* of social institutions, the normative expectations, social demands, political rights and utopian hopes of the individual participants within them, as well as the principles gained in political conflicts on the ground, and principles that concern their overall social purposes and their contributions to different constituencies.[21] This is what social science in the strictest sense could never produce, much less legal doctrine create from within itself. At the same time, however, the law will, in juridifiying partial social rationalities, enforce its own particularist-universal orientation above the particularist-universal orientations of other forms of reflexive practice. For example, when it comes to structural corruption, law needs to distance itself from the results of social practices. Sociological jurisprudence, currently cloaked in the mantel of scientific study, should thus, in fact, be identified as a specific legal mode of dealing with the collision between different social rationalities.[22]

[20] Luhmann, *Law as a Social System* (n 2 above) chs 1 and 11.

[21] These are phenomena that normative sociology focuses on, particularly, L Fuller, *The Morality of Law* (New Haven, Yale University Press, 1969); P Selznick, *Law, Society and Industrial Justice* (New York, Russell Sage, 1969); P Selznick, *The Moral Commonwealth: Social Theory and the Promise of Community* (Berkeley, University of California Press, 1992); F Ewald, *L'État providence* (Paris, Grasset, 1986); R Friedland and R Alford, 'Bringing Society Back In: Symbols, Practices, and Institutional Contradictions' in P DiMaggio and W Powell (eds), *The New Institutionalism* (Chicago: Chicago University Press, 1992) 232–63.

[22] For an elaboration, G Teubner, 'Altera Pars Audiatur: Law in the Collision of Discourses' in R Rawlings (ed), *Law, Society and Economy* (Oxford, Clarendon Press, 1997) 149–76.

II.3 (a) Business Studies

It is noteworthy that several legal studies on hybrid networks have now developed a heightened sensitivity for business studies—in our words, for a reflexive social practice that formulates the normative preconditions for business success. These legal forays across the borders have proved successful, since they have discovered the opportunities and risks posed by hybrid networks, and have allowed this material to inform their legal solutions. The pioneering analyses of franchising made early detailed reference to business studies and established their legal concepts in close proximity to the organisational demands of franchising systems.[23] The resulting legal typology maps interest-conflicts into different types of franchising (subordination, co-ordination, coalition and federation), subjecting each type to a specific regulatory regime (relational contract, partnership and corporate groups). Risk analyses of new forms of 'systemic' dependence in just-in-time arrangements base themselves upon detailed organisational studies that have unveiled, in particular, the importance of computer-based integration as compared to merely contractual or corporate dependence, and, via analogy of the law of corporate groups, have drawn legal conclusions.[24]

II.3 (b) Legal Economics

Indeed, reference to reflexive social practices in business management has been fruitful, especially where legal concepts of network phenomena need to be developed according to the motivation of actors. Nonetheless, if the task is one of reconstructing the network revolution in its relevance for economy and society as a whole, then the business perspective is far too narrow. Empirical business studies tend to focus only upon network effects on individual firms and fail to recognise general economic and social implications. Their normative viewpoint is similarly limited, since they concentrate upon the efficiency, effectiveness and (occasionally) legitimacy of the individual network. This is far too restricted a basis for a legal appraisal of network opportunities and risks.

[23] M Martinek, *Franchising: Grundlagen der zivil- und wettbewerbsrechtichen Behandlung der vertraglichen Gruppenkooperation beim Absatz von Waren und Dienstleistungen* (Heidelberg, Decker & Schenck, 1987) 231 *et seq*.

[24] B Nagel, B Riess and G Theis, 'Der faktische Just-in-Time-Konzern: Unternehmensübergreifende Rationalisierungskonzepte und Konzernrecht am Beispiel der Automobilindustrie' (1989) 42 *Der Betrieb* at 1505 and 1506 *et seq*; B Nagel, B Riess and G Theis, *Just-in-Time-Strategien: Arbeitsbeziehungen, Gestaltungspotentiale, Mitbestimmung* (Düsseldorf, Hans-Böckler-Stiftung, 1990).

A step forward can be made here by taking into account the reflexive theories of economic practice and, above all, ideas from transaction-cost theory, property rights theory and economic institutionalism. Certainly, such theories conceive of themselves not as reflexive social practices, but as integral parts of the scientific-knowledge system. 'Pure' scientific theorems, however, devoid of all preconceptions, would never handicap themselves with normatively-loaded concepts and orientations, such as the *homo economicus* or 'economic efficiency'. Taking normative orientations, particularly efficiency concerns, as their starting point, legal studies of money transfer systems and other networks in the private sector are seeking to analyse and come to terms with the innovative, yet highly controversial category of a 'network contract'.[25] Other studies on symbiotic contracts, inspired by institutional economics, have successfully demonstrated the efficiency gains of networking and consequently advocate their legal institutionalisation.[26] Economic studies on network effects and their various legal implications are similarly profitable.[27]

II.3 (c) Social Theory

However, if law is concerned with embedding business networks within their broader political and social contexts, it must engage in a legal reconstruction of sociological network theories.[28] If law is to develop 'socially-appropriate' legal concepts, the analysis of market-networks

[25] W Möschel, 'Dogmatische Strukturen des bargeldlosen Zahlungsverkehrs' (1986) 186 *Archiv für die civilistische Praxis* 211–36; M Rohe, *Netzverträge: Rechtsprobleme komplexer Vertragsverbindungen* (Tübingen, Mohr & Siebeck, 1998) 66 *et seq* and 81 *et seq*, and *passim*.

[26] E Schanze, 'Symbiotic Contracts: Exploring Long-Term Agency Structures Between Contract and Corporation' in C Joerges (ed), *Franchising and the Law: Theoretical and Comparative Approaches in Europe and the United States* (Baden-Baden, Nomos, 1991) 67 *et seq* and 89 *et seq*; E Schanze, 'Symbiotic Arrangements' (1993) 149 *Journal of Institutional and Theoretical Economics* 691 *et seq*; C Kirchner, 'Unternehmensorganisation und Vertragsnetz: Überlegungen zu den rechtlichen Bedingungen zwischen Unternehmensorganisation und Vertragsnetz' in C Ott and H-B Schäfer (eds), *Ökonomische Analyse des Unternehmensrechts* (Heidelberg, Physica, 1993) 196 *et seq*, and 202 *et seq*; C Kirchner, 'Symbiotic Arrangements as a Challenge to Antitrust' (1996) 152 *Journal of Institutional and Theoretical Economics* 226 *et seq*; C Kirchner, 'Horizontale japanische Unternehmensgruppen (keiretsu) im deutschen Konzernrecht' in T Baums, KJ Hopt and N Horn (eds), *Corporations, Capital Markets and Business in the Law: Liber Amicorum Richard M. Buxbaum* (London, Kluwer Law International, 2000) 339 *et seq*, and 351 *et seq*; for a fruitful legal-economic analysis of cooperation contracts, see R Kulms, *Schuldrechtliche Organisationsverträge in der Unternehmenskooperation* (Baden-Baden, Nomos, 2000) 55 *et seq*, and 240 *et seq*.

[27] MA Lemley and D McGowan, 'Legal Implications of Network Economic Effects' (1998) 86 *California Law Review* 479 *et seq*.

[28] The social embedding of economic interchange is the objective of economic sociology, which has a closer empathy with the analytical interests of legal scholarship than do purely economic analyses. Representative, NJ Smelser and R Swedberg (eds), *The Handbook of Economic Sociology* (Princeton, Princeton University Press, 1994).

must be broadened to take the reflexive practices of other social environments into account. We are concerned here—all cognitive hurdles notwithstanding—with a legal reconstruction of the normativity inherent to social practice. As for networks, 'social theory-informed' legal forays into status-based and contractual relationships within franchising are particularly noteworthy, since they unveil the semi-autonomous status of network participants, and attempt to give them legal security.[29] Studies of standard term contract regulation for just-in-time contracts reveal the role which case law can play in the promotion of productive networks and in limiting institutional misuse.[30]

III. TRANSLATION PROBLEMS: NETWORKS AS CONNECTED CONTRACTS

However, I repeat: '"Network" is not a legal concept'. All joyous legal contact with reflexive social practices notwithstanding, legal arguments only begin where other reflexive theories end. The debate is on the appropriate form of regulation for business networks, virtual business, just-in-time systems, franchising chains and other co-operative contracts. They are generally established through bilateral contracts, and yet give rise to multilateral (legal) effects. Hybrid networks are remarkably disruptive social phenomena. They can neither be subsumed under the category of market, nor under the category of organisation. Following long indecision, sociologists and economists have responded to this confusion with theories that characterise networks as autonomous institutions, which are very different from the usual forms of economic co-ordination.[31] How is law to respond, however? Should it, as

[29] C Joerges, 'Status and Contract in Franchising Law' (n 11 above) 17 *et seq*.

[30] S Casper, 'How Public Law Influences Decentralized Supplier Network Organization: The Case of BMW and Audi', WZB-Discussion Paper FS I 95–314 (1995); S Casper, 'The Legal Framework for Corporate Governance: Explaining the Development of Contract Law in Germany and the United States' in PA Hall and D Soskice (eds), *Varieties of Capitalism: The Institutional Foundations of Comparative Advantage* (Oxford, Oxford University Press, 2001) 387 at 397 *et seq*.

[31] For an economic theory of networks most prominent, see O Williamson, *The Economic Institutions of Capitalism: Firms, Markets, Relational Contracting* (New York, Free Press, 1985); O Williamson, 'Comparative Economic Organization: The Analysis of Discrete Structural Alternatives' (1991) 36 *Administrative Science Quarterly* 269–96; O Williamson, *The Mechanisms of Governance* (Oxford, Oxford University Press, 1996). For a sociological theory of networks most prominent, see WW Powell, 'Neither Market nor Hierarchy: Network Forms of Organization' (1990) 12 *Research in Organisational Behaviour* 295–336.

innovation-friendly lawyers suggest, declare networks or symbiotic contracts to be *sui generis* legal institutions sailing in the Bermuda-triangle between contracts, torts and corporations?[32]

In my opinion, 'network' is not suited to play the role of a technical legal concept. Networks traverse private law concepts. Legally speaking, they can take the form of corporate, contractual or tortious special relationships. For this reason alone, legal doctrine cannot simply adopt the term 'network' as a legal concept. Yet, the disciplinary barriers are even higher. The current ideas about knowledge transfer are misleading. Law cannot simply accept the social structures of networks at face value; the social preconditions for intensive co-operation are an example of this. Nor can it simply adopt particular elements within social science definitions, such as the economic formula 'hybrid between market and hierarchy', or the sociological formula 'trust-based exchange system'. Instead, it must itself reconstruct anew the constitutive contours of the correlating legal definition out of its own path-dependent evolutionary logic.[33]

However, any attempt to subsume networks simply under traditional private law concepts is, to cut a long story short, doomed to failure.[34] First, company law is inappropriate for market networks, since the pooling of resources and joint decision-making do not suit the decentralised network structures. Secondly, given the radical individualism of the single nodes in networks, contract law is, indeed, the correct systematic arena, but needs to be considerably transformed for the opportunities and risks of market networks. Thirdly, an independent legal category of a 'network contract', based on the traditional law of agency, is not appropriate for the decision structure of business networks. It follows that doctrinal qualifications of networks need be based upon the development of an 'organisational contract law'—the law of 'controrgs', if you like—which recognises their hybrid nature through the inclusion of 'organisational', ie, not only the relational, but also the multi-lateral, elements within the contract.[35] Here,

[32] For symbiotic contracts as a third institution between contract and organisation, see Schanze, 'Symbiotic Contracts' and 'Symbiotic Arrangements' (n 26 above); Kirchner, 'Unternehmensorganisation und Vertragsnetz', 'Symbiotic Arrangements as a Challenge to Antitrust', and 'Horizontale japanische Unternehmensgruppen (keiretsu) im deutschen Konzernrecht' (n 26 above). For network contracts as an institution *sui generis*, see Möschel, 'Dogmatische Strukturen des bargeldlosen Zahlungsverkehrs' (n 25 above); Rohe, *Netzverträge: Rechtsprobleme komplexer Vertragsverbindungen* (n 25 above).

[33] See M Amstutz, 'Vertragskollisionen: Fragmente für eine Lehre von der Vertragsverbindung' in M Amstutz (ed), *Festschrift für Heinz Rey* (Zürich, Schulthess, 2003) 161 at 164 *et seq*, for a particularly clear distinction between social system and legal system.

[34] For more details, see G Teubner, *Netzwerk als Vertragsverbund: Virtuelle Unternehmen, Franchising, Just in Time in sozialwissenschaftlicher und juristischer Sicht* (Baden-Baden, Nomos, 2004) ch 2.

[35] For a special law of 'controrgs', ie, an 'organisational contract law' for networks, see G Teubner, 'Beyond Contract and Organization? The External Liability of Franchising Systems in German Law' in C Joerges (ed), *Franchising and the Law: Theoretical and Comparative*

one needs to exploit the developmental logic of a rudimentary, but already established, form of organisational contract law. In German law, the notion of *Vertragsverbund* ('connected contracts') has been developed—a doctrine that is ripe for further evolution in the network sphere.

To quote a doctrinal authority from Germany,

> [t]he notion of connected contracts is used to describe any plurality of contracts which refer to each other within either bilateral or multilateral relationships, whose interconnection gives rise to direct legal effects (of a genetic, functional or conditional nature), whether these simply result in the effect of one contract to the other (or others), or whether one can also observe mutual effects.[36]

It is the 'economic unity' of several bipolar contracts which is determinant for the connected contracts. However, this concept also entails a strange paradox which, time and time again, gives rise to a harsh critique of the entire construction: multiple contracts are directed to a single economic goal, which can only be achieved if all contracts are performed, but which is, again, also entirely dependent upon the legal independence of each of the contracts. Legally speaking, this results in the strained formula that each and every contract is legally distinct, but also builds an economic unity upon which the law can focus.

However, the critique that this is all quite arbitrary[37] leads us astray. Instead, in order to understand the mystery of connected contracts, we must make productive use of this 'unbearable contradiction'. The undeniable contradiction found within the notion of the 'economic unity of distinct contracts' is not simply to be regarded as a yet-to-be-corrected logical mistake within doctrinal reasoning, but is, instead, itself the exact juridical correlate of the social reality of hybrids, the bedrock for their productivity, and the source of those risks to which the law must find appropriate responses.[38]

Approaches in Europe and the United States (Baden-Baden, Nomos, 1991) 105 at 129 *et seq*; G Teubner, 'Piercing the Contractual Veil: The Social Responsibility of Contractual Networks' in T Wilhelmson (ed), *Perspectives of Critical Contract Law* (Dartmouth, Aldershot, 1993) 211 at 231 *et seq*; G Teubner, 'Hybrid Laws: Constitutionalising Private Governance Networks' in RA Kagan, M Krygier and K Winston (eds), *Legality and Community: On the Intellectual Legacy of Philip Selznick* (Berkeley, Berkeley Public Policy Press, 2002) 311 at 320 *et seq*; Teubner, *Netzwerk als Vertragsverbund* (n 34 above) ch 3.

[36] J Gernhuber, *Das Schuldverhältnis: Begründung und Änderung, Pflichten und Strukturen, Drittwirkungen* (Tübingen: Mohr & Siebeck, 1989) 710. Similarly, K Larenz and M Wolf, *Allgemeiner Teil des Bürgerlichen Rechts*, 8th edn (Munich, CH Beck, 1997) 469 *et seq*; J Esser and E Schmidt, *Schuldrecht: Ein Lehrbuch. Allgemeiner Teil I 1*, 8th edn (Heidelberg, Müller, 1995) 214.

[37] E Wolf, *Lehrbuch des Schuldrechts. Zweiter Band: Besonderer Teil* (Cologne, Heymanns, 1978) 62 *et seq*.

[38] The relationship of network building to contradictory external demands made on business is the focus for many social science analyses, albeit dealing with different aspects of the problem: KS Cameron and RE Quinn, 'Organisational Paradox and Transformation' in Quinn and Cameron (eds), *Paradox and Transformation: Towards a Theory of Change in*

IV. THE ROLE OF LAW IN SOCIAL DE-PARADOXIFICATION PROCESSES

This contradiction is absolutely central to networks. Private law must respond with sensitivity to the *coincidentia oppositorum* manifest within networks. The main thesis is as follows: certain economic developments expose actors to a 'double-bind' situation, which they react to with the aid of an internally-contradictory network structure. The double-bind situation typical for networks arises where: (1) The social environment makes ambivalent, contradictory or paradoxical demands of the business entities to which they must respond; (2) such demands are so central to business survival that they cannot be simply ignored; and (3) their explicit thematisation is highly problematical.[39] The institutional answer to these problems is neither contract nor organisation, but the hybrid network, since this construct allows for the transformation of external incompatibilities into internally-manageable contradictions. In turn, private law needs to respond in two ways, with innovative doctrinal concepts: on the one hand, it normalises and stabilises network-specific contradictions; on the other, it combats the various consequences of these contradictions.

In more detail, hybrid constructions within the triangle of contract, organisation and network, facilitate escape from the double-bind situation. They constitute institutional arrangements that make network-logic—as opposed to simple contractual or organisational logic—resistant to contradictory social environmental demands. More precisely, hybrids react to paradoxical situations (in their broadest sense) that threaten the operational capacities of the actors. They do so through their ambivalence (*A* is or is not *A*), their contradictory nature (*A* is not *A*) or their paradoxical character (*A* because not *A*).[40] Generally speaking, there

Organisation and Management (Cambridge MA, Ballinger, 1988) 1 *et seq*; Buxbaum, 'Is "Network" a Legal Concept?' (n 1 above) 701; M Funder, *Paradoxien der Reorganisation* (Munich, Hampp, 1999); D Sauer and C Lang (eds), *Paradoxien der Innovation: Perspektiven sozialwissenschaftlicher Innovationsforschung* (Frankfurt, Campus, 1999); N Luhmann, *Organisation und Entscheidung* (Opladen, Westdeutscher Verlag, 2000) 407 *et seq*; H Hirsch-Kreinsen, 'Unternehmensnetzwerke—revisited' (2002) 31 *Zeitschrift für Soziologie* 106 at 107.

[39] On the paradoxical double-bind situation, see the classic text by G Bateson, *Steps to an Ecology of Mind* (New York, Ballantine, 1972); P Watzlawick, JH Beavin and DD Jackson, *Pragmatics of Human Communication: A Study of Interactional Patterns, Pathologies, and Paradoxes* (New York, Norton, 1967). For the application of the double-bind to organisations, see FB Simon, *Die Kunst, nicht zu lernen: Und andere Paradoxien in Psychotherapie, Management, Politik* (Heidelberg, Carl-Auer-Systeme, 1997).

[40] 'Paradoxes' in their narrowest sense, denote situations such as 'A because not A'. In a wider rhetorical sense, 'paradoxes' include ambivalence and contradictions that inhibit thinking within a given framework. Social science and law are best served by the wider definition that encompasses inhibition effects, as well as the potential to overcome them. For a general pragmatic perspective on contradictions and paradoxes, see HU Gumbrecht

are two modes of escape from such imbroglios. The first is repressive, suppressing contradictions by admitting only one of the contradictory instructions, and dismissing the other. The second is constructive, seeking to make paradoxes fruitful, to the degree that it establishes a more complex representation of the world. This is what is meant by 'morphogenesis', which Krippendorff suggested for dealing with paradox:

> Unless one is able to escape a paradoxical situation which is what Whitehead and Russell achieved with the theory of logical types, paradoxes paralyse an observer and may lead either to a collapse of the construction of his or her world, or to a growth in complexity in his or her representation of this world. It is the latter case which could be characterised as morphogenesis.[41]

If, in a double-bind situation, people choose contractual arrangements, they tend to repress one of the two contradictory messages. If they choose integrated hierarchical organisations, they do the same thing for the other message. Under certain conditions, however, hybrid arrangements provide for an institutional environment in which paradoxical communication is not repressed; not only is it tolerated, it is also invited, institutionally facilitated and, sometimes, rendered productive. Hybrids, as a highly ambiguous combination of networks with contracts and organisations, seem to be the result of a subtle interplay between different and mutually-contradicting logics of action.

In the particular context of hybrid networks, the double-bind stems from the imposition of environmental demands upon actors to obey different and contradictory operational imperatives simultaneously. Some of these demands derive directly from contradictory economic pressures. Others result from a collision of economic requirements, on the one hand, with scientific, cultural, medical and political principles, on the other.

and LK Pfeiffer (eds), *Paradoxien, Dissonanzen, Zusammenbrüche: Situationen offener Epistemologie* (Frankfurt aM, Suhrkamp, 1991); Watzlawick, Beavin and Jackson, *Pragmatics of Human Communication* (n 39 above) ch 6. On paradoxical situations within economic enterprises, see O Neuberger, 'Dilemmata und Paradoxa im Managementprozess' in G Schreyögg (ed), *Funktionswandel im Management: Wege jenseits der Ordnung* (Berlin, Duncker & Humblot, 2000) 173 at 187 *et seq*. On the legal treatment of paradoxes, see GP Fletcher 'Paradoxes in Legal Thought' (1985) 85 *Columbia Law Review* 1263–92; P Suber, *The Paradox of Self-Amendment: A Study of Logic, Law, Omnipotence and Change* (New York, Lang, 1990) and http://www.earlham.edu/~peters/writing/psa/index.htm.

[41] K Krippendorff, 'Paradox and Information' in B Dervin and MJ Voigt (eds), *Progress in Communication Sciences* Vol 5 (Norwood, Ablex, 1984) 45 at 51 *et seq*. On paradox and morphogenesis in social systems, see N Luhmann, 'Sthenography' (1990) 7 *Stanford Literature Review* 133–7; N Luhmann, *Die Gesellschaft der Gesellschaft* (Frankfurt aM, Suhrkamp, 1997) 57 *et seq*. On exemplary reactions to the paradoxical demands of just-in-time systems, K Eisenhardt and B Westcott, 'Paradoxical Demands and the Creation of Excellence: The Case of Just-in-Time Manufacturing' in RE Quinn and KS Cameron (eds), *Paradox and Transformation: Towards a Theory of Change in Organisation and Management* (Cambridge MA, Ballinger, 1988) 169 at 191.

Contradictory demands can be traced to economic trends that have increasingly overburdened individual firms and have forced them to engage in networking:

> trends such as increased technological complexity, increased pressure on productivity and costs, as well as simultaneous market demands for a high degree of flexibility.[42]

Empirical studies on intra-company co-operation have systematically researched the particular contradictions to which firms are exposed. Increasingly, the market demands 'flexible specialisation'. Following the demise of standardised mass production, the demand is for 'client-specific mass production'. This goal gives rise to a barely surmountable contradiction between flexibility and efficiency. The trend in production is towards 'systemic rationalisation'. This optimisation standard cloaks a contradiction between complexity and reliability. Similarly, business organisation is required to follow the goal of 'decentralised self-direction', which lays itself open to a contradiction between the autonomy of, and oversight over, de-centralised business units. Business organisation is then left with the question of whether they can choose only one organisational structure, or whether they must set off on the far harder path of combination, fusion and trade-offs.[43]

Networks are confronted with the problem of how to translate contradictory demands into internal structures, so that operational burdens are sustainable.[44] The determinative innovation of networks is that they transform external contradictions into a tense, but sustainable, 'double-orientation' within the operational system. One and the same operation is exposed both to individual network node orientations and to the collective orientation of the network, and is simultaneously both constrained *and* liberated by the demand that it must find a balance in each context.[45]

[42] Hirsch-Kreinsen, 'Unternehmensnetzwerke—revisited' (n 38 above) 107.

[43] K Semlinger, 'Effizienz und Autonomie in Zulieferungsnetzwerken: Zum strategischen Gehalt von Kooperation' in WH Staehle and J Sydow (eds), *Managementforschung 3* (Berlin, de Gruyter, 1993) 309 at 313 *et seq*.

[44] Semlinger, 'Effizienz und Autonomie in Zulieferungsnetzwerken: Zum strategischen Gehalt von Kooperation' (n 43 above) 332; Hirsch-Kreinsen, 'Unternehmensnetzwerke—revisited' (n 38 above) 120.

[45] On the key concept of 'double-attribution', see Teubner, 'Beyond Contract and Organization?' (n 35 above) 119 *et seq*; Teubner, 'Piercing the Contractual Veil' (n 35 above) 226 *et seq*; Teubner, 'Hybrid Laws: Constitutionalising Private Governance Networks' (n 35 above) 324 *et seq*. For double-attribution from a social science perspective, see FW Scharpf, 'Die Handlungsfähigkeit des Staates am Ende des Zwanzigsten Jahrhunderts' (1991) 32 *Politische Vierteljahresschrift* 621 at 621 *et seq*; P Littmann and S Jansen, *Oszillodox: Virtualisierung—die permanente Neuerfindung der Organisation* (Stuttgart, Klett, 2000) 69 *et seq*; A Windeler, *Unternehmungsnetzwerke: Konstitution und Strukturation* (Wiesbaden, Westdeutscher Verlag, 2001) 194 *et seq*, and 224. For double attribution in the law of networks, H

In contrast to contracts or organisations, which exhibit either an individual or a collective orientation, networks have created a double social orientation for individual operations. Each operation within the hybrid must simultaneously meet both the normative demands that stem from bilateral relations between individual actors, and those that stem from the network as a whole. The result is a remarkable degree of self-regulation within networks. This furnishes the key explanation for the conclusion by economists that networks and nodes engage in a specific form of profit-sharing, which is clearly distinguishable from the forms of profit-sharing found within other social contexts.[46] Whilst the law of corporations first attributes profit to the corporation and then oversees its distribution to its members, networks provide for a simultaneous distribution to the net and its nodes. All transactions profit both the network and the individual actors.[47] This type of profit-sharing acts as a constraint, since all transactions must pass the double test. At the same time, however, it acts as an incentive, since all network gains are always related to individual gain.[48]

V. LEGAL CONDITIONS: DUAL CONSTITUTION OF CONNECTED CONTRACTS

How is the law to respond to this transformation of external contradictions into an internal—simultaneously individual and collective—orientation? Law cannot just map network structures into its concepts. Under the network irritation, it has to find its own answers: in terms of legal facts, through the dual constitution of connected contracts; and in terms of legal consequences, through a selective double attribution to individual contractual partners and to the network as a whole.

Any attempt to reconstruct the legal conditions for a business network must pay due regard to the internal evolution of doctrine. It is for this reason that the legal concept of 'connected contracts', which has now

Collins, *Regulating Contracts* (Oxford, Oxford University Press, 1999) 248 *et seq*; A Supiot, 'Les nouveaux visages de la subordination' (2000) 63 *Droit Social* 131 at 135.

[46] JA Brickley and FH Dark, 'The Choice of the Organisational Form: The Case of Franchising' (1987) 18 *Journal of Financial Economics* 401 at 411 *et seq*; AW Dnes, 'The Economic Analysis of Franchising and its Regulation' in C Joerges (ed), *Franchising and the Law: Theoretical and Comparative Approaches in Europe and the United States* (Baden Baden, Nomos, 1991) 133 at 136 *et seq*. For an especially interesting empirical study, see SW Norton (1988) 'An Empirical Look at Franchising as an Organisational Form' (1988) 61 *The Journal of Business* 197 at 202 *et seq*.

[47] Dnes, 'The Economic Analysis of Franchising and its Regulation' (n 46 above) 136 *et seq*.

[48] Norton, 'An Empirical Look at Franchising as an Organisational Form' (n 46 above) 202 *et seq*; see, also, B Klein and LF Saft, 'The Law and Economics of Franchise Tying Contracts' (1985) 28 *Journal of Law and Economics* 345 at 349 *et seq*.

been incorporated into the German Civil Code,[49] is so attractive for networks. Its particular characteristics derive from the legal logic of synallagmatic contracts.[50] To date, in German law, the purchase money loan has been the major object of the law of connected contracts. Moving away from its peculiarities, in order to attempt to develop a more general legal concept of connected contracts that also encompasses business networks, we can extrapolate from both case law and recent legislative advances and thus define three legal conditions.[51] Together, these three conditions constitute the surplus value of the dual constitution of the connected contracts as opposed to a simple mass of disconnected bilateral contracts within a market.

1. Reciprocal reference of bilateral contracts to one another, either found within the document and/or distilled from contractual practice ('multilaterality');
2. a contractual reference to the overall project of the connected contracts ('relational purpose'); and
3. a close and significant co-operation relationship between the participants within the multilateral relation ('economic unity').

Does this mean that business networks are simply made up of a multitude of bilateral contracts? Is their only distinguishing characteristic that a relational agreement should be added to more commonplace agreements? No. What lurks beneath the three legal conditions is the social specificity of networking, which cannot, as such, be captured within legal categories. As we said, sociological jurisprudence is an oxymoron. 'Network' is not a legal concept. There is good reason why lawyers work with mysterious formulations in this area: 'purposive nexus', 'unity despite division', 'accessory acts', and '*causa consumendi*'.

Seen from the distance of systems theory, the entire matter can be understood as a difference between two closed systems: social practices and legal doctrine. From the sociological standpoint, it is the network's specific characteristic that a contractual system observes its environment in a somewhat unusual manner. Usually, contracts focus their observations on markets and market conditions—in particular, market prices—and adapt their decisions and internal structures to them. The network situation differs from this 'normality': where simple market observation no longer suffices, the system redirects its observation away from general market conditions and observes other contractual systems within the

[49] § 358 BGB (Verbundene Verträge).

[50] Gernhuber, *Das Schuldverhältnis* (n 36 above) 710 *et seq*.

[51] For a recent restatement of doctrine and jurisprudence of connected contracts, see Habersack in *Münchener Kommentar zum Bürgerlichen Gesetzbuch*, 4th edn (Munich, CH Beck, 2003) § 358, at 26 *et seq*, and 36 *et seq*.

market, and orients itself in line with changes here, rather than the changes within the market.[52] Systems thus use networking to attempt to establish a symbiotic relationship with other systems, so that they can gain greater control of their environment. The fusion within such hybrid networking does not create 'unity' out of individual contracts; instead, each contract remains autonomous in relation to its own function and its contributions to the environment.[53] Thus the 'relation' between contracts becomes a mutual observation between two separate contracts, each of which autonomously pursues its own project, but which adapt themselves to one another through internal reflection.[54] It is simply not possible that this sociological picture of reciprocal reflection appears on the screens of the law. Instead, what we see on these screens are the three legal conditions of the connected contracts mentioned above—'mutual referencing' of contracts, 'relational purpose', and 'co-operative relationship'—which establish the legal connectedness of the contracts.

If this is true for the legal construction of networks, then classical contract law needs to undergo some considerable modifications. In contractual networks, a heteronomous private order superimposes its demands on autonomous bilateral contracts. The reference of one contract to another entails the inclusive acceptance by the contractual partners of a foreign private order. Each bilateral contract must submit to a coherent overall system that needs to be respected. In practice, contractual conclusion is more or less reduced to a simple decision to enter into a homogeneous private order. Reference to other contracts is similar in nature to regard for standard contract terms, for the customs of the market, or for the social and technical norms. All in all, bilateral contracts are caught in the institutional logic of networks: entry as a bilateral access to a multilateral order, trust-based interaction, de-central co-ordination of a quasi-organisation, and orientation of individual operations to the network purpose.

Taken together, the three conditions reconstruct the legal equivalent of a non-contractual 'spontaneous social order' which emerges from a multiplicity of bilateral contracts. This is the proprium of social networks reconstructed in law as connected contracts. However, in marked contrast to Hayek's spontaneous order for the discovery processes of competitive markets, it is networking and co-operation, rather than the market and competition, that are the sources of spontaneous order.[55]

[52] Luhmann, *Organisation und Entscheidung* (n 38 above) 407 *et seq*.

[53] M Castells, *The Rise of the Network Society* (Oxford, Blackwell, 2000) 187; Teubner, 'Hybrid Laws: Constitutionalising Private Governance Networks' (n 35 above) 330.

[54] Amstutz, 'Vertragskollisionen' (n 33 above) 164 *et seq*.

[55] On spontaneous ordering in competitive markets and legal evolution, see FA von Hayek, *Law, Legislation and Liberty. Volume 1: Rules and Order* (London, Routledge & Paul, 1973) 72 *et seq*; V Vanberg, 'Spontaneous Market Order and Social Rules: A Critical

Within such spontaneous orders, the stability of the relationship between legally independent units is deduced by going beyond bipolar provisions.[56] And it is this going 'beyond' bipolar provisions that is the core of the argument. Various social co-ordination mechanisms of a non-contractual nature—reciprocal observation, anticipatory adaptation, co-operation, trust, self-binding, responsibility, negotiation, and stable relationships[57]—constitute the overarching order of networking, and stamp the network's character upon each bilateral contractual relationship.

VI. LEGAL CONSEQUENCES: SELECTIVE DOUBLE-ATTRIBUTION TO CONTRACT PARTIES AND TO THE NETWORK

What holds good in relation to the legal conditions of the network as connected contracts, also holds good for its legal consequences. The double orientation in networks, which are the result of the subtle interplay between contradictory logics of action, must also find its resonance within the law.[58] This is true both for internal relations between participants within the network, as well as for its external relations. The appropriate legal response is a selective (!) double-attribution of network acts to the contract parties and to the network. The attribution varies according to the different structural contradictions within the network.

VI.1 First Contradiction: Bilateral Exchange versus Multilateral Association

There is a first—maybe we should say, 'the standard'—configuration of hybrid networks in which they appear as the result of contradictory demands from the market. Economic transactions, especially when they

Examination of F.A. Hayek's Theory of Cultural Evolution' (1986) 2 *Economics and Philosophy* 75 at 79 *et seq*; RD Cooter, 'Decentralised Law for a Complex Economy' (1994) 23 *International Review of Law and Economics* 443 at 447 *et seq*. On the important distinction between different types of spontaneous order, especially between markets and relational contracts, see R Gordon, 'Hayek and Cooter on Custom and Reason' (1944) 23 *Southwestern University Law Review* 453–60.

56 Windeler, *Unternehmungsnetzwerke: Konstitution und Strukturation* (n 45 above) 240.

57 For discussion on the mechanisms and effects of such non-market spontaneous orders, see Gordon, 'Hayek and Cooter on Custom and Reason' (n 55 above) 459; J Sydow and A Windeler, *Steuerung von Netzwerken: Konzepte und Praktiken* (Opladen, Westdeutscher Verlag, 2000) 1 *et seq*, and 12 *et seq*; Windeler, *Unternehmungsnetzwerke: Konstitution und Strukturation* (n 45 above) 240 *et seq*.

58 'Resonance' is not deployed here as a metaphor, but instead forms an important element within the theory of structural coupling. For the resonance of social problems within the law, see Luhmann, *Law as a Social System* (n 2 above) ch 10.

deal with knowledge-based products, are simultaneously exposed to the contradictory demands of bilateral exchange and multilateral relations.[59] An important explanation for the contradictory nature of behavioural expectations is the uncertainty of economic actors about future market development. Despite their antagonistic interests, this uncertainty forces the parties to long-term exchange contracts to develop closely co-ordinated behavioural patterns, be they constructed along hierarchical or heterarchical lines.[60]

The traditional solution to such a collision between operational logics was a simple 'either-or' decision. The suggestions made in the literature that we should qualify networks either as exchange contracts or as a 'corporation' derives from this tradition. The result is the well-known rigid separation between market and hierarchies supported by similarly rigid rules of anti-trust law, contract law and corporation law. However, the enforced dichotomy between market/organisation, or between contract/corporation censors a more productive solution. Each institutional answer—market or hierarchy, contract or organisation—represses the paradox. Each predominantly favours one of the contradictory orientations while pushing the other into the darkness of informality where it is sometimes discovered by subversive sociologists interested in the dark side of formal institutions.

The various routes out of these conflicts, which we characterised above as 'morphogenesis', converge within the specific institutional logic of networks. The relevant concept within organisational theory is 'de-totalisation'. In order to react to external paradoxes, the network must give up its monolithic unity and 'recreate external diversity within its own institutions and functions'. In such a process, 'antagonistic relationships (in this case, bilateral exchange and multilateral co-operation) are nurtured with one and the same partner—which cannot but prove to be a paradox should sectoral and temporal differentiations be ignored or 'totalised'.[61] Empirical studies have demonstrated that this internal division and re-combination of exchange and co-operation is, in fact, possible on the ground. Within successful business networks, actors have simultaneously been able to maintain the logic of exchange within 'contractual' sectors, such as logistics, quality, quantity and pricing, and combine it

[59] On contradictory environmental demands as a network building impetus, see the sources in n 38 above. In addition, M Reiss, 'Mythos Netzwerkorganisation' (1998) 4 *Zeitschrift Führung & Organisation* 224 at 224 *et seq*; H-D Köhler, 'Auf dem Weg zum Netzwerkunternehmen? Anmerkungen zu einem problematischen Konzept am Beispiel der deutschen Automobilkonzerne' (1999) 6 *Industrielle Beziehungen* 36 at 36 *et seq*; Sydow and Windeler, *Steuerung von Netzwerken* (n 57 above) 6 *et seq*.

[60] Kulms, *Schuldrechtliche Organisationsverträge in der Unternehmenskooperation* (n 26 above) 227 *et seq*.

[61] Neuberger, 'Dilemmata und Paradoxa im Managementprozess' (n 40 above) 207 *et seq*.

with trust-based co-operation within 'relational' sectors such as R & D and joint-planning and construction.[62] 'De-totalisation' strategies thus aim to instutionalise new internal differences within a business 'totality' that is indelibly marked by contradictions. The notion 'de-totalisation' thus means internalising external contradictions, in order to legitimate them as simple tensions, and contribute to their contextual resolution through internal differences.

In stark contrast to the duties of good faith which govern exchange contracts on the one hand, and the duties of loyalty to the association on the other, the legal category that is best suited to capture the network logic, to give it institutional support, and to compensate for some of its negative implications, is surely the duty of loyalty to the network. This duty is distinguished by virtue of its double orientation within one formula, to both network and contract. This duty explicitly adopts the contradiction between individual and collective elements within the network.

The primary achievement of this duty is the internal translation of externally-imposed insoluble contradictions into manageable conflicts between different levels and sub-systems within the network—between nodes, relations, the centre, and the network in its entirety.[63] The duty of loyalty, therefore, fulfils the following task in law: that of creating an internal differentiation between various temporal, social and functional sectors, in order to translate initially contradictory demands into clear, contextually-determined, expectations.

The legal formula is thus as follows: to distinguish situations in which an intensified duty of loyalty to the network exists, from situations in which only the contractual duty of good faith will apply, even though each obligation must be modified with reference to the other. The legal task is one of distinguishing between contractual good faith and the duty of loyalty to the network. At the same time, however, care must be taken to ensure that this duty is not simply equated with the duty of loyalty within corporation law, but that, for its part, it is given a de-centralised bias. Such differences clearly educe from the repeatedly discussed distinction between a network and a collective: the pervasive combination of autonomy and association. This combination is better served by a contractual, legislative and judicial apportionment of duties of

[62] D Bieber, 'Probleme unternehmensübergreifender Organisation von Innovationsprozessen' in D Bieber (ed), *Technikentwicklung und Industriearbeit: Industrielle Produktionstechnik zwischen Eigendynamik und Nutzerinteressen* (Frankfurt aM, Campus, 1997) 111, especially at 124 *et seq*.

[63] See Semlinger, 'Effizienz und Autonomie in Zulieferungsnetzwerken' (n 43 above) 332.

loyalty—in contrast to resource-pooling—which assumes the task of the context-dependent fine-tuning of autonomy and association.[64]

VI.2 Second Contradiction: Competition versus Co-operation

Here, we are concerned with a second type of configuration in which hybrid networks evolve as an answer to external contradictions. Especially in the case of knowledge-based products, economic decisions are not merely subject to the tensions between bilateral exchanges and multilateral organisations, but are also subject to the conflict between competition and co-operation.[65] Paradoxical commands given to network participants are to be able to 'co-operate with one another!' and, simultaneously, be able to 'compete against one another!' Knowledge-oriented production gives rise to a contradiction between two fundamental forms of social experience. Within competition, individual goals can only be achieved at the cost of other goals, while within co-operation, individual goals are wholly compatible with those of others. This justifies the usual practice of institutionalising a strict distinction between the two: the market or the organisation.

Recent business studies nonetheless suggest that it is possible to conceive of alternatives to the rigid institutional separation of competition and co-operation. And these alternatives do work in practice. The increased incidence of hybrid networks can be seen as a refined reaction to the contradictory demands of co-operation and competition.[66] 'Co-opetition' is the new magic formula that promises that competitive advantages will flow out of the combination of co-operation and competition, which manages to combine organisation and contract with network elements.[67] 'Co-opetition' would, therefore, constitute a social model that would allow—even demand—that competitors would be congruent with co-operation partners.

One should nonetheless keep a certain distance from such purely combinatory approaches and emphasise 're-entry' effects in this context.

[64] See Kulms, *Schuldrechtliche Organisationsverträge in der Unternehmenskooperation* (n 26 above) 231 and 261.

[65] For the co-operation/competition conflict, see J Sydow, *Management von Netzwerkorganisationen* (Wiesbaden, Westdeutscher Verlag, 1999) 279 at 299 *et seq*; Littmann and Jansen, *Oszillodox: Virtualisierung—die permanente Neuerfindung der Organisation* (n 45 above) 64 *et seq*; K Semlinger, 'Kooperation und Konkurrenz in japanischen Netzwerkbeziehungen' in J Sydow and A Windeler (eds), *Steuerung von Netzwerken* (Opladen, Westdeutscher Verlag, 2000) 130 *et seq*, 141 *et seq*.

[66] See, in particular, JC Jarillo, *Strategic Networks: Creating the Borderless Organisation* (Oxford, Oxford University Press, 1993); Neuberger, 'Dilemmata und Paradoxa im Managementprozess' (n 40 above) 207 *et seq*.

[67] See Littmann and Jansen, *Oszillodox: Virtualisierung—die permanente Neuerfindung der Organisation* (n 45 above) 64 *et seq*.

A simple mixture of competitive and co-operative behavioural patterns does not provide an easy exit out of paradoxical oscillation. In the technical sense defined by Spencer Brown, re-entry has nothing to do with ending the division between the two sides of an 'either-or' decision.[68] On the contrary, the distinction between competition and co-operation must not be ended, and must, instead, be strictly maintained and institutionalised in a legal form. At the same time, this same distinction makes a second appearance. Now, however, it is re-introduced to one side of the institutional divide, and once again it is institutionalised within it.

Mixed competition/co-operation forms only cease to be ideological, in the sense that they simply pursue only one orientation under the semantic cloak of 'combination', if and when they are subject to re-entry conditions. By the same token, they do not simply squander the gains of each social model which only become apparent by virtue of their institutional separation. Instead, and in so far as re-entry secures the stable identity of the distinction, they can maximise such advantages. This, however, seems only possible under three conditions:

1. Sustainable institutionalisation of market competition through the conclusion of parallel and distinct bilateral contracts (ie, precisely not by the creation of a unitary organisation).
2. Institutionalisation of the re-entry of the co-operation/competition distinction within the system of contracts, so that market competition is overlaid by a sphere of operational co-operation.
3. Situationally-defined internal demarcation between operational spheres.

Any attempt to institutionalise hybrids legally must pay due regard to such complications. It is precisely this complex of questions to which German private law has yet to find a response. We are faced here with the difficult question of whether legal obligations can be established at all between network participants who are not contractually bound to one another. The problem is whether legal sanctions exist for the incorrect behaviour of a participant within a delivery chain or a system of networked contracts.[69] The legal postulate of mutual contractual liability of non-contractual partners within the network is becoming increasingly

[68] See GS Brown, *Laws of Form* (New York, Julian Press, 1972) 56 *et seq*, and 69 *et seq*.

[69] E Picker, 'Vertragliche und deliktische Schadenshaftung: Überlegungen zu einer Neustrukturierung der Haftungssysteme' (1987) 42 *Juristenzeitung* 1041–58; idem, 'Gutachterhaftung: Außervertragliche Einstandspflichten als innergesetzliche Rechtsfortbildung' in *Festschrift für Dieter Medicus* (Cologne, Heymann, 1999) 397–447; Möschel, 'Dogmatische Strukturen des bargeldlosen Zahlungsverkehrs' (n 25 above) 187 *et seq*; Rohe, *Netzverträge: Rechtsprobleme komplexer Vertragsverbindungen* (n 25 above) 98.

pressing. It is the result of increased network relations within the provision of goods and services. The privity of contract principle notwithstanding, arguments of fairness and prevention demand restitutionary liability in such cases. The liability of strangers to the bilateral contract within the network to claims for damages is the consequence.

VI.3 Third Contradiction: *Unitas Multiplex*

In a third configuration, hybrid networks appear as a response to contradictions within the attribution of social action. Who, in the positive sense, benefits from success and profit; and who, in the negative sense, suffers loss and liability—individual or collective actors? Is the network simply a trust-based relationship between individual actors, or does it form an independent collective, making its appearance as a new actor which in itself becomes a point of attribution of action and responsibility?[70] In this case, too, the traditional approach of a strict division between contract and organisation, found both in sociological theory and in legal doctrine supplies inappropriate solutions. Social practice within hybrid networks has, however, identified its own solution: 'double-attribution'. This attribution technique is one of the most important characteristics of hybrid networks, facilitating the distinction between simple attribution to individual actors in the case of the contract, and attribution to collective actors in the case of the organisation. One and the same economic transaction is doubly attributed; to individual actors as network nodes and to the overall network.

This new form of attribution, however, gives rise to new risks which, in turn, demand a new legal form of network responsibility to external actors, that is distinguishable both from individual liability and from the collective liability of organisations. Although the 'piercing of the contractual veil' proves its worth as a general formulation to establish network

[70] For networks as mere relations between individual actors and not as collective actors: see W Heydebrand, *The Network Metaphor as Key to the Analysis of Complex Production and Service Relation in a Global Economy* (Stuttgart, Akademie für Technikfolgenabschätzung in Baden-Württemberg, 1999); V Tacke, 'Netzwerk und Adresse' (2000) 6 *Soziale Systeme* 291 at 317. For networks as collective actors, however, under specified conditions: G Teubner, 'The Many-Headed Hydra: Networks as Higher-Order Collective Actors' in J McCahery, S Picciotto and C Scott (eds), *Corporate Control and Accountability* (Oxford, Clarendon Press, 1993) 41 at 54 *et seq*; G Teubner, 'Piercing the Contractual Veil' (n 35 above) 226 *et seq*; J Sydow and A Windeler, 'Organising and Evaluating Interfirm Networks' (1998) 9 *Organisation Science*, Special Issue: Managing Partnership and Strategic Alliances 265–84; Castells, *The Rise of the Network Society* (n 53 above) 177 *et seq*, 187, 209 and 214; Windeler, *Unternehmungsnetzwerke: Konstitution und Strukturation* (n 45 above) 225 *et seq*. A salomonic solution: Luhmann, *Organisation und Entscheidung* (n 38 above) 408: Networks will 'become social systems of their own, once they constitute clear boundaries and a history of recursive events on which trust will be based'.

liability, a distinction must be made between two typical situations, ie, between centralised and de-centralised networks. Various hybrid networks are so centralised and the autonomy of their nodes so limited that they are little more than hierarchical organisations in contractual clothing. Such networks are just a strategic effort to evade the imperative provision of law. Empirical data confirms the suspicion that companies deploy disaggregation strategies in order to avoid the application of tort and labour law.

In the case of de-centralised networks, we return to our example of the marketing of private vehicles. Although the external liability of the network, and not just that of its individual nodes, should be legally guaranteed, the 'piercing of the contractual veil' should not result in unitary collective liability. Instead, the appropriate form of liability is a de-centralised, multiple and collective combination of network liability and the liability of nodes which have, in fact, participated within the operation under scrutiny. In contrast to comprehensive collective liability in the case of formal organisations, this leads to a re-indivualisation of collective liability within networks. Analogous to the well-known concept of 'market share liability', one might make use of the notion 'network share liability'—a form of liability that is particularly significant in situations where the root cause of damage cannot be traced back to individual nodes, but only to the network itself. Such cases do not involve a traditional collective actor whose assets might serve as the object of liability claims. Nonetheless, the network does serve as a point of reference for the attribution of liability, and as the springboard for the re-individualisation of liability amongst individual nodes. Such a re-individualisation is particularly to be promoted in cases where the individual contributions of nodes to damage can no longer be clearly distinguished. In such a situation, liability could be met through the pro-rata liability of participating nodes, calculated in accordance within their degree of participation within the network.

VI.4 Fourth Contradiction: Intersystemic Networks

A final conflict between different operational logics becomes apparent within a third configuration/group of hybrids. In the effort to promote technological transformation, the state provides extensive grants to joint research projects between particular industrial branches and independent research institutions. This results in a loosely organised network, which establishes close relationships between the relevant industries and both the participating research institutions and the public authorities that have an interest in such co-operation. The network is charged with the pursuit of successful innovation. Its attitude to transaction costs, however, is as irrational and extravagant as a series of UN conferences.

This is a conflict between different social rationalities that again disturbs institutional arrangements. The participating actors demand to be allowed to behave in accordance with different and contradictory behavioural logics. The case of public-private research networks would require rational actors to observe three mutually-incompatible categorical imperatives. Hybrid networks, in this case, appear as manna from heaven, being exactly tailored to bridge multiple contradictory rationalities. They facilitate mutual interference between rationalities without the imposition of a hierarchical order.

Can a legal concept of network respond to such demands? In the case of mixed network regimes, the simple evolution of legal norms to support the transaction-cost advantages and efficiency gains of networks, as opposed to contractual or corporate arrangements, is clearly not enough. In reality, such networks only offend against the imperatives of transaction-cost minimisation and allocative efficiency. Nonetheless, they are successful innovators. The roles of legal concepts of the network are, therefore—in this case of mixed public-private regimes—far more those of developing principles of institutional autonomy, of establishing fundamental rights, of securing procedural fairness, of ensuring the rule of law and of fostering political responsibility.

This points to one of the central tasks of a law of hybrid networks. In contrast to traditional legal concepts, such as 'contractual purposes' or 'business interest', this involves the evolution of a legally-applicable concept of 'network interest'. As a counterpoint to instrumental autonomy, I call this the legally-secured 'reflexive autonomy' of individual sub-units within the network. Within integrated organisations, be they private concerns, public corporations or mixed form, rules on organisational procedure are always oriented in line with the common purpose. The character of this common goal is determinative in the case of a de-centralisation or a delegation of functions. De-centralised units are afforded the freedom to use their local knowledge in order to choose the appropriate concrete means of pursuing the common aims of the entire organisation, or, legally speaking, the 'business interest'.

This is entirely different within inter-systemic networks. Legal norms must not merely afford network nodes a heightened degree of protection for their autonomy. Instead, they must supply a different form of protection in that, despite centralisation, they must guarantee reflexive capacities, ie, the capacity of nodes to balance out (against network relations) their own independent concept of their social function and contribution to their environment. Within inter-systemic networks of scientific knowledge, politics and the economy, this leads us in the direction of a quasi-constitutional guarantee for scientific freedom in the face of political and economic inter-references within the borders of a mixed network. This idea is, in fact, generalisable. In contrast to the case of companies, in which legal guarantees of the autonomy of subsidiaries protect the profit interests of the parts against the whole, and vice versa, we are required, in the case of inter-systemic networks, to respect the institutional integrity of health, education, journalism, technology and art, not only within a de-central (not simply de-centralised) structure of autonomous nodes, but also within the inclusive network. Although it still makes sense to conceive of a common company interest in the form of procedural and material legal norms within corporation law, the 'network interest' can only be created out of the depths of the compatibility of autonomous network participants.

2

Network Contracts Revisited

ROGER BROWNSWORD*

I. INTRODUCTION

TWENTY YEARS AGO, in the English law of obligations, there was a serious doctrinal difficulty at the interface between the law of contract and the law of negligence.[1] The difficulty arose from the interaction of the principle of privity of contract (as a cornerstone feature of the classical law of contract)[2] and the apparent willingness, after the House of Lords's decision in *Junior Books Ltd v Veitchi Co Ltd*,[3] to allow negligence-based claims for purely economic loss. Contract lawyers were generally dissatisfied with a restrictive privity principle that not only shut out meritorious third-party claimants but also undermined reasonable expectations in some commercial contexts. Tort lawyers were fearful that *Junior Books* would open the floodgates, exposing too many negligent defendants to unlimited liability to unlimited classes of claimants. And, observers of the borderland that divides contract from tort were troubled by the way in which *Junior Books* seemed to allow claimants to by-pass the privity rule, and recover damages by pleading their actions in negligence rather than in contract.

In the event, this difficulty was resolved by doctrinal adjustment on both sides of the problem. First, in *Murphy v Brentwood District Council*,[4] a specially convened seven-member panel of the House of Lords had second thoughts about *Junior Books* and reverted to a much more restrictive approach to negligence-based claims for purely economic loss.

* Professor of Law, King's College London and Honorary Professor in Law at the University of Sheffield. I am grateful to my colleague at KCL, John Phillips, for helpful comments and conversations at various stages of work on this paper. Needless to say, the usual disclaimers apply.

[1] See R Brownsword, *Contract Law: Themes for the Twenty-First Century* (London, Butterworths, 2000) ch 8.

[2] *Dunlop Pneumatic Tyre Co Ltd v Selfridge & Co Ltd* [1915] AC 847.

[3] *Junior Books Ltd v Veitchi Co Ltd* [1983] 1 AC 520 (HL).

[4] *Murphy v Brentwood District Council* [1991] 1 AC 398 (HL).

Secondly, after further assaults on the privity principle in the case law and the accompanying jurisprudence, the rule was relaxed by the Contracts (Rights of Third Parties) Act 1999. Accordingly, by the turn of the millennium, English law had taken steps to mollify both contract and tort lawyers, and, with its new mixture of relaxation and restriction, it channelled third-party claimants towards an action in contract, rather than tort.

When the difficulties were at their peak, one suggestion for their resolution was that clusters of cognate contracts (such as the construction contracts in both *Junior Books* and *Murphy*, and carriage contracts, where there had been similar problems) should be treated as special sets, or 'networks', with their own distinctive rules.[5] In due course, it was proposed that the idea of a network, and, concomitantly, network contracts, might facilitate a focused relaxation of the privity rule that would support the reasonable expectations of the contractors.[6] For the purposes of this proposal, the default rule was that there would be a network (with relevant network effects) where a particular set of contracts was bound together by an overall unifying objective, such as a constitutive commercial project. Characteristically, there would be a principal contract (or a number of lead contracts) to which other contracts would be linked directly or indirectly.[7] It was implicit in this proposal that the lead contractors of what would otherwise be treated as a network should be free to disapply the network rules, but also that contractors involved in what would otherwise *not* be treated as a network should be free to adopt network effects for their contract.

Of course, the idea of a network, as outlined above, is not entirely original. In the English law of property, special rules for the running of covenants apply where a development is laid out as a so-called 'building scheme'[8]; the idea of a contractual structure has been relied on by some judges in order to prevent tort claims being used where this would be inconsistent with what are, in effect, network expectations[9]; and the network is not dissimilar to the concept of 'groups of contracts' as

[5] See JN Adams and R Brownsword, 'From *Jarvis* to *Junior Books*: Tortuous and Tortious Constructions' (1989) 5 *Construction Law Journal* 3, and JN Adams and R Brownsword, 'The Aliakmon and the Hague Rules' (1990) *Journal of Business Law* 23.

[6] JN Adams and R Brownsword, 'Privity and the Concept of a Network Contract' (1990) 10 *Legal Studies* 12, and *Key Issues in Contract* (London, Butterworths, 1995) ch 5.

[7] See, eg, *ibid*, 149.

[8] For the essentials of building schemes, see *Halsbury's Laws of England 4th edn*, vol 16(2) paras 624–5. NB, too, the possibility of a 'local law' being applied in other contexts, eg, where competing traders hold business leases within a single development, *ibid*, para 626 and *Williams v Kiley (trading as CK Supermarkets Ltd)* [2002] EWCA Civ 1645.

[9] See, eg, *Marc Rich and Co AG v Bishop Rock Marine Co Ltd (The Nicholas H)* [1996] AC 211.

developed in France by the first *chambre civil* of the *Cour de Cassation*.[10] That said, after the relaxation of the privity principle in the 1999 legislation, the effect of which was to allow for both claims and defences to run more freely in commercial contractual settings, is there any point in revisiting the idea of network contracts? Perhaps we would do better to file away networks as an idea whose time never quite came and which now has definitely gone.[11]

Against the proposition that networks should be consigned to history, I will argue that the idea of a network remains helpful for at least two reasons. First, where the law of contract aims to protect the reasonable expectations of parties to transactions, and where it judges the reasonableness of an expectation by reference to practice, the idea of a network will (in appropriate contexts) facilitate the articulation of the operative assumptions of contractors; and this will reach through to the particular decisions made by arbitrators and courts.[12] In applying such ideas, networks might be given a more radical application, bringing in consumers at the end of an integrated distribution system,[13] making some sense of the competition cases that puzzle contract lawyers,[14] helping in those corporate group cases where there is a gap between a guarantee as drafted and the actual implementation of the loan,[15] and perhaps having some potential for application to distributed contracting in electronic environments. Secondly, if we view a network as a particular kind of governance structure that is self-consciously engaged by contractors, then we have the key to distinguishing between genuinely contractual and other tort-like mechanisms for regulating transactions. Ironically, we find that where parties opt-in to a network governance structure, far from this being a deviant case, this is an ideal-typical instantiation of contractual obligation.

The paper is in three parts. First, I describe a doctrinal puzzle that has been created by the relaxation of the privity principle in conjunction with the modern judicial power to review the fairness and reasonableness of exclusion and limitation clauses (or, more generally, unfair contract terms). Stated briefly, the puzzle arises where a court must decide

[10] See B Nicholas, *The French Law of Contract*, 2nd edn (Oxford, Clarendon Press, 1992) 172–7.

[11] For critical (network-driven) comment on the Law Commission's proposals (Law Com No 242, July 1996) see JN Adams, D Beyleveld and R Brownsword, 'Privity of Contract—the Benefits and the Burdens of Law Reform' (1997) 60 *Modern Law Review* 238.

[12] Generally, compare G Teubner, '*Coincidentia Oppositorum*: Hybrid Networks beyond Contract and Organisation' in this volume.

[13] *Ibid*, at 2–3, discussing the judgment of the Karlsruhe Appeals Court in OLG Karlsruhe (1989) 2 *Neue Zeitschrift für Verkehrsrecht* 434.

[14] See, eg, *Clarke v Earl of Dunraven and Mount-Earl, The Satanita* [1897] AC 59 (HL).

[15] See, eg, *Amalgamated Investment and Property Co Ltd (in liquidation) v Texas Commerce International Bank Ltd* [1982] QB 84 (CA).

whether a term that has been included in a contract between *A* and *B* is a fair and reasonable one when the dispute is actually between *A* and *C*. Such a puzzle is more likely to arise between commercial contractors; but, in principle, it could also apply where consumer contractors are involved. In both cases, the root of the difficulty is that, as long as contracts are viewed as discrete unrelated bipolar transactions, rather than as connected contracts within a network, it is hard to find the right frame of reference for the question of fairness and reasonableness. The puzzle does not stop here—similar problems arise, for example, where the way in which a third-party beneficiary interprets a contractual term is at odds with the understanding of the principal contractors. Generalising the difficulty, we can say that, where the application of contract doctrine presupposes a context that focuses on the dealings between *A* and *B*, the law is in trouble once *C* (with a quite different history of dealing) comes on the scene. Doctrine might have been revised so that third-party beneficiaries are not altogether excluded, but there remains a sense in which third-parties are unexpected guests. In some such cases, at least, the idea of a network might be the solution.

Secondly, I distinguish two quite different justificatory bases for holding parties to a set of transactional ground-rules, whether these ground-rules concern third-party effects or the validity of exclusions and limitations. One justification rests on the consent of the parties, in the sense that the parties have freely engaged and chosen to be bound by a particular set of rules (just like players who agree to be bound by the rules of a particular game; or just like 'netizens' might sign up for a particular governance regime as they enter a particular sector of cyberspace).[16] This, I maintain, is the ideal-type of contractual obligation. The other justification does not rely on the parties having opted-in, but on the merits of the ground-rules themselves. The reason why the parties are bound, so it is claimed, is because the ground-rules are efficient, or fair, or right by reference to whatever background substantive criterion is adopted. If the first kind of justification is procedural and 'Lockean' (ie, one is bound only if one has freely signed up for the deal), then the second is substantive and 'Hobbesian' (ie, one is bound because this is the best available deal, irrespective of whether one has signed up for it). If the first kind of justification fits with, say, international trade where contractors self-consciously make a particular choice of law to govern

[16] Compare DR Johnson and D Post, 'Law and Borders—The Rise of Law in Cyberspace' (1996) 48 *Stanford Law Review* 1367; see also, G Teubner, 'Societal Constitutionalism: Alternatives to State-Centred Constitutional Theory' in C Joerges, I-J Sand and G Teubner (eds), *Constitutionalism and Transnational Governance* (Oxford, Hart Publishing, 2004) 3.

their dealings,[17] the second kind of justification seems to fit the mass-consumer marketplace where a governing law of consumer protection is imposed. If the first is truly contract, the second masquerades as contract, but actually belongs to another division of the law of obligations.

Thirdly, I return to the possible application of networks. One application, a paradigmatic contractual application as we now see it, is for parties to opt-in freely to a particular kind of governance structure for their transaction(s). This is contract working pure. A second application is to impose a network (with defined network effects) as a governance structure for a complex of transactions, not because it has been chosen by the parties but because it is judged, on its merits, to be substantively justified. And, a third application sees the idea of a network operating within and through the English law of contract, whether that particular body of law is chosen or imposed. It is probably the third of these applications that best responds to the particular doctrinal puzzle identified in the first part of the paper. However, it is the first two applications that are of more general significance.

II. THE CONTINUING RELEVANCE OF NETWORKS IN THE LAW OF CONTRACT

Following the enactment of the Contracts (Rights of Third Parties) Act 1999, where the contracting parties, *A* and *B*, intend that a third-party, *C*, should be permitted to enforce their contract, then *C* will have the right to do so.[18] *C* will also have the right to enforce the contract between *A* and *B* where it is the intention of the contractors that their agreement should be for the benefit of *C*—at any rate, this is so, provided that the contractors did not intend to deny *C* the right to enforce the agreement.[19] Applying these provisions, it should be possible to avoid some notoriously unfair outcomes, particularly in family third-party beneficiary cases such as *Tweddle v Atkinson*[20] and *Beswick v Beswick*.[21]

However, having addressed the simpler third-party beneficiary problem, the Act deals, in a somewhat back-handed way, with the kind of case that gave the courts most cause for concern during the period when pressure for reform of the privity rule gathered real momentum. This was the kind of commercial case where *A* and *B* were the main contractors and then *B* sub-contracted some of the work to *C* (for example, *B* might

[17] Compare G Teubner, 'Breaking Frames: Economic Globalisation and the Emergence of *lex mercatoria*' (2002) 5 *European Journal of Social Theory* 199.

[18] Contracts (Rights of Third Parties) Act 1999 s. 1(1)(a).

[19] Contracts (Rights of Third Parties) Act 1999 s. 1(1)(b) and (2).

[20] *Tweddle v Atkinson* (1861) 1 B & S 393 (QB).

[21] *Beswick v Beswick* [1968] AC 58 (HL).

be a carrier who sub-contracted the stevedoring work to *C*, or a builder who sub-contracted the electrical work to *C*, and so on). It was commonplace in such cases for *B* to contract with *A* for a restriction of liability that would cover not only *B* but also all other downstream sub-contractors such as *C*—such was the purported effect of so-called 'Himalaya' clauses. Although *A* would have no direct contractual action against *C*, *A* might sue *C* in negligence (typically, where *C* negligently damaged *A*'s property). If *C* responded by setting up the restrictions agreed in the main contract between *A* and *B*, or in the sub-contract between *B* and *C*, a strict application of the privity rule would disallow *C*'s purported reliance on these terms.[22] Scarcely reflecting the degree of difficulty presented by such cases, the Act simply provides that the relaxation of the privity rule (designed for single contract third-party beneficiary cases) also applies to enable a third-party to avail itself of an exclusion or limitation.[23]

With privity relaxed, there is, in principle, no reason why a third-party sub-contractor, such as *C*, should be denied the right to set up a restrictive term in the contract between *A* and *B* in order to respond to a claim made by *A*. However, what if the claimant, *A*, challenges the fairness or reasonableness of the restrictive term to which *C* (after the 1999 Act) has access? *A*'s point is not that *C* has no standing to rely on the term; that point is defeated by the new legislation. Rather, *A*'s point is that the term is not fair and reasonable; and, after the Unfair Contract Terms Act 1977 (UCTA), this is a challenge that *A* could make in many situations, most strongly as a consumer contractor, but also as a commercial contractor. The puzzle arises because *A* is taking this point against *C*, a contractor with whom *A* has no direct dealings, rather than against *B*, the party with whom *A* has contractual dealings and where there is evidence that is relevant to making a judgement of inter-personal fairness and reasonableness. Or, to put this another way, the difficulty arises not simply because it does not follow that what might be fair and reasonable as between *A* and *B* is also fair and reasonable between *A* and *C*, but because it is unclear which frame of reference should be used to assess fairness and reasonableness between *A* and *C*.

To revert to the standard case, if *A* were to challenge the fairness and reasonableness of a term (in the contract between *A* and *B*) on which *B* seeks to rely, the frame of reference for determining the fairness and reasonableness of the term would be the background dealings between *A* and *B*. Typically, the courts would have to determine whether the particular term was a fair and reasonable one to include in the contract,

22 See *Scruttons Ltd v Midland Silicones Ltd* [1962] AC 446 (HL).
23 Contracts (Rights of Third Parties) Act 1999 s. 1(6).

having regard to such considerations as the relative bargaining strength of the contractors (*A* and *B*), whether an inducement was offered to the complainant (whether *B* offered an inducement to *A*), who would be the better insurer (*A* or *B*), and so on. Making judgements of this kind is a long way from being an exact science. There is, for example, no scale for the measurement of a contractor's bargaining strength: we cannot say that *A* measures five on the bargaining power scale and *B* measures seven on that scale; all that we can say is that *B* has greater bargaining strength than *A*. Most importantly, the bottom-line judgement that a term is a fair and reasonable one to be included in a contract (relative to the dealings between *A* and *B*), does not signal that the term is the very apogee of fairness and reasonableness; rather, it merely signals that the term cannot be condemned as manifestly unfair and unreasonable, and that it falls somewhere within the margin of acceptability. Because relatively few unfair contract term cases are reported, it is difficult to know precisely how wide the margin of acceptability is. However, it is a fair bet that, in commercial contracts, the margin is rather wider than is the case in consumer contracts.[24] For present purposes, though, the capital point is that, whatever the width of the margin, it is the dealings between *A* and *B* that provide the frame of reference for making the judgement of fairness and reasonableness—that is, in the language of Section 11(1) of UCTA, the question is whether the term is:

> a fair and reasonable one to be included having regard to the circumstances which were, or ought reasonably to have been, known to or in the contemplation of the parties when the contract was made.[25]

Now, the difficulty that I am highlighting arises where it is *C*, not *B*, who seeks to rely on the particular restrictive term. The obvious question is this: Is it still the relationship and dealings between *A* and *B* that set the frame of reference for the purposes of determining the fairness and reasonableness of the term? Or, should some attempt be made to switch the frame of reference so that C is substituted for *B* (even though *A* will not have dealt directly with C)?[26] The legislation gives no indication as to how a dispute of this kind should be framed.

[24] See JN Adams and R Brownsword, 'The Unfair Contract Terms Act: A Decade of Discretion' (1988) 104 *Law Quarterly Review* 94. The margin tolerated in commercial dealings is clearly evident in cases such as *Photo Production Ltd v Securicor Transport Ltd* [1980] AC 827 and, more recently, *Watford Electronics Ltd v Sanderson CFL Ltd* [2001] EWCA Civ 317.

[25] This test, focused on the reasonableness of including the term at the time of contracting, was chosen in preference to a test focused on the reasonableness of reliance at the time of the dispute. Even if the latter test had been adopted, the puzzle highlighted in the text remains.

[26] It is true that there is a sense in which *B* will have dealt on behalf of C (that is, with a view to extending the protective benefit of the term in question to C); and this might prompt the thought that the contract between *A* and *B* is, after all, the right frame of

Before we proceed to consider the problem of how to frame the question of fairness, one technical point needs to be cleared out of the way. According to Section 7(2) of the 1999 Act,

> [s]ection 2(2) of the Unfair Contract Terms Act 1977 (restriction on exclusion etc. of liability for negligence) shall not apply where the negligence consists of the breach of an obligation arising from a term of a contract and the person seeking to enforce it is a third party acting in reliance on Section 1.

Although this provision anticipates one issue arising from the intersection of the new privity rule and the UCTA, it does not have any purchase on our problem case. To see why this is so, we need to focus on the closing condition which specifies that the person seeking to enforce the term is a third party who relies on the enforceability provisions in the 1999 Act.

Let us suppose, first, that *A* seeks to enforce the contract between *B* and *C* by relying on the 1999 enforceability provisions and claiming that, in breach of contract, *C* has failed to take reasonable care (*C* has been negligent). Further, let us suppose that *B* and *C* concede that these provisions apply because it was their intention to contract for the benefit of *A*, and let us suppose that *C* admits the breach of which *A* complains. Now, the effect of Section 1(4) of the 1999 Act is to bring *A* into the contract on the same terms as *B*, from which it follows that, if there are exclusions or restrictions of liability (shielding *C*) in the contract between *B* and *C*, *A* is bound by those terms. If *A* entertains thoughts about challenging the fairness and reasonableness of such terms, Section 7(2) of the 1999 Act disables *A* from invoking Section 2(2) of UCTA (which would otherwise be available to support a challenge to the fairness and reasonableness of a contractual restriction on *C*'s liability for negligence (this not being a case of the negligence causing death or personal injury)).[27]

reference for handling a dispute between *A* and *C*. However, this thought might be taken up in more than one way. If it is suggested that it is as though *A* has dealt directly with *C*, this, surely, is unconvincing. After all, this is not a case in which *B* is acting as an agent on behalf of a disclosed principal, *C*; and *C* might be no more than an, as yet, unidentified member of a specified class of sub-contractors, or the like. Seemingly, a more promising suggestion is that the protection of *C* is part of the package negotiated between *A* and *B*. However, what begins to crystallise from this more promising thought is that *A* and *B* are not simply negotiating a contract but a set of governance rules for a group of contractors—and this introduces the idea of the network as the relevant frame of reference. In other words, the contract between *A* and *B* might be the appropriate frame of reference (for disputes between *A* and *C*, *A* and *D*, *A* and *E*, and so on) but not so much as a discrete commercial transaction between *A* and *B* but as a constitutive act for a group of contractors (as a mini-constitution).

[27] Where negligence does cause death or personal injury, s. 2(1) of UCTA precludes reliance on any term that purports to exclude or restrict the liability of the negligent party.

By contrast, the scenario that troubled the courts in the run-up to the 1999 Act, and which is our model, starts with *A* suing *C* directly for *C*'s negligence. *A*'s cause of action does not depend on the 1999 Act and thus Section 7(2) simply does not apply. In such a case, *C* might set up, by way of a response, an exclusion or restriction of liability found in (i) the contract between *A* and *B* or (ii) the contract between *B* and *C*. Other things being equal, the 1999 Act allows *C* to rely on the former (keeping faith with the intentions of *A* and *B*) but it has no effect on the latter, which continues to be a difficult case under the common law.[28] Our test-case, therefore, is one in which *A* sues *C* in negligence, without relying on the 1999 Act to get the claim up and running, and where *C* purports to rely on an exclusion or restriction of liability for negligence in the contract between *A* and *B*, such term being intended to confer a benefit on C. Once again, the question is: Does it make sense for a court to evaluate the fairness and reasonableness of an exclusion clause that is central to a dispute between *A* and *C* by reference to the dealings between *A* and *B*?

Consider how the factor of relative bargaining power might play and, for the sake of illustration, let us suppose that the context is one of construction. In the straightforward case, where the dispute is between *A* (the client) and *B* (the main contractor), a court will determine whether there is an asymmetry of bargaining power between *A* and *B* and, if so, whether the party with greater bargaining strength has unfairly exercised it. Similarly, where the dispute is between *B* (the main contractor) and *C* (a sub-contractor), the court will follow the same process, except, of course, that it will be the dealings between *B* and *C* that are material. Where the dispute is between *A* and *C*, how is the relative bargaining strength of the parties to be factored into the judgement of the fairness and reasonableness of the term on which C seeks to rely?

If we take account of the relative bargaining strength of all three parties, *A* and *B*, *B* and *C*, and *A* and *C*, there are six possible permutations (effectively, three pairs of permutations depending upon whether it is *A*, *B*, or *C* who is in the strongest bargaining position). To simplify, and bearing in mind that it is *A* who challenges the fairness and reasonableness of the term on which *C* relies, there are two variations, as follows:

(V1) (*A>B>C*; *B>A>C*; and *B>C>A*). *A* is in a stronger bargaining position relative to *C* than to *B*; and

(V2) (*A>C>B*; *C>B>A*; and *C>A>B*). *A* is in a stronger bargaining position relative to *B* than to *C*.

[28] See *Morris v CW Martin and Sons Ltd* [1966] 1 QB 716.

Where the pattern is as per V1, *A* will argue that *C* is over-protected because, had *A* been dealing directly with *C*, less would have been conceded (ie, less than *A* has conceded to *B*); the exclusion or restriction of liability would not have had the same breadth or depth. It follows, argues *A*, that even if the court would have accepted the term as fair and reasonable in a negotiation between *A* and *B*, it should not do so relative to *C*. In other words, *A* argues that it is unfair for *C* to take the benefit of the *A*/*B* contract when, had *A* been dealing with *C*, *A* would not have allowed such benefits.

Where the pattern is as per V2, there seems to be little mileage in *A* rehearsing the V1 argument: for, if *A* has allowed a certain level of exclusion or limitation to *B*, *A* cannot plausibly assert that a more favourable deal would have been struck with *C* (who, ex hypothesi, is a stronger bargaining party). Instead, *A*'s argument has to be that it is unfair for *C* to take the benefit of the exclusion or restriction that *A* allowed to *B* as a quid pro quo for some balancing consideration given by *B*, when *C* (as a stronger bargaining party) would not have reciprocated in this way. In other words, *A* argues that it is unfair for *C* to take the benefit of the *A*/*B* contract when, had *C* been dealing with *A*, *C* would not have made the balancing concessions.[29]

A's arguments invite several lines of objection. For one thing, *A* seems to want to have it both ways, opportunistically pleading both its relative bargaining strength (in V1) and its relative vulnerability (in V2) against the fairness and reasonableness of the term. Moreover, the argument assumes that the parties negotiate in an adversarial way that in fact might not fit at all well with a relational approach. However, *A* surely has a point in inviting the court to construct a frame of reference that facilitates assessment of the term as fair or reasonable when it is *C*, not *B*, who seeks to rely on it. The difficulty is that there are no direct dealings between *A* and *C* on which to found such a frame of reference.

Let us change the context, from commercial to consumer contractors, and from construction to cleaning. Imagine that *A* is a consumer contractor who regularly deals with *B*, a commercial cleaner; *B* often sub-contracts cleaning work, using various sub-contractors, including *C*. Our test case arises where *C* damages *A*'s property, *A* sues *C* for the latter's negligence, and *C* replies by setting up protective terms in the contract that *A* has with *B*. Suppose that, on this occasion, *B* has offered *A* an

[29] When the Law Commission brought forward its proposals for relaxation of the privity principle (see n 11 above) some concerns were expressed about setting up a doctrinal tension between a relaxed third-party enforceability rule and the retained requirement of consideration for formation of the main contact. There are echoes of this tension (albeit not in a particular scenario envisaged by the Commission) in *A*'s complaint that *C* is, in effect, free-riding.

inducement (a substantial discount on the normal price) in return for a more extensive limitation of liability. *A* concedes that it would be fair and reasonable for *B* to rely on this special limitation, but does not accept that *C* should enjoy the same benefit. Or, again, suppose that *B* rarely notifies *A* of the contractual terms and conditions until after the contract has been made but that, by virtue of the 'previous dealings' principle, *B*'s terms will be treated as incorporated.[30] *A* concedes that *B*'s limitations of liability are incorporated relative to *B* but does not accept that they are incorporated for the benefit of *C*. As in the construction case, *A* is arguing that what might be fair between *A* and *B* does not carry through necessarily to the relationship between *A* and *C*. And the problem once again is not just that inter-personal fair dealing does not carry through, but that it is not clear what frame of reference would be just and appropriate here.

Another relatively recent development in English contract law further accentuates the puzzle. This is the explicit adoption, notably by Lord Hoffmann in *Investors Compensation Scheme Ltd v West Bromwich Building Society*,[31] of a new contextual approach to the interpretation of commercial contracts. According to Lord Hoffmann, '[a]lmost all the old intellectual baggage of 'legal' interpretation has been discarded'[32] and, in particular, an abstracted 'literalism'. Whilst the latter is wedded to application of the plain, natural and ordinary meaning of the language used by the contractors, new contextualism seeks out

> the meaning which the document would convey to a reasonable person having all the background knowledge which would reasonably have been available to the parties in the situation in which they were at the time of the contract.[33]

Contextualist interpretation, then, draws on three elements: the meaning of a contract is that which would be conveyed to (i) a reasonable person, (ii) put in the situation of the parties at the time that they made their agreement, and (iii) who is informed by the background knowledge that they would have had at that time. As these three elements make very clear, though, it is the dealings between the particular contractors (*A* and *B*) that set the immediate context for interpretation.

Since *Investors*, it has become apparent that even straightforward disputes between *A* and *B* are capable of defying swift contextual

30 See, eg, *McCutcheon v David MacBrayne Ltd* [1964] 1 All ER 430 (HL).

31 *Investors Compensation Scheme Ltd v West Bromwich Building Society* [1998] 1 All ER 98 (HL). In similar terms, see, too, the speeches of both Lord Hoffmann and Lord Steyn in *Mannai Investments Co Ltd v Eagle Star Life Assurance Co Ltd* [1997] 3 All ER 352 (the latter case dealing specifically with contractual notices).

32 *Investors Compensation Scheme* [1998] 1 All ER 98 (HL) 114.

33 *Ibid*.

resolution[34]; but at least the context is that of the dealings between *A* and *B*. If *C* enters the picture, claiming the benefit of a term in the contract between *A* and *B*, but reading the term in a way that is at odds with the understanding of *A* or *B*, we are in deeper difficulty. Which frame of reference is to be applied?

By now, the general shape of the difficulty should be clear. In the straightforward case, it makes sense to resolve contractual disputes by reference to the dealings between the disputing parties. However, where a third-party enters the dispute, there is no self-selecting frame of reference. If we refer to the dealings between *A* and *B* and the contract as they negotiated it, in order to judge a dispute between *A* and *C*, then this seems to be acting on the wrong standards. On the other hand, if we try to construct dealings between *A* and *C*, we are engaging in fiction. It is at this point that it is tempting to see the network as a better way of both handling the problem and keeping faith with the parties' expectations. For, the network does not force a choice to be made between two sets of dealings, treating them as unrelated. Instead, it seems to give the opportunity to put the question into a context that maps more satisfactorily on to the transactional situation in which the disputants are actually located. And, there is the promise here that we might generate results that are more in line with the reasonable expectations of the parties.[35]

What these opening thoughts suggest is that the idea of a network contract remains a live and relevant proposal. However, to appreciate its full significance we need to step back to clarify two different justifying approaches—that is, two ways of justifying the enforcement of the expectations of a contractor. Surprisingly, what we see is that the enforcement of obligations under a network regime is actually the ideal-typical case of contractual obligation and not some crazy deviation or exception.

[34] See R Brownsword, 'After *Investors*: Interpretation, Expectation and the Implicit Dimension of the 'New Contextualism' in D Campbell, H Collins and J Wightman (eds), *The Implicit Dimensions of Contract* (Oxford, Hart Publishing, 2003) 103.

[35] Compare, for example, the case of 'charge-back' clauses that are found in contracts between credit card companies and retailers (such contracts being one member of a larger credit-facilitating network): for discussion, see R Brownsword and J MacGowan, 'Credit Card Fraud' (1997) 147 *New Law Journal* 1806 (response by S Ward at: (1998) 148 *New Law Journal* 7; and reply at: (1998) 148 *New Law Journal* 133); R Brownsword, 'Judicial Revision of Abusive Contractual Terms: Credit Card Fraud and Charge-Back Clauses' *Revista de Direito Bancário*, Special Edition (Proceedings of the First International Symposium of Banking Law: *Banking Law and the Globalization of the Financial System*) (São Paulo, Brazil, 1998) 668; and PW Heermann, in this volume. For a further example, consider the case of minimum term membership clauses in contracts offered by fitness clubs: for discussion, see G-P Calliess, in this volume. And, for a very recent, and exemplary, illustration of network thinking, see *The Office of Fair Trading v Lloyds TSB Bank plc and Others* [2006] EWCA Civ 268; [2007] UKHL48.

III. TWO JUSTIFYING APPROACHES

Where *A* is in contract with *B* and where *B* is in contract with *C*, we run into difficulties where (i) contract doctrine presupposes a single contract frame of reference for contractual disputes, and (ii) the contractual dispute is between *A* and *C*. It is not clear why such a dispute, between *A* and *C*, should be determined by reference to the quite different relationship and transaction between *A* and *B* (nor, for that matter, the transaction between *B* and *C*); and it is not clear how a contractual relationship between *A* and *C* might be constructed for this purpose. Networks, I have suggested, might enable the courts to place the dispute between *A* and *C* in a more adequate context, but quite how this would work has yet to be explored. In the present section, I want to distinguish between two quite different strategies for dealing with this difficulty—indeed, with any question relating to the reasonable expectations of contractors. One of these strategies relies on a procedural justification (on the fact that the parties have freely engaged the governing rules); the other relies on an 'on the merits', substantive, justification (not on the fact that the governing rules have been freely engaged by the parties, but that the rules that govern are the best available for that purpose).

To begin at the beginning: *A*, *B*, and *C* do not necessarily need a formal body of doctrine, marked up as the 'law of contract', in order to transact with one another.[36] However, without the cover of the law of contract, commercial people would tend to take fewer risks and operate in a more defensive manner; and, for consumers, there might be an even more limited fall-back when things go wrong. Put somewhat crudely, we can say that the law of contract confers (enforceable) rights which parties otherwise do not have, and that, functionally, it encourages contractors to trade beyond the boundaries of trust. But, in marketplaces where we take it as read that the law of contract is in play, it is as well to remember that markets can function without the law of contract.

In principle, there are two ways in which the law of contract can be brought into play. First, *A* and *B* might agree that their dealings will be regulated by the law of contract. Where they agree to this, they are then precluded from complaining about the relevant rules of contract being applied to resolve any subsequent dispute arising from their dealings. To be sure, the relevant rules might be ugly and unfair, but, if the parties have authorised their application, they have no cause for complaint. Such is procedural justification. Secondly, *A* and *B* might not have given any thought to whether their dealings are regulated by the law of contract but

[36] For some examples, see T Daintith, 'Comment on Lewis: Markets, Regulation and Citizenship' in R Brownsword (ed), *Law and the Public Interest* (Stuttgart, Franz Steiner Verlag, 1993) 139 and 144–5.

the state has already decreed that dealings of this kind are covered by the law of contract. For example, when *A* (the consumer in our hypothetical scenario) takes his clothes to *B*'s shop to be dry-cleaned *A* does not give a moment's thought to the bearing of the law of contract on his dealings with *B*. Yet, it is already decreed that the law of contract is in play. If the parties are not permitted to disapply the law, the justification for its application has to be substantive; the state will need to defend the applicable regulation on its merits (whether by reference to some theory of justice or efficiency, or the like). Where *A* and *B* are permitted to disapply the law (in English law, by declaring that they do not intend to create legal relations),[37] and where *A* and *B* have not opted out, it is arguable that a procedural justification remains available. However, in mass-consumer markets, this view is unrealistic. For the most part, the parties do not realise that the law of contract is in play, let alone appreciate that they have the option of opting out. Accordingly, where the law of contract is, for all practical purposes, imposed on the parties, rather than being freely engaged by the parties themselves—that is, where opt-out is very much de jure rather than de facto—a substantive justification is called for.

Given its centrality to this paper—ie to the idea that contractors might adopt a network (or network effects) for their dealings—a few more words need to be said about the nature of procedural justification. Ideal-typically, before *A* and *B* enter into any dealings with one another (before *A* begins to negotiate with *B* for the construction work that is required) they should agree that these dealings will be regulated by a particular set of rules. In other words, there has to be an auxiliary agreement that decides the rules that are to govern the main contract dealings. To avoid an infinite regress running back from an auxiliary agreement to cover the main contract, and a pre-auxiliary agreement to cover the auxiliary agreement, and so on, there need to be some imposed ground-rules that cover the auxiliary agreement. Essentially, what we need is a jurisprudence that delineates what constitutes a valid (authorising) auxiliary agreement.[38] Depending upon how we theorise consent, the exercise of power by agents, etc, we will have a particular specification of what constitutes a free and informed choice by the parties, where the threshold for capacity lies, how their agreement is signalled (by opt-in or opt-out and the like), how any matters of interpretation are to

[37] See *Rose and Frank Company v JR Crompton and Brothers Ltd* [1925] AC 445.

[38] See, further, R Brownsword, 'Contract, Consent, and Civil Society: Private Governance and Public Imposition' in P Odell and C Willett (eds), *Civil Society* (Oxford, Hart Publishing, 2008).

be resolved, and so on. These are difficult questions, but, for our present purposes, it suffices to note their existence.[39]

Let us suppose that these difficulties are behind us and that the jurisprudence of auxiliary agreements is comprehensive and settled. The state might place some bodies of regulation off limits[40]; but, subject to any such restriction, the parties are then free to engage whatever rules they so wish to govern their dealings. In principle, this might be the local 'law of contract', or it might be a regional (eg, European) code of contract, or it might be an informal set of rules, or the rules of a commercial club (eg, those adopted where electronic bills of lading are used), and so on. Whichever rules are mandated by the auxiliary agreement, their application is procedurally justified.

If a set of rules, specifically designed to regulate network transactions, were to be developed, one of the choices available to the parties would be to engage these rules. In other words, *A* and *B* would agree that their dealings would be regulated by 'the rules for network contracts' and neither *A* nor *B* would have cause for complaint if these rules were applied. However, one of the distinctive features of this kind of procedural justification is that it holds good only between the parties to the auxiliary agreement. *A* is precluded from complaining about the application of the network rules; and so, too, is *B*. But, this still does not bind *C*, or any other third-party. To complete the procedural justification, therefore, *C* and other third-parties must also commit to the auxiliary agreement and agree that their dealings will be regulated by the chosen body of rules. In this way, two awkward questions concerning networks—namely, how insiders and outsiders are identified and how relations between internal network members and external parties are regulated—are answered. If the justification for applying network rules is procedural, then insiders are those, and only those, who have committed themselves to the auxiliary agreement; and, if network effects are to be applied to external parties, the justification will have to be substantive rather than procedural.

The next step is to understand how consenting to the terms of the auxiliary agreement is prior to, and distinct from, consenting to the main contract itself. It is widely assumed that the basis of contractual obligation is consent, and that it is consent that distinguishes contractual

[39] For a full discussion, see D Beyleveld and R Brownsword, *Consent in the Law* (Oxford, Hart Publishing, 2007).

[40] Where national courts act as enforcers of the parties' chosen rules, there might be some resistance to recognising model sets that lack the pedigree of a formally authorised source. Compare, R Goode, 'Usage and its Reception in Transnational Commercial Law' (1997) 46 *International Comparative Law Quarterly* 1 (dealing with codes and model sets such as the *lex mercatoria*, the UNIDROIT *Principles of International Commercial Contracts*, and the *Principles of European Contract Law*).

obligations from obligations imposed by regimes of tort, property, restitution or whatever.[41] And, so it is. However, contrary to common belief, it is not consent to the terms of the main contract (be it the phenomenon of agreement, or offer and acceptance) that is the key to contractual obligation; instead, it is consent in relation to the auxiliary agreement that is fundamental and the deeper source of obligation. Notice how a contract crystallises in the following four stages.

1. *A* and *B* reach an auxiliary agreement that their dealings will be regulated by, let us say, 'the English law of contract';
2. By virtue of consenting to the terms of the auxiliary agreement, *A* and *B* have now adopted the rules of the English law of contract as the governing law of their transaction;
3. According to the governing law of contract (freely engaged by *A* and *B*), a transaction will only be regarded as legally enforceable if it meets various criteria, one of which is that the parties must come to terms (ie, must reach agreement) and must do so in a way that involves neither coercion nor deception; and
4. *A* and *B* duly consent to a deal that satisfies the conditions for enforceability set by the governing law (ie, the law engaged by *A* and *B*).

Where the governing law that has been engaged by *A* and *B* specifies consent as one of the conditions of an enforceable transaction, we find consent double-banked. First, the parties must consent to the terms of the auxiliary agreement, and then they must consent to the terms of the main contract. While the jurisprudence of the auxiliary agreement will provide for the necessary and sufficient conditions for a valid authorising consent (how free, how informed, it has to be and the like),[42] it is the rules within the engaged governing law that specify what counts as consent for the purposes of an enforceable transaction. There is a sense, therefore, in which we have a double consent theory of contract. Moreover, we might also think of 'freedom of contract' as being double-banked: first, under the auxiliary jurisprudence where the parties are free to engage their own governing law (or rules or principles)[43] for their dealings; and secondly,

[41] See, eg, H Kötz and A Flessner, *European Contract Law: Volume One* (Oxford, Clarendon Press, 1998).

[42] Compare R Barnett, 'The Sound of Silence: Default Rules and Contractual Consent' (1992) 78 *Virginia Law Review* 821.

[43] In principle, parties might engage a model set such as the UNIDROIT Principles for International Commercial Contracts, or the Lando principles, or the like. However, each legal system would have to decide whether transactions governed by such principles would be recognised as legally enforceable in the civil courts. The availability of such sets would test the boundaries of freedom of contract (in relation to the auxiliary agreement). Compare Goode, 'Usage and its Reception in Transnational Commercial Law' (n 40 above).

within the governing law so engaged. On this analysis, the key to freedom of contract is not so much that the parties are permitted to set their own transactional terms, but that they are permitted to engage their own governing law.

Before taking up the question of networks again, it is necessary to say a few words about the protection of reasonable expectations. In the case of ideal-typical procedural justification, if *A* and *B* have freely engaged 'the English law of contract' as the governing law for their dealings, then they expect, quite reasonably, that the rules of English contract law will be applied to their transaction. The idea of reasonable expectation, however, is also susceptible to double-banking. This is because, internal to the English law of contract, there might be various rules that are designed to protect the reasonable expectations of the contractors, with the basis of reasonable expectation being doctrinally elaborated in a particular way. The new contextualism, after *Investors Compensation*, for instance, bases the reasonable expectations of the contractors less on the literal reading of the agreement, and more on the inter-subjective understanding of the parties. Accordingly, once *A* and *B* have freely engaged a particular set of governing rules, these rules may or may not develop the idea of protecting reasonable expectations, and, if they do so, they might articulate this idea in more than one way. Whatever the approach taken by the governing law, the most basic reasonable expectation of *A* and *B* is that their chosen rules will be applied to their disputes.

This all contrasts, quite markedly, with the deployment of doctrines concerning the protection of reasonable expectation where the justification is substantive. One view of English contract law is that there has been a shift from a static market-individualist approach (where the rules are set to guide and govern the practice of business contractors) to a dynamic market-individualist approach (where the rules are set in a way that is guided by, and tracks, the practice of business contractors).[44] On the former approach, the rules drive practice (or, at least, that is the intention); on the latter, it is practice that drives the rules. On the former, an expectation is reasonable if it is rule-based or rule-reliant; on the latter, an expectation is reasonable if it is practice-based or practice-reliant. There is also the possibility that doctrine might articulate an idea of reasonable expectation that is based neither on the existing rules nor on the relevant sector of business practice, but on some external standard that identifies the parties' entitlements, instead.[45] Whichever approach is

[44] See R Brownsword, 'Static and Dynamic Market Individualism' in R Halson (ed), *Exploring the Boundaries of Contract* (Aldershot, Dartmouth, 1996) 48.

[45] R Brownsword, 'After *Investors*: Interpretation, Expectation and the Implicit Dimension of the "New Contextualism"' in D Campbell, H Collins and J Wightman (eds), *The Implicit Dimensions of Contract* (Oxford, Hart Publishing, 2003) 103.

taken by a particular set of rules, in the absence of the parties having mandated the application of such rules, it is incumbent on the state to develop a substantive, 'on the merits', justification for its rejection or rendition of the idea of the protection of reasonable expectation.

Finally, what is the general shape of network thinking relative to these two justificatory strategies? First, if *A* and *B* have freely engaged 'the law of networks' then, whatever the network rules are, their application is procedurally justified (although not necessarily substantively justified). Secondly, if the set of rules freely engaged by *A* and *B*—whether it be the English, French or whatever law of contract—has a doctrine of networks or network effects, then the application of the rules so chosen is procedurally justified (although not necessarily substantively justified). Thirdly, if *A* and *B* have not freely engaged any set of governing rules, no procedural justification will be available. Fourthly, in the absence of a procedural justification, the rules that are imposed will have to be substantively justified—and this applies whether networks or network effects are imposed directly or indirectly (eg, via a practice-based doctrine of reasonable expectation).

IV. TWO TYPES OF NETWORK

Broadly speaking, we might expect procedural justification to have some support in commercial contracting (where the parties are concerned to tailor the governing law to the transaction, and where they are professionally advised as to their options).[46] However, it is hard to imagine a similar level of support in the field of consumer contracts. Here, the state will impose a package of rights and obligations that it will seek to justify substantively as an appropriate settlement of consumer and business interests, or something of that kind. It follows that, in our first test-case (a commercial construction project) we might meaningfully consider how networks might be procedurally justified; but, in our second test-case (cleaning for a consumer customer) the introduction of networks would have to be substantively justified. How might the network principle be elaborated and how might these respective justifications go?

In both instances, the *general* principle that is to be applied runs along the lines that, although *A* and *B* and *B* and *C* are parties to their own contracts, these contracts are part of a network of contracts and this is a consideration to be taken into account in determining questions of fairness and allocation of risk, and the like, where they arise between the

[46] Compare E Schanze, 'Hare and Hedgehog Revisited: The Regulation of Markets that Have Escaped Regulated Markets' (1995) 151 *Journal of Institutional and Theoretical Economics* 162.

parties. Negatively, this means that the frame of reference for settling disputes between the parties will not be limited to an examination of the dealings between the parties to one particular contract (the discrete, bipolar view). Positively, it means that the dispute will be set in the context of the network within which that dispute arises (that is, that the network provides the larger frame of reference for the determination of the dispute). Depending upon the particular regime that governs the parties' dealings, we can expect this general network principle to be elaborated in a set of concrete provisions—and this will be so, irrespective of whether the parties freely engage a tailored network governance regime or the state imposes a network solution.

As we begin to fill in the substantive detail, one of the key questions to be addressed by the particular governance regime will be the extent of the positive obligations owed by each network contractor to fellow network members. Assuming that it is characteristic of networks that they involve a co-operative ethic,[47] an intensified duty of loyalty, and the like, what remains to be settled is how far these responsibilities go. For example, in a franchising network, how far do the economic interests of fellow franchisees constrain a particular franchisee's right to terminate; and to what extent is the franchisor under an obligation to pass on to franchisees the financial benefits that have been negotiated only by virtue of the franchisor's position as procurer for the network?[48] Or, again, if the letting of retail units at a shopping centre is constituted as a network, what are the responsibilities of the linchpin retailers to fellow members who rely on the former to attract customers to the shopping centre[49]; and, conversely, what are the responsibilities of the smaller retailers to support the larger retailers (say, supermarkets) and their suppliers in the event of a price war with their competitors (viewing these rivals as competitors to the *network*)?[50] And, if account or loyalty card-holding consumers are to be treated as members of such a network, what are the responsibilities of the retailers at the shopping centre to their regular customers (for instance, in the event of a stock shortage)?[51]

Turning to the hypothetical construction test-case, the difficulty is that it is unclear how to frame the question of the fairness and reasonableness of a term negotiated between *A* and *B* when it is *C*, rather than *B*, who

[47] See R Brownsword, 'Individualism, Co-operativism and an Ethic for European Contract Law' (2001) 64 *Modern Law Review* 628; and G Teubner, *Coincidentia Oppositorum*: Hybrid Networks beyond Contract and Organisation (n 12 above).

[48] Compare R Böhner, 'Asset-sharing in Franchise Network. The Obligation to Pass on Network Benefits' (ch 9), in this volume.

[49] See *Co-operative Insurance Society Ltd v Argyll Stores (Holdings) Ltd* [1998] AC 1.

[50] See H Collins, 'The Weakest Link: Legal Implications of the Network Architecture of Supply Chains' (ch 10), in this volume.

[51] *Ibid.*

seeks to rely on that term. If the parties are committed to an auxiliary agreement under which their dealings and disputes are governed by a bespoke package of network rules, these rules will not only offer up a network frame of reference, they will resolve the issue. Moreover, because the parties have authorised the application of these bespoke rules, they are procedurally justified. If the parties have not engaged a bespoke set of network rules as such, but have engaged a body of doctrine that incorporates a network principle, then the application of that principle (possibly with less predictable results) is again procedurally justified. For, in both cases, *A* and *C* have, so to speak, previous dealings in relation to the auxiliary agreement; and it is this auxiliary agreement that binds them in to the effect of the network. It is only if the parties have not self-consciously engaged a governing set of rules that the network principle or more concrete network provisions will need to be imposed and substantively justified. This, naturally, leads us to the consumer test-case.

In the consumer test-case a number of difficulties were mooted, all of which arose from the fact that there is a frame of reference based on *A* (the consumer's) dealings with the cleaners (*B*), but the dispute is now between *A* and a sub-contractor *C*. If the network principle is to be legitimately imposed in such a case, it must be because it is judged to be substantively justifiable. Where doctrine poses the question of whether it would be fair and reasonable for *C* to rely on a term in the contract between *A* and *B*, or whether reliance by *C* would be in line with the parties' reasonable expectations, the network principle allows the court to put the question in the larger context of the related dealings between the parties. This is not necessarily conducive to more predictable decision-making, but it might be defended as having the merit of locating the dispute in a context that fits better with the parties' own perceptions of the matter.

What happens if we combine the test-cases? Imagine that *A*, who is a housing developer, contracting for the construction work with *B*, and *B* with *C*, sells a finished house to *Z*, a consumer. As we have said, if the application of network rules is to be procedurally justified, it will only be those parties who have committed to the auxiliary agreement who are bound by the network rules. In the hybrid scenario, this will mean that *A*, *B*, and *C* are in a network, but that *Z* is unlikely to be so bound—indeed, *Z* will have a legitimate cause for complaint if network effects are applied and then defended by reference to a procedural justification. Having said this, if the application of a network is defended by reference to a substantive justification (possibly one that gives proper recognition to *Z*'s interest as a private house-purchaser), the question is not whether *Z*, *A*, *B*, or *C* have signed up for it as their chosen governance regime but whether its imposition can be justified on the merits.

This leaves one further general issue. If the state judges that an imposed network is the best way of achieving a fair balance of interests between house-purchasers such as *Z*, and developers and contractors such as *A*, *B*, and *C*, it will be necessary to limit the freedom of the latter to engage a legal regime that does not recognise network effects. This is simply akin to denying contractors the freedom to bargain round an imposed tort rule, to self-regulate, so to speak, beyond regulation[52]; and, as I have said, the deeper meaning of freedom of contract is found at the auxiliary point of engaging a chosen set of rules rather than at the later point of coming to terms relative to the main transaction.

V. CONCLUSION

When the idea of network contracts was first proposed, there were a number of loose ends. In particular, it was unclear whether a network would arise only where the parties so intended, or whether it would be found (irrespective of the parties' intentions) where it mapped on to the transactional infrastructure. With hindsight, we can see that these loose ends concerned the difference between the parties engaging a governing law with network features and the imposition of a network. We can also see that this distinction expresses the far more important difference between obligations that are procedurally justified and obligations that are substantively justified.

Obligations that are procedurally justified are distinctively contractual. Where rule-sets are brought into play *qua* governance regimes that are consensually adopted by the participants, then, far from being a deviation, this is contract law working itself pure. This is the proper realm for freedom of contract (in relation to setting the terms of governance) and sanctity of contract (holding parties to the terms of the agreed regime).

Currently, we look at contract the wrong way round, through the wrong end of a telescope. Choice of law clauses, declarations of intention to be bound in honour only, authorisation of network governance, and the like are not exceptions but paradigms of authentic contractual activity; such matters go to the essence of contractual obligation. By contrast, in the consumer marketplace, where there is an uncritical submission to the local law of contract, 'contract' so-called in practice rules by imposition. Contract by failure to opt-out is the death of contract. Contract by opt-in is the ideal-type; and network governance in commercial contracting fits with this.

More generally, the network based on consent is a micro-version of the idea, if not the reality, of the social contract (a governance regime

[52] See Schanze, 'Hare and Hedgehog Revisited' (n 46 above).

authorised by the consent of the participants), of governance in clubs and competitions, and so on.[53] It is not strange. It is not deviant. What is strange is that even after the relaxation of the privity principle we continue to be fixated with contract as a bipolar transaction and, as a result, this has blocked us from seeing something that is staring us in the face. On the one hand, the parties might freely engage network rules; on the other, the appropriate context for contractual disputes will sometimes be a network.

[53] Compare Teubner, 'Societal Constitutionalism' (n 16 above).

3

The Return of the Guild? Network Relations in Historical Perspective

SIMON DEAKIN*

I. INTRODUCTION

AS MARC AMSTUTZ and Gunther Teubner put it,[1] one of the challenges posed by the rise of the network form in the final decades of the twentieth century was its incompatibility with the legal categories of contract and association, which roughly corresponded to the division between market and enterprise that had been predominant since the industrial revolution. This chapter seeks to take up the challenge of more precisely locating network forms in relation to the long-run process of industrialisation and of assessing the relevance, in this context, of the legal framework of enterprise. How would we view the network phenomenon if, instead of seeing it as a manifestation of the 'post-industrial society' of the late-twentieth century, as argued by Manuel Castells,[2] we recognised that network forms also preceded the emergence of the modern industrial enterprise?

Prior to the industrial revolution, the predominant form of economic organisation in Western Europe and North America was the corporate guild. Guilds possessed many of the features now associated with networks. Guilds were neither firms nor markets, but loose associations of independent producers, with strong local or regional identities, in which co-operation and competition were combined, and the benefits of innovation shared by the trade as a whole. The values expressed by guild forms were those of communitarianism, producer solidarity, and the

* Professor of Law, University of Cambridge. I am grateful for comments received from Ana Lourenço, Steve Pratten and Frank Wilkinson, and from the participants at the conference 'Contractual networks: legal issues of multilateral co-operation', in particular, Poul Kjaer.

[1] 'Contractual networks: legal issues of multilateral co-operation', conference held at Fribourg, 6–9 October 2005, home page: http://www.unifr.ch/obligations/conference/home.htm.

[2] M Castells, *The Information Age: Economy, Society and Culture. Volume 1—The Rise of the Network Society* (Oxford, Blackwell, 1999).

defence of the collective property of the trade as an 'intellectual commons'. These same values could also be interpreted as collusion, restriction and exclusion—literally, as the English judges put it in the seventeenth and eighteenth centuries, a 'conspiracy' against consumers and the interests of wider society. At the same time as the common law was reshaping the boundaries of criminal and civil liability for unlawful 'combinations' and developing the doctrine of 'restraint of trade', guild forms were also being condemned by the legislation of the French Revolution and by the post-revolutionary codes on the continent of Europe. But while the decline of the guilds paved the way for the emergence of the integrated business enterprise, the transition was far from seamless; and elements of the guild lived on under conditions of industrial capitalism, albeit in niches and segments which were continuously under threat of encroachment.

The guild and the network are not synonymous; but the guild does represent a particular sub-division of the network form, based, as it is, on 'lateral or horizontal patterns of exchange, interdependent flows of resources, and reciprocal lines of communication'.[3] Using a historical perspective, the fate of the guild may be particularly instructive. This chapter will argue that, if present-day network forms are not to be consigned to the margins of (post-) industrial capitalism, as their predecessors were, we need, if not necessarily a legal analogue to the network form, then, at the very least, a set of legal concepts and techniques which can underpin and protect network relations, in the same way that the law permits the organisation of firms and markets.

With this end in view, the argument in this chapter unfolds as follows. The next section considers some issues concerning the economic and legal definitions of the network form, and the relationship between networks, markets and firms. Then, the focus shifts to an historical analysis of the legal changes which, first, underpinned guild relations, and then accompanied their decline. This is followed by an outline of the role played by competition law and policy in reshaping organisational boundaries in a prototypical 'post-industrial' sector, the cultural industries. This is followed by the concluding section.

II. 'MARKET', 'FIRM' AND 'NETWORK' AS ECONOMIC AND LEGAL CONCEPTS

A key question is whether markets, firms and networks are mutually exclusive categories. Transaction cost economics in the tradition of RH

[3] W Powell, 'Neither market nor hierarchy: network forms of organisation' (1990) 12 *Research in Organizational Behaviour* 295 at 295.

Coase[4] and Oliver Williamson[5] portrays firms and markets as alternative modes of economic organisation. However, it has not been convincingly shown that networks constitute a distinctive form of governance in this sense. Jeffrey Bradach and Robert Eccles[6]—having identified 'price, authority and trust' as potentially alternative mechanisms of co-ordination for the market, firm and network, respectively—in the end have to accept that these are no more than ideal types which are useful in model-building and do not represent the reality of industrial organisation. As control mechanisms, while they may be 'separate', they are also, in practice, 'overlapping, embedded, intertwined, juxtaposed and nested'. The assumption of mutual exclusivity, these authors conclude, 'obscures, rather than clarifies, our understanding'.[7]

Walter Powell, likewise, sets out with the aim of identifying

> a coherent set of factors that make it meaningful to talk about networks as a distinctive form of co-ordinating economic activity.[8]

Networks, in his presentation, are 'more social—that is, more dependent on relationships, mutual interests and reputations'[9] than markets, while being 'less guided by a formal structure of authority'[10] than hierarchies. As distinct from markets, networks embody mechanisms for social learning and information transfer, while, by contrast with hierarchies, they depend on a 'mutual orientation' and norms of reciprocity.[11] The difficulty with this analysis is that the characteristics described by Powell as belonging specifically to networks can convincingly be ascribed to the other two forms as well. Markets, as FA Hayek has shown,[12] function to mobilise and encode knowledge. While Hayek's account perhaps overplays the extent to which this is a necessary or universal feature of market-based activity, it is unquestionably present in many market settings. Conversely, many enterprises, if clearly not all, exhibit a high degree of trust and co-operation between workers and managers, without losing their character as hierarchical modes of organisation.

Despite all this, there is a case for regarding networks as possessing distinctive features. The problem with the existing accounts is that they

[4] RH Coase, 'The nature of the firm' (1937) 4 *Economica* 386.

[5] O Williamson, *The Economic Institutions of Capitalism* (New York, Free Press, 1986).

[6] J Bradach and R Eccles, 'Price, authority and trust: from ideal types to plural forms' (1989) 15 *Annual Review of Sociology* 97.

[7] *Ibid*, 116.

[8] Powell, 'Neither market nor hierarchy' (n 3 above) 298.

[9] *Ibid*, 298.

[10] *Ibid*, 298.

[11] *Ibid*, 302.

[12] Above all, in FA von Hayek, *Law, Legislation and Liberty. A New Statement of the Liberal Principles of Justice and Political Economy* (London, Routledge, 1982).

start with the Coasean assumption that firms and markets are alternatives: the firm displaces the market as the costs of organising transactions through external exchange increase. This is, essentially, a static presentation, offering at best, as Coase put it, a 'moving equilibrium'.[13] From an evolutionary or historical perspective, the firm and the market have to be seen not as alternatives, but as complements to one another. The rise of the vertically integrated enterprise, and the related organisational techniques of mass production, went hand in hand with the emergence of markets based on mass consumption of standardised goods. In the language of modern systems theory, we might say that they 'co-evolved'.[14] The process was spelled out—although without using this particular terminology—in JR Commons's classic and, latterly, unduly neglected account of industrial evolution, which appeared in 1909 (in the now unlikely setting of the *Quarterly Journal of Economics*).[15] Commons's highly detailed, 'micro-institutional' analysis tracks the evolution of the footwear industry in America, from the guilds of the early colonial period, through to the factory labour of the age of mass production. As Commons recognised, the original or 'primitive'[16] guild 'represented the union in one person of the later separated classes of merchant, master and journeyman'.[17] Its principal function was to exclude 'bad ware',[18] which often amounted, in practice, to shifting contractual risk on to the consumer. The subsequent fragmentation of the guild was not simply the result, Commons argued, of changes in the technological or organisational forms of production, although these played a part. It was, above all, the consequence of the development or 'widening out' of product markets.[19] This led to the separation of wholesale and retail product markets and thereby to a decisive shift in economic power from producers to consumers:

> [T]hus it is that the ever-widening market from the custom-order stage, through the retail shop and wholesale-order to the wholesale-speculative stage, removes the journeyman more and more from his market, diverts

[13] Coase, 'The nature of the firm' (n 4 above).

[14] On co-evolution and systems theory with regard to the evolution of legal form, see generally G Teubner, *Law as an Autopoietic System*, (Oxford, Blackwell, 1993); MT Fögen, 'Legal history—history of the evolution of a social system. A proposal' (2002) *Rechtsgeschichte*, September, English version available on line at: http://www.mpier.uni-frankfurt.de/Forschung/Mitarbeiter_Forschung/foegen-legal-history.htm.

[15] JR Commons, 'American shoemakers, 1648–1895: a sketch of industrial evolution' (1909) 24 *Quarterly Journal of Economics* 39.

[16] *Ibid*, 43.

[17] *Ibid*, 42–3.

[18] *Ibid*, 43.

[19] *Ibid*, 50.

attention to price rather than quality and shifts the advantage in the series of bargains from the journeymen to the consumers and their intermediaries.[20]

These changes occurred without a major shift in the techniques of production, and prior to the emergence of the factory, which in Commons's account is simply the accompaniment to the final stage in the extension of the market, which he saw, in the age of mass production, as encompassing 'the world'.[21]

To identify vertical integration with the extension of markets to a global level jars with the more recent association of globalisation with a 'flexible', post-industrial and, fundamentally, fragmented economic structure.[22] But what Commons was describing was a process which contemporary commentators understood as disempowering labour. In the early years of the twentieth century, vertical integration was resisted by craft-based unions and small producers alike, aware that it signalled a threat to their independence.[23] The legal category of the 'contract of employment' was emerging at this time in large part as a consequence of a desire by employers for a unitary status which embodied the 'subordination' of all waged and salaried workers to the authority of management.[24] We have since become used to thinking of the large, vertically-integrated corporation, and the 'permanent' or indeterminate contract of employment, as institutions protective of the interests of labour, which have been placed under threat by the fragmentation of the firm; but this is not how they began, and not how Commons, writing in 1909, would have seen them.

In stressing the co-evolution of firms and markets as a consequence of the extension of competition, Commons's account also points to the marginalisation of network forms. If the firm and the market were complementary, their joint rise pushed network relations to the fringes. This was the consequence, on the one hand, of the incorporation of independent units into the firm, and, on the other, of the eclipse of customised production by mass consumer markets. Networks endured, but in isolated contexts, segments and niches, which struggled to survive when placed in direct competition with integrated industrial forms.

[20] *Ibid*, 67.

[21] *Ibid*, 84 ('Appendix II. Shoemakers—Industrial Stages, Causes, and Organizations', Column 1 ('Extent of Market') final row.

[22] Castells, *The Rise of the Network Society* (n 2 above).

[23] See S Jacoby, *Employing Bureaucracy: Managers, Unions, and the Transformation of Work in American Industry 1900–1945* (New York, Columbia University Press, 1985); D Marsden, *A Theory of Employment Systems: Micro-Foundations of Societal Diversity* (Oxford, Oxford University Press, 1999); P Cappelli, 'Market-mediated employment: the historical context' in M Blair and T Kochan (eds), *The New Relationship. Human Capital in the American Corporation* (Washington DC, Brookings Institution, 2002) 66–90.

[24] S Deakin and F Wilkinson, *The Law of the Labour Market: Industrialisation, Employment, and Legal Evolution* (Oxford, Oxford University Press, 2005).

To sum up this part of the argument: networks are, indeed, a distinctive form, but they provide an alternative mode of economic organisation not to firms on the one hand and markets on the other, but to the conjunction of the vertically-integrated firm and mass consumer markets. As part of the unfolding of industrial capitalism, networks were, for the most part, marginalised by the firm-market conjunction. They never disappeared altogether, and in some contexts they thrived, but these situations were the exception.

What was the role of the legal-institutional framework in this process? The next section considers the role of changes in the legal framework in England which accompanied the transition to industrial capitalism.

III. THE LEGAL STRUCTURE OF GUILD PRODUCTION AND THE TRANSITION TO INDUSTRIAL CAPITALISM IN ENGLAND

Guild production in early modern England was not a hold-over or relic of the medieval period. Historical research has recently re-evaluated the role of the guilds, suggesting that they were far from being the obstructive force portrayed by the political economy of the time. They appear to have played a significant role in sustaining the 'proto-industrial' forms of production, based on complex chains of contractual relations between merchants, wholesalers and producers, which characterised industry before the coming of the factory.[25] Guilds were underpinned at this time by an elaborate and extensive legal structure.[26] As late as the mid-eighteenth century it was still necessary to serve a seven-year apprenticeship in order to again entry to certain artisanal trades. The status of apprenticeship was only partially integrated into the cash economy—it involved payment in kind and living in as part of the master's household. Journeymen were those who had completed their apprenticeships in the relevant trade; they were generally paid wages at a daily rate, although they were normally hired for longer than this. A journeyman could be admitted to the group of masters not simply on showing that he had the resources and qualifications to be an independent trader, but also according to the rules of the guild which placed strict limits on the numbers of masters. At this stage, the terms 'master' and 'employer' were not synonymous.[27] The 'master' was one who had the right to direct the apprentices and journeymen whom he employed by virtue of his

[25] See M Daunton, *Progress and Poverty: An Economic and Social History of Britain 1700–1850* (Oxford, Oxford University Press, 1995) 155–8.

[26] See Deakin and Wilkinson, *The Law of the Labour Market* (n 24 above) for a fuller account of this, on which the present section draws.

[27] RA Leeson, *Travelling Brothers: The Six Centuries' Road from Craft Fellowship to Trade Unionism* (London, Allen & Unwin, 1979) 30.

knowledge of the trade, and, in many instances, by virtue of his status as a freeman of the relevant guild or city corporation. The master could, in turn, be 'employed' as an independent contractor on either a regular or intermittent basis by third parties, such as merchants or wealthy clients.

The artisanal system can be distinguished from the capitalist forms of employment which developed later by the preservation of control over the form and pace of work by the 'trade'; in other words, the collectivity of producers who were subject to the rules of guild membership. The master's relationship with his suppliers and customers, even when regular and stable, was never that of an employee (as that term later came to be understood), while a journeyman, although paid wages which were calculated by the day or by the piece, could only be directed to work within the limits of his apprenticed trade, while, at the same time, being protected from low wage competition by restrictions on the numbers of apprenticeships and by the general controls on entry into the trade. Thus, the 'artisan wage relationship' was one in which the journeyman

> worked with, not for, his master, and during slack times he was likely to be kept on for as long as the master could manage,

while the guild rules gave the master a

> protective independence . . . [which] existed within a body of custom and law which prevented competition and encouraged solidarity between producers of the same trade.[28]

The rules of the guilds were underpinned by the Statute of Artificers of 1562, a legislative measure which, to a large degree, codified laws going back to the fourteenth century and local practice with an even longer lineage. The apprenticeship sections of the Statute of 1562 were, to some extent, a liberalising influence: they made earlier property qualifications applying to the parents of apprentices less onerous, and introduced a number of exemptions to the rules on entry, as concessions to some of the larger corporate guilds.[29] In other respects, however, the Statute confirmed the guild model. Under the Statute, it was an offence punishable by repeated fines of 40 shillings for each month for any person to

> set up, occupy, use or exercise any craft, mystery or occupation now used or occupied within the realm of England and Wales, except he shall have been brought up therein seven years at the least as an apprentice.[30]

[28] J Smail, 'New languages for labour and capital: the transformation of discourse in the early years of the industrial revolution' (1987) 12 *Social History* 54 at 55.

[29] D Woodward, 'The background to the Statute of Artificers: the genesis of labour policy, 1558–63' (1980) 33 *Economic History Review* 32–44.

[30] Statute of Artificers 1562, 5 Eliz I, c 4, s 21.

The Statute also made it an offence to employ persons who had not been properly apprenticed in these occupations and to employ more than three apprentices for each journeyman.[31] In addition, in certain cities, including the major urban centres of London and Norwich, there was regulation in the form of by-laws made by the local guilds and city corporations. Numerous corporations and guilds which had been established by Royal Charter had the power to exercise legal controls over local trade and conditions of employment, subject to minimal supervision by local justices.[32]

The effect of these provisions was that the emerging capitalist forms of industrial organisation, based around the vertically-integrated enterprise, were, in effect, unlawful. No employer could operate in an industry for which he had not served an apprenticeship. The Act could also be interpreted as preventing an employer from hiring workmen from different trades to work alongside each other, since the effect would be that he was then exercising a number of trades in addition to his own.[33]

The regulatory scope of Act was tested in the King's Bench in *Hobbs v Young* (1689).[34] Even at early stage in industrialisation, it is possible to see the pressures to which the Act was being subjected by the new model of economic organisation. A merchant-capitalist who had employed journeymen cloth-workers in his house for a month to make goods up for export was successfully prosecuted for a breach of the Act. The argument of the prosecuting Counsel was that

> he who cannot use a mystery himself, is prohibited to employ any other men in that trade; for if this should be allowed, then the care which has been taken to keep up mysteries, by erecting guilds or fraternities, would signify little.

The majority of the court agreed:

> [T]he exercise of [the trade] by journeymen and master workmen, or an overseer for hire, is not an exercise of it by them, but by him that employs them; he provided them materials and tools, and paid them wages: by law, he is esteemed the trader who is to run the loss and hazard; the whole managery was to be for his profit, and the workmen are to have no advantage but their wages.

Even then, one of the three judges dissented on the grounds that

[31] *Ibid*, ss 21 and 23.

[32] See, generally, Leeson, *Travelling Brothers* (n 27 above); C Dobson, *Masters and Journeymen: A Pre-History of Industrial Relations* (London, Croom Helm, 1980).

[33] See *Re Statute of 5 Eliz, Apprentices* (1591) 4 Leon 9, and the discussion of this case law by Lord Mansfield CJ in *Raynard v Chase* (1756) 1 Burr 6.

[34] *Hobbs v Young* (1689) 1 Show KB 266.

> no encouragement was ever given to prosecutions upon this Statute . . . it would be for the common good if it were repealed, for no greater punishment can be to the seller than to expose goods for sale, ill wrought, for by such means he will never sell more.

By the early nineteenth century, this view had become the new orthodoxy. However, the demise of the extensive regulatory framework of the 1562 Act was not a sudden event. There was no equivalent to the peremptory prohibition of the guilds, which was embodied in the relevant legislation of the French Revolution, the *decret d'Allarde* and *loi Le Chapelier*. In England, the process of change was more gradual, but highly contested for over a century or more. Thus, the statute of 1814,[35] which finally abolished the apprenticeship provisions of the Statute of Artificers, brought about a change which was more than purely symbolic. The 1814 Act was passed precisely because there had been a vigorous and concerted attempt to uphold the Act of 1562 by its supporters in the urban guilds, a campaign which involved extensive strike action as well as parliamentary petitions and litigation aimed at enforcing the Act's provisions.[36]

The Act of 1562 received a hostile interpretation from the courts almost from the very start. Looking back on this process in a 1792 judgment, Lord Kenyon commented:

> When [the Act] was made, those who framed it might find it beneficial, but the ink with which it was written was scarce dry, ere the inconvenience of it was perceived; and Judges falling in with the sentiments of policy entertained by others have lent their assistance to repeal this law as much as it was in their power.[37]

The principal weapon used by the courts was the doctrine of restraint of trade. Under this legal doctrine,

> at common law, no man could be prohibited from working in any lawful trade . . . and therefore the common law abhors all monopolies.[38]

Such restraints required either 'ancient custom' or an Act of Parliament: thus,

[35] 54 Geo III, c 96.

[36] See, generally, I Prothero, *Artisans and Politics in Early Nineteenth Century London: John Gast and His Times* (Folkestone, Dawson, 1979).

[37] *Smith v Company of Armourers and Braziers of the City of London* (1792) Peake 199.

[38] *Case of the Tailors of Ipswich* (1615) 11 Co Rep 53a.

> without an Act of Parliament, none can be in any manner restrained from working in any lawful trade... ordinances for the good order and government of men of trades and mysteries are good, but not to restrain anyone in his lawful mystery.[39]

On this basis, courts struck down rules which imposed additional entry requirements on apprentices and which sought to limit guild numbers.[40] Then, the courts went further, ruling that the 1562 Act only applied, even in the case of a pre-1562 trade, if, in the court's view, 'an apprenticeship could possibly be expedient', since the Act could only govern 'such trades as imply mystery and craft, and that require skill and experience'.[41]

The second technique used by the courts was the restrictive interpretation of statutes which were deemed to have carved out an exception from the general common law. In was on this basis that the courts ruled that the Act of 1562 had no application to trades or techniques which had not existed at the time of its passage.[42] This doctrine was used in the eighteenth century to remove from the scope of the Act several of the emerging industrial trades, including cotton spinning, coach building, and framework knitting. In *The Wealth of Nations*, Adam Smith caught the prevailing view, arguing that

> the manufactures of Manchester, Birmingham and Wolverhampton, are many of them, upon this account, not being within the statute, not having been exercised in England before the 5th. of Elizabeth.[43]

'The pretence that corporations [ie, guilds] are necessary for the better government of the trade', he went on, 'is without any foundation', since

> the real and effectual discipline which is exercised over a workman, is not that of his corporation, but that of his customers.[44]

Hobbs v Young was decisively circumvented 10 years before the publication of *The Wealth of Nations*, in a judgment of Lord Mansfield in *Raynard*

[39] *Ibid*. See also *Case of Monopolies* (1602) 11 Co Rep 84b at 87b: only Parliament, under 5 Eliz I, c 4, could restrain a person from exercising any trade.

[40] *Case of the Tailors of Ipswich* (n 38 above), striking down a rule that no person should exercise any of the specified trades until he had appeared before the master and wardens of the society to prove that he had served his seven years as an apprentice; *R v Coopers' Company, Newcastle* (1768) 7 Term Rep 544 (a case of a by-law restricting numbers of indentured apprentices: 'a prohibition not to take more than a certain number of apprentices is a bye-law in restraint of trade' (Kenyon CJ)).

[41] *R. v Fredland* (1637) Cro Car 499.

[42] See *Tolley's Case* (1615) Calthrop 9; *R v Housden* (1665) 1 Keble 848; *R v Paris Slaughter* (1700) 2 Salk 611; *R v Harper* (1706) 2 Salk 611; *Pride v Stubbs* (1810) 6, Esp 131.

[43] A Smith, *An Inquiry into the Nature and Causes of the Wealth of Nations* (edn with an introduction by JS Nicholson) vol I (London, T Nelson & Sons, 1886; originally published 1776) ch 10 at 50.

[44] *Ibid*, 55.

v Chase in 1756.[45] This ruling decided that a non-apprenticed merchant or financier could be the owner of a business and employ others in it without infringing the Act if he acted in partnership with one who was qualified in the relevant trade. By these means, the courts relaxed the prohibition on workers from different trades being employed alongside one another.[46] In other cases, the courts took a loose view of the entry requirements themselves. In *Smith v Company of Armourers* (1792)[47] the Court of the King's Bench ordered the defendant company to admit the manager of an iron foundry to membership, on the grounds that, although he had not served an apprenticeship and 'did not know how to manufacture the commodity by his own personal labour', he had been employed in the business for seven years,

> during the greatest part of which time he conducted the whole of their extensive works, received all the orders, gave directions to the workmen, *etc.*, . . . he knew how to conduct the business as well as any master in London.[48]

Finally, just prior to the repeal of the Act, in *Kent v Dormay* (1811)[49] Lord Ellenborough CJ simply refused to convict an unapprenticed textile mill owner, on the grounds that

> the valuable mills at Wakefield, Leeds, *etc.*, were the property of several persons of the first families in this kingdom; but who would be liable to informations, or would be required to serve regular apprenticeships as millers, if the defendant could be considered as within the meaning of the Statute.

Underlying the repeal of the apprenticeship provisions in 1814 was the political economy of the time, which argued for the desirability of unhindered competition. Joseph Chitty's textbook on *Apprenticeship*, which had appeared in 1812 in response to the demand caused by 'numerous recent prosecutions' under the Act of 1562, drew on Adam Smith, TR Malthus and William Paley to advocate the repeal of the Statute. The efforts to see the law enforced

[45] *Raynard v Chase* (1756) 1 Burr 6.

[46] *Coward v Maberly* (1809) 2 Camp 127, where it was held that a coachmaker could directly employ a blacksmith to manufacture coach wheels: 'blacksmith's work may be required in building a bridge; but the builder who employs a journeyman properly qualified to do that work, is not himself to be considered as carrying on the trade of a blacksmith' (Lord Ellenborough CJ).

[47] *Smith v Company of Armourers* (1792) Peake 199.

[48] On this basis 'serving an apprenticeship' became simply a matter of time serving, as anyone who worked for seven years without interruption as master, servant or apprentice could now qualify under the Act.

[49] *Kent v Dormay* (1811) Kingston Assizes, 14 August 1811; see J Chitty, *A Practical Treatise on the Law Relating to Apprentices and Journeymen, and to Exercising Trades* (London, W Clarke & Sons, 1812) 122.

> have been uniformly instituted, not with a view to any advantage that might result to the public, but purely on behalf of journeymen, in order to keep up the high price of wages;

repeal would bring about that 'competition incident to the freedom of employment' which Adam Smith had argued for, with benefits for all:

> Where there is free competition, the labour and capital of every individual will always be directed by him into the channel most conducive to his own ultimate interest; of that interest each is himself, from a thousand circumstances, the best possible judge; and the interests of the whole community must in general be most effectually insured, when that of each individual is most judicially consulted.[50]

Lord Kenyon had earlier asserted that the 'natural reason' of the market, rather than guild controls, was the appropriate solution for the manufacture of poor quality goods:

> [t]he reason for making [the Act] was that bad commodities might not be spread abroad; but natural reason tells us, that if the manufacture is not good, there is no danger of its having a favourable reception in the world, or answering the tradesman's purpose.[51]

The social upheaveal which accompanied the defence of the Act of 1562 can be seen as a last effort to shore up a decaying legal and economic order. Yet, this was never simply a matter of resistance to technological change. The violent Luddite protests in Nottinghamshire in 1811–12 began when local magistrates refused to convict hosiery employers who were acknowledged to have flouted local norms governing the use of non-apprenticed labour and respect for customary wage levels. Machine-breaking was the response to the spread of these 'illegal' terms and conditions of employment. As EP Thompson suggested, Luddism arose

> at the crisis-point in the abrogation of paternalist legislation … a violent eruption of feeling against unrestrained industrial capitalism, harking back to an obsolescent paternalist code.[52]

But, for the defenders of the guild model, the refusal of the courts to enforce trade controls was also an 'unconstitutional' expropriation of the 'mystery' or property of the trade. Machine-breaking was simply the traditional sanction for breach of the customary rules of guild production. As Martin Daunton has more recently put it,

[50] *Ibid*, 2.

[51] *Smith v Company of Armourers* (1799) Peake 199 at 201.

[52] EP Thompson, *The Making of the English Working Class* (Harmondsworth, Penguin, 1968) 555.

> [t]he response of workers should not be interpreted in terms of disorder and ineffectuality, but as part of a well-developed and articulate 'corporate discourse' which stressed stability, regulation, and the need to observe strict limits to innovation which threatened independence and accountability. Workers threatened by the rise of 'dishonourable trades' appealed for the state to protect their property in skill in the same way as other property, and to recognise their social value. The rejection of legislative support for this set of assumptions was political, and workers continued to press for its restoration. Luddites who continued to urge the implementation of laws which no longer existed were, according to some historians, not adjusting to new realities. This fails to comprehend their attitudes and assumptions, and gives priority to the ideology of their opponents.[53]

The upheaval which accompanied the demise of the guilds arguably had long-standing consequences for British industrialisation. On the continent, the post-revolutionary codes repeated the condemnation of the 'corporations' of the *ancien régime* which had been embodied in the *loi Le Chapelier* of 1791. But beneath this sweeping legal prohibition, certain aspects of guild production were carried over into emerging forms of industrial organisation. A combination of competition and co-operation, and the preservation of solidaristic ties between independent producers, came to characterise the 'industrial districts' of Italy and their equivalents in France, Germany and Japan, which economists rediscovered in the final decades of the twentieth century.[54] In Britain, organisational ties across independent production units were much more tenuous than on the continent, which was a reflection, to some degree, of common law values which were hostile to 'restraint of trade', but also a legacy of a particular pattern of industrial development. In Britain, although guild relations persisted in the craft-based trade unionism, centred on the institution of the closed shop, collectivism on the employer side was weak and reactive. Industrial concentration and an increasing trend towards vertical integration were the predominant tendencies of the twentieth century.[55]

Recently, this trend has been reversed. Is it possible to see in the vertical disintegration of production and the growth of network forms of economic organisation, a revival of the guild?

[53] Daunton, *Progress and Poverty* (n 25 above) 499.

[54] See, generally, M Piore and C Sabel, *The Second Industrial Divide: Possibilities for Prosperity* (New York, Basic Books, 1984).

[55] See Deakin and Wilkinson, *The Law of the Labour Market* (n 24 above) chs 2 (on vertical integration and the rise of the employment model) and 4 (on the retention of guild-like features of control of the trade in modern British trade unionism).

IV. CONTRACTING IN TODAY'S 'NETWORK ECONOMY': VERTICAL DISINTEGRATION IN BROADCASTING

According to the thesis influentially advanced by Manuel Castells,[56] a combination of technological and organisational changes produced, at the end of the twentieth century, a reconfiguration of capitalism, which saw the rise of a 'network society'. In Castells's model, the 'network' infuses both the market and the firm, displacing the (by now) traditional vertically-integrated firm with more loosely-coupled organisational units, and dividing mass consumption markets into distinctive segments. Product market de-regulation, the liberalisation of trade flows and the growing role of the capital markets in the restructuring of firms play their part in ushering in a globalised economic system. In this account, it is, however, technology, above all, which is driving social and economic change, as it was (according to Castells) in the original industrial revolution. The 'networking' logic of new information technology and the life sciences is reproduced in the flexible social structures of the 'new economy':

> [T]he 'spirit of informationalism' is the culture of 'creative destruction' accelerated to the speed of the opto-electronic circuits that process its signals.Schumpeter meets Weber in the cyberspace of the network enterprise.[57]

Within this new frame, the basic economic unit is neither the individual subject, nor a collectivity such as the corporation or the state, but the network itself,

> made up of a variety of subjects and organisations, relentlessly modified as networks adapt to supportive environments and market structures.[58]

The essential question in assessing Castells's thesis is whether the trends that he describes amount to a genuinely new phenomenon, or simply to another phase in the familiar dynamic of industrial capitalism, with its conjunction of the enterprise and the market. In the spirit of Commons's 'micro-institutionalism', a study of industrial evolution in the context of a particular industrial sector may help. The cultural industries, and television production in particular, are an appropriate sector to choose, since there we find all the elements of the 'new economy': a prominent role for information technology (represented here above all by the shift to digital broadcasting), the vertical disintegration of established firms, and the seeming reconstruction of economic relations in the form of malleable

[56] Castells, *The Rise of the Network Society* (n 2 above).
[57] *Ibid*, 199.
[58] *Ibid*, 198.

network forms. Above all, we find an element which while not completely absent from Castells's account, is not especially prominent either: a role for competition law as a catalyst for economic change.[59]

Broadcasting in the United Kingdom is a particularly interesting case, since we can see here two parallel attempts to foster network relations in place of vertically-integrated organisational structures: on the one hand, there is government encouragement for the growth of an independent production sector, supported by quotas for sub-contracting, and a specialised set of contractual terms of trade; on the other, there is an 'internal market' within the main terrestrial broadcaster, the BBC, which 'mimics' contractual relations within an organisational frame. The entire structure continues to be supported, directly or indirectly, by a substantial degree of public funding, and is heavily regulated.

The process of institutional change began in the mid-1980s with the government-commissioned Peacock Report, which set out a vision of 'a sophisticated system based on consumer sovereignty' for broadcasting in which it was recognised that

> viewers and listeners are the best ultimate judges of their own interests, which they can best satisfy if they have the option of purchasing the broadcasting services they require from as many alternative sources of supply as possible.[60]

The full application of this logic would have led to a system based on pay-per-view, since this was the 'only system' under which viewers could 'register their preferences directly' for particular types of programming. On the supply side, liberalisation implied 'freedom of entry for any programme maker who can cover his costs or otherwise finance his or her production', and the imposition of public utility-style common carrier obligations upon operators of transmission equipment.[61]

This did not happen; instead, the Peacock Report also found a place for the concept of public service broadcasting, arguing that consumers were willing to fund television production 'in their capacity as voting taxpayers' in order to achieve greater diversity and quality of programme production, and that

[59] This part of the paper draws on ideas developed in joint work with Steve Pratten and Ana Lourenço; see S Deakin and S Pratten, 'Reinventing the market? Competition and regulatory change in broadcasting' (1999) 26 *Journal of Law and Society* 323–50, and S Deakin, S Pratten and A Lourenço, 'No third way for economic organisation? Networks and quasi-markets in broadcasting', forthcoming, *Industrial and Corporate Change* (2008) , for a more complete account of the institutional background to vertical disintegration in broadcasting.

[60] A Peacock (Chairman), *Report of the Committee on Financing the BBC*, Cmnd 9824 (London, Home Office, 1986) para 592.

[61] *Ibid*, paras 547–8.

> public support of programmes of this type can be accepted by those who believe that viewers and listeners are, in the last analysis, the best judges of their own interest.[62]

Thus, the White Paper of 1988 and the Broadcasting Act of 1990 stopped short of imposing complete liberalisation. However, a key part of the new structure was a requirement that the BBC and ITV should contract out 25 per cent of the volume of their programme-making to independent producers: as the White Paper put it,

> independent producers constitute an important source of originality and talent which must be exploited and have brought new pressures for efficiency and flexibility in production procedures.[63]

Vertical disintegration within the BBC took the complementary form of internal administrative arrangements under which a series of producer-provider splits were implemented.[64] The context for these reforms was a perception by senior management, and in particular, by the then Director-General, John Birt, of the limitations of the traditional organisational structure of the corporation, which saw the BBC as

> a vast command economy; a series of entangled, integrated baronies, each providing internally most of its needs; all the many faceted inputs to the complex business of programme making; programme departments, resource facilities and support services, all separately and directly funded.[65]

With this diagnosis of the problems facing it, the BBC entered into a two-phase programme of reform. The first stage, known as Producer Choice, was introduced in April 1993. It essentially took the form of a purchaser-provider split at the level of the relationship between programme-makers and the suppliers of production resources. The purpose was two-fold: to enable the BBC's management to obtain information on the indirect, overhead costs of its programmes, in particular, accommodation and capital depreciation; and to benchmark the costs of internal resource provision against those of external providers, thus making it possible to carry out market testing. By these means, potential inefficiencies would be identified and costs brought under control. The second stage involved the introduction of a number of separate internal units or 'directorates' in the autumn of 1996. Programme-makers were

62 *Ibid*, paras 550–51.

63 Home Office, *Broadcasting in the '90s: Competition, Choice and Quality* Cmd 517 (London, HMSO, 1988) para 41.

64 See Deakin and Pratten, 'Reinventing the market?' (n 59 above).

65 J Birt, cited in J Spangenberg, *The BBC in Transition: Reasons, Results and Consequences* (Frankfurt, Deutscher Univeritäts Verlag, 1998) 103.

allocated to the Production directorate and commissioners to the Broadcast directorate. An internal commissioning system for television production was then put in place, to operate in addition to the 25 per cent external quota which had been imposed by legislation. The imposition of the external quota was one of the principal factors behind the decision of BBC managers to introduce an internal market of their own.

To critics of the pre-reform BBC, the absence of choice and competition implied that producers had the power to set their own agendas for programme content and quality:

> British broadcasting was effectively run by producer élites, while the economic rewards went disproportionately to the workforce. This unusual arrangement arose from the twin features of monopoly funding and a Reithian ethos—television should be good for you. The definition of what was good for you was left to the programme departments of the BBC and ITV companies, self-perpetuating oligarchies which shared a common value system, supported by managements and regulators who themselves started their careers in the broadcasting organisations.[66]

At the same time, this 'common value system' sustained production capabilities of a certain kind. These can be understood not simply in terms of the extensive training system which the BBC operated during these years, but also in the shared knowledge and values which it perpetuated. The advent of Producer Choice, the producer-broadcaster split and, more generally, the regulatory encouragement of the independent sector marked a fundamental challenge to these established values.

Paradoxically, it was the apparently monolithic BBC which had provided the setting for a latter-day guild-like culture to flourish. The sociologist Tom Burns's longitudinal studies of the BBC, carried out in the 1960s and 1970s, stressed the degree to which BBC staff during this period

> seemed to be devoting themselves—and consciously so—to individual ends and values which were consistent with those of public service broadcasting without being necessarily derived from them,

thereby creating what a personnel manager of that earlier era called 'an increment you don't pay for'.[67] The nature of the issues involved here can be gauged by this comment on the 1990s reforms, made by an employee representative:

[66] B Cox, 'Two tiers for TV' (March 1997) *Prospect* 21–5.

[67] T Burns, *Description, Explanation and Understanding* (Edinburgh, Edinburgh University Press, 1994) 91.

> [W]hen the independent quota came in, and outsourcing of cleaning, catering and security began, most employees, far from saying 'what an opportunity', were fighting to hold on to their jobs,

with the result that

> it was like working for any other broadcasting organisation; it didn't matter to the staff that it was the BBC any more.[68]

As the quotation we referred to earlier from John Birt makes abundantly clear, the reorganisation of the BBC which began with Producer Choice was viewed by its proponents in terms of a shift away from this producer-led, bureaucratically-driven production process, which was said to be stifling creativity. The introduction of market-like processes and flexible organisational forms would, it was hoped, release creative abilities and enhance innovation. The same perspective was at work in the efforts made to promote the growth of the independent sector. In this context, one of the other public service broadcasters, Channel 4—which had always relied on external producers to supply its programmes—was held out as an example of what could be achieved in terms of innovative production through reliance on externally-sourced production.

In each case, however, there was more at stake than a straightforward move 'from firm to market'. Peacock's proposal to empower the ultimate consumer would have implied the complete 'unbundling' of production from distribution, the break up of the BBC and ITV companies, and a move to individualised pay-per-view. This was rejected as a series of steps too far, on grounds that included the ill-defined, but nevertheless still powerful, notion of 'public service broadcasting'. Instead, what emerged was a 'quasi market' in which separate production and commissioning stages were established within organisational boundaries in the case of the BBC, and beyond them in the case of outsourcing to the independent sector. In the late 1990s the internal market of the BBC was stabilised through the use of guaranteed output deals, which protected in-house suppliers while limiting the scope for influence on the part of the independents.[69] But, more recently, partly as a consequence of government pressure for the reform of the BBC, there has been a renewed emphasis on externalisation of production functions, which has led to a further increase in the share of production available to the independent sector,[70] and down-sizing within the organisation.

[68] Cited from interview notes, Deakin, Pratten and Lourenço, 'No third way for economic organisation?' (n 59 above).

[69] Deakin and Pratten, 'Reinventing the market' (n 59 above).

[70] The so-called 'window of creative competition' announced in 2004, which was intended to come into effect upon the renewal of the BBC's Charter in 2006, opened up an additional 25% of the BBC's programme expenditure to competition between the BBC's in house producers and the independent sector, on top of the 25% already guaranteed for

Within the independent sector, at the same time, there has been a move away from guaranteed supply contracts, in favour of a re-allocation of property rights under the terms of trade governing broadcaster-supplier contracts. The effect of this is to ensure that intellectual property rights to the re-use of television programmes vest in the programme-makers and not in the broadcasters. This has enabled a small segment of the independent sector to build up a valuable economic resource in the form of secondary and tertiary rights to sell on the right to broadcast the programmes that they make, and this has led, in turn, to an increase in the external financing of the industry by venture capital and private equity firms.[71]

According to a review of independent sector carried out by the industry regulator, the Independent Television Commission (ITC) in the early 2000s, 'a healthy and competitive TV programme supply market is a vital part of our creative economy',[72] and this, in turn, requires an independent sector which is 'viable and sustainable in its own right, rather than reliant on the quota for its existence'.[73] Pointing to the successes of the reform process, the review claimed that the United Kingdom has 'strong production capabilities', in part due to the role, first, of Channel 4, and then due to the role of the independent production quota in

> [opening] up the programme supply market to many hundreds of independent producers, responsible for adding to the creative and innovative programming available to viewers.[74]

But the review was also required to acknowledge that, in many respects, the current industry structure was less than ideal:

> [T]he independent production sector remains fragile—producers lack the scale to diversify their risks, and lack the rights base which would allow them to attract external finance—only a few independents have been able to grow sizeable and sustainable businesses at home; and fewer still have made inroads in the international marketplace.[75]

outsourcing. For discussion of the implications of the BBC's move to ever greater use of the independent sector, see W Hutton, Á O'Keeffe and N Turner, *The Tipping Point: How Much is Broadcast Creativity at Risk? An Independent Report commissioned by the BBC* (London, The Work Foundation, 2005).

[71] Deakin, Lourenço and Pratten, 'No third way for economic organisation?' (n 59 above).

[72] Independent Television Commission, *A Review of the UK Programme Supply Market* (London, ITC 2002) para 9. The ITC was subsumed into the current industry regulator, Ofcom, in 2003.

[73] *Ibid*, para 10.

[74] *Ibid*, para 12.

[75] *Ibid*, para 13.

Worse still, the 25 per cent quota, while 'a success in its original terms', was becoming part of the sector's problems:

> [I]t addresses only some of the issues that are required for a healthy programme supply market, and has its own disadvantages as well as advantages. Some broadcasters use it as a ceiling, not a floor, and many have said that it risks creating a 'welfare culture' of small independents who depend on the quota, rather than their own competitive strengths, for their continuing existence.[76]

The solution advanced by the ITC was one based on the further intensification of competition: by limiting perceived abuse of market power by the BBC, moving to terms of trade previously used by the ITV companies, and attempting to dis-embed the commissioning processes, the independent sector would be released from the forces holding it back. The expectation was that as old-style 'cottage industry' firms were sidelined, the survivors, now able to assert control over secondary and tertiary rights, would be better equipped to attract external capital.

But there is a rival narrative running through the recent experience of the television production sector. The model of cost-plus financing which was introduced in the wake of the Broadcasting Act 1990, while making it difficult for some of the smaller independents to grow, also protected them from the downside risks of cost shortfalls which are a common feature of television production, and which only the larger suppliers have the scale and reserves to deal with. A fully level playing field for the independents would probably require the formal unbundling of the broadcasting and production functions of the BBC; but as the ITC was compelled to recognise, the

> structural separation of the BBC's broadcasting and production businesses might have the effect of creating a more level playing field between the BBC's own producers and independents, but would likely impose significant costs on the Corporation.[77]

The BBC's own evolution since the late 1990s, which has seen a significant modification of the internal market put in place by John Birt's reforms, further points to the potentially disruptive impact of organisational fragmentation upon production capabilities.[78]

If we observe here a role for network-type relations, with a web of contracts centred on the 'nodes' of the main broadcasting organisations, and a wide variety of organisational forms springing up to meet

[76] *Ibid*, para 18.

[77] *Ibid*, para 31.

[78] See, generally, G Born, *Uncertain Vision: Birt, Dyke and the Reinvention of the BBC* (London, Vintage, 2005); Hutton, O' Keeffe and Turner, *The Tipping Point* (n 70 above).

demands for diversified quality production, then we also see the potential limits to the process of network construction in a highly de-regulated environment. The push to marketise the sector has very quickly led to concerns about the quality of production, in an environment where the existing conventions of quality are proving fragile. The effect of the reforms has been to undermine a 'guild-like' autonomy for producers, which previously served as a guarantor of quality standards.

V. CONCLUSIONS

At the outset of the debate over new forms of economic organisation in the 1980s, Michael Piore and Charles Sabel[79] argued that vertical integration of production was not an historical inevitability, but rather a contingent outcome of a particular phase of industrial capitalism. In predicting the re-emergence of network forms, they pointed to the possible revival of types of regulation which predated the first great 'industrial divide' of the nineteenth century. Twenty years on, there is little sign of this regulatory revival becoming a reality. The considerable promise held out by network forms is in danger of being displaced by a neo-Schumpeterian view of industry and society, in which technological determinism leaves little or no scope for institutional variety. The crucial issue here is the nature of competition policy. Policy must be capable of recognising both the multiplicity of forms which competition can take, and the necessity for regulatory measures to foster the mechanisms which traditionally underpinned producer autonomy in the face of hierarchical control on the one hand, and the homogenising force of mass markets on the other. This is the case for the return of the guild.

[79] In Piore and Sabel, *The Second Industrial Divide* (n 54 above).

4

Post-Hegelian Networks

Comments on the Chapter by Simon Deakin

POUL F KJAER*

I. INTRODUCTION

SIMON DEAKIN EXPLORES whether we can observe a 'return of the guild' in the era of the post-industrial society.[1] This question has been raised regularly since the final dismantling of the guild institutions in Europe in the *époque* of the French Revolution.[2] Deakin, however, gives the question a new twist by relating it to more recent literature on networks and by exploring whether it is possible to see the concept of the guild as a useful metaphor for the emerging structures of the so-called network society.[3]

Taking up this theme, this contribution will seek to identify the societal functions reproduced by the guild as well as by its institutional successors in modern and late-modern times. Admittedly, this exercise will take a stylised form in the sense that a distinction will be made between three 'ideal types', which represent pre-modern feudal society, modern society, and the radicalised modernity of contemporary society. Using this background, Deakin's question concerning a possible 'return' of the guild will be addressed.

* Research Fellow, Cluster Of Exellence 'The Formation of Normative Orders', Goethe-University, Frankfurt am Main. He has previously studied and researched in political science, sociology and law at the University of Aarhus, Humboldt University Berlin, University of Bielefeld and the European University Institute, Florence.

[1] See S Deakin, 'The Return of the Guild? Network Relations in Historical Perspective' (ch 3), in this volume.

[2] See, eg, AJ Penty, *Old Worlds for New. A Study of the Post-Industrial State* (London, George Allen & Unwin, 1917) 44–57, and *Post-Industrialism* (London, George Allen & Unwin, 1922) 84–123.

[3] M Castell, *The Information Age: Economy, Society and Culture. Volume 1, The Rise of the Network Society* (Oxford, Blackwell, 1999).

II. FEUDALISM

The word guild (more correctly, spelt gild) was derived from the Anglo-Saxon term 'gildan', which means 'to pay'. Guilds were, in other words, associations based on membership fees. Originally, several forms of guilds co-existed: religious guilds, frith (or peace) guilds, merchant guilds and craft guilds.[4] Each type of guild took up a specific function: religious commemoration; the handling of security concerns in the absence of a state monopoly on violence[5]; and, for the merchant and craft guilds, economic regulation, in terms of standard-setting—the regulation of inclusion and exclusion to the market and the setting of prices. Standard-setting performed a quality assurance function for products placed on the market and also contributed towards a reduction of—in today's terminology—non-tariff barriers to trade. An additional function of merchant and craft guilds was to reproduce knowledge through the regulation of educational measures such as apprenticeships.[6]

Although considerable regional differences can be observed in the development and organisation of the guild institutions throughout Europe, one common feature seems to be that the merchant and craft guilds rose in importance from the tenth century onwards, whereas the other types of guilds tended to fade away. This development can also be described as a 'merger' in the sense that the guild institutions largely became merchant or craft guilds, which were, at the same time, committed to, and were embedded in, a religious framework that provided guidelines for the conduct of business.[7] In the same way they tended to develop autonomous security capacities in order to safeguard production and commerce. The move towards concentration, however, did not lead to the establishment of centralised organisations, in so far as most regions continued to be characterised by a large number of competing and partly overlapping guilds, and competition from non-organised merchants and craftsmen was a continuous source of irritation. Moreover, the guild institutions took up a representative role in relation to other elements of

[4] A Black, *Guilds and Civil Society in European Political Thought from the Twelfth Century to the Present* (London, Methuen, 1984) 3, and G Clune, *The Medieval Guild System* (Dublin, Brown & Nolan Limited, 1942).

[5] N Elias, *Über den Prozess der Zivilisation: Soziogenetische und Psychogenetische Uuntersuchungen, Band 2* (Basel, Verlag Haus zum Falken, 1939).

[6] SR Epstein, 'Craft Guilds, Apprenticeship, and Technological Change in Preindustrial Europe' (1998) 3 *The Journal of Economic History* 684–713.

[7] For examples, in relation to the religious inspired concept of 'just price', see R de Roover, 'The Concept of the Just Price: Theory and Economic Policy' (1950) 4 *The Journal of Economic History* 418–34; M Weber, *Wirtschaftsgeschichte* (Leipzig, Duncker & Humblot, 1923) 127–48, and W Sombart, *Der moderne Kapitalismus: historisch-systematische Darstellung des gesamteuropäischen Wirtschaftslebens von seinen Anfangen bis zur Gegenwart. Band 2* (Leipzig, Duncker & Humblot, 1924) 180–98.

society, aimed at stabilising relations and ensuring the greatest possible level of autonomy for both the guilds and their constituencies. The commitment to a shared frame of reference in the form of a common system of religious beliefs, whose validity applied to society as whole, provided an essential platform for this kind of representation. As part of security efforts, insurance schemes were also developed to cover losses due to risk exposure such as premature death, accidents or damage arising from the kind of violence which, in modern times, usually would be described as either war or crime.

The rise of guild institutions can be seen to be a result of a hybrid form of societal differentiation, in the sense that the regions where the guilds gained the strongest positions were typically characterised by a strong differentiation between the centre and the periphery as well as a high level of stratification. The differentiation between the centre and the periphery was usually particularly strong when one region achieved a dominant role in long-distance trade, hence establishing a structural basis for the development of merchant and craft guilds in the first place.[8] Stratificatory differentiation—in the sense of a relatively inflexible order of ranks between different segments of society—is also related to the centre/periphery distinction in so far as the creation of a centre allows for stratification within the centre, thereby allowing the centre to increase its internal complexity.[9] Accordingly, independent segments of merchants and craftsman seem to have out-differentiated (*ausdifferenziert*) themselves as layers of the stratified society, originally providing a 'support function' for the centre, which had a similar trajectory at the level of the clergy and the nobility. Consequently, each of these levels developed internal forms of organisation, such as orders of chivalry, monastic orders, and, in the case of merchants and craftsmen, the guilds. These organisations seem to have taken up equivalent functions within their respective layers of society, in terms of providing security and internal cohesion, the reproduction of knowledge through education, and acting as representatives for their particular layer of society. This was the case even though the orders of chivalry and the guilds were placed at opposite ends of the emerging distinction between rural and urban structures.

Besides handling the exchange between centres and their peripheries, the guilds, monastic orders and orders of chivalry also acted as forms for the establishment of links between centres, leading to the creation of European-wide networks. The clearest example of the guilds' role in establishing such networks was the development of the North European

[8] N Luhmann, *Die Gesellschaft der Gesellschaft* (Frankfurt a M, Suhrkamp, 1997) 663.
[9] *Ibid*, 663.

Hanseatic League. The League started as associations of guild members who were more or less permanently based in cities other than their native towns. Over time, however, it developed into an inter-city conglomerate occupied with the maintenance of European-wide trade connections.[10] The double function of the guilds—which, on the one hand, exercised a support function within the centre and, on the other hand, connected centres with their peripheries and other centres—reflected the need to ensure a stabilisation of the double differentiation between centre/ periphery and stratification. Thus, the guilds can also be considered as a long-term transitional phenomenon that evolved in the period between the breakdown of mainly segmented societies and the rise of mainly stratified ones. Consequently, the guild structure experienced a slow but continued weakening from the fifteenth century onwards, in so far as the centre/periphery distinction increasingly lost its societal significance with the rise of the modern territorial state.

Guilds, as well as the orders of chivalry and monastic orders, can—at a first glance—be regarded as structures which reproduce functions equivalent to those undertaken by hierarchical organisations within the modern functionally-differentiated society, especially since their emergence seems to have been closely related to the internal reproduction of coherence within their respective layers of society on the basis of inclusion/exclusion distinctions. However, the function of ensuring integration for society as a whole was mainly reproduced by the household, an institution that acted as a container for members of different layers of stratified society, thereby enabling them to act as structural couplings between these layers.[11] Moreover, in terms of internal organisation, guilds were fundamentally different from modern organisations, in the sense that their internal structure reflected the structure of the society within which they operated. Again, massive regional differences can be observed, but generally guilds were based on a mixture of de facto hereditary positions and the occasional inclusion of newcomers, which reflected the hybrid nature of a society based upon a mixture of stratificatory and centre/periphery differentiation.

[10] NJG Pounds, *An Economic History of Medieval Europe* (New York, Longman, 1974) 378–86; JW Thompson, *Economic and Social History of Europe in the Later Middle Ages (1300–1530)* (New York, The Century Co, 1931) 126–79. Although long-distance trade was an important element in Medieval economic interaction, the local market seems to have been just as important. See RC Epstein, 'Regional Fairs, Institutional Innovation, and Economic Growth in Late Medieval Europe' (1994) 47 *The Economic History Review, New Series* 459–82.

[11] MM Knight, *Economic History of Europe. To the End of the Middle Ages* (London, George Allen & Unwin, 1928) 162–98; R Latouche, *Les origines de l'eéconomie occidentale, IVe-XIe sieècle* (Paris, A Michel, 1956) 221–42, and N Luhmann, *Die Gesellschaft der Gesellschaft* (Frankfurt aM, Suhrkamp, 1997) 678.

In today's terminology, one could also be tempted to contemplate guilds as being somewhere in-between markets and hierarchy, and therefore, as being a kind of lateral, or horizontal, network.[12] However, this description does not capture the distinction between the centre/periphery and stratification which were reproduced within all layers of pre-modern society. Modern markets do not have a centre and a periphery in the pre-modern sense,[13] and modern hierarchal organisations are not based on stratificatory differentiation in the form of a largely hereditary and religiously embedded order. Moreover, the breakthrough of modernity, through functional differentiation, must be regarded as a paradigmatic shift. This makes attempts to establish directs links between pre-modern and modern elements a futile exercise. Even if a continuity of structures could be observed, such structures are likely to fulfill significantly different societal functions and to be ascribed radically different meanings when operating within a fundamentally different societal setting. However, attempts to transfer essentially modern concepts back to a time when they did not exist and to analyse the institution of the guild according to such premises is a classical exercise. Thus, the guilds have been described as a form of 'civil society' that existed between the state and the family, or between *Gemeinschaft* and *Gesellschaft*,[14] or have been regarded as structures which perform an integrating function similar to the integrative functions of unions and syndicates in the modern era.[15] In addition, by imposing the class semantics of the nineteenth century on the distinction between merchant and craft guilds, the guilds have even been described as part of a the class struggle between privileged and less privileged groups.[16]

III. MODERNITY

GWF Hegel (1770–1831) can be considered as the modernist par excellence. At the beginning of the nineteenth century, the young Hegel raised the question of why Germany had not become 'modern', in the sense that he asked why Germany had not become a modern state like France or the United Kingdom. Hegel's answer was that Germany had not overcome the stratified structures of pre-modern society. The German state was

[12] See S Deakin, 'The Return of the Guild? Network Relations in Historical Perspective' (ch 3), in this volume.
[13] N Luhmann, *Die Wirtschaft der Gesellschaft* (Frankfurt aM, Suhrkamp, 1998) 91–130.
[14] F Tönnies, *Gemeinschaft und gesellschaft; Grundbegriffe der reinen soziologie* (Berlin, Karl Curtius, 1887).
[15] JC Filloux, *Durkheim et la socialisme* (Geneva, Librairie Droz, 1977) 335–53.
[16] JW Thompson, *Economic and Social History of Europe in the Later Middle Ages* (London, The Century Co, 1931) 396–414.

nothing other than a conglomerate of private legal structures in the sense that each prince, each estate, each city and each guild regulated itsself in a way that did not establish a coherent whole.[17] Hence, Hegel regarded the guilds—although they were not the prime target of his criticism—as part of a pre-modern structure that prevented the realisation of a modern, functionally-differentiated society.

Twenty years after his devastating critique of feudal Germany, however, Hegel was able to develop a detailed theory of a functionally-differentiated society and a modern state. He could now claim that, as a result of the upheaval created by the French Revolution and the Napoleonic wars, Germany had moved far closer to the realisation of modern structures; a move that was mainly the result of the Prussian reform movement in the first two decades of the nineteenth century, which, to a large extent, copied French structures of state organisation. Accordingly, his *Philosophy of Right* [1821] was essentially concerned with the question of how the modern, functionally-differentiated society could be conceptualised as a coherent whole. Thus, Hegel was the first to raise the question which later on was to become the key question of modern sociology, in so far as his main concern was how functionally-differentiated society could be conceived of as an integrated society. Hegel's answer lay in the concept of the state, in the sense that that he called for the stabilisation of the relationship between the different spheres of society through their compliance with the rationality of the modern state. For Hegel, this, in practice, meant compliance with the rationality of modern organisation, and, accordingly, he developed a theory of bureaucracy that incorporated all the essential elements of the theory later developed by Max Weber.[18]

Although it addressed public administration, this model was essentially valid for the description of modern Continental European economic organisation as well, in so far as the starting point of Continental European industrialisation was mercantilism and—later on—state capitalism.[19] Industrial organisations were often established on the basis of government decrees, usually in order to fulfill military needs. Industrial organisation in Continental Europe was based upon a copying of the organisational structures of the state, thereby making the organisation of the state administration the role model for industrialists. Moreover, this was one of the reasons why public law became the role model for private law within Continental European legal systems during the nineteenth

[17] GWF Hegel, *Die Verfassung Deutschlands [1800–02], Werke 1* (Frankfurt aM, Suhrkamp Verlag, 1971) 451–610, especially at 467.

[18] GWF Hegel, *Grundlinien der Philosophie des Rechts [1821], Werke 7* (Frankfurt aM, Suhrkamp, 1970) § 287–97.

[19] M Weber, *Wirtschaftsgeschichte* (Leipzig, Duncker & Humblot, 1923) 289–315.

century. One of the many consequences of the rise of modern state organisation was that the state took over the functions which had previously been handled by the guilds. Security issues became the exclusive purview of the state, which had gained the monopoly of power. The regulation of the economy became a primary concern of the state. Issues such as standard-setting, therefore, became a public function.[20] It was the same case with the regulation of competition and price-setting. The state, moreover, played a central role in the secularisation of society, thereby contributing to the break-down of the religious embeddedness of the economy.

From a Hegelian perspective—which, to a large extent, corresponded with the empirical realities of Continental Europe in the nineteenth and early twentieth centuries—modern society was functionally differentiated, but this functional differentiation was counter-balanced by territorial differentiation, in that functionally-differentiated society unfolded itself within the framework of the nation state. But the framing was not only territorial. A central function of the modern state was to ensure a sufficient stabilisation of the new stratified class structures which emerged as a consequence of industrialisation and urbanisation.[21] In practice, this meant that, whereas pre-modern economic structures had been framed by a religious universe, the rationality of the modern economy was—at organisational level—subsumed under the larger frame of *Étatisme*, in that the economy became the subject of a 'double-binary coding'. Economic organisations reproduced themselves on the basis of the distinction property/non-property, at the same time as they faced the demand to operate in accordance with the rationality of the state, which was based on the distinction between ruler and ruled. Consequently, the distinction between state and society was mainly reduced to a distinction between state and economy. This created the basis for the establishment of structural couplings through the kind of corporatist economic constitutions that developed over the course of the nineteenth and most of the twentieth century in most European countries; constitutions which ensured the legal stabilisation of the triangular relations among the state, employers and employees. In organisational terms, these structural couplings were intrinsically state-centred, in the sense that the labour market organisations which evolved tended to mirror the organisational forms of the state administration or even to see themselves as parts of the state.[22] Consequently, there was little room for

[20] H Schepel, *The Constitution of Private Governance: Product Standards in the Regulation of Integrating Markets* (Oxford, Hart Publishing, 2004).

[21] GWF Hegel, *Grundlinien der Philosophie des Rechts [1821], Werke 7* (Frankfurt a M, Suhrkamp, 1970), § 250–56.

[22] A Brodocz, 'Strukturelle Kopplung durch Verbände' (1996) 2 *Soziale Systeme* 361–87.

non-hierarchical organisational structures in the time of modernity. In Deakin's words, 'networks were confined to the margins of modern society'.[23] Accordingly, the concept of networks was only useful for the description of the kind of policy networks that tend to surround the hierarchical peaks of any modern organisation.[24]

IV. THE RADICALISED MODERNITY

The Hegelian nation-state society achieved its zenith with the rise of welfare societies in the 1960s. Since then, the nation-state container has increasingly broken down, just as class society has been increasingly dissolved through the replacement of class distinctions with inclusion/exclusion mechanisms, along the borders of functionally-differentiated systems.[25] In other words, the level of functional differentiation has been radicalised and territorial, and stratificatory forms of stabilisation have increasingly lost their relevance. Consequently, what is often being described as post-modern society is, in fact, only a society where the intrinsic modern logic of functional differentiation has become an even stronger characteristic of society than before.[26]

Moreover, the state is increasingly facing 'capacity-problems' in relation to its capabilities to reproduce the societal functions that it used to monopolise. The other functional systems, and, in particular, the economic system, are less and less confined within the nation-states. The state, which, for Hegel, had three meanings—(i) the political system; (ii) society as a whole; and (iii) the nation-state, understood as a container demarcating one society from other societies[27]—is increasingly being reduced to one functional system among others.[28] Consequently, only the first of Hegel's three meanings of the state continues to have empirical validity. The relative weight of the state in relation to other functional systems is therefore steadily diminishing. But even though world society, which is almost fully functionally-differentiated, is, in principle, based upon heterarchy—since no functional system is directly subsumed within the rationality of another functional system—the economic system has progressively emerged as the 'market leader' among functional systems. This final victory of the commercial spirit (*Handelsgeist*), as

[23] See S Deakin, 'The Return of the Guild? Network Relations in Historical Perspective' (ch 3), in this volume.

[24] G Grabher (ed), *The Embedded Firm* (London, Routledge, 1993).

[25] N Luhmann, 'Inklusion und Exklusion' in Luhmann, *Soziologische Aufklärung Band 6* (Opladen, Westdeutscher, 1995) 237–64.

[26] N Luhmann, *Die Gesellschaft der Gesellschaft* (Frankfurt aM, Suhrkamp, 1997) 1143–9.

[27] GWF Hegel, *Grundlinien der Philosophie des Rechts [1821], Werke 7* (Frankfurt aM, Suhrkamp, 1970) § 257–360.

[28] N Luhmann, *Politik der Gesellschaft* (Frankfurt aM, Suhrkamp, 2000).

foreseen by Kant,[29] means that the form of economic re-reproduction has become the ideal model which other functional systems seek to imitate. Consequently, private law has increasingly become the role model for public law. Moreover, the organisation of the political system, and especially of its bureaucratic sub-system, is undergoing profound changes due to the system's adoption of the economic semantics of efficiency, market orientation and customisation. This has also been illustrated by Deakin, who used the example of public broadcasting.[30] These changes profoundly undermine the modern illusion of the state as a unity.

The re-organisation of the political-bureaucratic system on the basis of economic rationality means that the political system—at organisational level—is increasingly faced with a double-binary coding. Its operations unfold on the basis of the known distinctions between ruler and ruled, and attached parasitic distinction between government and opposition, at the same time as the system adopts the logic of the economic system. This changes the way in which the political system engages with its environment. The political system increasingly acts as a societal co-ordinator or 'broker', and far less as a Weberian instrument of rule (*Herrschaftsinstrument*). Accordingly, the state is increasingly aligning itself with concepts such as social corporate responsibility and self-regulation, rather than exclusively with hard legal regulation. This is the case, especially in relation to the European Union (EU), which can be seen as an avant-garde structure[31] in the sense that the EU largely performs regulatory functions suitable for the late-modern risk society, and not the kind of redistributive functions that characterise the modern welfare-state.[32] Consequently, the EU's relations to the economic system and other parts of its environment are regulated mainly through lobbying networks, rather than through hierarchical corporatist organisations.

Thus, the economic system is increasingly faced with a need to perform functions that no longer are being exclusively handled by the political system. For example, the main security threats to economic entities today are often related to the increased use of information technology. This is an area where the territorially-based state experiences

[29] I Kant, 'Zum Ewigen Frieden' [1795] in A Buchenau, E Cassirer and B Kellerman, *Immanuel Kants Werke, Schriften von 1790–1796* (Berlin, Bruno Cassirer, 1914) 425 at 454.

[30] See S Deakin, 'The Return of the Guild? Network Relations in Historical Perspective' (ch 3), in this volume.

[31] K-H Ladeur, 'Towards a Legal Theory of Supranationality—The Viability of the Network Concept' (1997) 3 *European Law Journal* 33–54.

[32] G Majone, *Regulating Europe* (London, Routledge, 1996).

difficulties in providing the necessary protection, thereby forcing economic entities to find alternative, and largely private, modes of protection.[33] As pointed out by Harm Schepel, standard-setting is increasingly being outsourced to private actors, because it is becoming difficult for public authorities to handle its complexity.[34] In fact, the safeguarding of competition seems to be the only area where the state continues to hold a strong position. It is, therefore, not surprising that almost the only area where the EU, as an emerging late-modern 'state', possesses exclusive competence is in the area of competition policy.[35]

With the increased erosion of the political system's framing of the relations between the economic system and its social environment—through the reproduction of indirect structural couplings between the economic system and, for example, the functional systems of science, education and the environment—the economic system has been forced to seek alternative ways of ensuring the compatibility of its operations with the operations of the systems in its social environment. The economic system is faced with a functional need to substitute the indirect structural couplings, which were established via the political system, with direct structural couplings. It is in the context of this background that the expansion of the phenomenon of networks should be understood: in the sense that the establishment of network-based 'partnerships' between firms and other organisational systems, which are often reproduced within the spheres of other functional systems, is one of the strategies being invoked by the economic system (as well as other functional systems) in order to ensure its embeddedness within society. In particular, larger companies are no longer restricting their activities to engaging with traditional corporatist organisations, but instead are actively seeking to participate in networks concerned, for example, with self-regulation of marketing norms, standard-setting, and dialogue with a multiplicity of public authorities, research institutions, environmental groups, advocates of fair trade and so forth.[36] Accordingly, representation within the wider social environment is increasingly becoming a matter that is handled directly by the firms in question. In other words, any major economic entity is increasingly faced with the need to develop

[33] G-P Calliess, *Globale Kommunikation—staatenloses Recht* in M Anderheiden, S Huster and S Kirste (eds), *Globalisierung von Gerechtigkeit und Steuerungsfähigkeit des Rechts, ARSP-Beiheft* (Stuttgart, Franz Steiner, 2001) 61 at 79.

[34] H Schepel, *The Constitution of Private Governance: Product Standards in the Regulation of Integrating Markets* (Oxford, Hart Publishing, 2004).

[35] EC Treaty §§ 81 and 82.

[36] Royal Dutch/Shell's change of communication strategy after the Brent Spar affair is a very good illustration. See http://www.shell.com/home/Framework?siteId=uk-en&FC2=/uk-en/html/iwgen/zzz_lhn.html&FC3=/uk-en/html/iwgen/about_shell/brentspardossier/dir_brent_spar.html.

self-reflexive strategies for the handling of uncertainty and the irritations that originate from its social environment. Networks, understood as a specific form of structural coupling between organisational systems operating under the condition of the simultaneous activation of interaction systems,[37] fulfill exactly this function.

Thus, networks are acquiring a fundamentally different role within the radical late-modernity to that conducted in the Hegelian era, where the concept, as already indicated, was only a useful tool for describing the very limited kind of interaction systems which tend to surround the peaks of hierarchical organisations. Present-day networks are also fundamentally different from the guild institutions, since their main function is to act as integrative measures under the condition of radical functional differentiation.[38] Moreover, networks must be seen as inter-hierarchical phenomena; ie, they link modern organisations. The intrinsic modern concept of the hierarchical organisation thus remains the central starting point[39] upon which parasitic networks can thrive. Accordingly, what has changed is not so much the form of organisations as the form by which such organisations ensure their embeddedness in society. Employing the metaphor of the guild to describe contemporary networks is, therefore, not particularly useful, as it tends to evoke neo-medieval connotations rather than an understanding of the conditions of operating within a radicalised modernity. That said, historical explorations of the network phenomenon remain crucial if the present wave of social and legal network theory is not to become more than just another fashion that will disappear as quickly as it emerged. Moreover, any quest for legal diversity must start from the insight that the current situation may be different because, in the past, things also used to be different.

[37] For this specific definition of networks, see E Kämper and JFK Schmidt, 'Netzwerke als strukturelle Kopplung' in J Weyer (ed), *Soziale Netzwerke. Koncepte und Methoden der Socialwissenschaftlichen Netzwerkforschung* (Munich, Oldenburg, 2000) 211–35.

[38] For a somewhat similar line of thinking and an illustrative example, see A Abegg, 'Regulation of Hybrid Networks at the Intersection between Governmental Administration and Economic Self-Organisation' (ch 14), in this volume.

[39] The vision of Piore and Sabel concerning a possible breakdown of vertical integration of production has therefore not materialised. See MJ Piore and C Sabel, *The Second Industrial Divide: Possibilities for Prosperity* (New York, Basic Books, 1984).

5

The Path to the Law—The Difficult Legal Access of Networks

JEAN NICOLAS DRUEY*

WHAT FOLLOWS, tries to sort out the methodological steps of a phenomenon-oriented legal science with regard to the network phenomenon.

I. LAW IS AN ORACLE, NOT A MANAGER

There is no tie provided by nature between 'law' and 'network'. Their relationship is one of a mutual lack of concern, and thus of mutual passivity. Looking from the point of view of the *law*, this has nothing to do with the network phenomenon in particular, whether the term is registered in the body of law or not, because it is due to a very general quality of law. Law is information and can only trigger something when it is confronted with a question. Maybe the intention behind any legal rule is to steer and shape something: technically, however, law is only an offer to inform about rules.

In this sense, law is an oracle and not a manager who actively seeks to achieve his or her goals by influence; it is Pythia of Delphi and not the lightning-throwing Zeus on Mount Olympia. This means that the law exclusively draws on its own resources when answering the question of which rules are applicable to any specific phenomenon, be it known to the law or be it new. The water and steam of Castalia come out of the mountain. Autarchy as to its content is what makes law into what it is; its norms are 'legalised' by their source.

* Professor of Private Law and Commercial Law, University St Gallen, Director, Forschungsstelle für Informationsrecht.

This may sound very positivistic. However, it stands under the reservation of the openness of law that HLA Hart insists upon.[1] The generality of legal terms, and, I would add, the hierarchy of the norms, allow answers to unexpected questions by referring to the ideas that lie behind the face of the rules. This is also an opportunity for the network phenomenon.

I leave it open as to whether, in this description, law appears as a *system* in the sense of the respective (and respected) theory, and whether this appearance of new phenomena is adequately described as an irritation. In our context, the focus is elsewhere, since the type of link we are considering is not that of action and reaction, but that of informing and becoming informed. To put it more precisely, systems theory clearly has much to do with information, but information is considered in the sense of influence and impact, ie of actions and reactions, whereas we have to abstract from this, in order to separate the information acquired from law, or by law, from its potential consequences.

II. FACTS PRIMARILY DO NOT ASK FOR LAW

Turning to the other side and looking from facts to law, the situation is the same. Facts are not the product of law; they exist whatever the law says about them. However, they must fear action based upon law, which can hinder their evolution, be it by providing intervention or by attributing individual rights in a selective manner. Facts are 'interested', so to speak, in ascertaining the law as a relatively cheap and relatively important prognosis. The factual world is not only open for legal information, but it is eager to obtain it. This means that the necessary conditions for communication are given: there is, on the one hand, a party ready to give information, and, on the other, there is a party taking the initiative for the transfer.

Thus, as a factual structure, networks continue to exist independently of whether or not the law says something about them, and even if its statement is negative, be it in the sense that legal relevance is denied to them, or in the sense that law forbids their existence. This is all the more so if the law's attitude is positive, be it that, by its rules, it helps to stabilise the set-ups, or that it grants individual rights to them. Knowing that law attaches consequences to something which is a network is, in any case, valuable information as an indication on future influence.

So, let us now try to titillate the law with the term 'network'.

[1] HLA Hart, *The Concept of Law* (Oxford, Clarendon Press, 1961) 121–32.

III. LEGAL ANALYSIS OF CONCEPTS STARTS FROM COMMON LANGUAGE

Now, no less than the law, the world of facts needs concepts to be grasped intellectually. Questioning the law thus implies a translation process, and when looking at it sufficiently closely, this is twofold, because the approach of the language must occur in both directions: not only have the terms been originated by facts in order to find their legal counterparts, but the legal terms have to be analysed to determine what phenomena they fit with.

The reaction when realising the need to overcome this division is usually the call for a dialogue between the respective *sciences*. The chance of obtaining neatly prepared definitions is, of course, best when the concepts have undergone scientific cleansing. However, this is not what is sought. Each science has its own questions and methods. Its definitions are streamlined under the aspect of what it considers to be rewarding and feels fit to take under its scrutiny. By this, the phenomena may either be grossly narrowed or broadened. When the law has to determine its own position, it therefore needs a proper analysis of the respective facts, and since it cannot do so without taking concepts as mediators for facts, it should take the language as close as possible to where the facts are *lived*—independently of the position taken in the old law-in-the-books/law-in-action-issue. This is common language.

Looking at common language use, the term 'network' is first of all intriguing, for its enormous recent use. This signals an important factual presence and raises corresponding questions for the law. What is even more intriguing, however, is that the network is certainly not a new fact, but is, instead, a new name for structures that are tied to human life as such. The network-wave is connected to a discovery, not an evolution. This renders the legal task more complex. There is a substantial chance that the network or its conceptual constituents may appear under other denominations in the legal vocabulary, and the phenomenon to be considered is not merely the network itself, but the growth of interest in the term. In other words, the question for the law is not only what to do about the network, but also what everyone means—from a legal standpoint—when they use the word.

IV. CONFRONTATION, DECONSTRUCTION, AND LIMITATION ARE THE LEGAL STRATEGIES TOWARDS FACTUAL CONCEPTS

What does the law do with the concept of network presented to it?

A first possibility is processing. This means that the term 'network' is, as such, confronted in the register of legal terms. The result is probably equally easily described for all legal orders: there is no entry. Maybe we would have a greater chance of defining it when specifying: co-operation network, electronic network, or—in the light of the subject of this volume—contractual network. But this is no answer when 'the' network is looked for. In this sense, Richard Buxbaum's statement repeatedly cited by my co-authors is certainly correct: 'Network is not a legal concept'.[2]

Even if the juristic antennae do not react to the term as such, there are further possibilities. One means is to break it down into its constituent qualities. What are the qualities which make the network what it is? Considering linguistic practice, for example, by looking the word up on Google, there are several requirements which are deemed essential for a network. These include:

- horizontal structure;
- informality;
- openness to access;
- non-exclusivity with respect to other links.

The last three criteria are merely negative and could only be constituents together with horizontality as a positive description. But horizontality appears not to be generally understood as a characteristic of networks.[3] One is therefore tempted to add a second sentence to Buxbaum's: 'Don't worry, network is not a concept anywhere'.

However, as already observed, law may create its own language, since it has the option of linguistic isolationism. In this sense, it can make a choice which, for practical reasons, should not excessively depart from common usage, but which can, to some degree, channel the floodtide of meanings. Legally, there would be good reasons to choose horizontality as the criterion; it would be the feature that is lacking in the traditional legal systems.[4] However, I feel that isolation of the law would be going too far, and would be detached from the active world. Instead, the orientation is to be found in network science *proprement parlé*,[5] which

[2] RM Buxbaum, 'Is "Network" a Legal Concept?' (1993) 149 *Journal of Institutional and Theoretical Economics* 698 at 704.

[3] For example, the German business administration doctrine sees the very idea of networks as a mixture of horizontal *and vertical* structures (see J Sydow, *Strategische Netzwerke—Evolution und Organisation*, (Wiesbaden, Gabler, 1992) 78 *et seq*. However, not any kind of mixture is eligible, but only an 'intelligent' one; thus, the network is something which *allows* the intelligent mixture (which is, of course, the interesting aspect under the auspices of business administration), and the definition remains open.

[4] For more details, see JN Druey, 'Organisationsnetzwerke' in M Amstutz (ed), *Die vernetzte Wirtschaft* (Zürich, Schulthess, 2004) 123 at 127 *et seq*.

[5] See A-L Baraba'si, *Linked*, 2nd edn (London, Penguin, 2003). Since the network-concept is the very starting point, there is a chance that this science comes close to common language.

conforms to sociological terminology.[6] For these sciences, the point is simply that a plurality of distinguishable units is *linked* together.

Whether this makes sense in the legal perspective remains, of course, to be seen. The primary condition is that the factual concept can be *understood* by the law; translation requires comprehension.

V. CONCEPTS HAVE A RHETORICAL DIMENSION

Concepts, besides being the keys to some kind of reality, bear within themselves additional associations. In terms of semiotics, it is, beside the denotative power, the connotative power of a concept. Or to put it in another way: concepts are of interest not only because they are a clothing to any reality, but because a good phrase can be fascinating in itself. The clothing does not tell, it only suggests, it does not describe, it only promises.

This second, rhetorical dimension is of great importance in networking. There is hardly any concept which has gained so much in linguistic appeal during the past few decades as that of the network. This is certainly not entirely due to an increase of networks in the real world, but, as I said, has probably much more to do with the *discovery* that there exist structures which up to now remained nameless. The open term of network, on the other hand, is suggestive but vague and offers itself as an umbrella for a variety of kinds of such discoveries. The weakness of the concept, its lack of precision, is also its strength in that it stimulates the fantasy of discoveries.

This important rhetorical dimension of the network term enlarges the gap for the law since it multiplies the meanings, the interests, and thereby the questions for the law. But, at the same time, the frequency of use enhances the necessity to bridge it.

VI. UNDER LEGAL AUSPICES, SOCIAL NETWORKS AND OBJECT-NETWORKS ARE NOT THE SAME

Networks link persons or objects together—Hauriou's distinction of '*institution personnes*' and '*institution choses*' may appear here.[7] Thus, the knots are either human beings or non-human elements. Thus, if we speak of contractual networks, these could be (personal, social) networks *by*

[6] Referring to AR Radcliffe-Brown, 'On Social Structure' in (1940) 70 *Journal of the Royal Anthropological Institute of Great Britain* 1 at 8.

[7] Cited from M Hauriou, *Die Theorie der Institution und zwei weitere Aufsätze, Schriften zur Rechtstheorie 5*, R Schnur (ed), (Berlin, Duncker & Humblot, 1965) 35.

contracts, or (real) networks *of* contracts. In the former sense, 'contract' appears as the construction principle of personal relationships, in the latter, which is the subject of this volume, it appears as a constituent of the entity.

Social networks, in themselves, are of legal interest, because the grouping of persons, namely, organising, is a task of law. But they are not, in themselves, of a legal nature. Law—in the sense of an autonomous conflict rule as exposed by Amstutz—is not prepared to deal with any specific kind of organisation. It offers a *numerus clausus* of organisational forms with the twofold liberal idea not only of giving a choice among several legal forms, but also of granting the option to the parties to stay without the law by choosing none of these forms. This says that—legally—a contract and an organisation do not stand on an equal footing. In a contract, the willingness to be bound means *eo ipso* to be bound legally; it is a mutually promised programme for action. An organisation only provides for how future common action programmes are to be settled. The constituting act is not necessarily a promise, but can be an autonomous availability to integrate the proper intentions.

Although here is not the place to explore this distinction in depth, or to criticise the tendency to make contracts omnipresent, it should be seen that social networks have a good chance of delivering the *experimentum crucis* on this issue. Any multitude of relationships can be understood as a sum of contracts, but do we thereby grasp the essence of networks? Our two already stated elements of the negative answer are that, first, networking effects do not depend on the existence of legal strings, and that, secondly, organisational law is guided by the *numerus clausus* of associative forms. Taken together, this means that there *must* be non-legal organisations and that networks exist among them.

For networks other than social ones, ie the '*réseau-chose*' to remain in Hauriou's categories, things are easier, since the elements are of the same stuff. The internet, today's most prominent network, is not a creation of law and the links it provides are not legal. We may call it a communicative or an electronic network. The molecule, as another example, is a chemical, and the atom a physical, network—in any case the link is not legal and the legal relevance therefore is not attached to the phenomenon as such, but maybe to some consequences: cyber-law may deal with the validity of electronic signatures or the prohibition of sex. By contrast, a contract is something primarily legal. Thus, a network of contracts is always and necessarily a legal matter, because the ties must emerge from those contracts.

VII. A SOCIAL NETWORK IS ORGANISATIONAL BY NATURE

Let us take up the topic of organisation for another moment. I have described the organisation as a purely potential set-up. It attributes functions which can trigger action depending on the situation.

Networks always have an organisational character; they provide links which can later be used for purposes set by one or several of the persons integrated. Clearly, contracts may come into the picture as well. Take, for example, a network between law firms: the basis for it is probably contractual, and consists of one or several contracts, which may provide for certain regular performances (*'Leistungen'*) by the member firms, such as quarterly bulletins on recent developments in their sector. Thus, there is a network of contracts and an action programme is established. But what makes it a social network is that the channel is seen as something different from its content. A subscription to a quarterly report is, in itself, not a network. To call this structure a network is saying that it has a *potential*; it will be used for exchanges which are not yet determined when the set-up is made.

Potential means organisation. An organisation is a description of functions or procedures which will, in the future, produce behaviour plans for the selfsame entity. An organisation is not per se a *legal* organisation, and this is not saying that there is, in the law, a loophole which is simply to be closed. It reflects the idea of freedom; organisations should not be placed under the hat of the law if they do not wish to. This self-restraint of the law has to do with an innate 'stiffness', so to speak, which renders it inadequate for some kinds of organisations. Let me briefly elaborate on this, as a final reflection.

VIII. PRIVATE LAW IS A SERVANT OF PRACTICE, BUT A STUBBORN ONE

Private law lowers transaction costs by making available standard moulds for private organisations. It does so with a view to the insiders as well as to the outsiders. Whilst the insiders find a ready-made order which helps to equilibrate the positions among them, the outsiders are told as to whether, and in what respects, they are confronting a separate entity and who acts for it.

Up to now, the law does not offer any ready-made cloth which could dress 'the' network. If, according to common understanding, horizontality is to be a feature of networks, there is no fitting model to be found. In particular, the various forms of associative structures—associations, partnerships, companies—do not allow an extrapolation towards the network, since their members do not constitute the organisation. Instead, they unite to *set up* an organisation, ie an entity employing usually many more persons than the constituents, say, of a company. For all involved, a *goal* and a hierarchy are set which co-ordinate the activities. Even if the common goal is simply to harvest a field of potatoes, it has to be determined where the truck is to be filled, what to do with the potatoes, etc, and all this necessitates decisions, and hence requires a subordination of the people under the authority of the competent persons and bodies. A network does not.

If this is so, could and should there not be an additional form of law called 'network' to reflect the great popularity of this mode of associating? I think that, given its function, law is unable to do this, at least, if it aims to achieve a sweeping coverage of networks per se.[8] In networks, links are not the means of reaching a specific goal; they are the goal in themselves. What, then, would be the typical objects of the regulation of networks as such? We do not know what kind of links there should be, whether the set-up is open to further access or not, whether communication is confidential or not, whether, when and with effect for whom membership can be withdrawn—just to mention a few of the issues. None of the possible answers to all these questions can generally claim more fairness than another; everything depends on the ideas prevailing in the respective case.

To follow the approach from language adopted by this paper, this means that the law cannot undertake the full responsibility for translation in transferring facts into norms. Despite the law's serving function, it can only take-up phenomena which have been conceptualised beforehand. Its starting point is a cluster of statements which express what are, at least, typical (not necessarily stringent) features of the phenomenon. The law stands between the will of those involved to shape their relationship, and the political will to regulate. The input from the 'users' must allow a generalised ruling, and the law's equilibration and specification task can only be fulfilled when the necessary material is available; the idea received needs to be sufficiently complete to permit derivations. This is not the case with networks today. It goes without saying that the frequency of the use of the term today, due simply to its popularity, contributes more to it being blurred than clarified.

This being the case, I also doubt whether the *mixture formula* which describes the network as a combination of hierarchy and market, and thus having vertical *and* horizontal structure, is eligible to be sheltered by

[8] For more detail, see Druey, 'Organisationsnetzwerke' (cited in n 4 above) 127–9.

law. In the legal perspective, this formula has repeatedly and impressively been purported by Gunther Teubner.[9] Here, again, I would say that the law appears to be too 'stiff' or, to say it more respectfully, it requires more precise input in order to integrate the concept. On the level of logic, a structure is horizontal *or* vertical; horizontality means that there *is no* hierarchy. Undoubtedly, life is at all times confronted with the task of absorbing contradictory tendencies or principles, and so are organisations. One might even say that the mixture of both hierarchy and market is the very engine keeping an organisation in action: everyone engaged in it has, on one hand, a manifold horizontal orientation—he or she is permanently selling himself or herself (for more money, influence, career, etc), is informally seeking and giving information, or is entering coalitions, etc—but he or she is also (vertically) directed by orders which indicate the intended targets of the organisational activities. Any person in an organisation is pushed from two (or more) sides. Teubner, with his rich catalogue of illustrative institutions, brings to our attention a problem which can hardly be overestimated. My question only concerns the role of networks in this. I would think that the tensions of this kind are typical for more or less all functions in an organisation. I do not see what should be the specific quality of the network in that respect—not even the specific *possibility* it should offer. The mixture formula pre-supposes precisely the elasticity that the law is unable to offer.

IX. CONCLUSION: THE WAY OF CONCEPTS INTO LAW IS LONG

The preceding considerations aimed to show that the concept of network needs more differentiation in order to be a candidate for legal ruling. Grasping the general phenomenon and such possible differentiations, and determining what the law can do about this is a long way off. Our times somewhat lack patience in this respect, I am afraid. The network, maybe now at the peak of its terminological bestseller-career, has grown in awareness in a very short time, if one compares it, for example, with the term *societas* and its unfolding in a long series of centuries. Undoubtedly, pressure to do something legally about it is legitimate, simply on the basis of the frequent use of the term, but it cannot be the law's function to provide an order for factual concepts. It would seem to be necessary to wait until the dust has settled. Patience is also asked for in legal science. We all know the long route of the concept of *societas* into the

[9] G Teubner, *Netzwerk als Vertragsverbund: Virtuelle Unternehmen, Franchising, Just-in-time in sozialwissenschaftlicher und juristischer Sicht* (Baden-Baden, Nomos, 2004). See also G Teubner, '*Coincidentia Oppositorum*: Hybrid Networks beyond Contract and Organisation' (ch 1), in this volume.

law. Today, a tendency to derive a task of the law from any phenomenon is growing; the '... and the law'—publication titles show, in this sense, the laudable eagerness to keep the law up-to-date. But the aim cannot be to suck the world into the law.

X. THREE EXAMPLES—THREE TYPES

X.1. Auditing Companies

Certain worldwide auditing organisations have no ties in terms of capital participation between the national member companies. These use the same company name, have a partly common education programme, and a central governing body decides on general policy matters and ensures that the rules of independence applied to one company are observed by all the others. The contracts with the clients and the billing are performed by the individual companies in their own names. International mandates are split up into national mandates. They do not officially call themselves a network, nor do they use any other term to characterise the overall organisation, but internationally and in informal contacts, the common word is, indeed, network.

What are the alternatives in legal categories? One which should be considered is the partnership. This would mean that all debts are borne by all members *in solidum*. But the fact that the clients only have privity with individual companies and that no action by other member companies can be expected, as well as individual billing and earning clearly exclude this possibility.

The second variant would be the '*Konzern*', ie a group of companies with common management. This could also mean a certain extension of liability beyond the individual service-performing companies. But it would not be substantial; one reason for this is that it would only apply to the central managing company, which, precisely for this reason, is equipped with a minimum of assets. On the other hand, in the case of a *Konzern*, it is more likely that national legislators require all companies to respect the rules of independence.

A third possibility, to mention just these, might be to classify the external appearance as simply inspiring the 'warm feeling'. Although the network presents itself as a homogenous block (shown by the actual language, eg 'Big Four'), it avoids specifying what the public can expect from the linking, except that one can hope for companies working along the same formal standards throughout the world. This would mean that the linking, despite the common name, has essentially no legal bearing. This third classification is not entirely satisfactory, either, since, in the case of international mandates, the referral of clients by one member company to others is not made by optimised choice, but is based on membership only. This is usually accepted by the clients, based on vague ideas that the transfer is merely 'internal'. It would seem to be fair that this concept of an entity be reflected in one way or another in an extension of liability, but the law, as yet, is not sensible to such considerations.

Thus, it is interesting to see that the suggestive power of new concepts like the network can be used very well to grant the user the advantages flowing from them without burdening them with the disadvantages. To get to the point, being unclear is rewarding when suggestive concepts such as that of the network are put forward. This would mean turning upside-down the classical saying *periculum est stipulatoris*, ie, that the risk of misunderstandings lies with the party phrasing a statement.

X.2. Money Transfers

Here, I refer to Amstutz's presentation of the Swiss Federal Court's decision.[10] In a transfer from *T*'s account in bank *Z* to *B*'s account in bank *Y*, the recipient bank *Y* allowed *B* to dispose of the amount, disregarding an order of *Z* to hold the money blocked for a certain time. *T* then sued *B* for breach of contract, although he had a contract with his own bank *Z* only. And he won the case. As Amstutz notes, the court obviously refused to base its finding on any of the several specific instruments which the law and doctrine on contracts have elaborated to help in this sort of triangular relationship, and, to the fury of the scholarly specialists, decided simply on the grounds that transferors need to be protected. In the reader's impression, the opinion leaves a big blank here, just as if they meant 'the network' but did not want to say it.

And I would add, as does Amstutz, that there *is*, in fact, a network here. The banking system provides channels for inter-banking and thereby inter-client money transfers, which are thoroughly regulated by agreements drafted by the Swiss Bankers' Association and signed by the participating banks—agreements with each other and with the central clearing agency set up for this purpose. In this sense, it is a contractual network, but it is organisational in so far as it is a mechanism ready to work upon the respective input. However, this organisation fits into no legal form, at least (which is essential here) not from an external view. Liability—to restrict ourselves to this aspect—cannot tackle the organisation as such, because most of the participants have nothing to do with the respective transaction. This is not a service of the organisation. And, after

[10] *BGE* 121 III 310.

all, it is *not* an organisation: there is no product elaborated by common forces, no common goal and no hierarchy enforcing it.

Does this mean that the next step in the legal process would simply be to lift the veil which the Federal Court has left over the concept of network? Clearly, it thought that it was not its job to decide upon complementing the law in this sense. From the outset, the network was not the court's problem. It was concerned in the first instance with the choice between the various theories offered to cover damage caused to an unrelated party. All these constructions appeared to be too daring to the judges. Clearly, this was no atmosphere for inaugurating such a new and fundamental concept as the network. The Federal Court might even have received some criticism for bringing the certainly less far-reaching notion of '*Konzernvertrauen*' into the system. Whereas these constructive 'triangle'-theories were at least intensely and explicitly examined by the court, there is no mention at all of the term 'network' in the opinion delivered by the court. Silence is the most negative of all answers. I understand this intriguing (and practically important) decision as a 'try harder'-appeal to doctrine to refine and corroborate the tools offered by existing law which portray the *elements* of networks relevant in the case, but also as a refusal to prepare for the birth of the network as such.

X.3. Health Services

As my last example, I would like to take up one of these innumerable situations of very informal and open use of the term 'network' in actual day-to-day-life, of friendships, neighbourhoods or other interactive relationships which have existed since the birth of humanity, but have only recently been called 'networks'. The viewpoint is, in a way, opposite to the prior example, in that it does not analyse the non-use of the notion, but the very use. The question, however, is again the same: the 'way into law'.

I let pure chance decide upon the case which I use to illustrate here. By chance, I followed a presentation on TV about health services yesterday. As usual, it was first the image, and only secondarily the text, speaking. The doctor who was the focus of the presentation did wear the 'doctoral' white overcoat, but only very loosely. This was obviously to fit with the quasi-omnipresence of the word 'network' throughout, predominantly used as a verb ('*vernetzt arbeiten*', ie 'networking'). What did the concept and what did the words used around it convey?

The message was clear: that health-care personnel should co-operate more closely. 'Network', here, was not an entity in a juridical sense. The set-up remained entirely open and the persons coming to participate were determined by their functions, not by an act of access. Their functions were not attributed by the so-called network. The purpose was to minimise the obstacles in order for a patient to obtain optimal help. Part of the core idea is informality, the readiness of the medical professionals involved to contribute wherever both need and capacity exists. Everyone works with everyone. Another part is hierarchical. There have to be orders, of course, for the functioning of the set-up: physicians instruct the care personnel; the chief co-ordinator calls on the specialists required, etc. The only legal implication that I can find is a purely negative one: it is to tear down all obstacles of professional confidentiality within the 'network'.

In the context presented, the message was nothing but a homily: 'Do make sure you work together when you are close to a sick person.' If it had been backed up by law, a lot of difficulties and obstacles would appear, and there would be substantial risk that it would lose the selfsame flexibility that it purports to seek. The doctor's principles on TV represent the most elementary level (in an evolutionary sense) of a culture in which networks can grow. They are neither referring to law nor to socio-ethical principles, but merely to rhetoric. This does not necessarily say something against their value.

Part II.

Internal Network Relations: Generalised Reciprocity

6

The Status of Multilateral Synallagmas in the Law of Connected Contracts

PETER W HEERMANN*

I. INTRODUCTION

WITHIN THE GENERAL framework of 'contractual networks' and 'legal issues surrounding contractual multilaterality', the following remarks will clarify the concept of trilateral (multilateral) synallagmas that I developed in the second half of the '90s[1] within the law of connected contracts. To this end, I will:

- present the model of trilateral (multilateral) synallagmas using a credit card transaction as an example;
- outline Teubner's model of the network as connected contracts[2] using a bank transaction as an example;
- posit his view against my position into the current discussion; and
- challenge some of Teubner's assumptions, and, in some cases, illustrate them.

The first two sections will be limited to an outline presentation of the discussion as it currently stands. However, half of the article will be devoted to the last two sections, since, in this connection, the discussion on the law of connected contracts should be critically elucidated, advanced, and, perhaps even to a certain extent, enriched.

* Professor of Civil Law, Business and Commercial Law, Comparative Law and Sports Law at the University of Bayreuth and former Judge at the Regional Appeals Court in Nuremberg (2001–2005).

[1] PW Heermann, *Drittfinanzierte Erwerbsgeschäfte—Entwicklung der Rechtsfigur des trilateralen Synallagmas auf der Grundlage deutscher und U.S.-amerikanischer Rechtsentwicklungen* (Tübingen: Mohr & Siebeck, 1998) 92 *et seq*, 200 *et seq*; see also PW Heermann, *Geld und Geldgeschäfte* (Tübingen: Mohr & Siebeck, 2003) 78 *et seq*.

[2] G Teubner, *Netzwerk als Vertragsverbund—Virtuelle Unternehmen, Franchising, Just-in-time in sozialwissenschaftlicher und juristischer Sicht* (Baden-Baden, Nomos, 2004) 109 *et seq*. See also G Teubner, '*Coincidentia Oppositorum*: Hybrid Networks beyond Contract and Organisation' (ch 1), in this volume.

II. MODEL OF THE TRILATERAL (MULTILATERAL) SYNALLAGMAS

II.1. The Concept of Individual Performance

The concept of individual performance ('*Leistungsbegriff*') forms the basis of the point of departure for my model of reasoning, in which connection the concept of 'individual performance' should be understood in a purely factual sense.[3] For the following deliberations, the legal term 'individual performance' will be ascribed the following definition:

> an intentional and directly commercial bestowal or transfer of assets from the debtor to the creditor based on a contractual obligation.

II.2. The *do ut des ut det*- exchange of performance

In a credit card transaction[4] which, for the sake of simplicity, will be limited to three participants (credit card issuer, credit card holder, and authorised merchant), the trilateral synallagmatic exchange of performance is represented as follows:

In the underlying debt relationship (credit card issuer/authorised merchant), the credit card company assumes the obligation to compensate the authorised merchant at specific intervals of time—often weekly—the amount due, which arises from the credit card use at its current nominal value with the deduction of a percentage discount (Performance A). In the relationship between the authorised merchant and the credit card holder, the authorised merchant has the duty to transfer ownership and surrender possession of the object or service being acquired (Performance B). In the relationship between the credit card holder and the credit card issuer, the credit card holder meets the obligation of making, in most cases, monthly payments of money, in an amount which reflects his or her credit card transactions, to the credit card issuer, as well as to offset the (lump sum) costs of using the card in a foreign country, if applicable (Performance C). Performances A through to C are linked together in a relationship that can be described with the Latin phrase *do ut des ut det* (or to be more exact: *do ut tertio des ut tertius mihi det*).

Such a trilateral synallagma can be established in numerous other triangular configurations especially with assignments of debt,[5] qualifying

[3] See also Heermann, *Drittfinanzierte Erwerbsgeschäfte* (n 1 above) 92 and 246.

[4] On credit card transactions, see, eg, Heermann, *Geld und Geldgeschäfte* (n 1 above) 263 *et seq*, and 464 *et seq*.

[5] Heermann, *Drittfinanzierte Erwerbsgeschäfte* (n 1 above) 130; Heermann, *Geld und Geldgeschäfte* (n 1 above) 664 *et seq*.

Figure 1

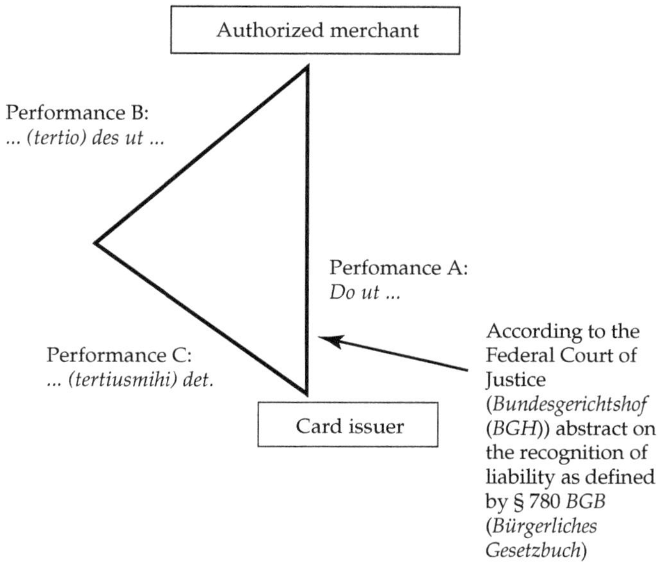

contracts for the benefit of third parties,[6] instalment plan businesses financed by third parties,[7] finance leasing transactions,[8] as well as in various collateral security transactions, such as a contract of suretyship,[9] additional assumptions of debt,[10] bank guarantees,[11] documentary credit operations,[12] and assignments by way of security.[13]

II.3. The Basic Principles of the Trilateral Synallagma

Once a trilateral (multilateral) synallagmatic exchange of performances in connected contracts has been shown—and in the absence of agreements among the parties or legal opinions to the contrary—the legal consequences can be deduced from the basic principles of the genetic, conditional, and functional synallagmas.

[6] Heermann, *Drittfinanzierte Erwerbsgeschäfte* (n 1 above) 131.
[7] *Ibid*, 147 *et seq*; Heermann, *Geld und Geldgeschäfte* (n 1 above) 435 *et seq*.
[8] Heermann, *Drittfinanzierte Erwerbsgeschäfte* (n 1 above) 152 *et seq*; Heermann, *Geld und Geldgeschäfte* (n 1 above) 482 *et seq*.
[9] Heermann, *Geld und Geldgeschäfte* (n 1 above) 540 *et seq*.
[10] *Ibid*, 600 *et seq*.
[11] *Ibid*, 616 *et seq*.
[12] *Ibid*, 642 *et seq*.
[13] *Ibid*, 665 *et seq*.

II.3.(a) The Genetic Synallagma

The basic principles of the genetic trilateral synallagma[14] can be summarised in simplified form as follows: if one of the individual performance obligations in the trilateral synallagma is invalid, provisionally invalid, or has not accrued in the first place, then this also applies for the remaining links of the performance chain around the triangle and all the residual performance obligations of the entire three-sided and mutual legal transaction. The legal-enrichment-minded reverse transaction of invalid trilateral-synallagmatically entwined performances takes place within the parameters of each performance relationship. Thus, the re-conveyance of these performances occurs in the opposite direction in the performance chain around the triangle.

II.3.(b) The Conditional Synallagma

With the conditional synallagma, one perceives the dependence of the exchanged performances on their continued existence. In question is the shifting of the genetic synallagma in the phase after the creation of the obligation. The following can be said concerning the basic principles of the trilateral conditional synallagma[15]: If the performance obligations of a bilateral contractual relationship are cancelled, taking the *do ut des ut det* legal transaction as a basis, then simultaneously both the other trilateral-synallagmatically entwined performance obligations, and, in the end, also all the remaining performance obligations of the entire three-sided and mutual legal transaction, are discontinued. The subsequent discontinuance of one of the links which, in itself, effects the chain of performance obligations around the triangle, causes the discharge of every performance obligation standing within the three-sided or two-sided synallagma. The reverse transaction, with an eye towards unjust enrichment, occurs once again in the opposite direction of the performance chain around the triangle.

II.3.(c) The Functional Synallagma

Under the functional synallagma, one perceives, in general, the reciprocal dependence that the performance obligations present in the exchange relationship by their enforcement and achievement. The questions present in this context are regulated—in German law—in the provisions

[14] In detail, see Heermann, *Drittfinanzierte Erwerbsgeschäfte* (n 1 above) 163 *et seq*; Heermann, *Geld und Geldgeschäfte* (n 1 above) 129 *et seq*.
[15] In detail, see Heermann, *Drittfinanzierte Erwerbsgeschäfte* (n 1 above) 168 *et seq*; Heermann, *Geld und Geldgeschäfte* (n 1 above) 134 *et seq*.

of Sections 320 to 322 *BGB* (*Bürgerliches Gesetzbuch*), which govern the mutual-reciprocal contract. The functional synallagma has effects in the following way during *do ut des ut det* legal transactions[16]: If Participant *A* should fulfill its performance in the tripartite performance chain with respect to Participant *B*, without Third Party *C* having already fulfilled his duty to *A* in due form or completely, *A* can make a valid claim for an unfulfilled contract. This phenomenon can be described with the catch-phrases 'enforcement network liability' ('*Einwendungsdruchgriff*') or '*exceptio ex iure tertii*'.

II.3.(d) Division of the Risk of Insolvency or Financial Risks

The risk of the inability to pay due debts on the part of a participant in a *do ut des ut det* legal transaction[17] is apparent in the absence of legal insolvency protection mechanisms, especially in cases when, in the setting of a reverse transaction, the fulfilled action of the financing party (for example, the credit card issuer) proves to be irrecoverable from the receiver (the authorised merchant).[18] The remaining two parties will split the resulting insolvency risk basically in equal amounts. Such a division of risk appears appropriate, because, with respect to their profit expectations, all the participants are equally dependent on each other, ie, on the co-operation of each and every participant, and all respectively wanting to obtain personal advantage. This mutual dependency finds its expression—in insolvency cases—in the fundamental division of this risk.

Let me herein cite an example from recent German court decisions[19]: Credit card issuers often reserve the right, in their general terms and conditions forms, by so-called recovery clauses ('charge back' clauses) to reclaim a payment already made to the authorised dealer. This is valid when the card holder brings a claim against the authorised dealer with respect to his promised performance, has a complaint, or—with telephone and mail order procedures—denies that the order was made or that the signature is genuine and, for these reasons, refuses payment vis-à-vis the credit card issuer. Finally, the Federal Court of Justice (*Bundesgerichtshof* (*BGH*)) has declared impermissible such 'charge back' clauses at least with respect to telephone and mail order cases. In the

[16] In detail, see Heermann, *Drittfinanzierte Erwerbsgeschäfte* (n 1 above) 184 *et seq*; Heermann, *Geld und Geldgeschäfte* (n 1 above) 141 *et seq*.

[17] In detail, see Heermann, *Drittfinanzierte Erwerbsgeschäfte* (n 1 above) 267 *et seq*; Heermann, *Geld und Geldgeschäfte* (n 1 above) 144 *et seq*.

[18] Regarding this special problem, see Heermann, *Geld und Geldgeschäfte* (n 1 above) 281 *et seq*.

[19] BGH (2002) *Zeitschrift für Wirtschaftsrecht* (ZIP) 974 at 977 *et seq*.

opinion of the court, however, clauses would be permissible in which the credit card issuer and the authorised merchant shared the risk of misuse.

III. MODEL OF THE NETWORK AS A CONNECTED CONTRACT

III.1. Characteristics (By Example of a Bank Transfer of Funds)

With a deeper understanding, networks—as connected contracts as defined by Teubner—exhibit three characteristics:

III.1.(a) 'Multi-dimensionality'

First of all, the 'multi-dimensionality' of these kinds of networks is typical, characterised by reciprocal references to each other in bilateral contracts.[20] This 'multi-dimensionality' can find its expression in the performance programme and/or in the execution of the contract. When, for example, a bank transfer is completed, usually at least five participants are joined together. The transfer of an amount of money is thereby effected through a stringing together of different mutual contractual relationships. These contracts regularly bear relation to each other.

III.1.(b) 'Network Purpose'

Above and beyond 'multi-dimensionality', connected contracts require a so-called 'network purpose,' ie, a reference in their contents to the common project of the contractual association.[21] With a bank transfer, the 'network purpose' can be seen in that the participants want to convey the cashless transfer of a given sum from the account of the transferring party to the account of the receiver of the transfer.

III.1.(c) 'Economic Unity'

Finally, connected contracts should encourage an 'economic unity'.[22] In this regard, Teubner understands a legally relevant and closely co-operative relationship between the participants in the connection. It can be assumed that in a bank transfer there is the presence of such a co-operative relationship.

[20] See Teubner, *Netzwerk als Vertragsverbund* (n 2 above) 125 and 133.
[21] See *ibid*, 156 *et seq*.
[22] See *ibid*, 125.

III.2. A Bank Transfer is not a Multilateral-Synallagmatic Legal Transaction

All the pre-requisites of a network are present within a bank transfer. Nevertheless, it is definitely not a question of a multilateral-synallagmatic legal transaction.[23] Indeed, all the banks that conduct transfers certainly have performance duties to fulfill by forwarding the amount of the remittance. And yet, these contractual or legal duties exist only vis-à-vis the remitter, as a rule, though not vis-à-vis the payee (third party beneficiary). This would be the pre-requisite, however, in order to be able to establish a chain of synallagmatically entwined performance duties.

III.3. Legal Consequences

In looking at networks as connected contracts, divergent types of legal consequences, differing from each other in their details, have already been developed. Hereinafter, four central aspects should be briefly illuminated in particular.

III.3.(a) Profit Sharing?

The notion of profit sharing[24] is especially explosive. According to this notion, 'network advantages' are, in principle, above all accrued to the co-ordinated parties and then divided among the members according to the equitable treatment principle, and between them and the central office in accordance with the fairness aspect.

III.3.(b) Division of Risk?

Networks are characterised by the fact that all participants in a network are promised a profit from their participation. However, by this action, the network does not turn into an association. Certainly, such a constellation should make

> a proportionate division of risk, with regard to a just salary in accordance with defined, dispositive statutory law as defined by a judge, conditionally necessary among the co-ordinated parties.[25]

Control and insurance aspects should play a rôle in the division—aspects that we recognise from the school of economic analysis of the law.

[23] In detail, see Heermann, *Geld und Geldgeschäfte* (n 1 above) 225 *et seq*.
[24] Teubner, *Netzwerk als Vertragsverbund* (n 2 above) 164 *et seq*, with further references.
[25] *Ibid*, 175 *et seq*, with further references.

III.3.(c) Piercing Liability within the Network

One characteristic for a network as connected contracts is the possibility of 'veil-piercing' liability within the network.[26] Under this concept, one perceives the reciprocal contractual liability of non-contractual partners with each other within the network.

III.3.(d) External Network Liability

Teubner's model is confusing at first glance, and strikes one as strange as it addresses external network liability.[27] He illustrates his concept with an example of a third party financed time payment transaction.[28] In it, he maintains that the 'economic unity' between the institute issuing credit and the seller is the real co-operation network that, vis-à-vis the customer, constructs external contacts. From this perspective, then, the veil-piercing liability within the network appears as external network liability on the economic unity of the network. This selective accountability liability from third parties in financed acquisition transactions could serve in general as a prototype for connected contracts.

III.4. The Regulation Model in German Law (Sections 676a to 676h *BGB*)

As previously stated,[29] a bank transfer does not constitute a multilateral-synallagmatic legal transaction. Some years ago, the German legislature interpolated, for the first time, special provisions contained in Sections 676a to 676h *BGB* concerning bank transfers under the civil law.[30] Here, the legislature expressly associated the bank transfer transaction with neither the connected contract concept nor the controversial model of a network contract,[31] despite detailed academic preparations. Instead, the legislature chose an independent stance that fundamentally assumed that a bank transfer is composed of several mutual contracts. First, as secured through extremely detailed legal regulations, when obstructions or interruptions arise in the inter-bank relationship, the remitter can make a

[26] *Ibid*,188 *et seq*, with further references.
[27] In detail, see *ibid*, 212 *et seq*, with further references.
[28] *Ibid*, 145.
[29] See Section III.2 above.
[30] For a detailed description, see, eg, Heermann, *Geld und Geldgeschäfte* (n 1 above) 202 *et seq*.
[31] See W Möschel, 'Dogmatische Strukturen des bargeldlosen Zahlungsverkehrs' (1986) 186 *Archiv für die civilistische Praxis* (*AcP*) 211 at 223; M Rohe, *Netzverträge—Rechtsprobleme komplexer Vertragsverbindungen* (Tübingen: Mohr & Siebeck, 1998) 85 *et seq*, and 356 *et seq*; see, critically, Teubner, *Netzwerk als Vertragsverbund* (n 2 above) 104 *et seq*, with further references in fn 114.

valid claim against its bank, under a so-called 'money back' guarantee. Thereupon, the bank can seek recourse from its subsequent contractual partner, from the first intermediate bank, etc. In summary, in this way, the damages remain with the actual originator. With the exception of the remitter, every party only has the insolvency risk of its contractual partner. An exception occurs in specific cases legally connected with strict pre-requisites, namely, for veil-piercing liability within the network of the remitter by the intermediate bank or the payee's bank. In addition, the remitter's bank can, under certain circumstances, make a claim for piercing liability within the network against an intermediate bank with which it does not have a contractual relationship.

Figure 2

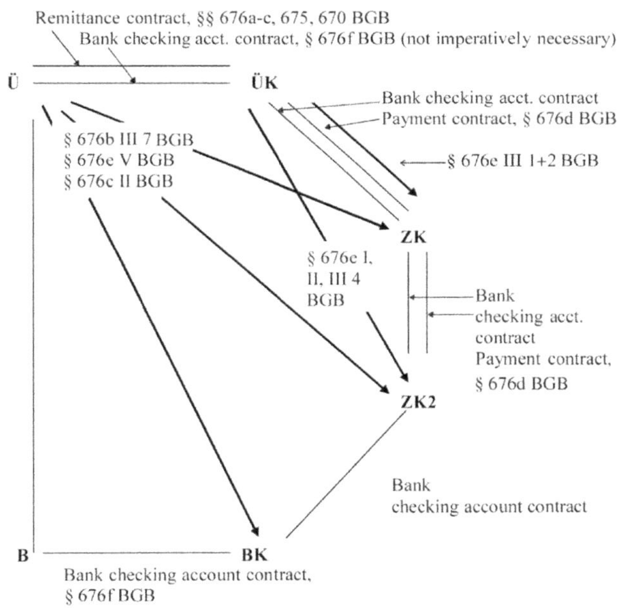

R = Remitter
RB = Remitting Bank
IB 1 = (first) Intermediate Bank
IB 2 = (second) Intermediate Bank
BB = Beneficiary's Bank
B = Beneficiary

IV. STATUS OF THE MODEL OF THE MULTILATERAL SYNALLAGMA IN THE LAW OF CONNECTED CONTRACTS

IV.1. Sub-category of the Concept of Network as Connected Contracts

The previous reflections have shown that connected contracts with trilateral-synallagmatic structures form a sub-category of the entirety of contractual networks. In this article, the examples of a credit card transaction and a bank transfer were consciously chosen in order to elucidate that, given the increasing number of participants within a network, the probability of proving a multilateral-synallagmatic structure decreases. Nevertheless, one should not neglect the fact that the configurations with a trilateral-synallagmatic exchange of performances consequently form 'mini' networks, a thoroughly meaningful sub-group of the networks as connected contracts which, to a substantial degree, determine economic activities. Here, only the following have been mentioned: third party financed time payment agreements, finance leasing transactions, credit card transactions, and different forms of credit security transactions.

IV.2. 'Landmark' Function for Connected Contracts without Synallagmatic Structures

What, then, is the model of the multilateral synallagma in the system of networks as connected contracts capable of performing? On this question, Teubner determined that, with networks, there is often a very much looser reciprocal intertwining of the contracts, a 'generalised reciprocity', that does not provide for every performance around a certain or particular intention. On the contrary, there are also thoroughly independent performances in the network, which have the indeterminate expectation of future network advantages.[32] How their internal interdependence is to be legally qualified cannot be answered by the concept of a trilateral synallagma. The specialised structure of a *'do ut des ut det'*, that genuinely could only be realised in a ring of exchanges and could sensibly be extended perhaps to a financed acquisition transaction, would soon find its limits in larger networks. A generalised reciprocity here would supplant synallagmatic intertwined individual performances.[33]

It should come as no surprise that, as the midwife for the entire legal system inherent in the concept of the multilateral synallagma, I suggest

[32] Teubner, *Netzwerk als Vertragsverbund* (n 2 above) 128 *et seq.*
[33] Teubner, *Netzwerk als Vertragsverbund* (n 2 above) 142 *et seq.*

that we make a finer distinction than Teubner does on this point. He neglects the fact that the concept of the trilateral (multilateral) synallagma does not aspire to include, in a legal sense, all forms of connected contracts. It is only a sub-category thereof. If, however, one follows the model of the trilateral, or as the case may be, the multilateral, synallagma, then far-reaching consequences can be extracted even for connected contracts in general:

1. Just as with bilateral performance exchanges, connected contracts of the type with synallagmatic structures can also be distinguished from those without thoroughly synallagmatic structures.
2. Concerning connected contracts *with* synallagmatic structures, the legal consequences are primarily derived from the previously discussed basic principles of the trilateral or multilateral synallagma.[34] Contractual autonomy is allowed a certain amount of room for interpretation here. If it is not employed, the basic principles of the multilateral synallagma reflect 'the fundamental basic notions of the legal regulations' or the 'fundamental rights and obligations that arise from the nature of the contract' (Section 307 II no 1 and 2 *BGB*.
3. With connected contracts *without* thoroughly synallagmatic structures, the actual, and thereby also legal, interdependencies are less intensively developed. Thus, the concept of the multilateral synallagma can serve as a *first landmark* for developing the legal consequences of contractual associations without synallagmatic structures in all points. Moreover, with non-synallagmatic connected contracts—as compared to *do ut des ut det* legal transactions—broader room has to be given for contractual autonomy.
4. A *second landmark* for identifying the legal consequences regarding contractual associations is formed from the legal consequences derived from the law of associations.

The legal categorisation of connected contracts without synallagmatic structures in all respects, as well as the legal consequences associated with it, are to be established between these two elements. Thus, an important standard is constituted in each case.

Some legal scholars bemoan the fact that the legislature, the court decisions, and, not least of all, most commentators, are rather indifferent in the face of the study of the problematics of connected contracts and their legal consequences. In such a situation, we cannot afford not to

[34] See Section II.3 above.

direct our attention to trilateral or multilateral synallagmas in all applied orientation points in the legal system.

IV.3. Effects of the Characteristics of Networks as Connected Contracts

As is generally known, the characteristics of networks as connected contracts can be summarised in three catchwords or phrases: 'multi-dimensionality,' 'network purpose,' and 'economic unity'.[35] Meanwhile, all these signifiers allow us to miss contours that are still sharp, and thus are much closer to being descriptive in nature. At least for the sub-category of trilateral (multilateral) synallagmatic networks, the previously mentioned pre-requisites can be defined in concrete terms: the decisive question is whether a *do ut des ut det* (*ut det*) legal relationship can be proven to exist. Such relationships are, in every case, multi-dimensional; they produce the requisite network purpose; and they can also be classified as an economic unity.

IV.4. Effects on Legal Consequences from Networks as Connected Contracts

Clearly, the more interesting question is how far the model of multilateral synallagmas can be applied to the list of legal consequences, which are, for the most part, as yet unclear, regarding networks as connected contracts. In this regard, I would again like to tackle the concepts of profit sharing, division of risk, piercing liability within the network, and external network liability.

IV.4.(a) Profit Sharing

Profit sharing of the type suggested for networks[36] shows a significantly stronger connection to solutions with partnership agreements as opposed to reciprocal agreements. Thus, this point of reference poses more questions than it purports to solve. Is it really justifiable to divide 'network advantages' in equal shares? Does the system of profit realisation in bilateral contract relationships—in the end, an emanation of private autonomy—really need correcting? How should the division of profits be executed? In the end, it is a question of a bold proposition when it comes

[35] See Section III.1 above.
[36] See Section III.3.(a) above.

to the postulate of profit sharing. Because, in such a measure, the advantages will not even be 'socialised' in an association, as Teubner also recognised.[37]

Proceeding from the model of the multilateral synallagma, there is no doubt that, with synallagmatic 'mini' networks, the profits sought in single bilateral contractual relations remain with the respective parties to the contract and are not 'socialised'. *Do ut des ut det* (*ut det…*) legal transactions are, in contrast to other connected contracts, characterised by their especially intensive legal interdependencies, without which—as is evident so far—an equal-share profit sharing in this regard would never have been discussed. From these points of departure, the postulate of profit sharing exhibits its lack of justification, which it attempts to overcome if one subscribes to the position for the entirety of connected contracts.

IV.4.(b) Division of Risk

With respect to *do ut des ut det* legal transactions, I have already tried to establish at an earlier point that, in the German *lex lata*, intellectual points of contact for the division of risk are present.[38] Within the parameters of *do ut des ut det* legal transactions, the connection cannot be considered as an association in fractional parts as defined in Sections 741 *et seq*, *BGB* because the participants lack common possession of a right. However, the participants certainly form an association of common interests in a *do ut des ut det* legal transaction upon which the regulations of Sections 742 *et seq BGB* can be appropriately applied to pay heed to the purpose of the legislation. In trilateral synallagmatically connected contracts, the participants thus found the aforementioned coalition or association through contractual, and, simultaneously, through personal, interdependencies. The defining characteristic is not the common position before the law of several persons; instead, what is far more typical is a mutual dependency. Within such associations of common interests, however, recourse can be taken to the dominant idea of fundamental equality in Sections 741 *et seq*, *BGB* as well as to the general concept of proportionate burdens and responsibility for costs that lies behind Section 748 *BGB*. This appears imaginable at least for performances which are similar in monetary values for the three participants. Thus, from the preceding assumptions can be drawn an equable division of insolvency risk or risk of non-payment within the association of those bearing risk. From the *do ut des*

[37] Teubner, *Netzwerk als Vertragsverbund* (n 2 above) 169.

[38] Heermann, *Drittfinanzierte Erwerbsgeschäfte* (n 1 above) 272 *et seq*; Heermann, *Geld und Geldgeschäfte* (n 1 above) 144 *et seq*, each with further references.

ut det connection of the performance obligations and the resulting reciprocal interdependence, the participants realise that they are all 'in the same boat' and want to take responsibility for each other in an emergency from the time that the legal transaction is prepared, through its execution, and up to the necessary (reverse) settlement, if it occurs.

At this point, one could also attempt to make these connections to the *lex lata* useful for non-synallagmatically connected contracts. Whatever one's decision, in the end, the following should be heeded: Between the decisions concerning profit sharing/individual profit realisation, on the one hand, and risk splitting/individual bearing of risk, on the other, no differences in valuation can be allowed to occur.

With regard to credit card transactions, Teubner[39] would like to have risk division in networks in the same way that connected contracts conform to the legal opinions of the Federal Court of Justice (*BGH*), which did, after all, express sympathy for a division of risk in an obiter dictum. This position of the judiciary is, in my opinion, a direct effect of the principles of multilateral synallagmas (without requiring reference to the fundamentals of the economic theory of law) and those are not—or at least conditionally would not be—assignable to connected contracts without synallagmatic structure! With the latter, in each case, contractual autonomy is to be preserved in strong measure because all participants are not 'in the same boat' in the same way. What, then, is the qualitative difference? For connected contracts without synallagmatic structures, the people in the boat are only partially acquainted with each other from the outset and, accordingly, cannot gauge the insolvency risk of each individual network member! This would speak against the equal division of risk for non-synallagmatic connected contracts.

IV.4.(c) Piercing Liability within the Network and External Network Liability

A central problem of complex connected contracts can be traced back to the cast-iron principle of the relativity of obligations (principle of privity). In as far as there is no contractual relationship between the aggrieved party and the damaging party, any fashioning of the enforcement of liability against the damaging party would be difficult from both a dogmatic and a practical perspective. The special charm of the concept of networks as connected contracts lies in the aspect of the legal consequences of piercing liability within the network, ie, in the reciprocal contractual liability among parties who did not sign a bilateral contract within the network. In addition, Teubner[40] recently contributed an external network liability. The 'economic unity' between banks and the seller

[39] Teubner, *Netzwerk als Vertragsverbund* (n 2 above) 175 *et seq*, with further references.
[40] Teubner, *Netzwerk als Vertragsverbund* (n 2 above) 145.

with third party acquisitions would approximate the real 'co-operative network' that would set up external contacts vis-à-vis the customer. From this perspective, the enforcement network liability of the customer would then appear as an external network liability upon the economic unity of the network. This selective accountability in network liability from outside parties for financed acquisition transactions could serve as a general model for contractual associations.

But is this so-called external network liability not perhaps exactly a case of piercing liability within the network? Teubner neglects that, at least concerning networks with multilateral synallagmas (as well as third party financed payment transactions), all the direct participants in the exchange of performances are themselves members of the network as connected contractors—in this respect the customer also constitutes an individual network member. However, in as far as a customer is entitled to enforce piercing liability within the network, the question presents itself as to whether an external network liability can even be additionally required. This is all the more valid since the preconditions for 'economic unity' or for a 'co-operative network' remain confused and indistinct as an opposing claim. Therefore, a so-called external network liability should only be considered if the damaged party himself is not a member of the network. In cases of mutual contracts that the damaged party concluded with an individual network member, reciprocal reference to at least one of the other contracts belonging to the network (and thus a characteristic of connected contracts) will be lacking.

In conclusion, the question is to be briefly elucidated, using a bank transfer as an example, as to how piercing liability within the network can be dogmatically substantiated by the example of a single case. According to Teubner's view, related legal decisions produce an especially massive impact on bank check department networks.[41] At one time, these decisions had made the contract with protective effect for the benefit of third parties into the main instrument of access for performance default with bank check department networks. Such a dogmatic stance is conceivable, but, in this point, it is classified by Teubner as being inadequate for a network because an external element to the contract is attached.[42] It appears as if the *lex lata* holds no satisfactory theoretical starting point. Should one, therefore, *de lege ferenda* introduce a new type of piercing liability within the network? At the very least, the German legislature has, in the meantime, decided otherwise. Remember, yet again, the remitter's legal money-back guarantee (Section 676b I *BGB*)[43]: a valid guarantee claim can be made by the remitter against his bank for

41 Teubner, *Netzwerk als Vertragsverbund* (n 2 above) 230 *et seq*, with further references.
42 *Ibid*, 199 *et seq*.
43 See Section III.4 above.

defaults that occur in the inter-bank relationship. The bank can, in turn, have recourse to the subsequent contractual partner, the first intermediate bank, etc. Finally, in this way, the damages are left hanging with the party that caused them. This stance should not be lost sight of in the future development of piercing liability within the network.

V. CONCLUSION

Multilateral synallagmatically connected contracts form a sub-category of network contracts. For networks with multilateral synallagmatic structures, the legal consequences can be deduced from the applicable basic principles in the complete collection of the legal regulations of the multilateral, genetic, conditional, and functional synallagmas. Simultaneously, a 'landmark' function is also attached to this position for connected contracts without synallagmatic structures. The law of associations develops the opposing 'landmark'.

7

Third Party Effects of Bilateral Contracts within the Network

MARINA WELLENHOFER*

I. THE NETWORK PHENOMENON

I.1. Forms of Contractual Networks

CONTRACTUAL NETWORKS MAY appear as chains of contracts.[1] Modern supply chains contain several links, such as the producer of raw materials, the manufacturer, the retailer and the consumer, with each link connected to the next link by a contract. Other examples of contract chains can be found in the energy sector concerning the energy supply, or in the transportation industry[2] when a number of carriers is operating consecutively. Furthermore, leasing and sub-leasing may establish a chain of contracts.[3]

In addition to chains of contracts, we can observe contract networks[4] in star-like formations. In this case, a natural or legal person concludes several parallel contracts with a number of other persons. Franchising may be a good example. And the franchisee, again, is meant to conclude many contracts with his suppliers or clients. Or in the car industry, we find automobile manufacturers co-operating with suppliers who are, in turn, supplied by their sub-contractors. These arrangements are characterised by one firm as a head office in the centre of the network. The

* Professor of Private Law at Johann Wolfgang Goethe-Universität, Frankfurt am Main.

[1] For this topic, see H Collins, 'The Weakest Link: Legal Aspects of the Network Architecture of Supply Chains' (Oxford, Hart Publishing, 2006) and ch 10 in this volume.

[2] See K Larenz and M Wolf, *Allgemeiner Teil des bürgerlichen Rechts*, 9th edn (Munich, CH Beck, 2004) § 23 Rn 128 *et seq*.

[3] See M Amstutz, 'Die Verfassung von Vertragsverbindungen' in M Amstutz (ed), *Die vernetzte Wirtschaft: Netzwerke als Rechtsproblem* (Zurich, Schulthess, 2004) 45 and 60.

[4] Against the expression 'net', see P Krebs, *Sonderverbindung und außerdeliktische Schutzpflichten* (Munich, CH Beck, 2000) 314 *et seq*.; he only wants to see chains of contracts, not networks. But the objection could be made that the word 'net' as well as the catchword 'network' are not meant to be strictly figurative.

contracting parties on the other side are not legally connected among themselves. They may have met and may even know each other (like the employees in the same firm or several franchisees in the same city) or even co-operate in some way, but it is also possible that there is no connection at all.

I.2. The Structure of Interests

In reference to this outward appearance of contractual relationships, these networks are looked upon as a new category between market and hierarchy, between contract and corporation.[5] We observe a collision of selfish and common interests, similar to the structure of interests in companies and partnerships. But the difference is that the importance of the common interests is inversely proportionate to that which exists in companies. Within networks, the common interests are only secondary; the individual orientation prevails.[6]

As a consequence, the structure of the interests within these networks is characterised by a strained relationship of autonomy and rivalry[7] on the one hand, and mutual integration into the network and a collective orientation on the other.[8] As a certain degree of co-operation and co-ordination seems to be necessary to fulfill the purpose ('*Zweck*') of the network, we may talk of a use or purpose of a network.[9] This purpose may be the production of any type of goods or merchandise, the realisation of a major building or construction project, or the successful marketing of a product.

Looking at contracts in general, there is always the interest of both parties to realise the exchange of goods and services as agreed, and without interference. But, in addition to this general purpose of contracts, the single contract within a network also indirectly serves to achieve the network purpose. However, this network purpose does not show the quality of a corporate purpose as we know it from company or partnership law — eg § 705 *BGB* (German Civil Code) — where the agreement on a certain object of the company is a constitutional element of the company agreement. As for networks, we talk of a category in between. And this category will be described best by the expression 'network purpose' ('*Netzzweck*').

[5] See M Rohe, *Netzverträge* (Tübingen, Mohr & Siebeck, 1998) 491.

[6] G Teubner, 'Profit sharing als Verbundpflicht?' (2003) *Zeitschrift für das gesamte Handels- und Wirtschaftsrecht* 86.

[7] In my opinion, to talk of contradictory expectations of behaviour is going too far; but, see G Teubner, *Netzwerk als Vertragsverbund* (Baden-Baden, Nomos, 2004) 80.

[8] Teubner, 'Profit sharing als Verbundpflicht?' (n 6 above) 86.

[9] *Ibid*, 85 with further references.

I.3. The Legal Problem

But do the network phenomenon, the affirmation of the network purpose and the specific structure of interests within networks really necessitate new legal constructions? This may be the case, if, from these network contracts, new legal problems, which cannot be resolved adequately by the means of present law, really accrue. Some colleagues share this opinion and call for the recognition of new legal principles; for instance, Möschel[10] and Rohe,[11] who plead for the so-called '*Netzvertrag*', which will arise irrespective of any declarations of intent. However, for reasons of strong dogmatic objections,[12] this idea could not prevail. Even Rohe himself has had to admit that many of the desired results can already be achieved only by the interpretation of the contracts.

In fact, the question is one of whether there are problems that cannot yet be regulated by individual contracts. Within the network, much can be achieved through the standardisation of contracts, either in the form of general terms and conditions, or by referring to other contracts. In cases of the violation of special legal interests, tort law, under §§ 823 *et seq BGB*, provides for sufficient protection. In extreme cases, § 826 *BGB* covers pure economic loss.

Thus, it is questionable whether a real demand for further legal instruments, such as the extension of contractual protection vis-à-vis third parties or the creation of new non-contractual or quasi-contractual claims, actually exists. Does a representative number of cases involving measurable damages and parties willing to go to the court really exist so as to justify the development of new legal principles?

From my point of view, the current legal concepts represent instruments which are basically flexible enough to provide appropriate solutions for network-specific problems. But this does not mean that law should ignore the network phenomenon. On the contrary. It is our task to clarify the characteristics of networks in order to take them carefully into consideration when it comes to the interpretation of contracts, to the determination of contractual duties, and/or the control of general terms and conditions. As a result, in the following section, I am going to analyse the implications of the integration of the single contract into the network and its consequences for the structure of contractual duties.

[10] W Möschel, 'Dogmatische Strukturen des bargeldlosen Zahlungsverkehrs' (1986) 186 *Archiv für civilistische Praxis* 211.

[11] Rohe, *Netzverträge* (n 5 above).

[12] U Hüffer, 'Die Haftung gegenüber dem ersten Auftraggeber im mehrgliedrigen Zahlungsverkehr' (1987) 151 *Zeitschrift für das gesamte Handels- und Wirtschaftsrecht* 106 *et seq*; H Heinrichs in Palandt, *Bürgerliches Gesetzbuch*, 64th edn (Munich, CH Beck, 2003) before § 305 fn 16; K Schmidt, *Handelsrecht*, 5th edn (Cologne, Heymanns, 1999) § 35 III.

II. NETWORK INTEGRATION AND INTERPRETATION OF DUTIES

The starting point of my consideration is, therefore, the single contract, especially as it is the individual orientation that prevails in most contract networks. The individual will is primarily focused upon the conclusion of a contract and not on following the purpose of the network.

However, the mere examination of the individual contract is not sufficient. In fact, it should be indisputable that the integration of the contract into the whole system has to be considered, too.[13] Though many economical contracts are somehow interlinked, the relationship in the networks is different. It seems to be characteristic for networks that their boundaries are definite or can, at least, be defined by all the network participants. For instance, the number and the headquarters of the companies of a franchise system or a just-in-time delivery system can easily be determined. Furthermore, all the participants are — on a higher level — united by the pursued network purpose, the so-called '*Netzzweck*'. This purpose covers, more or less explicitly, the contents of every contract within the net. As a consequence, the network regularly appears as a unity towards other market participants. To sum up, we can speak of systematic, long-term co-operation, based on mutual trust and confidence.[14]

For the interpretation of the contract and its liabilities, it is substantial that each contract also includes the superior net context, which has to be defined and evaluated individually.[15] Often, the rights, duties and objectives which refer to the network purpose are already determined in the text of the contracts. But, even then, concerning the controlling of general terms and conditions ('*AGB-Kontrolle*'), there is the problem of finding out the limits of these rights and duties, and of developing appropriate valuation standards. If special agreements are missing, the question is, what type of rights and duties can generally be derived from the network integration of the single contract? Thus, the next step will be the determination of the contents and scope of protective duties and accessory obligations.

[13] K Lange, *Das Recht der Netzwerke* (Heidelberg, CF Müller 1998) fn 465; Möschel, 'Dogmatische Strukturen des bargeldlosen Zahlungsverkehrs' (n 10 above) 235.

[14] Teubner, *Netzwerk als Vertragsverbund* (n 7 above) 42.

[15] M Stoffels, *Gesetzlich nicht geregelte Schuldverträge* (Munich, CH Beck, 2001) 262.

III. DUTIES OF PROTECTION AMONG NETWORK PARTICIPANTS

III.1. Duties of Co-operation

III.1.(a) Duties of Co-operation in General

Networks are characterised by the fact that a great number of parties or companies co-operate in an organised and systematic way. Every member of the network knows that a certain degree of co-operation is necessary to keep the system running.[16] Individual profit may be very important, but the overlapping interest of all companies is, nevertheless, geared towards successful co-operation in order to create a competitive product, a great building project, etc, because the existence of the individual companies depends on the common success.

From this necessity of co-operation, we can easily infer what the duties of co-operation are. They can refer to the forwarding of information received, or to the documentation of any process. Then, network participants may be obliged to consider the consequences of their actions for the whole network and to take into account the interaction of all the contractual relationships. But such a duty of co-operation is already derived from the individual contract and its objectives. In point of fact, immediate contact and a direct exchange of goods or services only take place between the contracting parties. An active duty of specific co-operation between non-contracting parties will not be found in any network, neither in franchise arrangements nor in 'just-in-time' supply systems. And, moreover, I think there is no necessity for it. If the parties want another arrangement in the particular case, they will come to individual agreements, for example, about research projects or promotion campaigns.

So my conclusion is that the duties to co-operate only take effect within the individual contractual relationship. They do not go beyond these relationships. The network purpose may charactarise the nature and the scope of these duties to a certain degree, but, for the individual company, there is no immediate obligation towards third parties.

III.1.(b) Duties of Loyalty

An interesting question is whether giving notice at an inopportune time is an offence against the duty of co-operation or loyality. In the German Civil Code, we have the general rule of law that a termination or notice at

[16] H Wiedemann and O Schultz, 'Grenzen der Bindung bei langfristigen Kooperationen' (1991) 12 *Zeitschrift für Wirtschaftsrecht (ZIP)* at 1 and 3, where they speak of a '*Kooperationsgemeinschaft*'.

an inopportune time is effective but is, nonetheless, illegal.[17] As a result, it may result in a liability for damage.

As for networks — building projects or just-in-time-delivery — one could imagine the situation in which a participant has the right of termination and complies with the termination period, but that the time chosen is incompatible with the interests of the third parties. In this case, the termination may, for instance, lead to a delay and cause substantial damage to other companies in the network. Under these circumstances, we may not have a breach of contract, but relating to the other members within the network, we can possibly speak of a violation of a network-specific fiduciary duty, a '*Verbundtreupflicht*'.[18] A franchising case adjudged by the Federal Court of Justice (*Bundesgerichtshof* (*BGH*)),[19] gives us another example. A franchisee, who was obliged to maintain a transport and distribution system for frozen foods, had terminated his contract without prior notice, and, in this way, had brought the system to a standstill. As a consequence, there was the danger that the food would not be forwarded to the next agent in time and would probably go bad. In this case, the '*Verbundtreupflicht*' may temporarily exclude the franchisee's right of termination. Thus, the franchisee may be obliged to wait for the right moment, as far as this can be expected from him or her. I will come back to this point later.

III.1.(c) Duty to Support the System

As for franchising, we also talk about a '*Systemförderungspflicht*', an obligation of all the participants to follow uniform and parallel behaviour as far as the design of the shops, goods and packaging, the methods of production or promotion, etc, are concerned. This is because the standardisation of quality and the homogeneous appearance of the products are highly important to keep the system running. Thus, the customers' trust in the product will increase and all participants in the system will take advantage of it. But the condition is that everybody meets the requirements and adheres strictly to the standards of quality.

A famous case in point, adjudged by the Federal Court of Justice (*BGH*),[20] related to the termination of a McDonald's franchise, whose operator did not observe the exact temperature for grilling hamburgers.

[17] See §§ 627(2), 671(2), 675 and 723(2) *BGB* (German Civil Code), 'Kündigung zur Unzeit'; C-W Canaris, 'Kreditkündigung und Kreditverweigerung gegenüber sanierungsbedürftigen Bankkunden' (1979) 143 *Zeitschrift für das gesamte Handels- und Wirtschaftsrecht* 113 at 114; KJ Hopt and PO Mülbert, *Kreditrecht, Bankkredit und Darlehen im deutschen Recht* (Berlin, de Gruyter, 1998) § 609, fns 23 and 32.

[18] Teubner, 'Profit sharing als Verbundpflicht?' (n 6 above) 90.

[19] See BGH (1999) 52 *Neue Juristische Wochenschrift (NJW)* 1177.

[20] See BGH (1985) 38 *NJW* 1894 and 1895.

In this case, the violation of duty may seem rather insignificant; and thus the termination of the franchisee's contract may seem quite unreasonable at first sight. However, if you take into consideration the above-mentioned aspects which call for a general duty to support the system, the termination has to be looked upon as an appropriate measure because it is necessary to protect the image of the brand and is, therefore, also necessary as a preventive measure.

But notwithstanding this, we cannot discover an immediate effect of contractual duties vis-à-vis third parties. Yet, the McDonald's case shows quite clearly that a regulation, which seems to be inadequate within the individual contract to justify termination, could be subject to different criteria of assessment due to the integration of the contract into the network. As a result, intensified duties are created for individual members within the network.

III.2. Duties of Information

Furthermore, the phenomenon of network contracts may lead to specific duties regarding information or warning.[21] On the one hand, this refers to preliminary duties and the duties to furnish details when entering into the system. Here, the new potential franchisee may be under the obligation to disclose his or her lack of know-how or his or her inability to perform within the network as agreed. On the other hand, there will be duties of information for all the system partners concerning their own acts or failures to act. Regarding contracts on the performance of a continuing obligation (*Dauerschuldverhältnisse*), it is already a consequence of the general fiduciary duty that the other party has to be informed about all the relevant facts in time.[22] Such facts may include imminent interference with performance, delay of performance, or modification of the materials used. Besides this, the head office of a franchise or just-in-time system is obliged to inform all participants about all relevant changes within the network, such as a new sales organisation, a new distribution chain, other systems of supply, etc.

However, it has to be noted that all these duties of information are only directed towards the individual contracting party. There is no need for

[21] Teubner, *Netzwerk als Vertragsverbund* (n 7 above) 159.

[22] D Medicus, *Schuldrecht I*, 16th edn (Munich, CH Beck, 2005) fn 14; L Weyers, 'Typendifferenzierung im Werkvertragsrecht' (1982) 182 *Archiv für civilistische Praxis* 67; P Ulmer, 'Kündigungsschranken im Handels- und Gesellschaftsrecht — Zum Einfluss der Treupflicht auf die einseitige Vertragsbeendigung' in *Festschrift für Philipp Möhring* (Munich, CH Beck, 1975) 295 and 296; A Saxinger, *Zulieferverträge im deutschen Recht* (Baden-Baden, Nomos, 1993) 147; H Oetker, *Das Dauerschuldverhältnis und seine Beendigung* (Tübingen, Mohr & Siebeck, 1994) 27.

duties of information towards third parties, because normally you can expect that the other party to the contract will pass on the information to his or her further contracting parties if this seems to be necessary for them. Thus, it can be assumed that the flow of information within chains of contracts is working.

In the case of connected contracts, all interference with performance can cause a sort of chain reaction; for instance, because the delay with a just-in-time delivery will continue and progress onto the next level of customers. Thus, the damage may increase exponentially. In this case, the duty to inform the other party will become very urgent. Nevertheless, it does not seem to be a network-specific problem. Wherever contracts are connected in chains, there will be the danger of multiplied damage. Furthermore, parties normally make provisions for cases of emergency. And, the greater the risk of damage may seem, the more the parties are expected to carry out their duties of information or warning. The same goes for the case in which the damage only occurs at another level. This is because, even in this case, the possibility of a recourse claim can never be excluded. The other party to the contract may have to pay damages to his or her contracting parties or be confronted with other disadvantages. But this gives us no reason to assume that non-contractual duties of information directly towards third parties actually exist.

III.3. Duties of Non-Disclosure

Teubner put forward the opinion that duties of non-disclosure towards third parties turn out to be specific duties of connected contracts.[23] He gives the example of a manufacturer passing on know-how or models of his or her supplier to another supplier.[24] However, in most cases, duties of non-disclosure will be expressly stipulated in the contract. Otherwise, duties of non-disclosure would regularly result from the interpretation of the contract. Consequently, there is no need for further explication backed up by the network concept.

[23] Teubner, *Netzwerk als Vertragsverbund* (n 7 above) 161; Teubner, 'Profit sharing als Verbundpflicht?' (n 6 above) 88.

[24] Teubner, *Netzwerk als Vertragsverbund* (n 7 above) 161.

III.4. Duties of Equal Treatment

Another issue concerns duties of equal treatment (*'Gleichbehandlungspflicht'*).[25] In point of fact, a franchising firm striving for rationalisation and simplification is supposed to be highly interested in the equal treatment of all participants. At the same time, equal treatment contributes to the unification of standards of performance and also to enduring peace within the network. This is why all the participants usually receive the same terms and conditions of contract.

But does this also mean that there is a duty of equal treatment within contract networks? There are lots of reasons against this hypothesis; for example, the freedom of contract and the principle of free competition. This is also why duties of equal treatment are an exception to the rule in private law. But in German labour law, the principle of equal treatment is acknowledged to be a legal rule according to the fundamental constitutional right of equal treatment, Article 3(1) *GG* (*Grundgesetz*, Constitution of the Federal Republic of Germany). However, in contractual networks, we are not dealing with legally-dependent persons nor with constitutional standards. The participants of networks are legally independent, autonomous companies.

Nevertheless, as far as networks are concerned, the opinion is held that intensified duties of equal treatment can exist.[26] Thus, the principle of equal treatment is looked upon as a counterweight to the directive authority of the head office or centre of the network.[27] Indeed, a duty of equal treatment may arise from the general fiduciary duty (*'Treupflicht'*).[28] The justification for the assumption of fiduciary duties — for employment relations as well as for just-in-time contracts — lies in the fact that one party is deeply integrated into the organisational structure of the other party, and is thus subject to the influence and domination of that party. In correspondence to these possibilities of influence over the legal interests of the other party, the fiduciary duty serves as a compensating and restricting element.[29]

Fiduciary duties require that the dependence and inferiority of the other party, both of which are consequences of integration, be taken into account. And fiduciary duties set limits to the arbitrary exercise of rights.

[25] G Hueck, *Der Grundsatz der gleichmäßigen Behandlung im Privatrecht* (Munich, CH Beck, 1958).

[26] Teubner, 'Profit sharing als Verbundpflicht?' (n 6 above) 89.

[27] Teubner, *Netzwerk als Vertragsverbund* (n 7 above) 162.

[28] Lange, *Das Recht der Netzwerke* (n 13 above) fn 715 for franchising; Teubner, 'Profit sharing als Verbundpflicht?' (n 6 above) 89.

[29] M Wellenhofer-Klein, *Zulieferverträge im Privat- und Wirtschaftsrecht* (Munich, CH Beck, 1999) 424 *et seq*.

Consequently, fiduciary duties are an expression of an intensified commitment in long-term contracts, which are significantly characterised by co-operative and integrative elements as well as by exclusiveness and dependence. Thus, the responsibility connected with this specific legal power is achieved in the fiduciary duty. The dogmatic roots can be found in § 242 *BGB* (German Civil Code), in the principle of good faith.[30]

If the fiduciary duty thus sets limits to the arbitrary exercise of rights, it also prohibits the head office from arbitrary unequal treatment. And fiduciary duties demand that damage to the other party be avoided and that its interests be taken into account. This is why it would be contradictory to this duty if another participant should be treated in a better way for no reason; because this would indirectly put the other parties at a disadvantage. As a consequence, the fiduciary duty can also result in a duty of equal treatment. This means, for instance, that the same starting conditions have to be granted to all franchisees as well as the same conditions of termination. Or, in cases of bottle-necks, there should be the duty to supply all parties proportionally.[31]

However, duties of equal treatment only exist in contractual relationships and not towards third parties. These duties may require a number of parallel contracts or contractual relationships in a star-like form, but only have effect on the respective contractual parties and do not create rights or duties vis-à-vis third parties.

III.5. Profit-sharing

Regarding the *Apollo franchising* case, adjudged by the Federal Court of Justice (*BGH*),[32] Teubner wrote an interesting paper about the so-called '*Vorteilsweiterleitungspflicht*'. In the *Apollo franchising* case, the head office had got suppliers to agree to quantity discounts, but had not passed on this advantage to the franchisees. According to the Federal Court of Justice (*BGH*), a duty to pass on these advantages resulted from the contracts and its terms. Thus, it was a question of interpretation of the contracts. Not surprisingly, this opinion made Apollo immediately changed the terms and conditions of the franchise contracts. Teubner, on the other hand, wants to derive this duty of profit sharing directly from the network concept.[33] Following this idea, we would not need any concrete contractual agreement on this issue. A duty to pass on the

[30] See, generally, with further references *ibid*, 424 *et seq*; as for fiduciary duties, see also Krebs, *Sonderverbindung und außerdeliktische Schutzpflichten* (n 4 above) 440 *et seq*, who uses this expression in a broader sense.

[31] Teubner, 'Profit sharing als Verbundpflicht?' (n 6 above) 89.

[32] See BGH (2003) 24 *Zeitschrift für Wirtschaftsrecht (ZIP)* 2030.

[33] Teubner, 'Profit sharing als Verbundpflicht?' (n 6 above) 80.

advantages received would just result from the network context. Indeed, it is true that a quantity discount can only be achieved by a bigger group of customers. So, one could speak of a network advantage because the advantage gained may be assigned to the whole group of companies. And thus every single company should participate. This is why Teubner takes the view that the principle of equal treatment and aspects of fairness call for profit sharing among the network participants.[34]

However, the comparison with labour law demonstrates that an employee has no chance of asking for profit sharing unless it has been agreed upon beforehand. So the question is one of whether the loose connection of contracts between the purpose of the network and the fact that all individual companies bear a part of the network risk can, in itself, justify the claim for profit sharing. Or is it exclusively the franchisor, as founder and organiser of the whole system, who deserves the extra profit? From my point of view, a duty of profit sharing may result from the individual contract in a particular case; but the assumption of a general duty of profit sharing in networks seems to overstep the limits of the interpretation of contracts and still needs justification.

III.6. Conclusion

It has been be demonstrated that the integration of the individual contract into the network does influence the contents and scope of the contractual duties. As a result, we may infer duties of equal treatment, in particular. Thus, the interests of third parties also influence the contents of contractual duties. However, as far as I can see, it is not possible to set up a fixed catalogue of fiduciary duties within networks. The existing variety of network concepts — such as just-in-time contracts on the one hand, and franchising contracts on the other — makes it quite difficult to define general network duties. However, one may be able to talk about '*situativ konkretisierte Verbundtreupflichten*', as Teubner does.[35] Notwithstanding this, these duties still continue to be contractual duties as defined by § 241 II *BGB*. Thus, in conclusion, as far as I can see, there is no need for a new innovative approach.

[34] Teubner, *Netzwerk als Vertragsverbund* (n 7 above) 169.
[35] Teubner, 'Profit sharing als Verbundpflicht?' (n 6 above) 86.

IV. THE LEGAL RELATIONSHIP OF NETWORK PARTICIPANTS UNCONNECTED BY A BILATERAL CONTRACT

IV.1. Case 'Constellations'

But there may be particular arrangements of relationships which raise the question of whether there are direct duties of protection towards third parties and whether these third parties may have a right of action to claim for damages in cases of violation. This problem refers to the internal relationships within the network as well as to the external relationship with other persons and companies outside the network. However, here, I wish to concentrate on the internal relationship alone.

With regard to franchise arrangements, we can imagine the situation in which a franchisee does not keep to the given standards, in order to gain a competitive advantage and to save costs at the expense of the other participants. Behaviour of this kind may cause damage to the whole franchise system because the quality and the image of the product will be affected. If the head office does not take action against the free-rider in time — for example, because of shortage of staff, sluggishness, or out of respect for the strong market position of this franchisee — then the question arises of whether the other franchisees who have suffered a decrease of sales can make claims for damages against this free-rider. In addition, I also wish to recall the above-mentioned case of termination at an inopportune time in this context. In this case, we also have to discuss the issue of a right for a '*Binnendurchgriff*'. Thus, we have to seek a basis and a legal foundation for an extra-contractual liability within the network.

IV.2. Contractual and Quasi-contractual Claims against Third Parties

From my point of view, the so-called contract with protective effects vis-à-vis third parties[36] ('*Vertrag mit Schutzwirkung zu Gunsten Dritter*') is not much help to our problem. This legal rule creates duties also vis-à-vis the employees or the family of the other party if these persons come into contact with the contractual performance, too. This rule does not apply with the multilaterality of network systems, because the perspective is always confined to bilateral relationships. Claims between participants who are not indirectly connected by a chain of contracts cannot be justified. Similar problems arise with regard to the concept of *Riesenhuber*,

[36] BGH (1985) 96 *Entscheidungen des Bundesgerichtshofs in Zivilsachen (BGHZ)* 9 and 17 concerning money transfer.

which wants to assume a special legal relationship between working colleagues, or between different tenants of the same apartment building, on the basis of a so-called *'Anschlussschuldverhältnis'* (connecting contractual obligation).[37]

Concerning the relationship between network members who are not directly connected by contracts, it might be a better idea to assume an obligation as defined by § 311 II No 3 *BGB*. According to this rule, a legal obligation with duties of protection can be created just by entering into business contact, namely by *'ähnliche geschäftliche Kontakte'*. We neither need a contract, contract negotiations, nor the intention to conclude a contract.[38] The only requirement is just a similar sort of contact based on mutual confidence and trust. For instance, contact on the occasion of a complimentary favour (*'Gefälligkeit'*) would be sufficient to establish collateral duties as defined by § 241 II *BGB*. The element of *'geschäftlich'* in § 311 II *BGB*, which refers to business or legal matters in contrast to mere social contact, does not seem to create any difficulties.

But the requirement of 'contact' may cause problems. Literally, contact means physical proximity and a meeting of parties. But this description does not fit when damage is caused only by a chain reaction or merely affects third parties as a reflex. Furthermore, the formulation *'geschäftlicher Kontakt'*, or business contact, stands for an intentional contact. Thus, it would seem to be quite doubtful as to whether the loose connection within the network, ie among several franchisees, can meet the requirements of § 311 II No 3 *BGB*. I, personally, do not think that it can. Contact is more than being a member of a network. But contact — as defined by § 311 II No 3 *BGB* — could possibly be assumed as far as major building projects are concerned. Building constructors working on the same building site will be obliged to co-ordinate their performance in many respects. As a consequence, they will inevitably come to more or less informal agreements on schedules, materials and other matters. Under these circumstances, it may be possible, in the particular case, to speak of a legal obligation with duties of protection as defined by § 311 II No 3 *BGB*. But this legal rule cannot be a general solution for our network problems.

[37] K Riesenhuber, *Die Rechtsbeziehungen zwischen Nebenparteien* (Berlin, Duncker & Humblot, 1997).

[38] Heinrichs in Palandt, *Bürgerliches Gesetzbuch* (n 12 above) § 311 fn 18.

IV.3. Application of § 826 *BGB*

IV.3.(a) Introduction

Eventually, we have to realise that contract law does not provide appropriate solutions for the problem of the '*Binnendurchgriff*'. But, possibly, we can resolve a part of our problems, as exemplified in the above-mentioned cases, by the application of § 826 *BGB*. This rule provides for liability in tort in cases of the intentional causation of damage involving violation of *bonos mores*. Liability is already triggered by pure economic loss. So, the above-mentioned circumstances, such as giving notice at an inappropriate time, as well as on-going violations against the directives and standards of a franchise system, are basically able to comply with the definitional elements of § 826 *BGB*.

IV.3.(b) Violation of Bonos Mores

The second requirement of § 826 *BGB* is that the damage has to be caused by an act *contra bonos mores*. Violations of *bonos mores* are generally defined as violations against the feeling of common decency, in German: '*das Anstandsgefühl aller billig und gerecht Denkenden*'.[39] Thus, the acknowledged commercial customs of trade and the *bonos mores* of the respective industrial sector are decisive.[40]

Consequently, with regard to contractual networks, we have to ask for the business practices and expectations of behaviour within the respective network of contracts to be taken into account. These practices will depend on the nature of the individual network and on the concrete industrial sector. However, based on all the previous analyses and investigations about networks, it should be possible to derive a basic standard of expectations and necessities concerning the behaviour of the participants, which would be generally indispensable for the efficiency of networks and which would therefore be an expression of the conventions and customs within the network.

With regard to this issue, it seems to be characteristic within networks that all participants inevitably expose themselves to the influence of the other participants when joining the network. Everybody knows that the network offers many opportunities for irresponsible and unfair behaviour. Notwithstanding this, the specific risks of the network are deliberately accepted. Furthermore, some firms, having made large-scale

[39] BGH (1953) 10 *BGHZ* 228 and 232, and *ibid*, (1977) 69 *BGHZ* 297; BGH (2004) 57 *NJW* 2668 and 2670.

[40] BGH (1953) 10 *BGHZ* 228 and 232; Heinrichs, in Palandt, *Bürgerliches Gesetzbuch* (n 12 above) § 138, fn 2.

investments, existentially depend on the success of the network. But even these companies accept the risks involved, because there is a general expectation of fairness on all sides. All participants implicitly expect that everybody will adhere to the rules of the network. Nobody is expected to strive for undue advantages at the expense of the other participants or at the expense of the network as a whole.

Here, we can draw a comparison with a sporting competition. Irrespective of playing in the same team or in competing teams, and irrespective of any individual interests pursued, all players rely on the rules of the game being observed by everybody. All players are expected to respect the basic rules of the game. Otherwise, nobody would be prepared to join in or to risk his legitimate interests, such as physical health, because there is no contractual relationship and there are no guarantees. Slight irregularities may be accepted as part of the game, but, in cases of obvious and severe violations of duties — so-called 'fouls' — we expect reasonable sanctions to be applied.

With regard to networks, we can draw the conclusion that damages cannot be sought simply because of the dangers being more or less common and immanent in the network. But things become very different if a member of the network accepts a substantial risk which endangers the whole system and the network purpose itself. In this case, it would be legitimate to talk about an act *contra bonos mores*. Thus, a fundamental violation of the rules of the game, represented here by the rules of the network, might be considered as a violation of *bonos mores* as defined by § 826 *BGB*.

IV.3.(c) Subjective Elements

The third and last requirement of § 826 *BGB* concerns the violator's intent. The concrete damage done has to be covered by the offender's intent. He must know about the occurrence of the damage, the causality of his or her act, and about all the facts which justify the assumption of a violation of *bonos mores*. A specific intent to cause damage is not required, *dolus eventualis* (conditional intent) will do.[41] The name of the injured person may not be known. All in all, the subjective elements of § 826 *BGB* do not cause any problems. In the above-mentioned cases, these elements of the offence will usually be fulfilled.

IV.3.(d) Results for the Application of § 826 BGB

Consequently, § 826 *BGB* may offer a possibility of justifying claims for damages within the net, respectively for the '*Binnendurchgriff*'. But we

[41] BGH (2000) 53 *NJW* 2896, and BGH (2004) 57 *NJW* 446.

have to be careful. § 826 *BGB* is not meant to be an all-purpose weapon or instrument. It is an exceptional provision to the principle of § 823 *BGB* in which only specific legal interests are protected by tort law. § 826 *BGB* breaks this rule for the rare case of damage caused by intentional violation of *bonos mores*. Under these restrictive conditions alone, damages for pure economic loss can be claimed, since any other provision would lead to an unbearable and incalculable restriction on freedom of action and freedom of decision. Thus, the restrictive wording of § 826 *BGB* fulfills the function of the necessary selection of cases.

Therefore, the application of § 826 *BGB* must not undermine a contractual spreading of risk. Furthermore, it has to be avoided that any kind of loss caused by fair acts of competition will be subsumed under § 826 *BGB*, because such damage is a normal and accepted consequence of competition. And § 826 *BGB* is also not meant to grant compensation in cases of diffuse damage occurring in a hardly measurable form to a vast number of persons.[42] And last, but not least, an uncertain and indefinite extension of liability to persons injured only in an indirect way has to be prevented.

However, these limits do not seem to be exceeded in cases of liability towards other participants in the network. The circle of the persons who possibly suffer damage and will possibly claim for damages is established right from the beginning. An excessive extension of liability can be avoided by taking into account very obvious and severe violations of duty alone, in other words, violations which have been directed against the network purpose itself and which have caused substantial damage. And on top of this, we must not forget that it is the injured person who bears the burden of proof and has to set forth all relevant facts.[43] Consequently, arbitrary claims by persons who have been damaged merely in an indirect or slight way are not to be expected.

Thus, the application of § 826 *BGB* has the advantage that it avoids any extension of contractual protection vis-à-vis third parties as well as the creation of new non-contractual claims, as both ideas are dogmatically dubious. Furthermore, a look at the rulings of the Federal Court of Justice (*BGH*) shows us that § 826 *BGB* has especially been applied in cases characterised by relationships of three or more persons. The Federal Court of Justice (*BGH*) has based the liability of auditors and tax consultants towards third persons on § 826 *BGB* for a long time.[44] The same applies to cases concerning the liability of experts.[45] Only now is

[42] G Wagner, in P Ulmer (ed), *Münchener Kommentar zum BGB*, 4th edn (Munich, CH Beck, 2004) § 826, fn 16.

[43] BGH (2004) 57 *NJW* 2664 and 2665.

[44] BGH (1973) 26 *NJW* 321, and BGH (1987) 40 *NJW* 1758 and BGH (1992) 55 *NJW* 2080.

[45] BGH (1999) 52 *BGHZ* 138, 257 and 260.

the jurisdiction also going to work with the contract granting protective effects to third parties. And last, but not least, in company law, measures performed by partners or shareholders which act at the expense of the company may be subsumed under § 826 *BGB*,[46] with the exception of the possibility of assuming that a violation of corporate fiduciary duties has occurred in these cases. The case that a disloyal partner concludes a contract in his or her own name, instead of signing in the company's name, may serve as an example. Consequently, it seems to me that § 826 *BGB* is the most appropriate provision to come to terms with cases which concern gross damage to third parties who are outside contractual relationships.

V. CONCLUSIONS

The fact that the integration of a contract into a whole system of connected contracts has effects on the determination of its contents and on the interpretation of the mutual rights and duties of the persons to whom it applies is no longer called into question, but is, instead, taken for granted. It seems to be evident that the contractual duties of protection are also specifically influenced by the common network purpose. As a consequence, the parties to a contract also have to take the potential effects of their behaviour on third parties within the network into account. Nevertheless, these effects remain restricted to the bipolar contractual relationship and do not create direct rights or duties for third parties in connection with the individual contract.

However, behaviour in breach of duty or in breach of contract, which causes damage to other network participants, may fulfill the requirements of § 826 *BGB* in a particular case, thus leading to a liability for damages to third parties. Clearly, we have to realise that § 826 is only meant to regulate the serious cases, but the restrictive wording of § 826 *BGB* ensures the necessary selection of cases. All the relevant facts and the gravity of the violation of duties have to be clear. These obvious cases will, at the same time, represent the cases in which it seems to be appropriate to solve the respective problems by legal means.[47] What still needs to be done is the further concretisation and definition of what was referred to above as '*Verkehrssitten im Netz*', that is to say, the minimum standard of expectations and necessities of behaviour of all network participants regarding the common network purpose. Considering the variety of contractual networks, this task can only be carried out by

[46] BGH (1992) 55 *NJW* 2821.

[47] See also Collins, 'The Weakest Link' (n 1 above), who refers to the question of whether non-legal sanctions are sufficient to solve network problems.

reference to certain groups of cases. But the case that a network participant is intentionally going to accept damage to other participants by termination without prior notice or at an inappropriate time, as well as the free-rider-cases, can basically be subsumed under § 826 *BGB*.

8

Internal Relations and Semi-spontaneous Order: The Case of Franchising and Construction Contracts

CORDULA HELDT*

FRANCHISING AND CONSTRUCTION co-operation? At first sight it seems that we are comparing an apple and a pear. Both types of contract network[1] indicate a structure of semi-spontaneous orders, which is legally reproduced as a multilateral special relationship (*'Sonderverbindung'*). They are two sorts of networks upon which the obligation structure of the special relationship reacts differently.

This study focuses on the internal relationships within the network. These are the legal relationships of the participants in a construction co-operation (networks of construction contracts) or in a franchise system, which are contractually unconnected, ie, the contractor/franchisee. The network qualities of franchising have been the subject of many innovative studies,[2] which is not true for construction contracts. In the 1990s, there was an impulse of work. It concerned the integrative structure, or intertwinement, of contacts in the construction co-operation. There was no link to the discussions concerning network combinations in other fields. In construction co-operations, the figure of the complex

* Researcher in law, Johann Wolfgang Goethe University, Frankfurt.

[1] In contractual networks, the bilateral contracts relate to each other in a certain way and create multilateral network effects; see G Teubner, *Netzwerk als Vertragsverbund* (Baden-Baden, Nomos, 2004); KW Lange, *Das Recht der Netzwerke* (Heidelberg, Verlag Recht & Wirtschaft, 1998) fn 10

[2] Dealing with Franchising are Teubner, *Netzwerk als Vertragsverbund* (n 1 above); A Schimansky, *Der Franchisevertrag nach deutschem und niederländischem Recht* (Tübingen, Mohr & Siebeck, 2003); M Rohe, *Netzverträge* (Tübingen, Mohr & Siebeck, 1998); R Kulms, *Schuldrechtliche Organisationsverträge in der Unternehmenskooperation* (Baden-Baden, Nomos, 2000).

long-term contract, which remained heuristic, developed.[3] Only few scholars have noted the similarity of the construction co-operation to that of the association.[4] The study of the internal relationships in networks is neglected in all fields, though. Many of the authors who generally approve of the legal relevance of contract networks deny legally relevant relations between contractually unconnected participants in a network with few categorical phrases.[5] Whoever takes the network idea seriously is bound to deal with the exact internal relationship in detail.

I. THE DISTINCTIVE STRUCTURE OF CONSTRUCTION CONTRACTS

The image of modern construction contracts is a heavy division of labour and specialisation. It is embossed by a complex technical and economic structure combined with deliveries and results, which normally can only be generated within a long period.[6] Unlike the unique exchange relationship that typically exists between two partners, many actors participate regularly in the planning and accomplishment of construction contracts, such as architects, specialists, consulting engineers, structural engineers and building contractors. The desired economic success cannot be obtained through the end of a mere contract.[7] The contract has a framework character, which needs constant adaptation in the accomplishment phase. Complex plants cannot be planned in detail beforehand.

The customer (*'Auftraggeber'*) can put the construction project out to tender as a whole and award it to a bidder. Or he can split it into several projects, by dividing the bids and awarding them to different bidders. The bidders can be sole traders, partnerships (*'Arbeitsgemeinschaften, Arge'*), or consortiums. They, in turn, can also award the project to a

[3] H Schlotke, 'Vertikale Verknüpfungen von Unternehmern verschiedener Produktionsstufen durch Qualitätssicherungssysteme und Just-In-Time-Lieferungen—komplexe Langzeitverträge besonderer Art?' in F Nicklisch (ed), *Verträge über Computertechnik in Forschung, Verwaltung, Wirtschaft und Technik* (Heidelberg, CF Müller, 1990)267 at 273.

[4] P Gauch 'Ein Bauwerk- mehrere Unternehmer' (1982) 118 *Zeitschrift des Berner Juristenvereins* 65 and 68; Schlotke, 'Vertikale Verknüpfungen von Unternehmern verschiedener Produktionsstufen durch Qualitätssicherungsysteme und Just-In-Time-Lieferungen' (n 3 above).

[5] Rohe, *Netzverträge* (n 2 above) 430 *et seq*; Kulms, *Schuldrechtliche Organisationsverträge in der Unternehmenskooperation* (n 2 above) 233, Schimansky, *Der Franchisevertrag nach deutschem und niederländischem Recht* (n 2 above) 117 *et seq*; see, also, KW Lange, *Virtuelle Unternehmen* (Heidelberg, Verlag Recht & Wirtschaft, 2001) 333.

[6] Schlotke, 'Vertikale Verknüpfungen von Unternehmern verschiedener Produktionsstufen durch Qualitätssicherungssysteme und Just-In-Time-Lieferungen' (n 3 above) 384.

[7] K Larenz and M Wolf, *Allgemeiner Teil des Bürgerlichen Rechts* (Munich, CH Beck, 1997) § 23 no 127; K Nicklisch and G Weick, *VOB Teil B* (Munich, CH Beck, 2001) Einleitung no 4.

sub-contractor (*'Subunternehmer'*). Thus, we have an image of a grid-shaped network or, more rarely, a star. If the contractor divides the work into bids and awards them by individual contracts, he is practically the sole party with whom all the participants have a contractual relationship. Then, he globally bears the responsibility for the association of all the partial performances of the individual participants (*'Schnittstellenrisiko'*, interface risk), and he alone bears the organisation and co-ordination charges.[8] According to the jurisdiction, sole contractors are liable independently of each other, for their individual task alone.[9] When the construction project is put out to tender as a whole, the customer discharges himself of the difficult co-ordination tasks which are brought about by the divided bids. With big projects, the *Arge* frequently acts as a general contractor (*'Generalunternehmer'*). As long as the customer faces more than one contractor, who assumes the risk warranty for the success of the 'turnkey' project, he still remains responsible for the interface risk.[10] The contractor's strong position inevitably results from the co-ordination charge. But construction co-operation does not have any strict hierarchic structure in which decisions always run from top to bottom. Due to the complexity of the project and the framework character of the contract, the decisions made during the realisation of the project must consecutively be made by either the customer or the contractor, or by both of them. Another necessity for collective decisions results when the plan and reality diverge. It may be that the project can only be finished when problems present are resolved during its realisation, ie, when the necessary alterations or realignments of the interlocking execution periods are made.[11]

The participants must co-operate, and must work together to achieve the objective. All the project participants are not just factually, but also legally associated in a network of intensive co-operation and communication.[12] The openness of these contracts for concretisation and alterations, combined with their long-term duration makes them very unstable. Not only the parties to the contract but also the participants of the project may be concerned by this instability, which creates the need to

[8] B Hautkappe, *Unternehmenseinsatzformen im Industrieanlagenbau* (Heidelberg, Verlag Recht & Wirtschaft, 1985) 27.

[9] A Barner, *Die Arbeitsgemeinschaft in der Bauwirtschaft als besonderer gesellschaftsrechtlicher Typus* (Munich, Schön, 1971) 16.

[10] W Koeble and M Schwärzel-Peters, 'Gesellschaftsvertragliche Ausgestaltung einer Arbeitsgemeinschaft am Beispiel der Bau-Arbeitsgemeinschaft' (1996) 34 *Deutsches Steuerrecht* 1734.

[11] Nicklisch and Weick, *VOB Teil B* (n 7 above) Einleitung no 4.

[12] H Schlotke, 'Mitwirkungspflichten bei Langzeitverträgen' in F Nicklisch (ed), *Der komplexe Langzeitvertrag* (Heidelberg, Müller, 1987) 377 at 379; V Zerr, 'Gesamtschuldverhältnisse im Bauwesen' (2002) 3 *Neue Zeitschrift für Baurecht und Vergaberecht* 241 at 241.

revise their contractual relationships.[13] The personal and trust-based network develops 'in the course of a necessary adaptive execution and therefore in its inner configuration an open network'.[14]

The conception of the complex long-term contract describes the complexity of construction contracts, and confronts the model of contracts for work and labour, which the *Bürgerliches Gesetzbuch* (*BGB*) forms, with the reality of modern construction co-operation. The law model is applicable to the making of a tailor-made suit as well as to industrial plants.[15] One of the results that the complex long-term contract brings to light is the concern as to why acceptance inspections and supplement payments require prescriptions other than those foreseen in the *BGB*. However, neither overall contract networks cohesion, nor the bilateralism of contracts is abandoned in any way.

II. THE DISTINCTIVE STRUCTURE OF FRANCHISING

Franchising is a 'vertical co-operative organised sales system of legally independent enterprises, on the basis of a continuing obligation'.[16] The aim of the system is to increase market efficiency through cost-cutting via standardisation of the production of goods, marketing or service delivery.[17] The franchisor concludes structurally similar bilateral contracts with the franchisees. The contracts oblige the franchisees to maintain the standards which provide a basis for the system to appear uniformly on the market. To secure the adherence of the system standards, the contracts contain an instruction and control system. The franchisor is the only person who contracts with all of them. Usually, no dependency develops between global, regional and local units, or internal performance allocations among the system participants.[18] The resulting network image takes the form of a star. In subordination franchising, it is a tough hierarchical structure, in which the control competence is assigned to the franchisor. He or she is the central point from which decisions proceed in a straight-line outwards.

[13] Nicklisch and Weick, *VOB Teil B* (n 7 above) Einleitung no 4.

[14] Schlotke, 'Vertikale Verknüpfungen von Unternehmern verschiedener Produktionsstufen durch Qualitätssicherungssysteme und Just-In-Time-Lieferungen (n 3 above) 381.

[15] *Motive zu dem Entwurfe eines bürgerlichen Gesetzbuches für das Deutsche Reich II* (Berlin, Guttentag, 1888) 470; HL Weyers, '"Werkvertrag" in Bundesminister der Justiz' ????(ed), *Gutachten und Vorschläge zur Überarbeitung des Schuldrechts Bd II* (Cologne, Bundesanzeiger Verlag, 1981) 1115 at 1122.

[16] This is a part of the definition created by the Deutscher Franchiseverband eV.

[17] Rohe, *Netzverträge* (n 2 above) 413 *et seq*.

[18] Rohe, *Netzverträge* (n 2 above) 357; Schimansky, *Der Franchisevertrag nach deutschem und niederländischem Recht* (n 2 above)108; R Struthof, *Führung und Organisation von Unternehmensnetzwerken* (Göttingen, Vandenhoeck & Ruprecht, 1999) 103 *et seq*, for heterarchic networks.

The goodwill of the network is dependant on the individual service provided by the participants. The system is vulnerable to disadvantages, which are caused by under-usage of the standard. The synergetic interdependencies can affect the sale figures of each franchisee both positively and negatively.[19]

III. COMPARISON BETWEEN CONSTRUCTION CONTRACTS AND FRANCHISING

What both network types have in common is that they have an overall project. In construction co-operation, it is the establishment of a building or plant by the division of labour, while in franchising, it is merchandising or sales promotion. In both networks, the overall context is either not mentioned contractually at all, or it is not given legal effect by contract. Both networks distinguish themselves through several factors. However, the difference does not lie in the fact that franchising is more of a strategic alliance, or that construction contracts are dominated by inherent necessities. Both constructors and franchisors can use other organisational forms. The contractor could join forces with the bidders in a consortium, of which the common goal is the creation of a common project, just as the franchisor could do with the franchisees. In construction contracts, the choice of the contract organisation is also a strategic decision. A difference between the two is brought about by the time factor. Construction contracts do not generally aim at continuance, but are defined by the project to be delivered. The network is terminated upon the completion of the project, the accomplishment possibly lasting several years. In the franchise system, there are no termination terms defined. Hierarchy represents another difference. Franchising is strongly built upon hierarchic rules with uniform obligation standards. The franchisor bears the responsibility for the network's unobstructed functioning. Indeed, the contractor is also responsible for the co-ordination interface, but as seen above, the decisions must be taken together.

One of the network types is limited in time, specific with regard to the results to be attained and can be defined as a heterarchical network. The other one is unspecific with regard to the result and duration, and is a hierarchic network. Differences can be observed in the multilateral special relationship's legal consequences.[20]

[19] Rohe, *Netzverträge* (n 2 above) 356; Schimansky, *Der Franchisevertrag nach deutschem und niederländischem Recht* (n 2 above) 108.

[20] See below 5. A.

IV. NETWORKS AS SEMI-SPONTANEOUS ORDERS

Schlotke[21] belongs to those who recognise, in a complex long-term contract, an overall cohesion between bilateral contracts, without using the grounds of legal transaction doctrine. In his opinion, it has to be essentially and clearly observed,

> how the participant's significant and possibly not intended association law related effects mutually intensify. 'Connections similar to those of company law are also effected if someone entering the system of complex long-term contracts once says "A" and so consequently is forced to say "B".' 'The point is to draw the attention to developments in the reality of law, that are not results of intentional use of power of single entrepreneurs in the first place, but rather results of self-adjustment (eigengesetzlich), often of side-effects out of non-legal inherent necessities, where the reality of law anticipates the legal pervasion.'[22]

Schlokte does not apply the concept, but describes nothing more than the circumstances of a spontaneous order's formation.

IV.1. Hayek's Spontaneous Order

The spontaneous order's terminology goes back to FA von Hayek, who describes the order as a state of affairs,

> in which a multiplicity of elements of various kinds are so related to each other that we may learn from our acquaintance with some spatial or temporal part of the whole to form correct expectations concerning the rest, or at least expectations which have a good chance of proving correct.[23]

Hayek differentiates between planned/made orders and grown/spontaneous orders. A planned order (*taxis*) distinguishes itself by the fact that someone proposes it and pursues the purpose. It is also described by Hayek as an organisation. In contrast, a spontaneous order (*kosmos*) is an order which exists without anyone being aware of having drafted it. The order has no purpose. The objectives that it serves are the particular objectives of every participant, in all their multifariousness and contrariness. It is an achievement of human action, but not of human design.[24] On the one hand, the underlying vision is of an order which is

[21] Schlotke, 'Vertikale Verknüpfungen von Unternehmern verschiedener Produktionsstufen durch Qualitätssicherungssysteme und Just-In-Time-Lieferungen (n 3 above) 268.

[22] *Ibid*, 268 and 274.

[23] FA von Hayek, *Law Legislation and Liberty, Volume 1 Rules and Order* (Chicago, University of Chicago Press, 1973) 36.

[24] *Ibid*, 37, refers to A Ferguson, who has written: 'nations stumble upon establishments, which are indeed the result of human action, but not the execution of any human design',

not only created by strength outside a system (exogenously), but also from strength inside (endogenously), which is self-engendering or spontaneous.[25] On the other hand, due to the epistemological assumption of the narrowness of human knowledge, individuals are required to submit to abstract rules.[26] Hayek assumes that the pursuit of different, de-centralised and independent objectives by individuals can establish an order when the individuals follow regularly given spontaneous rules in their reactions to their direct environment. These rules of conduct are evolutionary developed conventions, customs and practices, but are also legal rules. An individual obeys rules even though they do not have a forcible or constraining character, because they need them to reduce the complexity of their environment.[27] Since human beings are incapable of co-ordinating their actions successfully via a complete and explicit estimation of the whole range of alternative decisions and the knowledge of all circumstances and their corresponding consequences, they require—for each and every decision—a limit to their range of choices by means of abstract rules. For Hayek, it is the only instrument by which mankind can give a certain coherence to its actions. In doing so, it is exclusively the evolutionary rules that prevail over other behavioural patterns, which enable and secure a socially-differentiated life, the spontaneous order. This order must be beneficial to society so that the rules will, in general, be followed without constraint.[28]

Hayek differentiates further rules into abstract and concrete rules. The actor's action in spontaneous orders is based on abstract rules (*nomos*), which are applicable for an unknown number of future circumstances and persons. In (man-)made orders, according to Hayek, the action basically depends on concrete rules, commands (*thesis*), which are only adaptable for certain persons or merely serve the purposes of the organiser.[29]

An Essay on the History of Civil Society (Edinburgh, Edinburgh University Press, 1767) Part III, ch 2; also http://www.ecn.bris.ac.uk/het/ferguson/civil.htm.

[25] von Hayek, *Law Legislation and Liberty, Volume 1* (n 23 above) 37.

[26] FA von Hayek, *Studies in Philosophy, Politics and Economics* (London, Routledge & Kegan Paul, 1967) 23 and 39.

[27] von Hayek, *Law Legislation and Liberty, Volume 1* (n 23 above) 38.

[28] *Ibid*, 45; RD Cooter has proved this by a game: 'Decentralized Law for a Complex Economy' (1994) 23 *Southwestern University Law Review* 443 at 445.

[29] von Hayek, *Law Legislation and Liberty, Volume 1* (n 23 above) 38.

IV.2. Competition as a Discovery Procedure

Spontaneous orders have an important function in Hayek's theory: they can discover de-centralised, scattered and contextual individual knowledge.[30] For Hayek, this knowledge has an enormous economical and evolutionary significance for society. The process of competition can help the members of society to pursue their goals more successfully than they could with only their individual knowledge. Society needs the accumulation, co-ordination and realisation of knowledge as well as the generation of new knowledge. Hayek's opinion is that, in society, the realisation of knowledge can be achieved at its best through the price system.[31] It indicates hidden information by the alteration of scarcity, in the form of rising or declining prices, and always directs the self-interest guided activities to where rising prices signal scarcity. The legislator must not interfere, according to Hayek, in the 'natural market order' by direct commands, because it can affect its co-ordination efficiency.[32]

According to Hayek, this is the disadvantage of organisations which are co-ordinated by commands. Commands are concrete rules which are created by someone with only limited knowledge and serve purely his intentions. Relevant circumstances and information that are known only to individuals, but which could be of great interest for the organisation, cannot be discovered. Individuals in organisations can only make use of this knowledge when they are free to make their decisions, which is the case when abstract rules affect their actions. Organisations must therefore rely on rules in certain measures and cannot be conducted by commands alone.[33]

IV.3. Semi-spontaneous Orders

The presented networks are semi-spontaneous orders. The network participant's operations depend on the respective bilateral exchange agreements on the one hand, and depend on rules, which were not agreed by contract and established by a single actor, on the other. These are rules which are applied by the participant within the frame of his particular individual knowledge and objective. They originate from

[30] FA von Hayek, *Law Legislation and Liberty, Volume 3: The Political Order of a Free People* (Chicago, University of Chicago Press, 1973) 67; FA von Hayek, *Individualsim and Economic Order* (Chicago, University of Chicago Press, 1948) 53 and 95.

[31] FA von Hayek, 'Intertemporal Price Equilibrium and Movements in the Value of Money' in R McCloughry (ed), *Money, Capital, And Fluctuations: Early Essays* (Chicago, University of Chicago Press, 1984).

[32] von Hayek, *Law Legislation and Liberty, Volume 1* (n 23 above) 51; FA von Hayek, *Law Legislation and Liberty, Volume 3* (n 30 above) 110.

[33] von Hayek, *Law Legislation and Liberty, Volume 1* (n 23 above) 48, see also 50.

collective aims that the participant does not necessarily know about in all their aspects. The accomplishment will be partly contractually and partly spontaneously generated. The common project is the superior objective of all bilateral contracts. It brings order to the network.

> Neither the market nor competition has a role to play. Instead, networking and co-operation are the purveyors of spontaneous order.[34]

Since this order is not characterised by the complete absence of purpose, it represents a semi-spontaneous order.

In contractual networks, as in organisations, the operations of the participants depend on (man-)made, as well as spontaneous, orders. On the one hand, a contractual network resembles a complex organisation in which the customers or the franchisor acts as the organiser. It is this organiser who initiates the creation of the contract network. Unlike his contractual partners, he is basically the draftsman of the franchise system or the construction project. On the other hand, the contract is the instrument for the configuration of an organisation in private law, and this instrument is not used by the partners to establish an associational connection between the individual contracts. The agreement of the parties in the network remains strictly bilateral. The term 'made', in reference to networks, means only a multiplicity of bilateral organisations, which does not cross the barrier of a collective organisation. However, the participants of the network do not act as independent actors who, in their aims and plans, are completely different, in the spontaneous market process. Schlotke has accurately described how corporate, personal and trust-based co-operation beyond bipolar instruction emerges. The participants in major projects increasingly disregard formally-required notices, such as notices of defects, and begin to work more and more intimately and informally together. They increasingly see their contract as a share of problem-solving and not as a part of contractual accomplishment, and thus negate the primal juridical aspect of the relationship and of the contract's execution.[35] The obtained results, co-operation, communication, mutual observations, anticipated adaptation, trust, reciprocity, lasting relationship cohesion, self-responsibility, negotiation and reliability are the characteristics of the spontaneous order.[36] However, they are not the characteristics of a spontaneous

[34] Teubner, *Netzwerk als Vertragsverbund* (n 1 above) ch III 3.

[35] AR Börner 'Netzwerke komplexer Langzeitverträge: Möglichkeiten des multilateralen Interessenausgleichs' in F Nicklisch (ed), *Netzwerke komplexer Langzeitverträge* (Munich, CH Beck, 2000) 53 at 56; see also the study of S Macaulay, 'Non-Contractual Relations in Business: a Preliminary Study' (1963) 28 *American Sociological Review* 55–67 and http://www.law.wisc.edu/facstaff/macaulay/papers/non-contractual.pdf.

[36] Teubner, *Netzwerk als Vertragsverbund* (n 1 above) ch III 3.

competition process. Networks stand in a tension, but also in a continuum, between market and organisation. Thus, one of the characteristics of networks is the development of a superior collective purpose, a project, to which the actions of the participants and their expectations concerning the behaviour of others are directed, without being decided in detail by anybody. Accomplishing their contractual responsibility, the participants consider the project, but it does not fully superimpose the individual plans and objectives of everyone.[37] It is about a collective uniform purpose. The contract network illustrates a framework that leaves space for rules, instead of orders. It is, above all, essential in the 'knitting' of the network, in the area between the contractually unconnected participants.

IV.4. Hayek's Mixed Orders

Can this construction of a common project that puts an overall order over the network of bilateral contracts be a spontaneous order in Hayek's sense? How do the rules have to appear so that a spontaneous order can emerge? How must the spontaneous order appear? Hayek not only offers spontaneous and made orders, but also discusses mixed forms. According to Hayek, collaboration always depends on intended organisation as well as on spontaneous orders.[38]

> That even an order which rests on made rules may be spontaneous in character is shown by the fact that its particular manifestation will always depend on many circumstances which the designer of these rules did not and could not know. The particular content of the order will depend on the concrete circumstances known only to the individuals who obey the rules and apply them to facts known only to them. It will be through the knowledge of these individuals both of the rules and of the particular facts that both will determine the resulting order.[39]

Networks are a combination of both orders, that Hayek has not expressed, though. Hayek has made some remarks concerning spontaneous orders within organisation structures. These are co-operation groups which spontaneously form within the organisation. According to Hayek, in organisations, actions not only depend on commands, but also on rules. And these rules must be differentiated from the rules upon which spontaneous orders depend:

[37] Teubner, *Netzwerk als Vertragsverbund* (n 1 above) ch III 3, has figured out that it is the character of networks that individual and common purposes are pursuited simultaneously by the individuals.

[38] FA von Hayek, *Law Legislation and Liberty, Volume 1* (n 23 above) 46.

[39] *Ibid*, 46.

> Rules for an organisations presuppose the assignment of particular tasks, targets or functions to individual people by commands; and most of the rules of an organisation will apply only to the person charged with particular responsibilities. The rules in organisations will therefore never be universal in intent or end-independent, but always subsidiary to the commands by which roles are assigned and tasks or aims prescribed. They do not serve the spontaneous formation of an abstract order in which each individual must find his place and is able to build up a protected domain. The purpose and general outline of the organisation or arrangement must be determined by the organiser.[40]

First of all, it is important to stress that the network does not exceed the barrier of the organisation. The project brings order to a multiplicity of independent organisations (bilateral contracts). However, the rules which establish the overall cohesion regarding the whole project *are* comparable to the rules in an organisation. They orientate towards the project. They are not completely free of purpose, but unlike organisations, in which the objective is planned and must be accomplished by commands, the common project is developed by spontaneity and brings order to the network. This is not directly about the purpose of the customer or of the franchisor. At best, the objective is to be attributed to the bilateral contracts and here the parties are equal. 'It would be ridiculous to say that I am obeying another's will in fulfilling a contract'.[41] Thus, the project is a purpose in the sense of the 'function' of the network.[42]

Hayek's theory is to be seen against the background of his themes: he dedicates his theory to the fight against planned economy, Marxism and the protection of the 'natural market order'.[43] It concerns the allocation of resources, their stimulation, the problems of their control and allocation, and corporate welfare. The themes here are spontaneous rules and widespread information, which are relevant for the network! Thus, no abstract markets are examined, but de-limited networks, which are not organisations.

Hayek's attitude is ambivalent vis-à-vis unions and organisations.[44] They exclude competition by regulating their internal relationships and by threatening the competition efficiency of cartels. In his view, organisations have an aftertaste of the persecution of the individual and his or her particular objectives. Organisations and local customs are treated in his

40 FA von Hayek, *New Studies in Philosophy, Politics, Economics and the History of Ideas* (London, Routledge & Kegan Paul, 1978) 78.

41 FA von Hayek, *The Constitution of Liberty* (London, Routledge & Kegan Paul, 1960) 153.

42 See von Hayek, *Law Legislation and Liberty, Volume 1* (n 23 above) 39.

43 See, in general, FA von Hayek, *The Road to Serfdom* (Chicago, University of Chicago Press, 1944).

44 RW Gordon, 'Hayek and Cooter on Custom and Reason' (1994) 23 *Southwestern University Law Review* 453 at 457.

writings sometimes as good and other times as reactionary. Communities, such as markets that are embedded into face-to-face relationships, local customs, etc, are disregarded by Hayek.[45] They only receive his attention when they master the way into the abstract law by absorption through common law, and thus prevail in an evolutionary way. The meaning of spontaneous orders in small communities is emphasised by Gordon and Cooter. They respect the local narrowness and the particularity of local customs.[46] Cooter extracts the consequences that the set law must not reach within these relations, but is supposed to be reserved for cases of disagreement with strangers who are not part of the community.[47] However, he does not provide any instruction as to where the acquirement of relevant community and membership can be found.[48] Thus, this concept does not present the absence of a particular interest or purpose as a characteristic for spontaneous orders.[49] Compared to these spontaneous orders, networks go one step further. They do not include potential participants according to their profession or status, but according to their integration in a project. The common project defines and encapsulates the relevant 'community'. To accentuate this difference, the notion of semi-spontaneous order will be applied.

IV.5. Co-operation in Networks as a Discovery Procedure

In networks, not only does competition allow the discovery of knowledge, which has importance for the network participants, it also allows for co-operation. What Hayek did not observe was that inside the co-operation community, modified conditions must be applied for the discovery of knowledge. In networks, contractors and franchisors face the same problem as the draftsman of an organisation. For the network efficiency, they rely upon the network participants to pass knowledge which they possess and the contractors/franchisors do not. In addition, the other independent contractors need this knowledge, which can be pertinent to their work. It is about the knowledge that each participant possesses, but not the community of network participants altogether.

Knowledge cannot only be discovered by the market or by competition, because, in a network, both are not present in an absolute way. The

[45] Gordon has figured this out. His examples are medieval guilds, *ibid*, 458.

[46] Cooter, 'Decentralized Law for a Complex Economy' (n 28 above) 445.

[47] *Ibid*, 449.

[48] Gordon, 'Hayek and Cooter on Custom and Reason' (n 44 above) 457, emphasises this.

[49] So does the concept of JH Kaiser. Kaiser regards the Cyberspace as a spontaneous order: 'Das Recht im Cyberspace—Eine spontane Ordnung noch ohne Hierarchie' in *Festschrift, Günther Winkler* (Vienna, Springer, 1997) 397 at 402.

spontaneous co-operation within the network is useful not only for the discovery of this network knowledge, but also for the correction of information asymmetries. To illustrate this, here is an example in construction co-operation. Each party in a construction contract has the possibility of conducting operations which are not observed by the other parties (hidden action) or of handling basic information that is not known to other contract partners (hidden information).[50] For the better-informed party, an impulse of moral hazard may emerge. He would be tempted to neglect certain efficient operations if he had to support their marginal costs, whereas marginal revenues are divided between both parties. If the customer is not able to distinguish project delays that have been caused by the contractor from delays which have other origins, there is no incentive for the contractor to take all economically-justified measures to accelerate the project. If the delay in construction time does not result in any damage to the customer, for example, because the successive contractors make up for the delay, the customer will not make every endeavour to find out about the origin of the delay. Co-operation with the successive contractor, whose task will be attached to the work of the previous contractor, will quickly clarify the cause of the delay, through local communication or because the successive contractor might suffer damage. In contractual networks, in which there are dogmatic 'blind spots' related to contractually unconnected participants, co-operation will help to discover the relevant, or pertinent information. The network also gives an incentive to correct action concerning the contract that is directed towards the common project.

V. MULTILATERAL SPECIAL RELATIONSHIPS

The semi-spontaneous order is a legal, non-contractual, multilateral special relationship.[51] The necessity to stabilise the initiated expectations is the legitimating special relationship.

The reflections concerning the spontaneous order can be transferred to a bilateral relationship in order to explain why the semi-spontaneous order causes legal consequences even beyond contractual agreements. It is not to be dismissed that each exchange agreement that pursues a transaction purpose results in a bilateral order. By bilateral contracts, the

[50] T Eger 'Möglichkeiten und Grenzen der sozialen Kooperation durch langfristige Verträge' in C Ott (ed), *Effziente Verhaltenssteureung und Kooperation im Zivilrecht* (Tübingen, Mohr & Siebeck, 1997) 184 at 188.

[51] This is what Teubner, *Netzwerk als Vertragsverbund* (n 1 above) does for Franchising and Just-In-Time, and H Eidenmüller, in *Unternehmenssanierung zwischen Markt und Gesetz* (Cologne, Otto Schmidt, 1999) 608, pre-supposes for the people re-organising an ailing company.

range of alternative actions is limited, and complexity is reduced. The contract triggers expectations with each contractual partner independently of the concretely concerted terms of contract. These expectations are oriented towards the transaction purpose of the contract. However, this is not the reason why the contract is a special relationship. § 242 *BGB*, on good faith (*'Treu und Glauben'*), is the general clause in contract law by which expectations towards the other party are provided with rights-generating effects, just as the network motivates the expectations of the participants with regard to the behaviour of other participants. These expectations are justified as long as they are orientated towards the project. Spontaneous orders can appear in contract law as common usages (*'Verkehrssitten'*). The *BGB* refers to common usages on three occasions: in § 151 *BGB*, § 157 and § 242 *BGB*. Under § 242 *BGB*, the activity must be operated according to the principle of good faith. In refering to common usage there is an acknowledgment of non-governmental-controlled legal relations between individuals. However, § 242 *BGB* would not be the right choice for networks, just as the contract with protection effects for third parties (*'Drittschutzvertrag'*) could not reproduce the associative cohesion of the semi-spontaneous order.

One can argue that such unwritten rules and spontaneous orders are found everywhere. Not every ordinary rule compliance can lead to a multilateral special relationship. However, common usages, which can be seen as spontaneous orders, do not establish a special relationship between traders. In order to turn a spontaneous order into a multilateral special relationship, an ordering common project is required. This characteristic consists of a combination of contractual agreements and a spontaneous associative order, the common project, which not only limits the range of multiple alternative actions, but also limits the order's scope.

V.1. Legal Consequences of Special Relationships Concerning Contractually Unconnected Participants

Multilateral special relationships generate obligations that are obtained from the project. They can be designated as network obligations. It can concern co-operation, trust and protection obligations. Only network obligations have an overall reference, and it is only in respect of them that the contractually unconnected participants have to answer directly to each other. The exchange obligations (*'Austauschpflichten'*) of bilateral contracts must therefore be differentiated.[52] Here are a few examples:

[52] See, also, Teubner, *Netzwerk als Vertragsverbund* (n 1 above) ch V; Rohe, *Netzverträge* (n 2 above) 437; Kulms, *Schuldrechtliche Organisationsverträge in der Unternehmenskooperation* (n 2 above) 188 disagrees.

In the case of a delay in a construction project, it might occur that one contractor performs with a delay and the following contractor also begins his work late as a result. The preceding contractors's default alone is no infringement of a network obligation. It is a risk that could also have materialised during the realisation of an isolated task.[53] The network obligation concerns the other participants being informed immediately of the delay.

Defects are to be treated in the same manner. Faultless work is owed only to the other contract party. The network aspect is the combination of several tasks within the contract. A network obligation is breached when, in accomplishing his part of the building, the contractor disregards the common project; for example, if the preceding contractor does not take the succeeding task into account, by building an inadequate floor pavement for the chosen tiling. The individual tasks of the floor-layer and the tiler are both in line with the contract, but, taken together, they are out of line with the contract. The network obligation requires an exchange of information directly between both of them. In the multilateral special relationship, the one who infringes this obligation is liable not only to his contracting party but also directly to the other contractor(s). The constraint of this liability lies in the fact that the succeeding contractor has to check the preceding work according to his or her expert knowledge.

In franchise law, the problem of free-riding is covered by the multilateral special relationship. Free-riders reduce their costs and increase their profits by falling below the standards of the franchise system while the other franchisees maintain the standard.[54] They can harm the system's image, which can lead to a fall in sales. Because of the network interdependency, these standards are network obligations. Free-riders can be directly liable to the other franchisees. As the franchise system is a hierarchic network, the contractually-agreed hierarchy is to be observed. This closeness to the association weakens the spontaneity of the network. The special relationship takes this into account when it leaves the controlling competence to the franchisor. Teubner has proposed a limited direct liability taken from association law. It is the *actio pro socio*, a 'party' action,

> through which a single member enforces the claims of the entire corporation in his own name ... In doctrinal terms, the *actio pro socio* endows a cause of action upon an individual actor for the enforcement of a right possessed by the

[53] H Ganten, *Pflichtverletzung und Schadensrisiko im privaten Baurecht* (Bielefeld, Giesek-ing, 1974) 201.

[54] Schimansky, *Der Franchisevertrag nach deutschem und niederländischem Recht* (n 2 above) 118.

company. In practice, such actions arise where company law responsibility no longer functions due to massive internal conflicts.[55]

This would respect the primacy of the franchisor.

V.2. Special Relationship and Consortium

Through the network duties, the participants are more forcefully obliged to respect the common project. At the same time, liability for damages on which the individual participant had no influence is avoided. Via information and co-operation, the possible influence on the other participants grows concurrently, as does the control of risks. The result might be a complicated system of responsibilities and obligations; however, it is not unrealistic. Construction consortiums show similar structures. Like the *Arge*, the consortium takes over the accomplishment of the whole project in one bid. Internally, the bids are divided among the members via sub-contracts. The members accomplish their work independently at a fixed price. Thus, the project is not accomplished conjointly.[56] The members do not bring personnel or material into the consortium, so the consortium possesses no joint property. According to the prevailing opinion, these construction consortiums are associations under the BGB regime (*Gesellschaft bürgerlichen Rechts*).[57] The members are at one and the same time associates and sub-contractors of the consortium; they have a double status. As sub-contractors, they bear the risk warranty for fulfilling their individual task; as associates, they are bound by the common purpose, the accomplishment of the whole bid and have associative duties that are different from the exchange duties that they have as sub-contractors, ie, duties of co-operation and loyalty.[58] There is a unmistakable parallel to our multilateral special relationship.

[55] Teubner, *Netzwerk als Vertragsverbund* (n 1 above) ch 5.

[56] D Weitze, *Die Arbeitsgemeinschaft in der Bauwirtschaft* (Frankfurt aM, Peter Lang, 2003) 89.

[57] P Ulmer, in *Münchener Kommentar zum BGB* (Munich, CH Beck, 2004) § 705 no 80 *et seq*; W Hadding, in HT Soergel (ed), *Bürgerliches Gesetzbuch mit Einführungsgesetzen und Nebengesetzen* (Stuttgart, Kohlhammer, 1991) § 705 no 17.

[58] One could negate the character of a association here; see also Barner, *Die Arbeitsgemeinschaft in der Bauwirtschaft als besonderer gesellschaftsrechtlicher Typus* (n 9 above) 42. For consortiums, see HP Westermann, 'Das Emissionskonsortium als Beispiel der gesellschaftsrechtlichen Typendehnung' (1967) 22 *Die Aktiengesellschaft* 285 at 291.

9

Asset-sharing in Franchise Networks: The Obligation to pass on Network Benefits

REINHARD BÖHNER*

I. INTRODUCTION

THE LEGAL ANALYSIS of networks has not yet met with a response in the German jurisdiction. However, the Federal Court of Justice (*Bundesgerichtshof* (*BGH*)) has already had to decide, in three cases, upon a crucial issue that exists in franchise networks: the question of to whom network advantages belong in terms of purchase rebates, which are granted by suppliers to network partners for the acquisition of goods. The question is one of whether network advantages are granted to the initiator of the network for his or her organisational work or to the network partners, who fulfill the 'key account' conditions allowed to the network, ie, those who pay for the goods purchased from the listed supplier. The Federal Court of Justice (*BGH*) has resolved these questions with reference to the standard terms agreements of the parties who have priority. The Federal Court was thus able to avoid the question of whether the claims for the disclosure and the payment of purchase rebates could be justified on other legal grounds, such as agency or agency of necessity, (purchase-) commission, unjustified enrichment, or as a claim for damages for infringement against the prohibition of price-fixing or because of unjustified hindrance and the discrimination of franchisees in a dual distribution system.

The court decisions pronounced in *Sixt*, *Hertz*, and *Apollo Optik* are of particular interest, because the obligation to pass on network advantages was subject to standard contract clauses, which had to be interpreted.

* Rechtsanwalt, Commercial Law Firm, Munich.

According to Section 305c of the German Civil Code (*Bürgerliches Gesetzbuch* (*BGB*)), the principle of objective interpretation prevails.[1] Standard contract terms must be interpreted with reference to the understanding of an average client with no legal education—an interpretation which must further pay due attention to the way in which a reasonable and honourable party to the contract would understand them, and which also takes into account the interests which parties normally involved in such transactions would usually have.[2]

One may expect that, in the future, cases in which the franchisor has made no express contractual commitment to obtain and pass on network advantages (purchase rebates) will have to be decided upon. It will then be interesting to know whether the results which have arisen by the interpretation of single standard contract term based upon objective law will be applied to the interpretation of the contract as a whole. Whenever the complementary interpretation of agreements based on Sections 133 and 157 of the German Civil Code (*BGB*) is not possible, contract interpretation must be made according to the measure of good faith contained in Section 242 *BGB*, which influences the manner, the existence and the contents of an obligation independently of the intentions of the parties. Section 157 *BGB* concerns the legal intention, while Section 242 concerns the legal target.[3]

It is against this background that the potential future development of jurisdiction and jurisprudence, which is presented here with reference to the decisions of the Federal Court of Justice (*BGH*), is of particular interest for the development of network law.

II. EXTENSION OF 'KEY ACCOUNT CONDITIONS' OF A BRANCH NETWORK TO AFFILIATED FRANCHISEES—'THE *SIXT* CASE'

Purchase agreements on cars which are concluded by the industry directly with key account customers are characterised by particularly favourable purchase conditions, which are often better than the rebates of car dealers. In order to exclude possible claims for equal treatment such specific conditions are given fanciful names such as 'advertising contributions'. The car rental system 'Sixt' had already established an important network of car rental branches. Sixt wanted to expand through franchising, and made the following promise to the public:

[1] H Heinrichs in O Palandt, *Bürgerliches Gesetzbuch*, 65th edn (Munich, CH Beck, 2006) § 305c, no 15; BGH (1992) 45 *Neue Juristische Wochenschrift (NJW)* 2629.

[2] BGH (1952) 7 *Entscheidungen des Bundesgerichtshofs in Zivilsachen (BGHZ)* 368; BGH (1980) 77 *BGHZ* 118; BGH (1980) 79 *BGHZ* 119; BGH (1992) 45 *NJW* 2629; BGH (2001) 54 *NJW* 2165.

[3] BGH 16 *BGHZ* 8.

> [W]e will make key account purchase prices available to the franchisees. Our car park contains more than 20,000 cars; thus, our purchase conditions are particularly favourable.

This promise was the main reason for the entry of car rental enterprises into the Sixt branch network. In this way, a dual distribution system was established.

The franchisee received, to the same extent as Sixt, key account volume rebates when purchasing cars from car dealers. Such rebates were charged back by the car dealers to the car industry. However, this was not all. Sixt received, in addition, so-called 'advertising contributions' calculated on their own purchases of cars and on those of the franchisees. Such contributions were kept secret and were not passed on to the franchisees.

Eventually, Sixt fell under suspicion of discriminating against the franchisees. The latter started a court action for the disclosure and payment of all the purchase rebates which had not been disclosed. They based their action on the following wording in Section 3 of the Franchise Agreement:

> Section 3: Sixt shall support the franchisee in purchasing cars in a way that they are allowed to buy cars at the conditions agreed upon in the key account customer agreements, as far as the car industry shall agree to.

The franchisees had started a so-called 'graduated action'. The first step was the claim for disclosure regarding any and all payments and other advantages received by the defendant from the car manufacturers. The Court of Appeal shared the opinion of the franchisees, according to whom the wording of Section 3 of the franchise agreement obliged the defendant to pass on such payments without any reductions to the franchisees, in as far as they were paid in connection with purchases of rental cars made by the franchisees. In reasonable consideration of all the circumstances, Section 3 of the franchise agreement had to be understood in such a way that all price advantages and other benefits relating to large volumes of car purchases should be granted to the franchisees. This would include all advantages granted to the defendant Sixt, including 'advertising contributions' and other benefits in connection with the purchase of cars.[4]

The legal ruling of the court of appeal that the defendant was—according to the general principle of good faith—under an obligation to disclose to the franchisees the full extent of all benefits which the defendant had received and which had to be passed on to the franchisees, was correct according to the opinion of the Federal Court of

[4] OLG Munich (1997) 52 *Der Betriebsberater* (*BB*) 1429; R Böhner, 'Verbot von Preisempfehlungen im Sixt-Autovermietfranchisesystem nach § 38 Abs 1 No 11 GWB' (1997) 52 *BB* 1427–9.

Justice (*BGH*) . It is acknowledged in jurisdiction and jurisprudence that the debtor of an obligation can be obliged, according to the principle of good faith (Section 242 *BGB*), to disclose the necessary information which he needs to the creditor in order to enforce his right, if he cannot obtain such information otherwise, and if the disclosure of the information is possible and reasonable for the debtor.

Finally, the Federal Court of Justice (*BGH*) also had to answer the question of whether only such rebates (volume rebates) which had been granted at the moment of the purchase were to be considered as purchase advantages, or whether all other advantages which had been granted in connection with the purchase of cars by franchisees, such as advertising contributions, belonged to such benefits.[5] The answer was clear: advertising contributions were also to be considered as purchase advantages because Section 3 of the franchise agreement referred to the conditions of the key account customer agreements without limitation to volume rebates which were also the subject of such agreements. Such contributions are, in reality, not granted because of an obligation placed upon the franchisor to make provision for advertising. The franchisor conducts advertising campaigns in his own interest. The allowance of the contribution is only linked to the purchase of cars for the purpose of the car rental business.

In such cases, the evaluation by the tax authorities and the federal tax court is clear and justified: the advertising contribution is simply a price deduction, which is not granted independently from the delivery of goods by the party which grants the allowance; on the contrary, it is closely linked to the delivery.[6]

For the evaluation of standard contract terms in franchise and other network agreements, the principle of objective interpretation of standard contract terms is of major importance.[7] The interpretation of standard contract terms has to be uniform, is based upon the degree of understanding that is imputable to an average client with no legal education, further takes note of the manner in which reasonable and honourable parties to the agreement would understand them, and finally, pays due attention to the normal interests of all parties that would normally be involved in such transactions. However, the defendant had referred to the contents of the key account customer agreement, which were concluded with the car manufacturers. To this extent, the defendant had thus established a dual network which exceeded one market level: at the market level of distribution, the franchise network; and at the market level of procurement, the network with car manufacturers. According to

[5] BGH (1999) 52 *NJW* 2671 at 2675.

[6] OFD Hannover (1989) 44 *BB* 1393; BFH (1972) 27 *BB* 438.

[7] See n 2 above.

the Federal Court of Justice (*BGH*), the contents of framework agreements with the car manufacturers would only be taken into account for the interpretation of a standard contract term regulating the obligation to pass on network advantages, if such contents had been disclosed to the franchisees at the moment of the conclusion of the franchise agreement. The franchisees' understanding of the franchise agreement submitted to them could only have been influenced at this point.[8] The next question had to be answered with regard to a so-called 'manufacturers' exception clause' in the second part of the standard contract clause, under which the franchisor could only pass on purchase advantages with the prior consent of the car manufacturers. Is a car manufacturer entitled to differentiate, in such a way that he is able to grant advertising contributions in key account customer agreements only for the purchases of the franchisor for his branch network, while he can likewise refuse to grant the same network advantages for the purchases of the franchisees? The Court of Appeal considered the so-called manufacturers' exception clause to be invalid, because it did not meet the requirements of the principle of transparency (infringement of Section 9(1) of the Standard Contract Term Law, today Section 307 I *BGB*). It was not immediately transparent to the franchisee as to whether he could receive the key account advantages and which restrictions were the result of the manufacturers' exception clause. In addition, the franchisees would be unfairly discriminated against.[9] The Federal Court of Justice (*BGH*) did not follow this legal ruling of the Court of Appeal and decided this question in favour of the franchisor. The manufacturers' exception clause should be considered to be transparent information in a standard contract clause. The right of the franchisee would not depend on an arbitrary act of the franchisor, but would originate in the decision of a third party, in this case the car manufacturer. The franchisor would be subject to the manufacturer's decision. He himself would not need to make a claim for 'advertising contributions' on the purchases of the franchisees. In other words: if the franchisor himself has not received purchase advantages for his franchisees, he is not obliged to pass them on.

The Federal Court of Justice (*BGH*) rejected the counter-argument of the franchisees, according to which the manufacturers' exception clause would discriminate against them unfairly. The franchisor would neither be obliged to open up the purchase sources which he had developed himself, nor be obliged to pass on the advantages originating from such sources. This statement of the Federal Court of Justice (*BGH*) will presumably be a controversial issue with regard to the fair allocation of

[8] See n 5 above.
[9] OLG Munich (1997) 52 *BB* 1429 at 1433.

network advantages in franchising and other network agreements. The statement of the Federal Court of Justice (*BGH*) is taken as a precedent for the rejection of imposition of a general obligation upon the franchisor inherent to the agreement to negotiate advantageous purchase conditions for the franchisee.[10] The manufacturers' exception clause, which says that such purchase advantages will be passed on only with the consent of the granting manufacturer, is not regarded as a regulation which deviates from a guiding principle of a statutory provision. As the subject of a voluntary obligation on his side, the franchisor could, in principle, submit such an obligation and the amount of the allowance to the approval of his contractual partner. Such an exception clause could also be provided for in standard contract terms.

The legal basis for the claim of the franchisee for the transfer of purchase advantages in the form of advertising contributions was a standard contract term which needed to be interpreted. Thus, the Federal Court of Justice (*BGH*) had no grounds to take a position regarding the question of whether franchisors who want to avoid contractual regulations, keeping purchase advantages secret and withholding them from their franchisees, have to pass on purchase advantages by the 'nature of the franchise agreement' or by virtue of an agency agreement (Sections 675, 676 and 666 *BGB*). Some authors reject such an obligation, and refer to a statement of the Federal Court of Justice (*BGH*) taken out of context, ie

> the legal system does not know a legal obligation of the franchisor to pass on to his contractual partners all advantages resulting out of the purchase of goods from sources opened up by the franchisor.[11]

In order to understand this statement better, the importance of the word 'all' has to be emphasised. The Federal Court of Justice (*BGH*) has only recognised the power of the franchisor to shape the contractual conditions. He can—voluntarily—make a contractual commitment to the franchisees to pass on purchase advantages. However, he is entitled to limit the extent of such an obligation to pass on network advantages by a transparent regulation such as a manufacturers' exception clause.

In this context, one specific aspect has to be emphasised: the car rental franchisor 'Sixt' had not requested that his franchisees purchase cars from listed suppliers. The evaluation is entirely different if franchisors interfere with the autonomy of their franchisees by requesting the purchase of goods or services from certain listed suppliers, with the purpose of keeping secret and withholding from the franchisees specific purchase conditions which are granted by the suppliers, not only on the purchases

[10] K Metzlaff in Metzlaff (ed), *Praxishandbuch Franchising* § 8 no. 175.
[11] Metzlaff, *Praxishandbuch Franchising* (n 10 above) § 8 no. 172.

of the branch outlets of the dual system, but also on the purchases of the franchisees. In such cases, the subordination conditioned by the franchise system is extended from the franchisor to the listed suppliers. The purchase obligation of the franchisees is, for the suppliers, almost a guarantee of turnover. This is much more than just a chance of concentration of the voluntary purchases of the franchisees as a result of the advantageous price conditions of the listed suppliers.

The disadvantages which, from the angle of the franchisees, result from the loss of their entrepreneurial autonomy to choose their suppliers for themselves, call for compensation through the advantages which are generated by the bundling of the purchase power of all franchisees. These advantages in the form of price and rebate allowances are only derived from the suppliers' capital. Thus, it would not be reasonable not to transfer these advantages to the franchisee. The legal argument could only be different if the franchisor—in addition to the purchase obligation of his franchisees—made his own commitments towards the suppliers, for example, if he committed himself to making an advertisement campaign for the brand of the supplier. In this case, the payments of the suppliers could be justified as 'contributions to the advertisement costs' of the franchisor and not as elements for the calculation of the price of the cars which are purchased by the franchisees.

In the event of such a contractual agreement, the withholding of real advertising contributions would not be unreasonable.

III. INTERPRETATION OF A STANDARD CONTRACT TERM CONCERNING THE PASSING ON OF 'ADVANTAGES' IN THE DUAL DISTRIBUTION SYSTEM: '*APOLLO OPTIK*'.

Encouraged by the *Sixt* case, 17 franchisees of the franchisor 'Apollo Optik' had requested—at first, by an out-of-court action—disclosure of whether purchase advantages had been withheld from them. Following the purchase obligation, they had purchased goods from suppliers which were listed by Apollo Optik, and had obtained dealers' rebates on the list prices according to a 'official' list of rebates. The franchisees suspected that the suppliers had paid unofficial kick-backs on their purchases to their franchisor. This suspicion was quickly confirmed, when the franchisee received—by error—proof from which it became obvious that the suppliers had granted rebates of up to 52 per cent on the list price on all purchases coming from the 'Apollo Optik' network (branches and franchisees), of which only 38 per cent were passed on to the franchisees.

In addition, the franchisees raised a claim regarding forbidden economic price-fixing by the central advertising actions of the franchisor using fixed prices without indicating that these prices were not binding for franchisees. At first, the franchisees obtained a cease-and desist-order by injunction.[12] The controversy nonetheless escalated and finally the franchisees retained their obligation to make payment of franchise and advertising fees until the requested disclosure about the withheld purchase advantages. In addition, they started their claims against the franchise fees of the franchisor. The reaction of the franchisor was a mass cancellation of the franchise agreements of those franchisees who had formed a pool of interest in order to raise identical claims in a kind of class action.

The franchisees offered resistance against the cancellations and filed actions in 10 different courts. They made various claims, among which the claim for the disclosure and the restitution of the withheld purchase advantages was the most important. The judgments of the District Courts and later of six Courts of Appeal turned out to be diametrically opposed. Reference is made to the general position laid down in Haager.[13] The judgments of the Düsseldorf[14] and Bremen Courts of Appeal,[15] both of which were published, showed that the marked antagonism to judicial control of the contents of the 'Apollo Optik' franchise agreement was founded upon a completely different basic understanding of the obligations of the franchisor in a dual distribution system.

The judgments of the Courts of Appeal of Düsseldorf, Munich[16] and Koblenz[17] started from the understanding that franchising was a distribution system for goods, and was, therefore, characterised by the notion of a sales agreement.

In contrast, the judgments of the Courts of Appeal of Bremen, Frankfurt[18] and Karlsruhe[19] took as their basis the understanding that the commitment to pass on advantages was characterised as an obligation which resulted out of an agency agreement.

The Federal Court of Justice (*BGH*) rendered three judgments on 20 May 2003 in three test cases.[20] The judgments were based on the statement of the following facts. The franchisor, 'Apollo Optik' had established a chain of company-owned outlets of retail shops for optical goods—in 1999, it possessed about 150 branch outlets. In addition,

[12] OLG Munich, 'Festpreiswerbung eines Franchisegebers' (2000) 50 *Wirtschaft und Wettbewerb* DE-R 552, p 1112.

[13] B Haager, 'Die Entwicklung des Franchiserechts in den Jahren 1999, 2000 und 2001' (2002) 55 *NJW* 1463 at 1465.

[14] OLG Düsseldorf (2002) 48 *Wettbewerb in Recht und Praxis* 235.

[15] OLG Bremen (2002) 48 *Wettbewerb in Recht und Praxis* 224.

[16] OLG Munich, Judgment of 6 June 2002, Az: U (K) 2545/01.

[17] OLG Koblenz, Judgment of 13 June 2002, Az: U 422/01.

[18] OLG Frankfurt, Judgment of 23 July 2002, Az: 11 U (Kart) 55/00.

[19] OLG Karlsruhe, Judgments of 12 February 2003, Az: 6 U 129/01 and 6 U 130/01.

[20] BGH (2003) 57 *BB* 2254 and 2258, as well as *KZR* 29/02 (not yet published).

identical outlets (nearly 70) were operated by franchisees under the brand 'Apollo Optik'. The standard contract contained the following terms:

> Additional obligations of Apollo Optik.
>
> 6.1 Apollo Optik will give advice to the partner regularly in connection with questions regarding purchases, sales and promotional offers of the Apollo Optik retail shop and organisation questions. During the term of the agreement, representatives of Apollo Optik will, from time to time, visit the partner and will consult and support him in business matters.
>
> 6.2 ...
>
> 6.3 Apollo Optik shall take care of the partner with regard to the development of the business and the system-like operations and shall pass on advantages, ideas and improvements to the partner in order to obtain an optimum of business success.

Goods which were needed for the franchise outlets (especially lenses for eye-glasses) were purchased by the franchisees in their own names from listed suppliers.

For this purpose, Apollo Optik transmitted rebate schedules to its franchisees, indicating scales of rebates on the list prices for eye-glasses and optical accessories related to the volume of purchases. Such rebate schedules were based on 'framework agreements', which Apollo Optik had concluded for its own branches as well as for the outlets of its franchisees. However, the full amount of the agreed-upon rebates on each purchase of an outlet of the dual distribution network of Apollo Optik was not disclosed in the rebate schedules; the difference was kept secret. In contrast, Apollo Optik induced its suppliers to credit the so-called 'rebate differences' in the amount of the difference between the rebate granted to the network of Apollo Optik branches and its franchise outlets. The maximum rebate was 52 per cent of the list price and the lower rebates disclosed to the franchisees, according to the 'official rebate schedules' were a maximum of 38 per cent of the list price.

These 'rebate differences' were a closely-kept secret.

Because of the priority given to contractual grounds for the claim, the Federal Court of Justice (*BGH*) could leave it open as to whether the claim was justified under other legal headings, such as mandate, commission, unjustified enrichment (Section 812ss *BGB*) and damages based on infringement of the law on the limitation of competition, ie, unreasonable hindrance.

IV. CONSIDERATION OF THE INTEREST OF THE 'CIRCLES, INVOLVED IN A (FRANCHISE) NETWORK'

The Federal Court of Justice (*BGH*) was able to give priority to the wording of the clause when deciding that the network advantages had to be passed on to the franchisees. As the relevant contract clause was in use within the whole territory of the Federal Republic, its contents were subject to the control of the Federal Court of Justice (*BGH*).[21] The interpretation of general contract terms follows particular rules. General contract clauses are used in a variety of ways and therefore have to be interpreted in an objective way, in a manner in which they can and must be understood by the business circles which are normally involved in such business.[22]

When interpreting the general contract term, the Federal Court of Justice (*BGH*) did not limit its view to the bilateral contract, but also took the multilateral relations with suppliers into account. The legitimate interest of the franchisees to obtain 'purchase advantages' which were granted by the suppliers to the dual distribution system of 'Apollo Optik' as a key account customer, was taken into account, and proved to be the decisive aspect for the development of the jurisdiction on franchising. The obligations which have to be fulfilled in the triangular relationship between franchisor, franchisee and supplier are not simply reduced to the franchise contract, because the franchisor does not assume the function of delivering system goods to the franchisees. Deliveries are made directly by the listed suppliers. The franchisor does not assume the risk of the sales of the suppliers (capital risk, risk of insolvency of the franchisees); he delegates these functions and risks to the supplier. Thus, the franchise relationship and the sale and purchase relationship exist with different contractual partners.

On the other hand, the franchisor undertook measures with regard to the future sale and purchase relationship of his franchisees. Not only had he offered his know-how and his system concept, but he had also offered the franchisees access to the supply-chain system of his 150 branches, and, thus, even absent legal obligations in the franchise agreement, he had undertaken central dealings with suppliers for his own branches and for the 'third party' Apollo-outlets of his franchisees. He had concluded, by acting as a fiduciary intermediate, framework agreements on purchase conditions and rebates even in favour of his franchisees, who thereby had obtained a right of supply against the listed suppliers (Section 328 *BGB*).

[21] BGH (1986) 98 *BGHZ* 256, 258; BGH (1988) 105 *BGHZ* 24, 27.
[22] See n 2 above.

When undertaking such business for its own shops as well as for the third party franchise outlets, the bargaining power which can be exercised in dealings on prices and rebates is of decisive importance. First of all, the purchasing power resulting from the needs of 150 branch outlets is important. The shop managers have to follow the directives to purchase goods only from listed suppliers. The bargaining power of the branch network is enforced if the franchisor can bring in the third-party collective volume potential of the franchisees. Purchasing power is created automatically because of the restriction imposed on the franchisees to purchase up to 80 per cent of their needs only from listed suppliers. Such restriction of freedom to purchase systematically grants a mandate to the franchisor for central dealings with the suppliers and the right to represent the franchisees indirectly. Because of the identity restrictions (corporate identity), the collective bargaining power of the franchisees is increased with each new franchise agreement. Each franchisee takes part in the procurement system, which has been established by the franchisor, and takes advantage of the price and delivery conditions which have been granted to the branch network and to the 'collective group' of the existing franchisees.

For the supplier, it is not only a chance to obtain turnover with the franchisees through a favourable price performance relationship; he obtains a quasi-guarantee of turnover if the franchisees have to supply themselves from him (at least at a certain quota, in relation to other suppliers). This guarantee with regard to future sales permits considerable price reductions especially in the form of anticipated rebates, even for the first order of eye-glasses, and not just in the form of a bonus granted only after having attained a certain volume of purchases. With regard to the structure of the franchise system of Apollo Optik, it is not just the bilateral contract between franchisor and franchisee which has to be looked at. The relations between the franchisor and the single franchisee are determined by the network: ie the whole collectivity of the other franchisees who have to respect the same restrictions and their relations to the suppliers. The existence and the effects of their network cannot be neglected as facts for the legal evaluation. The franchise agreement has not only the function of organising the exchange of obligations between the franchisor and the franchisees within the franchise relationship, it also has an organisational object, because of the obligation of the franchisor to guarantee delivery to franchisees by listed suppliers, the obligation to pass on network advantages in order to obtain best business results (Section 6.3 of the agreement) and because of the restriction to buy only from the approved suppliers. These tasks, which are undertaken by Apollo Optik as the dominating enterprise of its network and the rights and obligations related to them, are not even expressly regulated in the franchise agreement, but are only supposed by the parties. This is to be seen in the preamble of the franchise agreement, under which the franchisee is granted access to the system of the Apollo shops developed by the franchisor. It was not expressly stipulated what action the franchisor had to undertake in relation to the approved suppliers in order to ensure unhindered supply to the franchisees and to secure the advantages that arose out of vertical co-operation. For the parties, the relationship with the franchisor's action with regard to purchases for his branch outlets and the franchise outlets was sufficient. With regard to this obligation, the franchisees relied upon the promise in the preamble:

> [O]nly close co-operation in good faith between the partners and Apollo Optik guarantees advantages for both sides and presents the basis of a successful business development.

Advantages for both sides are generated in the network: as a consequence of the network's 'corporate identity', the 150 branch outlets also benefit from the 70 franchise outlets. These franchise outlets assure a greater coverage of Apollo Optik shops and thus generally increase the reputation and the image of the network. On the other hand, the franchisees benefit from the existence of the 150 branch shops of the franchisor. However, it is legitimate that the natural economic interest of the franchisor is concentrated on his own branch shops, as the branch shops and franchise outlets are, in a certain way, competitors.

Here, a conflict of interests arises. Apollo Optik does not limit its role to that of the franchisor, but uses the franchise network for the benefit of its own branch shops (dual distribution system). This is acceptable as long as a symbiotic relationship exists between the two pillars of the dual distribution system, in which both partners—the franchisor with his branch shops, on the one hand, and the franchisees, on the other—participate in the same way. However, a disparity arises if the franchisor benefits unilaterally from the common profit obtained from the bargaining power of the dual distribution system, which is increased by the demand created by the collectivity of the franchisees and therefore—in addition to the transparent franchise and advertising fees—affects the conditions of competition detrimentally. The franchisor has bundled the bargaining power of his franchisees automatically with the restriction to buy only from approved suppliers in every franchise agreement, and, in addition, has combined it with the bargaining power of his own branch shops without passing on the full amount of the benefits which the suppliers have granted in exchange. Competition is negatively influenced in a considerable way by the fact that the maximum rebates which have been granted without discrimination by the suppliers are not given to all the clients of the dual Apollo Optik distribution system.

The franchisor receives, in the form of rebate differences, certain 'kick-backs' on the purchases of the franchisees payments (additional non-disclosed franchise fees), which result exclusively from the execution of the proper obligations of the franchisees and therefore belong to them. The franchisees' obligations consist, first of all, of their subordination to the franchisor and then of their assumption of the distribution risk in relation to the ordering, financing, and payment for the goods, and by their assumption of the risk involved in the resale of the goods. Compensation granted by the suppliers in exchange for these obligations accrues to the franchisees as advantages which are linked to their own performance. These advantages have been withheld by the franchisor from his franchisees, and he has directed the suppliers to credit him the difference between the disclosed rebates and the non-disclosed maximum rebates in the form of kick-backs. Consequently, the franchisor not only obtained a privileged position in competition because his own branch shops received the maximum rebates which were even increased by the additional bargaining power of the franchisees, he also pocketed the rebate differences which resulted from the purchases of the franchisees. Thus, the purchase conditions within the Apollo Optik system exhibited considerable differences. The franchisees' ability to compete, which already suffers from the contractual franchise and advertising fees, has been further damaged in a discriminatory way.

The differences in the conditions of competition have not been disclosed by the franchisor to his franchisees, and the promise that they would be treated equally is revealed to be false.

These network relations and the network advantages obtained through the delivery of goods by listed suppliers to franchisees are inherent in a dual-branch franchise network. Thus, they have to be taken into account when the courts interpret the contractual claims for 'advantages to obtain best business results'.[23] Teubner, in his profound critique of the judgment of the Federal Court of Justice (*BGH*), has already developed a new approach which goes far beyond the limits of the interpretation of standard contract terms. He identifies obligations from the object of the network as intensified obligations of good faith, in the form of the obligation to pass on all system rebates.

[23] G Teubner, 'Profit sharing als Verbundpflicht? Zur Weiterleitung von Netzvorteilen in Franchisesystemen' (2004) 168 *Zeitschrift für das gesamte Handels- und Wirtschaftsrecht* (ZHR) 78 at 92.

V. INTERPRETATION IN FAVOUR OF THE INTERESTS OF THE CUSTOMER OF STANDARD TERM CONTRACTS REGARDING THE PASSING ON OF ADVANTAGES

The Federal Court of Justice (*BGH*) did not accept systematic objections against its interpretation. The franchisor claimed that the passing on of purchase advantages should have been regulated under another head of the agreement, where stipulations regarding offers, supply and delivery were to be found. There, no wording could be found with regard to the passing on of these purchase advantages. This argument was rejected by the Federal Court of Justice (*BGH*), because it was in opposition to the factual behaviour of the franchisor, in that he had transmitted official lists of rebates at the moment of the conclusion of the agreement. In good faith, the franchisees might believe that these rebates represented the 'advantages' mentioned in Section 6.3; however, they could not know that the rebate differences had been withheld from them. The doubts which were raised by the franchisor were an argument against the apodictic interpretation of three Courts of Appeal, Düsseldorf, Munich and Koblenz, which had rejected claims that Section 6.3 only demanded that non-material advantages should have been passed on to the franchisees.

The doubts which had been raised led to the application of the rule on ambiguity of Section 5 of the General Contract Terms Law (old version), now Section 305c II *BGB*. The franchisor had to accept the Federal Court's interpretation of the clause. The reason given was that the interpretation by the three Courts of Appeal (Düsseldorf, Munich & Koblenz) could only lead to doubts, with regard to the Federal Court's interpretation. In such a situation of doubt, the franchisor, who was the author of the contractual clause, had to acknowledge the interpretation that was more in favour of the interests of the customer. Whoever offers General Contract Terms is responsible for a clear and unequivocal version of the stipulations formulated or used by himself.[24]

VI. LIMITATION OF THE CONTRACTUAL OBLIGATION TO PASS ON ADVANTAGES ONLY BY EXPLICIT REGULATIONS

The franchisor had presented different lines of defence:

1. A first line with the argument that Section 6.3 of the agreement did not mean financial advantages derived from his business relationship with the listed suppliers.

[24] BGH (1980) 79 *BGHZ* 117, 118 *et seq*; BGH (1987) 102 *BGHZ* 384, 389 *et seq*.

2. A second line with the argument that he had passed on at least the 'official' rebates indicated in the rebate schedule. The rebate differences were a financing instrument commonly used in the business, because the franchise fees would not cover the costs of the franchise system.

This second defence that the franchisees had been supplied with the optical goods that they ordered from the suppliers, exactly at the prices, conditions and rebates of which they had been 'officially' informed by the franchisor, is taken from an understanding influenced by a 'sale and purchase' interpretation of the relationship. The Federal Court's reaction to this strategy was to insist on the obligation to pass on all advantages based on the obligations derived from the franchise relationship.

This obligation could only have been limited by a transparent stipulation which stated that the franchisor's obligation to pass on network system rebates was limited exclusively to the 'official rebates' stated in the schedules to the contract.

VII. CLAIMS FOR DAMAGES BASED ON COLLATERAL NEGLIGENCE

If franchise relationships fail, claims for damages are often based on the legal ground of the violation of pre-contractual obligations.[25]

Under the pre-contractual disclosure rules, the franchisor has to inform the franchisee correctly and completely about the profitability of the system. The franchisor, Apollo Optik, had violated these rules in its relationship with the partners of the developing contract by withholding the information on the total amount of the system rebates agreed upon with the listed suppliers. However, it not only violated its pre-contractual duties, which were based on the principle of good faith, it also committed collateral negligence with regard to its duty to pass on all purchase advantages without limitation under Section 6.3 of the franchise agreement, by inducing the listed suppliers to pay out rebate differences to itself.

As a consequence, Apollo Optik's obligation to pay damages included the so-called 'positive interest' (expenses and loss of profit) while responsibility for loss caused by the violation of pre-contractual disclosure obligations was principally limited to the so-called 'negative interest', the

[25] OLG Munich (1988) 43 *BB* 865 with notes W Skaupy, 'Aufklärungspflichten bei Vertragsverhandlungen über Franchise-Vertrag' 865; OLG Munich (1994) 47 *NJW* 667—see also R Böhner, 'Schadensersatzpflicht des Franchisegebers aus Verschulden bei Vertragsschlusß' (1994) 47 *NJW* 635–6; OLG Munich (2001) 56 *BB* 1759, see also R Böhner, 'Bestand und Ausmaß der vorvertraglichen Aufklärungspflichten des Franchisegebers—das „Aufina"-Urteil unter der Lupe' (2001) 56 *BB* 1749–53.

right to be compensated only for the losses which would not exist if the franchisee had never concluded an agreement with the franchisor.

VIII. OBLIGATION TO PASS ON PURCHASE ADVANTAGES' BASED ON CONTRACTUAL PROMISES TO ASSIST THE FRANCHISEE OR ON AGENCY LAW?—*'HERTZ'*

In the cases *'Sixt'*[26] and *'Apollo Optik'*,[27] the Federal Court of Justice (*BGH*) could leave it open as to whether grounds other than contractual ones could justify damage claims, because of the withholding of purchase advantages. In *'Apollo Optik'*, the franchisees had invoked claims that were, in particular, based on mandate and agency law, on purchasing-commission and on unjustified enrichment.

Such legal grounds are theoretically well-founded; this can be drawn from the considerations of the Federal Court of Justice (*BGH*) in another car-rental case: *'Hertz'*. Like Sixt, Hertz International Ltd USA had established a dual car-rental network, which consisted of branch and franchise outlets, through its 100 per cent affiliate 'Hertz Deutschland GmbH' in Germany. 'Hertz Germany' had independently concluded framework agreements with various car manufacturers, under which so-called 'advertising contributions' were paid if the purchased cars were operated in the car-rental network created by Hertz. The Hertz standard franchise agreement, which is used worldwide, contains, in the English version, a commitment by the franchisor to support the franchisee, using the following language in Section 4f of the agreement:

> Hertz International agrees to assist the franchisee, in so far as is practical, in developing procedures for purchasing the various materials and equipment required in the franchise business.

The franchisees of Hertz claimed that the term 'equipment required in the franchise business' included, in particular, the vehicles needed for the car-rental business.

Hertz Germany had made the following promise in an additional standard term form which had to be signed by the Hertz-franchisees:

> [T]he undersigned ... (Hertz-licensee) is licensee of Hertz International Ltd., and participates in this capacity irrevocably at any time—in the purchase conditions for vehicles of Hertz Germany. Hertz Germany will inform the licensee at the beginning of each calendar year about the amount of special

[26] See n 5 above.
[27] See n 20 above.

conditions granted by the respective car manufacturers, especially about the amount of rebates, and/or key account—rebates, and advertising contributions.

The Hertz-franchisees started a 'gradual action', in order to disclose the 'kick-backs', against Hertz Germany as well as against Hertz International Ltd, with regard to the advertising contributions received from car manufacturers. The Court of Appeal of Stuttgart upheld the action against both defendants. The Federal Court of Justice (*BGH*)[28] confirmed the judgment against Hertz Germany, but dismissed the claim against Hertz International Ltd, with the following ruling: an agreement on the payment and collection of 'advertising contributions' had been concluded only between Hertz Germany and the franchisees. None of the parties had submitted the allegation that Hertz International had, in the past, collected advertising contributions and passed them on to the franchisees. Hertz International's obligation, under Section 4f of the franchise agreement, to assist the franchisees with regard to the purchase of material and equipment was only a general regulation, which could not justify the claims of the franchisees against Hertz International. In addition, Hertz International had not dealt with the car manufacturers on advertising contributions and had not collected them for the franchisees. No circumstances had been stated which could justify the conclusion that Hertz Germany had acted as an agent for Hertz International when it concluded agreements with respect to the payment of advertising contributions.

However, the Court of Appeal of Munich[29] did not follow this judgment of the Federal Court of Justice (*BGH*) in a similar case, and issued a judgment under which Hertz International and Hertz Germany were jointly liable to disclose and account for advertising contributions, using the following argument:

> [I]t would not be decisive for the judgment, whether franchisees are entitled to obtain disclosure on advertising contributions, based on the ground of the law of mandate.
>
> The obligation of the defendant Hertz International to disclose, would result with rare clarity from declarations under which Hertz Germany had undertaken expressly to inform the franchisee about advertising contributions. As Hertz International had used Hertz Germany for the fulfilment of its obligations as franchisor, it was also liable for disclosure and for accounting on advertising contributions.

[28] BGH (2002) NJW Rechtsprechungsreport RR 1554 and 1556.
[29] OLG Munich, judgment of 12 of December 2002, U (K) 3925/02

The *Hertz* cases show that it is particularly useful to examine the legal ground of claims for networking advantages on the basis of the law of mandate (Sections 675, 666 and 667 *BGB*). The law of mandate is permissive. In cases of mandate, the ranking of the rules applicable is as follows:

- Contractual agreements of the parties, as far as they are permitted by law, have priority;
- Specific stipulations in laws other than the Civil Code, especially those of the commercial code, shall apply secondarily;
- Most rules of the law of mandate have priority on agreements for work and service;
- In consideration of a specific agency agreement, the law of contracts on work and service shall apply if no specific rules exist.[30]

As the Federal Court of Justice (*BGH*) could not identify a contractual commitment of Hertz International within Section 4f of the franchise agreement, it became necessary to examine the claim of the franchisees with an eye to the legal obligation of the franchisor to restitute everything which he had obtained (Section 675, 667 *BGB*).

However, such a legal claim was rejected because Hertz International did not carry out the business itself, ie, it had not negotiated framework agreements itself with car producers and had not received 'advertising contributions' on account of the Franchisees. Therefore, the liability of Hertz International under Sections 675 and 667 *BGB* for the employment of Hertz Germany to execute its Franchisors obligations was rejected by the Federal Court of Justice (*BGH*).

IX. THE OBLIGATION TO PASS ON PURCHASE ADVANTAGES BY THE 'NATURE OF THE FRANCHISE AGREEMENT', EVEN WITHOUT A SPECIFIC CONTRACTUAL STIPULATION

Critics of the judgments in 'Sixt' and 'Apollo Optik' commit a basic error: they depart from the presumption that a commitment on the part of a franchisor who has established a dual distribution network to pass on network advantages would only be legally binding if it had been regulated in a specific stipulation.[31]

Such thinking is backward-minded and is influenced by the so-called 'legal terms jurisprudence'. However, legal obligations are not limited to dispositions of a statute. Legal provisions which can create the obligation

[30] H/Sprau 2005 in O Palandt *Bürgerliches Gesetzbuch* 65. edn. Munich CH Beck 2006, § 675, no 7.

[31] E Flohr, 'Der Franchise-Vertrag—Überlegungen vor dem Hintergrund der Apollo-Optik: Entscheidungen des BGH' (2004) 42 *Deutsches Steuerrecht* 93 at 95 and 97.

to pass on purchase advantages include the whole body of essential rights and obligations which may result out of the agreement. The Federal Court of Justice (*BGH*) has confirmed this principle on various occasions, when contract terms which deviated from legal provisions or modified them were subject to its control.[32]

When it comes to the control of the contents of the standard terms in agreements which are not regulated by dispositions of a statute, the contractual partner of the party who has stipulated the standard terms has to be protected against any unreasonable reduction of these rights that he was entitled to expect from the object and the purpose of the agreement.

In his review of the Apollo judgments, Teubner[33] has already given a description of the task of jurisprudence. It is the task to decide, based on *objective law*, whether purchase advantages have to be passed on to franchisees, even if no commitment in the form of an express contractual stipulation exists to that extent.

> The jurisprudence will be forced to decide this question based upon objective contractual structures at the latest when standard terms have been adjusted to the new case law (Apollo Optik) by weakening, deleting or excluding obligations to pass on purchase advantages.
>
> If obligations to pass on purchase advantages should simply be deleted in the future, it has to be decided, based upon objective law, whether the obligation of the franchisor to act in good faith includes an obligation to pass on rebates. Then, at the latest, the network character of franchise systems becomes legally relevant.[34]

'Objective law' means the essential rights and obligations which result from the nature of the agreement. The legislator presumes in Section 307 II *BGB* that such 'natural' contractual obligations exist. When controlling the contents of standard term clauses, it has to be examined whether they limit natural contractual rights in such a way that the purpose of the agreement is endangered. However, the achievement of the purpose of the agreement cannot only be endangered by a specific stipulation which excludes any claim for purchase advantages. The violation of an unwritten natural contractual obligation may endanger the achievement of the contractual obligations even more efficiently.

The franchisor who is the subject of a claim can try to reject his obligation to pass on network advantages by the defence that he is not obliged to do so without a specific contractual commitment to that

[32] BGH-Judgment of 14 October 1997 (1998) 51 *NJW* 383 = LM *AGBG* § 8, No 30; LM § 8 *AGBG*, No 8.

[33] See G Teubner, 'Profit sharing als Verbundpflicht?' (n 23 above) 93.

[34] *Ibid*.

purpose. Then, the franchisee will be forced to qualify the obligation to pass on network advantages as an essential obligation which is deducted directly and objectively from the particular picture of the atypical agreement, which means that he has to develop his own model of justice.

In the law suit, the 'real model' of the franchise agreement has to be supported by a normative structure model which is not based upon legislation but upon case law.

The rights and obligations which result from the nature of the agreement, which are decisive in the sense of Section 307 II Nr 2 *BGB* raise two questions which are linked in a hermeneutic way and which can hardly be separated. However, the idea of the nature of the agreement, which supersedes single rights and obligations, is helpful in order to obtain a guiding picture (*Leitbild*) and is a measure according to which the contractual stipulations can be controlled. Decisions on the nature of the contract should pay less attention to the concrete regulations agreed upon by the parties, and more attention to the model for consideration of exchange and justice to which the parties have impliedly committed themselves.

However, it would be erroneous to understand the wording of Section 307 II Nr. 2 *BGB* as a reference to natural justice conceptions. In contrast, the relevant guiding picture must be developed out of the contractual order itself. In order to avoid circular thinking, the data which have been provided by private autonomy have to be enriched by the generally valid principles and evaluations of objective law. They have to be viewed as a whole, and be united to a normative model of justice which overcomes the pure individual contractual picture of justice.[35]

The point of reference for the shaping of a concrete guiding picture is not the individual agreement but the specific 'type of contract' which has been called for in the agreement, even if it concerns a concept which is entirely new. This is the consequence of the abstract concept of general contract terms and standard contracts as the corresponding system of examination which looks for a generalisation and for contract types.[36] It also results from the notion of the very 'nature of the contract', which refers to a model of consideration exchange which supersedes the individual contract.

First of all, the general sense of each agreement, ie, to be bound by the given promise, is part of the 'nature of the contract'. However, no concrete rights and obligations can be deduced from this. Thus, the 'nature of the contract' is determined by the specific purposes which take into account and protect particular interests, and thereby characterise the

[35] See M Coester, in M Martinek (ed), *Staudingers Kommentar zum Bürgerlichen Gesetzbuch* (Berlin, Sellier-de Gruyter, 1998) § 9 *AGBG*, No 200–04.

[36] *Ibid.*

agreement. In the first place, the purposes and the expectations of the parties have to be considered, in the manner in which they are expressed in the individual agreement, because the agreement finds its basis in private autonomy.

If the purposes cannot be gleaned from the individual agreements, the purposes which are typically pursued in the relevant business have to be taken into account, ie those which guide an average, reasonable observer at the moment of the conclusion of the agreement and convince him to sign it.

The view of a reasonable observer and the manners of the relevant business, which have to be considered, are of importance in two regards:

- in order to exclude unreasonable purposes and expectations of the parties; and
- on the other hand, if the concrete purposes and expectations of the parties had not been laid down, it has to be determined what they would have reasonably pursued.

The purposes and expectations of the parties include:

- first, the specific purposes of the performance, which are inherent to the main contribution as typical in the business or by explicit agreement.
- in addition, the protection of the interests which are covered by the contractual regulation generally belonging to the 'nature of the contract'.

Thus, the nature of the contract is essentially determined by the interests which have to be reasonably considered and protected by the agreement. The nature of the contract is not only determined by its general character, but also by the individual parts of the agreement if they deal with interests which are worthy of protection.[37]

X. INVALIDITY OF STIPULATIONS EXCLUDING CLAIMS FOR NETWORK ADVANTAGES ART 307 II, NR 1 CIVIL CODE

To date, there are no judgments on obligations to pass on network advantages which are not based on a specific contractual stipulation; neither are there any judgments on the standard terms by which a franchisor has refused to pass on network advantages granted on purchases made by the franchisees who were bound to purchase goods only from approved suppliers.

[37] M Wolf in N Horn and W Lindacher (eds), *AGBG*, 3rd edn (Munich, CH Beck, 1994) § 9, numbers 83 and 84.

In order to examine the validity of such stipulations, the courts will have to define the characteristics of the guiding picture of the franchisor obligations, which result from the network agreement. There are no statutory provisions regarding the obligations of the franchisor to pass on any purchase advantages which he has received. In this context, a differentiation is necessary between:

- creating a conditional claim for participation in network advantages (key account rebates); and
- a claim to receive purchase advantages which the franchisor has negotiated and received not only on his own purchases, but also on the purchases of his franchisees.

Whenever the franchisor requests an obligation on the part of his franchisees to make purchases of approved products only from approved suppliers, a key account purchase volume of the network is created because of the multilateral connection of all the franchise agreements. This collective bargaining power can be used by the franchisor as a leverage instrument in his negotiations regarding the listing of the suppliers in order to obtain volume-related purchase advantages for the network. As a result of the nature of the 'network connected' franchise agreements, the obligation arises to allow the franchisees to participate in the purchase conditions negotiated for his own corporate stores as well as for the franchise shops.

To the extent that a franchisor employs the collective bargaining power of the dual distribution network in his negotiations with suppliers, and receives 'advantages' which are also granted on the purchases of the franchisees from them, not only does he look after his own interests, but also those of third parties. His dealings are part of the package of all the franchisor obligations for which he is paid by the franchise fees. As a result, the obligation to pass on purchase advantages by analogy to Sections 675 and 667 *BGB*, and Article 384(2) of the Commercial Code arises.[38]

XI. CLAIM FOR DAMAGES BASED ON ARTICLES 33 AND 20(1) S 2, 1 ANTITRUST LAW (*GWB*) FOR DISCRIMINATION AND OBSTRUCTION

In the event that no contractual obligation concerning the passing on of network advantages exists, the franchisees could consider basing their claims for purchase advantages which have been withheld from them openly or secretly, not just on the rights created by the contractual nature

[38] T Lenz in V Röhricht and F von Westphalen (eds), *HGB*, 2nd edn (Cologne, O Schmitt, 2002) § 384, No 12.

of the network ties. Legal claims could also come into consideration because of unjustified discrimination and obstruction by the franchisor and his authorised suppliers.

In a dual distribution network, the franchisors exercise a dual role:

- on the one hand, they maintain the interest of their own corporate store network; and
- on the other, they take care of the third-party interests of the independent franchisees within the dual distribution network.

In the face of claims for equal treatment of franchise shops and corporate outlets, they quote the prevailing opinion in both jurisdiction and the literature, which denies the application of Section 20(1) *GWB* (the law against restrictions of competition) on inter-corporate relations.

Within an entrepreneurial unit, it is admitted that specific conditions can be granted up to cost fee performance. Therefore, the legal condition for equal treatment, ie 'equivalent enterprises' would not exist[39] if competitors claimed to be treated in the same way as 'group-members'.

The underlying reason is that specific conditions granted within a group are, in the final analysis, little more than an indirect contribution of capital. Thus, the same result could also be obtained by making payments of the remuneration back and forth, which would be legal under antitrust law. This opinion, that the granting of special favours within a group does not meet the requirements of discrimination (ie, of other enterprises) could be left undecided for the moment. However, in the case of dual distribution systems, which have to procure their merchandise from third parties, ie, listed suppliers, the situation is different from group relations. The franchisor does *not* grant the specific conditions—the purchase advantages—which are offered without discrimination by the suppliers for each purchase made by any outlet of the network, corporate and franchise stores, *from his own means*. It is the total network of all the shops—situated at distribution level—which, by composite demand, creates new assets, ie, the claim to receive key account conditions from the network of listed suppliers, which are situated on the upper level of delivery of goods. These new assets in the form of the bundled claims for network key account conditions, are not part of the property of the franchisor. However, the property of bundled claims also includes those of the franchise shops.

By employing the composite demand of all the network shops of the dual distribution system, and, by the selecting and bundling of suppliers, the franchisor creates a network of listed suppliers as an 'enterprise with

[39] BGH (1982) 35 *NJW* 2775; K Markert, in U Immenga and E-J Mestmäcker (eds), *GWB*, 3rd edn (Munich, CH Beck, 2001) § 20, No 126.

a strong market position'. Here, in the field of antitrust law, the definition of 'enterprise' has to be dealt with without reference to corporate law.

The 'bundling of suppliers' is possible for the franchisor only because of his dual role as both franchisor and organiser of the dual distribution network. This dual role creates not only external effects in the relationship with the listed suppliers, but also internal effects in the relationship with the participants of the dual distribution system. The situation of demand competition is eliminated by the choice and listing of certain suppliers and by the rejection of others, not through a horizontal cartel, but through the establishment of a network by the franchisor as an intermediate instance. The franchisor is the organiser of a network at different business levels—the level of the delivery of goods and the level of distribution—and, as such, has a dual role. The relations between the listed suppliers and the franchisees are neither determined by the market nor by a horizontal cartel, but by the network.

The holder of the network and, consequently, the addressee of the standards established by antitrust law is the enterprise which operates the network. The stipulations of the statutory prohibitions of antitrust law apply to enterprises and/or the holders of enterprises.[40]

Since the introduction of Section 19(4) Nr 4 *GWB* (the law against the restriction of competition), the notion of network has come to the foreground. Examples of material networks include the classical nets for electric energy, natural gas and telecommunication and other networks. They have to be distinguished from other networks which consists of material establishments as well as of services and know-how. To this category belong postal, banking and other distribution networks. The service character is in the focus of this group. In addition, virtual networks represent a specific domain, such as booking and reservation systems for train, flight and hotel travel, and, for example, the S.W.I.F.T. system for international bank transfer without ready money.

The application of antitrust law stipulations on virtual networks is under discussion in the literature, although its results are uncertain. It corresponds to the intention of the legislator to include virtual networks, which can be justified by the common economic elements of such networks, which may lead to an access problem under antitrust politics.[41]

Franchisors constitute networks within different levels of the economy:

- the network of corporate stores and affiliated independent franchise shops, a network at distribution level;
- at the level of delivery of goods, they also constitute a network

[40] G Dannecker in Immenga and Mestmäcker (eds), *GWB* (n 39 above) before § 8, No 40.
[41] W Möschel in Immenga and Mestmäcker (eds), *GWB* (n 39 above) § 19, No 197.

> through the bundling of listed suppliers and by selecting certain goods for the line of the products of the system.

Today, both levels are very often linked together by the material instrument of intranet systems. This guarantees close inter-relationship, connection and electronic communication between both networks at different levels of the economy. In addition, multilateral contract networks, created by the connection of bilateral contracts, also exist.

Virtual networks correspond to the functional notion of enterprise in antitrust law. For the notion of enterprise, any activity in business, independently from legal statute and from the purpose of profit, is sufficient.[42] The franchisor with his corporate stores is dependent upon such virtual enterprise to the same extent as all the franchisees. The reason is that the suppliers grant the same conditions—without discrimination—to the whole body of network shops, and treat them, because of the bundled bargaining power for their purchases, as a unique key account client with respect to the conditions. The whole body of network shops is decisive, not just the very often greater number of corporate stores which are managed by the franchisor.

Because of the fact that the franchisor—in his dual role and in a conflict of interest—exercises the management power over the network of corporate stores as well as the role of being the holder of the network at different levels of the economy, he cannot claim that the passing on of favourable conditions to corporate stores and the withholding of such conditions from independent franchise shops would be 'inter-corporate dealings'. The reason for this is that the franchisee is not part of the group of the franchisor, although he is part of the dual distribution network.

In the case of a dual distribution network, the legal argument, that Section 20(1), Nr 2 *GWB* would not be applicable for internal network relations, because they are comparable to inter-corporate dealings, has no legal ground. The organisation of a network of listed suppliers for a dual distribution system (which consists of own corporate stores and of third party network shops) is not an event within a group.

In contrast to the '*Stuttgarter Wochenblatt*' case,[43] the franchisor does not grant the specific conditions from the means of his own group. He only constitutes conditional claims for specific conditions as the holder of the network.

Network advantages which have been obtained in multi-level networks do not belong to the franchisor but to the network, which is to be

[42] D Zimmer in Immenga and Mestmäcker (eds), *GWB* (n 39 above) § 1, No 30 *et seq*; K Markert in Immenga and Mestmäcker (eds), *GWB* (n 39 above) § 20 I, II, No 22; W Möschel in Immenga and Mestmäcker (eds), *GWB* (n 39 above) § 19 III.

[43] BGH (1982) 35 *NJW* 2775.

considered as a different, virtual enterprise in the sense of antitrust law. The franchisor is the addressee of antitrust stipulations as the holder of the network, and is therefore liable to be sued for claims of damages if he himself organises the discrimination against his own franchisees with respect to his own corporate stores.

XII. PROGNOSIS FOR THE DEVELOPMENT OF JURISDICTION: SYSTEM IMMANENT OBLIGATION TO PASS ON NETWORK ADVANTAGES

The jurisdiction of the Federal Court of Justice (*BGH*) with respect to the interpretation of the standard terms regarding the passing on of purchase advantages has led to the following results for dual systems which are constituted by corporate stores and franchise shops.

In the case of contractual stipulations which promise the granting of volume-related purchase advantages of a corporate store network also to the franchisees, all key account conditions have to fall under such stipulations if the promise was made without restrictions.

However, it is admitted that the amount of such claims for purchase advantages which are granted on a voluntary basis can be subject to the approval of the suppliers by a so-called manufacturers' exception, but not by an arbitrary decision of the franchisor (as in the *Sixt* judgment). If a franchisor wants to pass on the purchase advantages of his corporate store network on a voluntary basis only partially (for example, in the form of a list of reduced manufacturers rebates) the restriction of the amount of the obligation to pass on purchase advantages can be made only by a transparent contractual stipulation which, according to Section 307 II, nr 2 *BGB*, is subject to control by the judge. In the event of doubt the rule of ambiguity works in favour of the franchisee (as in the Apollo Optik judgment).

Contractual stipulations regarding the paying out of purchase advantages have priority over legal claims based upon the law of mandate. The requirement of a legal claim regarding the paying out of purchase advantages is that the franchisor has, in fact, carried out a mandate and has himself received purchase advantages which have been granted on purchases of franchisees who are part of the network (*Hertz*). The significance of this jurisdiction of the Federal Court of Justice (*BGH*) goes far beyond these terms of reference. The interpretation of a general abstract contractual stipulation, especially in the *Apollo Optik* cases, regarding 'advantages in order to obtain best business results' will be significant for the decision of future conflicts. The reason lies in the fact that—when balancing the interests of the parties—the Federal Court of Justice (*BGH*) has not only looked at the bilateral franchise relationship, but also at the expectations of a faithful franchisee who has legitimate expectations with respect to his membership in a network with strong bargaining power.

The franchisee never stands alone in his bilateral relations with suppliers when he makes purchases of merchandise. He faces the listed suppliers as a partner who possesses equal rights, and participates in a network with strong bargaining power, which is recognised as a 'buying association'.

This understanding of network advantages will not only be decisive in future conflicts on the interpretation of contractual stipulations regarding the passing on of purchase advantages, it will also be important when cases have to be decided where purchase advantages have been kept secret or where the passing on of such favours has been prevented, even though there had been promises in this respect.

Much more interesting are the cases in which the passing on of advantages granted to network partners with purchase obligations have been expressly, deliberately and transparently excluded. Such a contractual exclusion clause should, then, be reviewed with regard to whether it corresponds to the nature of the franchise agreement, and to the guiding picture of network relations in the triangle relationship between network members, franchisor and listed suppliers. In no event can the *Sixt* decision be transferred to the majority of typical franchise systems. In fact, Sixt had agreed upon the extension of the key account conditions granted in the framework agreements with car producers in favour of the franchisees on a voluntary basis. Thus, the franchisees were not obliged to make purchases from listed suppliers. On the other hand, in the case of Apollo Optik, the system ties and the system-subordination had been reinforced by the obligation to purchase products from approved suppliers. However, this was not decisive in the *Apollo Optik* case, because the Federal Court of Justice (*BGH*) came to the conclusion that all the purchase advantages had to be paid out, only through interpretation of the relevant contractual stipulation. The court was of the opinion that the publication of a so-called official producers' rebate list which contained reduced rebates was not a transparent regulation and was therefore an invalid attempt to reduce the amount of the obligation to pass on the purchase advantages.

The further moulding of the guiding picture of the network agreement should also be of great significance under the aspect of the interdiction of discrimination and obstruction under Section 20(2) , No 1 *GWB* (the law on the restriction of competition). For example, an obligation upon the franchisee to purchase merchandise exclusively from suppliers who have been approved by the franchisor is not unjustified when such obligation clearly serves as a guarantee of the quality of the contractual products. In such cases, purchase obligations serves the image of the franchise system and guarantees the functionality of the system even in the interest of small commercial business partners.[44] However, if the purchase obligations exclusively serve for the procurement of the purchase advantages which the franchisee has earned through his purchases and which, therefore, are an advantage which belong to him because of his own performance, it could be understood that this would be considered to be a restriction of the essential rights of a franchisee, which are generated by the nature of the franchise agreement. The reason for this assumption is that the Federal Court of Justice (*BGH*) has already recognised that the franchisee can expect to enjoy favourable purchase conditions by joining a network with strong bargaining power. This contractual purpose would be endangered by shortening or excluding the claim for purchase advantages. From this understanding of the interests of the parties in a network relationship there results a reciprocal connection between the system ties of the franchisees with the purchase obligations from the listed suppliers of the network and the obligation of the franchisor to pass on the advantages which are generated to the franchisee. However, in franchise relationships without purchase obligations, the franchisor is—as in the *Sixt* case—more free. He can reduce—through a transparent, express stipulation—the amount of his obligation to pass on the purchase advantages which he has granted upon a voluntary basis.

In the case of franchise agreements which do not contain any regulation with respect to purchase advantages, the question of the control of the contents of such a standard term could, naturally, not be raised. In such cases, the nature of the franchise agreement and of the purpose which is expressly or implicitly declared has to be defined. If the interpretation of the agreement has not led to an unequivocal result, then an evaluation of the factual behaviour of the franchisor should be decisive. If the franchisor has not clearly made a commitment to support the franchisee in procuring the material which is necessary for the system, and, on the other hand, he negotiates and receives kick-backs, his obligation to pay out purchase advantages can be predicted under Section 675 and 667 *BGB*, and Article 384(2) of the Commercial Code. This can be drawn from the jurisdiction of the Federal Court of Justice (*BGH*) in the *Hertz* case: if the franchisor negotiates framework agreements with producers, he is taking care—in a dual system—of his own interests (of his corporate stores) as well as of the third party interests of the franchisees. When taking care of such interests, he is bound by a fiduciary commitment and he receives the purchase advantages not as a

[44] Activity Report of the 'Bundeskartellamt' 1985–1986 in K Metzlaff, *Praxishandbuch Franchising* (Munich, CH Beck, 2003) 1175.

result of his own business relationship to the suppliers, but only as an indirect representative of the franchisees who are members of his network.

XIII. FURTHER DEVELOPMENT OF CONCEPT FORMATION IN NETWORK LAW

Network effects and network advantages are not limited to purchase advantages. Especially when networks act in the market like enterprises—be it at distribution level or at supply level—they are perceived as enterprises. Thus, rights and obligations are created for the organisers of networks as well as for the network partners. The legal terms which are used in the network partners' contracts have to be clarified. Here, a so-called submission decision of the Federal Court of Justice (*BGH*) is of interest.[45] The decision deals with the question of whether the car producer BMW was entitled to terminate dealerships with a shorter term of only 12 months by anticipation if the necessity to restructure the distribution network totally, or, at least, an essential part of it, exists. EC Regulation 1475/95 provides, in Article 5(3) sentence 1 for this extraordinary right of termination. The Federal Court of Justice (*BGH*) laid down the following opinion:

> without any doubt, it is correct, that—in cases of a pure interpretation of the wording of Article 5 para 3 sentence 1 first hyphen of EC regulation number 1475/95, a distinction has to be made between the distribution system, which has to be modified in accordance with the standards of the new group exemption regulation nr. 1400/2002, and the distribution network. On the other hand, the distribution system can also be understood to be a part of the structure of the distribution network, which does not consist only of the sum of the distribution partners (the producers on the one hand, the car dealers on the other hand) but is also characterised by the contractual structure of the legal relationship between the distribution partners *i.e.*, the distribution system. The producer and the dealers become a 'distribution network' only when they are linked together through a contractual set of rules by which the details of their co-operation in the distribution is structured. From this contractual set of rules which represent in their entirety, the distribution system cannot be separated.

This clarification of the definition is helpful even though it has, until now, been given only in the context of the specific distribution relationship between a (car) producer and the dealer.

If—in the case of franchise systems—the franchisor has to acquire for himself the merchandise which is necessary for the distribution from

[45] BGH, Submission Decision of 26 July 2005—Kfz-Vertragshändler II (2005) 55 *Wirtschaft und Wettbewerb* DE-R 1551, p 1141.

third suppliers, or if he has listed such suppliers so that the franchisees can order their supplies directly from him, the legal relations between the partners of the franchise agreement are not only characterised by the distribution system, but also by the supply system which is necessarily linked to it. This is particularly valid if the franchisor commits, legally or economically, the franchisees to purchase from sources which have been opened by him. The obligation to make purchases corresponds with the obligation of the franchisor to supply. Accordingly, he has to establish a supply system.[46]

If the franchisor—in looking after the interests of his franchisees—employs the bargaining power of the network in framework agreements with the suppliers, and achieves concessions from the suppliers with respect to purchase advantages (rebates) in favour of the franchisees (Section 328 *BGB*), the realisation of such network advantages in the execution agreements (related to the franchise agreement) is only caused by the performance of the franchisees, ie, the purchase and the payment of merchandise which is typical for the system. The franchisor does not contribute any performance of his own for this purpose. His organisational performance in connection with the conclusion of framework agreements on favourable conditions is already compensated by the franchise fee. As a consequence, the passing on of purchase advantages is an obligation upon the franchisor in his capacity as the organiser of the network which is 'system-immanent' and results from the obligation to grant the use of the procurement and distribution system.

In the *Sixt* case, the Federal Court of Justice (*BGH*) formulated one sentence which is quite often quoted by the opponents of an obligation to pass on purchase advantages:

> the law does not know a legal obligation of the Franchisor to pass on advantages to his contractual partners resulting out of the purchase of goods from sources which have been opened up by himself.[47]

In this context, it has to be recalled that, in the Sixt franchise system, no purchase obligation with respect to the acquisition of rental cars existed. Therefore, a statement of the Federal Court of Justice (*BGH*) on the *Sixt* case cannot be applied to franchise systems which impose a factual or legal purchase obligation. This was the case in *Apollo Optik*. The power of demand which is generated by the multilateral connection of franchise agreements with purchase obligations creates 'self-produced network advantages'. By evaluating the reciprocal interests, they belong to the

[46] Metzlaff, *Praxishandbuch Franchising* (n 44 above) § 8, No 150.
[47] BGH (1999) 52 *NJW* 2671 at 2675.

partner who executes the performance with respect to purchase advantages, who purchases and who pays for the merchandise. Thus, the obligation to pass on purchase advantages is inherent to the delivery obligation of the franchisor.

The jurisdiction and the literature will have to answer the question of whether the franchisor can—in a franchise system with purchase obligations—withhold purchase advantages totally or partially through a standard term clause, and will have to examine whether it represents a violation of the essential rights and obligations of the network agreement. For contractual relations in franchise networks, which are not only structured through a distribution network, but also through a procurement system, a normative guiding picture has to be developed.[48]

[48] M Coester in M Martinek (ed), *Staudingers Kommentar zum Bürgerlichen Gesetzbuch* (Berlin, Sellier-de Gruyter) § 9 *AGBG*, No 204.

Part III.

External Network Relations: State Regulation and Self-Regulation

10

The Weakest Link: Legal Implications of the Network Architecture of Supply Chains

HUGH COLLINS*

I. TWO STORIES ABOUT NETWORKS

I.1. The Prime Minister's 'Arm-lock'

A FEW YEARS ago, Prime Minister Tony Blair declared that he believed that the supermarkets in Britain had their suppliers in an 'arm-lock'. The implication of this remark seemed to be that, although consumers were benefiting from low prices owing to the intense competition between supermarkets, the suppliers to the supermarkets were suffering from the supermarkets' abuse of their dominant market position in groceries. The competition authorities carried out a lengthy investigation. They discovered all kinds of apparently abusive practices employed by supermarkets.[1] Under the practice of 'variable pricing', for instance, a supermarket would insist upon a retrospective price reduction by a supplier. In order to cover the costs of a sales promotion, such as 'buy one, get one free', the supermarket would unilaterally and retrospectively reduce its payment to its supplier. The competition authorities concluded that this practice, and many others, might be unfair to the suppliers. In a Code of Practice approved by the

* Professor of English Law, London School of Economics. As well as to the participants in the conference, special thanks to Ross Cranston, Georgio Monti, Keith Blois and Stefanos Mouzas for comments on earlier versions of this paper.

[1] Competition Commission, *The Supply of Groceries from Multiple Stores in the United Kingdom*, Cmd 4842 (London, October 2000).

national Competition Commission, the supermarkets agreed not to engage in variable pricing—except where they had given reasonable notice.[2]

From a traditional legal perspective, the issues in this story appear clear-cut. The retrospective, unilateral price reduction by the supermarket undoubtedly amounts to a breach of a fixed-price contract for the supply of goods. If litigation had been initiated, the supplier could have brought an action for the full, original price. In practice, no doubt, the suppliers decided that their long-term commercial interests lay in remaining part of the supply chain and keeping their largest customer, so they refrained from litigation for fear of future exclusion from a substantial segment of the retail market. This was the nature of the 'arm-lock': a bilateral monopoly in a long-term business relation with sunk investments.

The puzzling aspect of the story is not the discovery of the 'arm-lock', but the acceptance by the competition authority that it could ever be reasonable for the supermarkets to impose retrospective, unilateral price cuts. Variable pricing looks like a classic instance of opportunism or of taking advantage of a dominant position that ought to be deterred by legal regulation.

I.2. Remedying the Victims of 'Stock-outs'

Each week, I go to the local supermarket. In my hand is a shopping list, supplied by my family. I tour the aisles that display the products, fill up my trolley, cross off the items on the list, pay for the goods, and acquire points on my store loyalty card. On my return home, I sheepishly explain that I have not been able to buy a few items on the list because the supermarket was out of stock. This claim is never regarded as an adequate excuse, especially if the goods concerned were some type of hair-conditioner that is absolutely vital for a person to look her best. The rejection of my excuse is partly based on an assessment of its veracity (were the goods really not there or did the absent-minded professor simply forget to read the list?), and partly based on its inadequacy—I am at fault for going to the wrong shop, because it is so often out of stock (if

[2] Code of Practice on Supermarkets' Dealings with Suppliers, para 4: 'A supermarket shall not directly or indirectly require a supplier to reduce the agreed price of or increase the agreed discount for any product unless reasonable notice of such requirement is given to that supplier in writing before the relevant supplies of that product are made'. The Code of Practice is not legally binding, but it contains transparency requirements and a dispute resolution procedure, and if the Code is not observed there is the implicit threat that the Director General of Fair Trading may invoke legal enforcement powers against anti-competitive behaviour.

I am to be believed, that is). I have a good mind to complain to someone, even to sue them, because I am fed up with being the hapless victim of stock-outs.

A traditional legal analysis would not give my complaint the time of day. An empty shelf simply means that I cannot make an offer to buy, and the supermarket cannot accept that offer—there is not even an 'invitation to treat'. In the absence of a prior promise or representation that the goods would be available for sale at a particular location, I cannot complain to a seller if he or she does not have the goods that I happen to want to buy. My only remedy under the traditional legal analysis is to shop elsewhere in future, that is, a non-legal sanction. And, yet, I do not use this non-legal sanction, because the costs of finding alternative outlets have risen, as rival shops have become more distant; the opening of the supermarket coincided with the closure of nearly all other shops in the neighbourhood.

Is my desire to claim compensation for being the persistent victim of stock-outs a completely hopeless case? Perhaps, but it is worth highlighting a few details that suggest that I had some reasonable expectations, even if I did not actually have legal rights, to be protected from disappointment. For a start, it is important to point out that the supermarket knew that I was coming to the shop and also knew what I would be likely to purchase: data collected on the store loyalty card provides this information. We can, therefore, attribute to the supermarket reasonable foresight that the stock-out would cause discomfort to me. In addition, it seems likely that the supermarket could have taken steps to avoid the disappointment. It may be true that the supermarket is not entirely to blame—perhaps it was let down by the supplier of the product—but, without doubt, some combination of participants in the supply chain has caused the gap on the shelves, and the supermarkets have sufficient market power to discipline their suppliers. It is also true that my claim suffers from the weakness that it consists of non-pecuniary or non-material loss, unless I incur the cost of driving around the city to find another retail outlet that offers the missing product. Yet, such losses are sometimes recoverable for breach of contract,[3] as in the case of a disappointing holiday,[4] and, surely, the supermarket implicitly promised me a pleasurable shopping experience in its great bazaar of temptations?

Taking all these considerations into account, it might be argued that I had a reasonable expectation of being able to purchase the normal product range at the supermarket; through someone's fault, I have been

[3] *Farley v Skinner* [2001] UKHL 49, [2002] 2 AC 732; *Ruxley Electronics and Construction v Forsyth* [1996] AC 344 (HL).

[4] Case C-168/00 *Simone Leitner v TUI Deutschland GmbH* [2002] All ER (EC) 561 (ECJ); *Jarvis v Swans Tours Ltd* [1973] QB 233 (CA).

unable to do so, and, given the controlling power of the supermarket, it would be appropriate to hold it vicariously liable; and, as a result of this incompetence, I have suffered reasonably foreseeable non-material loss. Are these not sufficient elements to establish a civil claim for compensation? Is there not something unsatisfactory about a legal system that bluntly denies any possibility of such a claim for the victim of stock-outs?

II. A NETWORK ANALYSIS

These two stories concern supply chains and the legal position of actors within them. In both cases, the traditional legal response of private law may not produce outcomes that correspond to the reasonable expectations of the participants. The message of the first story is that, contrary to the private law of sales, it is sometimes reasonable for the supermarket to impose retrospective price variations on suppliers in breach of contract. And the suggestion of the second story is that, despite the absence of any binding explicit promises or representations on the part of the supermarket, consumers may have a legitimate sense of grievance against stock-outs because their reasonable expectations of supply have been dashed. How can we explain this apparent dissonance between the legal position in private law and the expectations, which may be reasonable ones, of the participants in these commonplace transactions?

A network analysis offers to provide a fruitful framework for the development of an answer to this question. In broad terms, a network analysis emphasises two significant alterations to the traditional legal reasoning of private law.

The first adjustment recognises that third parties to contracts may have legal rights and obligations that arise from their co-operation with, or dependence on, the parties to the contract. This variation is not a particularly revolutionary concept in private law systems, because most acknowledge, to a varying extent, that, in certain circumstances, third parties may acquire rights under a contract. Instead, the force of the proposed network analysis is to spread the possibility of third party effects far wider than hitherto recognised, and, perhaps more controversially, to include obligations as well as rights. We can observe this feature, for instance, in Teubner's theory of 'connected contracts', in which the obligations that arise under one contract affect the rights and obligations under another, on condition that they are linked by a network.[5] This kind of argument can be observed in other contexts involving triangular contractual relationships between three parties (without explicit mention

[5] G Teubner, '*Coincidentia Oppositorum*: Hybrid Networks beyond Contract and Organisation' (ch 1), in this volume.

of the network concept), as in the case of workers with a contract with an employment agency who perform services for a client without any explicit contract of employment with the client to complete the contractual triangle.[6]

The second, and more dramatic, departure from traditional private law concepts, is to imagine that, as well as the traditional legal categories for the regulation of business relationships —those of contract and recognised business entities, such as corporations and partnerships —there is a further legal category, which is neither a contract nor a business organisation, but which shares the qualities of both. In other words, in addition to markets composed of contracts and firms using techniques of vertical integration of production, there is a possible third, hybrid category that may be called a network. It is described as a hybrid because, although the participants remain independent legal entities, as in the case of contracts or markets, they are, nevertheless, bound, in certain circumstances, to respect the demands or needs of the group of actors within the network as a whole, which is similar to the need to respect the requirements or goals of an integrated firm. In short, a network business relationship has the divergent interests of market participants, but is simultaneously bound together by a common goal or purpose.

My two stories are designed to test the value of the apparently paradoxical concept of a network for legal analysis. If a network concept is useful, it should be capable of both explaining particular aspects of market behaviour involved in networks, and the problems for legal analysis in addressing this market behaviour. One kind of market behaviour that might be explained concerns breaches of bilateral contracts when the participants regard these breaches as justifiable or reasonable by reference to economic goals defined other than with direct reference to the performance of the contract. The example of variable pricing seems to present a suitable test case. It is an instance where one party breaches a contract, yet this conduct can apparently be regarded, in some circumstances, as reasonable. The question is whether the justification for this breach of contract can be explained by reference to the needs or goals of the supply chain as a whole, or what may be called the network entity itself. In other words, the hypothesis is that network goals can explain why the parties to contracts within a network do not invariably pursue their personal economic interests in their dealings with each other.

A second kind of market behaviour that might be explained by the network concept concerns the acknowledgement of links with, and obligations towards, parties that are not bound by direct contractual or

[6] G Davidov, 'Joint Employer Status in Triangular Employment Relationships' (2004) 42 *British Journal of Industrial Relations* 727–46; M Freedland, *The Personal Employment Contract* (Oxford, Oxford University Press, 2003) 33 *et seq*.

business organisation forms. A network concept suggests that we should expect such third party effects throughout a network, even though some parties do not have direct contractual links with each other. In a supply chain, for instance, although each buyer and seller has a direct contractual relationship, there is unlikely to be one between the original producer and the final retailer, or between that producer and the consumer. Despite this lack of formal contractual links, a network analysis may suggest that some third parties may have interests that deserve protection, and which are, in practice, acknowledged by the participants in the market. My second story about stock-outs is designed to explore this possibility of the third party effects of networks.

In order to examine the potential of a network analysis in addressing the puzzles raised by my stories, this essay proceeds by providing a more detailed account of the characteristics of supply chains in the retail grocery market. Following this account, the discussion considers whether these supply chains reveal dimensions that might be regarded as revealing the properties of networks. This discussion requires a more thorough analysis of the concept of network itself. Finally, the essay considers the potential implications of the network concept for legal claims from within and from outside networks. In particular, the possible legal implications for the solutions to the two stories with which we began will be considered. The exploration of these legal implications raises some further difficulties about networks and their normative implications.

III. THE ARCHITECTURE OF SUPPLY CHAINS

A supply chain comprises an elementary concept in micro-economics. It describes the route by which goods and services move from their originator to reach a consumer through a series, or chain, of market transactions. In the case of a washing machine, for instance, a consumer purchases the item from a retail store, the store purchases the goods from a manufacturer, or perhaps from a distributor standing as an intermediary between manufacturer and retailer, and the manufacturer purchases the components and raw materials from other producers, who, in turn, may have purchased components and raw materials from yet further producers down the chain. Each link in this supply chain contains a market transaction. In the case of washing machines, the transactions normally comprise a sale of goods. The way in which economics imagines that the chain works is that value is added at each link, so that the seller agrees a price which is greater than his costs, and the buyer, in turn, becomes a seller at a higher price, until the final purchaser, the consumer, selects the goods or services at the price and quality that he or she can afford. The traditional legal analysis shares most of this perspective. It regards each link in the supply chain as a separate contract, to which the normal legal rules of holding the parties to their bargain and the need to protect one's own interests apply. However, there are many features of contemporary supply chains that do not fit into the economic and legal image of a series of disconnected sales of goods.

Without doubt each supply chain has its distinctive combinations of elements. In different market sectors, the emphasis and labelling of the systems employed differs: for apparel companies, the goal is 'Quick Response'; for grocery companies, it is 'Efficient Consumer Response'. Where consumer demand is stagnant, competitive pressures intensify the search for improvements in the efficiency of supply chains that will benefit all the actors along the chain.[7] Here, five common deviations from the simple model of a chain of sale of goods transactions will be highlighted.

III.1. Seller's Orders

One departure concerns the purchasing decision. The simple sale of goods model assumes that the seller creates goods that are marketed, and that the buyer selects a quantity of the desired goods from the available market. But the business relationship under this supply chain reverses, or, at least, shares many of these decisions and roles.[8] Large retailers, such as supermarkets, acquire enormous databases about their customers on computerised systems governing stock control. Manufacturers and distributors seek access to these databases, so that they can know exactly when and what products on the shelves are being sold. Manufacturers and distributors can then institute an automated ordering system or continuous replenishment system, under which the retailer no longer orders the required goods, but the manufacturer, instead, supplies them as the products leave the shelves. An automated ordering process seems to mean that the seller of the goods (manufacturer, producer, distributor), rather than the buyer (retailer, distributor), makes the decision as to

[7] S Mouzas and L Araujo, 'Implementing Programmatic Initiatives in Manufacturer-Retailer Networks' (2000) 29 *Industrial Marketing Management* 293–303.

[8] The exact allocation of rights to determine ordering no doubt follows slightly different patterns according to industrial sector. For example, it is reported in Spain that distributors of cars determine the quantity of new cars and the models they order from the manufacturers, but this right must be qualified in view of the manufacturers' requirement that a minimum number of new cars across the range of models be held in stock, and the fact that the incentive payment system for sales ensures that unless the distributor sells about 100% of the sales target set by the manufacturer, the distributor will not make a profit: B Arrunada, L Garicano and L Vasquez, 'Contractual Allocation of Decision Rights and Incentives: The Case of Automobile Distribution' (2001) 17 *Journal of Law, Economics and Organisation* 257–84.

when the goods are required. This arrangement of continuous replenishment is to the buyer's advantage in the sense that the shelves will always be stocked, and, in particular, the buyer/retailer will not run out of fast-moving products, so that the buyer increases his or her volume of sales.

However, there is an obvious risk of misaligned incentives here: the seller might supply far more goods than the buyer requires. In order to counter this risk, the seller may bear all, or part of, the cost of surplus inventory. For example, an American supplier of spare parts to car dealers (Saturn) takes responsibility for managing the availability of parts at the dealers by making all stocking and replenishment decisions for dealers through its central computerised system. When a dealer turns out not having a part that it needs, the supplier pays for the cost of the emergency shipping costs. The supplier also shares the costs of excess inventory by buying back any particular part from a dealer if it is unused after nine months.[9] This arrangement reverses the traditional allocation of risks in supply chain ordering: the seller decides on the quantity of the buyer's purchases rather than the buyer determining its own needs; and the seller pays the cost of purchases in excess of requirements, instead of the buyer bearing the cost of its own inventory.

III.2. Marketing Decisions

A second departure concerns the allocation of roles with regard to marketing. In the traditional model, the retailer determines how to market the goods in the shop by choosing the layout and the allocation of shelf space to particular products. However, in modern supply chains to retailers, the distributor or producer often tries to determine how its goods are displayed in retail outlets, either by issuing instructions or using incentives to influence the retailer's decision. Thus, where the buyer of the product is a retail outlet, the arrangement with a producer may be better conceived, not so much as a sale as a rental agreement or a concession.

The retailer is renting out an identified part of its shelf space to a manufacturer in return for retaining a commission on sales (the mark-up), and this commission varies according to the exact location of the shelves on which the goods are presented to consumers. This perception of the relationship being as much a concession as a sale is strengthened when one considers the extent to which the supplier often determines where and when its goods should be displayed on the shelves. For

[9] HL Lee, 'The Triple-A Supply Chain' (2004) *Harvard Business Review* (October) 102 at 111.

example, following analysis of customer sales to consumers, the Japanese retail chain Seven-Eleven Japan requires its retail outlets to reconfigure store shelves at least three times daily so that the most heavily purchased items are readily accessible to cater for different consumer segments and demands at different hours.[10] As in this example, manufacturers can also use their databases to make suggestions to retailers about shelf design and brand visibility in order to maximise sales. For this purpose, it should be especially noted that producers and distributors can use information gained from monitoring one retail outlet to improve sales in another rival company's outlet. This perception of a shelf rental agreement or concession, rather than a sale, is strengthened when one observes the previous point about the sharing of the risk of over- or under-supply.

III.3. Information Disclosure

A third departure from the traditional model of the supply chain concerns the sharing of information. Instead of the parties dealing at arms' length and keeping their business secrets and knowledge private, the participants in the supply chain share information about demand from customers. The retailer, for instance, supplies the distributor or producer with up-to-the-minute information about customer purchases or consumer preferences. With this information, a producer and distributor may both ensure adequate stock replenishment for the retailer, but also arrange for their own suppliers to provide appropriate stock replenishment. Furthermore, it is possible to integrate this information exchange all the way down the supply chain. If a particular new fashion item is selling well in clothes shops in London, this information can appear not only on the distributor's computer but also on the manufacturer's computer on the other side of the world; in China, for example, or wherever the apparel is made.

The manufacturer can also gain information from the retailer's database early on about returns of goods, consumer complaints, etc, which may help to improve product quality and consumer satisfaction. This sharing of information reduces the extent to which the parties operate at arm's length, and, indeed, produces a situation in which the purchasing system is effectively jointly managed in their joint interests, leading to a situation of quasi-integration of the distribution system.

The sharing of the information by a computer network can also be used to obtain further efficiency and customer service. A distributor of products to small independent drugstores in the United States responded

[10] *Ibid*, 112.

to intense competition from chains of large stores by using computerised data processing not only to ship orders automatically to meet those needs, but also to pack the goods in crates that could be unloaded in an order that coincided with the lay-out of the retailer's shelves. The distributor also used the database to offer such services as warning consumers about the potentially dangerous drug combinations that they were purchasing and in order to help process health-insurance claims for prescription reimbursement.[11]

III.4. Joint Design

As a fourth departure from the traditional model of a chain of sales contracts, in modern supply chains, it is noticeable how responsibility for the design or composition of the goods to be sold is also shifted. Under the traditional model, a producer or manufacturer would create a product and then try to find distributors or retailers prepared to carry it as part of their inventory. Under contemporary practices, design decisions are often shared between the large retailers and the manufacturers. The retailer will describe in general terms the products it desires to a number of manufacturers, who then propose designs, which will be evaluated and refined. Once the final product has been chosen by the retailer, it will then issue orders for the product, not only, perhaps, to the manufacturer that originated the design, but also to other suppliers and competitors.[12]

The combining of information about customer preferences and technical knowledge seems likely to produce the items that consumers will prefer at the lowest cost. Again, the process of creating the design requires the disclosure of information that would traditionally have been kept secret, such as manufacturing techniques, sourcing issues, and data on customer shopping-patterns. Indeed, the 'total quality' management philosophy requires each participant in the chain to be concerned about all upstream decisions affecting the quality of products and services, which leads to increasing attempts to supervise the management of production in earlier links in the chain. The supermarket, for instance, is not only concerned about the hygienic qualities of the packing plant for chickens, but also needs to supervise, in some manner how the farmer has reared the chickens in the first place, so that it can make promotional

[11] R Johnston and PR Lawrence, 'Beyond vertical integration—the rise of the value-adding partnership' in G Thompson, J Frances, R Levacic and J Mitchell (eds), *Markets, Hierarchies & Networks* (London, Sage, 1991) 193, adapted from (July–August 1988) *Harvard Business Review* 94–101.

[12] K. Blois, 'B2B "relationships"—A Social Construction of Reality?' (2003) 3 *Marketing Theory* 79–95.

claims such as that the chickens are 'farm assured', 'free range', or from an unspecific Arcadia, such as the 'West Country'.

III.5. Architectural Coding

The final deviation from the traditional model of a chain of sale of goods transactions concerns the function of computers in these business relationships. Once two separate businesses establish a computer link to exchange information for the purpose of purchasing decisions, the code established by that link then regulates the relationship. In order for a product to be shipped, for instance, neither seller nor buyer need make a conscious decision if the coding of the computer link determines the need for the product. How the relationship operates depends on the coding of the software, rather than on decisions made by managers on a daily basis, let alone the terms of the contract.

Furthermore, the computer may well link together several members of the supply chain, from the supplier of fabric and other raw materials, to the manufacturer, the distributor, and the retailer. The same practical integration of decision-making may apply along the whole chain: to avoid a stock shortage in a shop, the computer may be coded to instruct the fabric supplier to ship fabric to the manufacturer, and so on down the chain so that the goods arrive in the shop just in time to prevent a stock-out. There are still contractual relationships down the chain, but performance under the contract is determined by the code of the software, rather than by reference to the terms of the contract: the software determines what will happen; the contract only if it does not. Furthermore, how the supply chain is linked together depends not so much on the contractual relationship as on the architecture of the computer software.[13]

IV. NETWORK DIMENSIONS

Putting together these five departures from the traditional model of a chain of sales contracts between opposing business interests, it becomes clear that there are more than elements of the integration of businesses here. Indeed, there seems to be little difference in practice in these supply chains from the rather rarer instance of a fully-integrated business, such as the Zara clothes chain, which designs, manufactures and sells clothes

[13] In talking about code and architecture, I am using the terminology of L Lessig, *Code and Other Laws of Cuberspace*. See: http://code-is-law.org/.

in its own retail outlets.[14] Nevertheless, the typical pattern in a supply chain remains the formal separation of businesses as independent economic entities or firms. The close co-operation involved in what is revealingly called in business schools 'supply chain management' does not require vertical integration.

A detailed examination of the reasons for the development of these quasi-integrated supply chains is beyond the scope of this paper, though there is no reason to doubt that they are motivated by traditional business concerns to maximise profits in a competitive economy. The operation of the supply chain in this manner is designed to maximise sales to consumers whilst maintaining a small inventory. The agility of the system is necessary in many business sectors in order to respond to sudden fluctuations in consumer demand and changes in competitive pressures. There also seem to be savings on transaction costs here to offset the investment in IT. For example, the buyer's purchasing and ordering department can be reduced in size, and the manufacturer's sales force can be similarly reduced, because in these long-term arrangements there is only an intermittent annual need to negotiate orders: in the meantime, the computer code determines requirements.

The question that requires examination here concerns the applicability and utility of a network analysis to the modern business practice of quasi-integrated supply chains. Apart from law, the concept of the network has been employed prolifically by most disciplines in the social sciences, from sociology through politics to anthropology, economics and business studies.[15] However, the meaning of the concept of network appears to differ between disciplines, though it is possible that these meanings are related in unexplored ways. In order to reflect on the network dimensions of supply chains for the purpose of legal analysis, it is, therefore, necessary to develop some relevant and adequate conceptual analysis of the notion.

In the commercial context of supply chains, it is perhaps most convenient to turn to institutional economics as arguably the most influential and pertinent discipline in this context of the study of markets and business relationships.[16] However, institutional economics does not

[14] K Ferdows, MA Lewis and JAD Machuca, 'Rapid-Fire Fulfilment' (November 2004) *Harvard Business Review* 104. One possible difference is, however, that Zara is quicker as a result of a better alignment of incentives in a vertically-integrated supply chain, since it claims to be able to take clothes from first design to the shelves of the world in 15 days.

[15] G Thompson, J Frances, R Levacic and J Mitchell (eds), *Markets, Hierarchies & Networks* (London, Sage, 1991).

[16] Perhaps sociological approaches to economic behaviour could make an equal claim, but their research involving networks has tended to focus on some of the social factors that economics tends to ignore, such as having a useful network of personal contacts for the purpose of obtaining jobs. For a recent overview, see M Granovetter, 'The Impact of Social Structure on Economic Outcomes' (2005) 19 *Journal of Economic Perspectives* 33–50.

prove to be as helpful to this enquiry as might be hoped. The main problem is that the central distinction drawn by institutional economics between markets and hierarchies is itself contested by the concept of networks as a type of hybrid. Nevertheless, it is instructive to identify in more detail the reasons for the difficulties of institutional economics in grappling with the phenomena described as networks.

In broad outline, the functional approach of institutional economics would explain the features of modern supply chains along the following lines. Although simple market transactions for the sale of goods work reasonably well—since it is easily possible to observe whether parties have conformed to the contract—these contracts create various risks for both supplier and purchaser. For the supplier, there are risks of over-production of a particular item for which the market diminishes as a result of changes in consumer taste and competitive pressures, and, by the same token, there are equivalent risks of under-production of a popular item. For the retailer or purchaser, there are matching problems of inventory control. Close co-operation and timely exchange of information can reduce these risks and their associated costs, although, at the same time, such measures create new risks, in particular, the loss of investments sunk into this specific co-operative business relationship and the consequent danger of opportunistic behaviour. To protect these sunk investments, such as IT expenses, and to deter opportunistic behaviour—such as taking advantage of the other's economic dependence on the chain relationship in order to obtain retrospective price variations—it becomes efficient for each business to engage in even closer monitoring of the other party and more elaborate governance relationships. Through these various steps, the parties move from a fairly pure market relationship to one that becomes closer to, though never reaching, the other end of the spectrum of vertical integration. In many instances, the close co-operation and incentive structures of the contractual relationships can be aptly described as symbiotic contracts.[17]

Although this type of account of the efficiency properties of the 'quasi-integration' of supply chains has considerable explanatory power, there are two features of modern supply chains that tend to resist explanation within the framework of institutional economics. These two features comprise the distinctive elements of the network architecture

[17] It has been argued that the producer-retailer relationship in food forms a symbiotic relationship, though it is also noted that the greater concentration of retail outlets combined with their lower asset specificity (the shelves can always be used to display a different product) contribute to retailer dominance of a the relationship: KP Kass, 'Symbiotic Relationships between Producers and Retailers in the German Food market?' (1993) 149 *Journal of Institutional and Theoretical Economics* 741–7.

that we are trying to understand: namely, the multilateral dimension of the co-operative architecture, and the economic interests of the network as a whole.

The first troubling feature of the modern supply chain for transaction cost economics arises from the presence of several parties, and from the nature of the diverse and multilateral links between them. Although transaction cost economics offers a functional explanation of the governance structures created between two market operators, in the case of supply chains it needs to have an analysis of why governance structures are created all down the chain, and back up it. In the relations between remote parties, who do not—between themselves—engage in exchange transactions, the decisions about governance structures are not directly connected to the make or buy question, that is, the question about vertical integration or contractual relations. Instead, they plan to co-operate with someone with whom they have no direct market relationship, in order to improve the efficiency of the performance of a contract they have with someone else or to gain a competitive advantage in the retail market. For example, the retailer sends information down the ordering system so that its suppliers, and their suppliers, know as soon as possible what the requirements of the retailer will be, and can respond to them appropriately in good time. The architecture of this supply chain is only partly comprised of market relationships; the crucial operational process involves the transmission of data throughout the chain. What requires explanation is the governance structure or co-ordination mechanism that handles efficiency problems of the network as a whole. If the kind of functional efficiency analysis offered by institutional economics can be useful here, it needs to be applied not only to the market transactions involved in the supply chain, but also to the efficiency of the operation of the network as a whole.

Furthermore, in so far as institutional economics imagines such non-market relationships, it tends to assume that they must comprise hierarchical systems of control that are designed to resolve the problems of co-ordination and to reduce transaction costs. In the case of the supply chain, however, it is not clear that the management of the chain should be regarded as a hierarchical structure. In the design of the co-ordination system, the emphasis seems to lie not on direction and monitoring of behaviour, but on the disclosure of information and mutual direction, instead. Recognising their economic interdependence, the parties agree to high levels of co-operation and intensive governance structures. These governance structures can often assume the architectural form of the software code of communications between computers: the parties fear cheating far less than the lack of timely information and mutual adaptation. As a result, the co-ordination mechanism may prove 'acephalous' or heterarchical.

A second troubling feature of modern supply chains for institutional economics concerns the motivations of the actors. One of the central tenets of transaction cost economics has been the plausible assumption that economic actors will not fulfill their contractual obligations if they believe they can avoid them without harm to their short-term and long-term interests. However, this assumption is put to the test in modern supply chains. The problem is that each party in the chain has an interest in securing successful business outcomes for every other party in the chain. If the retailer fails, for some reason, to sell the goods to consumers, not only are the retailer's profits damaged, but so too, at least in the long run, are the profits of *all* the businesses in the supply chain. Some earlier examples vividly illustrated this point. The distributor of products to independent drug stores realised that its business depended upon the ability of independent drug stores to compete with vertically integrated chains, so it intervened in various ways to improve the competitiveness of its customers, the drug stores, with the long-term benefit of its own survival. Similarly, the distributor of spares to the car dealers assumed most of the risks regarding the inventory because this permitted a more reliable supply to customers, which, in turn, enabled the car dealers to improve their market share, which finally secured the success of the distributor itself.

Modern supply chains share this feature that every member must be deeply concerned about the fortunes of its weakest link. Although each member needs to be concerned primarily about its own interests, it must also be concerned about the interests of the network as a whole. A deal that becomes onerous for other links in the chain threatens the success of the chain as a whole. Within the supply chain, each actor must conduct its business in order to maximise both its own profits but also those of the network as an entity.

Neither of these features of supply chains necessarily presents an insuperable problem for institutional economic analysis. In addressing the co-ordinating role of the network architecture between multiple parties, institutional economics needs to develop an alternative to contractual and hierarchical governance systems that can understand the 'acephalous' or heterarchical nature of the computerised co-ordination system within the network of the supply chain. Similarly, by extending the notion of the long-term interests of the participants in the supply chain, it may be possible to account for their need to act with reference to the interests of the weakest link in the chain. It is probably not essential for this purpose to posit the existence of an independent entity, such as a network with its own goals, provided that the notion of long-term interest includes the concern to ensure the efficient operation of remote actors in the supply chain with whom there is no direct contractual link, and provided that the tension between the immediate economic interests and the long-term welfare of *all* the participants in the supply chain is recognised. The advantage of the concept of a network lies in its utility of expressing both of these ideas: multi-party co-ordination without hierarchy and the promotion of the interests of *all* the participants in the chain by conceiving of the chain as an entity in itself.[18]

With these two points in mind, it seems possible to provide a concept of a network architecture that is apt for the present discussion. In this context of supply chains, a network comprises two or more long-term business relationships, which consist of an unending sequence of repeated transactions for the sale of goods, and in which common arrangements for co-ordination (or a governance structure) apply to all business relationships, rather than simply between the parties to each business relationship separately. In other words, networks require at least three parties, and therefore at least two long-term business relationships involving exchanges, but they share one co-ordination system. The co-ordination system may be regarded as a type of governance structure, but, in the case of supply chains, instead of its emphasis lying in the detection of deceit or betrayal, its primary concern is with the exchange of information up and down the entire chain with a view to promoting the competitiveness of the chain as a whole.

Under this concept of network architecture, there is both market and hierarchy within networks, but only in a special sense. There is a series of interconnected business relationships in the sense that one presupposes the functioning of the other, as in a chain of supply from producer, distributor, retailer, and consumer. These business relations are market relations in the sense that each actor is in business on its own account and will retain any residual surplus or profit from the transaction. This feature distinguishes a network from a corporate firm, where only one party, the shareholders, has the legal right to the residual surplus. The network differs from a simple chain of contracts because of the existence of a co-ordinating mechanism or governance structure, which links each node or actor in the chain. But this governance structure is not necessarily hierarchical because its primary function lies in co-ordination rather than detection of default. The co-ordination can be provided by the code in the software that governs the exchange of information.

This concept of a network architecture tries to explain the features of supply chains that differ from the traditional model of a series of market

[18] In the terminology of systems theory, the concept of network can be used to explain that the network creates a system of business communications that differs from the particular interests or subsystems of each business entity: 'The network architecture is a mechanism for a form of communication (including normative communication) that facilitates the merging of these subsystems into a system'. RM Buxbaum, 'Is "Network" a Legal Concept?' (1993) 149 *Journal of Institutional and Theoretical Economics* 698 at 704.

transactions. It may not be helpful to describe other kinds of institutions and business relationships that have also been described as networks. In the case of business format franchises, for instance, it seems clear that the governance structure operated by the franchisor is very much organised to detect default by franchisees, rather than to provide a mechanism for an exchange of information and to facilitate mutual adaptation. Many other examples of networks seem to share this kind of hierarchical triangular relationship, or the pattern of hub and spokes, in which the centre controls the peripheral business entities. However, in the concept of network architecture developed here, it is possible to analyse acephalous or heterarchical organisations as networks, since the co-ordinating architecture may not employ a hierarchical dimension. Supply chains are, however, not unique in fitting this model of a network architecture. Arrangements between banks for transfers of funds and for irrevocable documentary credits used in international trade seem to fit this pattern as well.[19] In these kinds of banking arrangements, the co-ordinating mechanism may be found in clearing systems and in the use of standardised documents formulated by the industry. Similarly, it is possible to describe complex construction projects as heterarchical networks,[20] though often a project co-ordinator employed by the commissioner of the building assumes a hierarchical position with regard to all other contractors.

To put these observations in a slightly different way, institutional economics has typically been interested in the economic functions of hierarchy or governance structures to solve problems of efficiency, especially transaction costs, in economic relations. Although this model can be useful for the analysis of the multi-party relationships in networks, in the case of relatively acephalous networks, the search for hierarchy may blind us to some of the distinctive elements of these relationships. In particular, the architecture for the relationships fixed by the software code itself functions as a system of control without an authority relationship, and co-ordinates remote actors without any formal legal links of contract or organisation.

In order to describe these features of supply chains, it is perhaps useful to denote them as a 'network architecture'. The use of the term architecture is also intended to stress both how the communication systems of the network are the product of deliberate design, and how, once instituted, they regulate the multi-party relationships by their codes of

[19] PW Heermann, 'The Status of Multilateral Synallagmas. In the Law of Connected Contracts' in this volume; M Amstutz, 'The Constitution of Contractual Networks' (ch 16), in this volume.

[20] C Heldt, 'Internal Relations and Semi-spontaneous Order: The Case of Franchising and Construction Contracts' (ch 8), in this volume; RG Eccles, 'The Quasifirm in the Construction Industry' (1981) 2 *Journal of Economic Behaviour and Organisation* 335.

operation. But like a building where the walls and doors control patterns of movement, the network architecture creates a framework that unconsciously steers and co-ordinates the operations of all the participants. A network architecture, in this sense, though lacking hierarchy, possesses a more substantial controlling mechanism than do some other business phenomena that have also been described as networks, such as the connections between small businesses in an industrial region where they both compete and co-operate in the same line of business. In such a local industrial network, there may be co-operation between businesses without any market relationships or hierarchical connections.[21] However, in a network architecture, there are multiple business relationships between more than two parties (the chain), and the architecture serves as a single co-ordinating mechanism for the chain as a whole.

V. NORMATIVE REORIENTATION

Turning, finally, to the legal regulation of supply chains, the question posed is the following one: does this conceptual analysis of the network architecture of modern supply chains either help to develop or require any normative reorientation of the law? The case for believing that some change in the law may be desirable or even necessary rests on the earlier observation that the modern supply chain differs in five dimensions from the traditional legal model of a horizontal chain of isolated sales of goods. Does the network architecture of supply chains require a rethinking of the conceptual analysis provided by the law in understanding and in regulating both these relationships and any disputes that occur within them? There are many reasons for being cautious in advancing an affirmative answer to this question.

First, the observation that the world is more complex than the law imagines it to be must be the normal situation for legal science, and cannot, in itself, be a reason for believing that there is a need to change the law. Since the law operates through norms that seek to have general application, its rules can never reflect all the diversity of concrete situations. The law copes with this problem by various devices, such as open-textured rules, general principles that can provide the source of exceptions, and more generally normative complexity that provides a rich texture of competing norms that can be employed to forge novel solutions in concrete cases. In this particular context of supply chains, there may be sufficient flexibility in the law of sales to permit marginal

[21] EH Lorenz, 'Neither Friends nor Strangers: Informal Networks of Subcontracting in French Industry' in D Gambetta (ed), *Trust: Making and Breaking of Co-operative Relations* (Oxford, Blackwell, 1989) 194–210.

adjustments to legal conclusions where they are either necessary or appropriate in order to reflect the particular details of the network architecture.

Secondly, there is a substantial problem in the context of networks in defining a normative orientation. Private law regulation takes as its starting-point a deceptively simple idea about corrective justice, so that the central justification for permitting a legal claim is to provide compensation for the harm caused to another's interests. Clearly, this simple idea turns out to be extremely complex as soon as one reflects upon issues such as what interests should be protected, and what amounts to adequate compensation. A network architecture presents an additional problem for the normative orientation of private law regulation. In so far that, unlike the traditional legal model of isolated sale of goods transactions, it suggests that there are interests in relationships outside explicit contractual relationships that need to be protected, we become engaged with the question of externalities. In other words, the interests of third parties are external to the interests of the parties to the explicit contracts, and, normally, the legal analysis of private law ignores these interests in order to concentrate on securing corrective justice between the parties to the contract. The task of dealing with externalities is usually assigned to regulatory interventions. The problem presented by the network architecture of supply chains seems to be that the limited palette of private law regulation cannot easily address externalities, even though these third-party relationships and the whole co-ordinating system seem to lie at the core of the distinctive features of modern supply chains. We could, of course, then declare that network architecture must be dealt with by non-private law regulatory interventions, and leave private law alone. But then the question arises of what policy goals should be pursued by regulation in relation to networks.

Thirdly, one should never overlook the potential significance of the fact that the remote parties in the network have not entered into explicit contracts. The absence of explicit contracts in this context is unlikely to be the product of transaction costs, the presence of which might have justified legal regulation. In the supply chain network, remote parties may have a good idea of the identity of each other, and, indeed, they may have dictated their identity, as in the case where the manufacturer dictates to suppliers of components the identity of their suppliers ('approved suppliers', 'nominated sub-contractors'). Explicit contracts are usually possible and may frequently occur even for mass transactions, as in the case of manufacturers' guarantees to the ultimate consumer. The absence of explicit contracts may, therefore, plausibly suggest that the parties have decided to rely upon non-legal sanctions to handle any disputes that occur, or to place the burden of seeking legal recourse on the immediate partner to an explicit contract in the chain. In these circumstances, to impose legal obligations directly between remote parties without explicit contracts may lead to an inefficient distortion of behaviour if these remote parties react by incurring additional transaction costs to ensure that no legal recourse is available, as, for example, by entering into contracts of indemnity or exclusions of liability. This reluctance to impose legal relationships where explicit contracts have been avoided appears to have been the normative orientation behind Buxbaum's famous pithy conclusion '"Network" is not a legal concept'.[22]

These brief observations are intended to advise caution in proposing any kind of normative reorientation of the law. The fundamental difficulty is how to move from facts to norms. Whilst it is vital to ground legal reasoning and criticism of legal thought in an appreciation of the dimensions of the social life being regulated, such an appreciation does not dictate any particular normative stance for the law to adopt. There is no simple move from the achievement of an understanding of a particular social phenomenon or sub-system to a programme for adopting a particular legal analysis. Such a translation is fraught with difficulty. A heavy burden of proof should, therefore, lie on those who argue for disturbing the legal regime of two-party discrete sale of goods contracts in order to capture the network aspects of supply chains in the normative orientation of the law. Combining the fact that networks exist and the problem that the law does not recognise their existence as a distinct form of business relationship does not necessarily lead to the conclusion that the law should construct a category that explicitly supports the functions of the network.

Nevertheless, if we are persuaded that a network architecture comprises a distinct form of economic relationship (or perhaps several analogous forms), not exactly like either a market relationship or an organisation, but one which includes elements of both—the conflicting interests of market relationships and, simultaneously and paradoxically, the unified objective of an organisation—we can argue, on the grounds of welfare maximisation, that the law should recognise this novel institution and support its potential economic benefits by inventing rules that sustain and promote its operations. In other words, the normative orientation of the law should embrace networks by protecting the reasonable expectations of the participants in such novel forms of economic relationships. Even having taken this step, however, it will remain a difficult and controversial issue how best to support the efficient properties of a network architecture without simultaneously distorting or

[22] RM Buxbaum, 'Is "Network" a Legal Concept?' (1993) 149 *Journal of Institutional and Theoretical Economics* 698 at 704.

subverting its qualities. These difficulties concerning the normative orientation of the law and the practical implementation of goals can be explored further by a reconsideration of my two opening stories. This investigation reveals both the potential normative implications of the theory of network architecture and the normative indeterminacy of this revelation.

V.1. Variable Pricing

Having observed the network dimensions of supply chains, it is now possible to understand why it may be reasonable for supermarkets to impose retrospective price cuts. Price variation seems to be necessary in the intensely competitive markets of grocery shopping. A sales promotion by one supermarket chain of charging 10p for a can of beans cannot go unanswered by the other chains for long, without a reduction in customers in their shops. Any supermarket, therefore, has to be agile in its pricing policy, even though it has narrow margins within which to operate because the market is so competitive. As a result, the supermarket needs to share the costs of this agility with its supply chain. To preserve its competitive position, the network as a whole has to bear the costs of price variations. These costs need to be shared throughout the entire chain, since each member of the chain must be concerned about the fortunes of the weakest link—in this case, the supermarket.

Following this analysis, it might be suggested that we need to adjust the normative orientation of the law that 'fixed-priced sales are fixed', that unilateral variations are repudiatory breaches of contract, and that even agreed variations of price reductions are suspect because they can only usually be explained by the exercise of coercion or opportunism. In the network architecture described above, one would instead expect that the governance structure would share the risk of price variation in response to competition down the chain. What may be wrong about the commercial practices observed by the competition authorities is not the unilateral price variation by the supermarket, but the possible absence of a mechanism to share the risk of price variation proportionately throughout the network, instead.[23] We can, therefore, begin to make sense of the supermarkets' suggestion that sometimes price variation is a reasonable commercial practice. It would be reasonable when it was a necessary or

[23] As another example of risk sharing in the chain, in the former Marks and Spencer supply chain, the arrangements (which were explicitly understood not to comprise any contractual undertakings) included a unilateral price and quantity variation clause, but provision was made for reimbursement of suppliers for the cost of raw materials and components already purchased by the supplier: K Blois, 'B2B "relationships"—a social construction of reality?' (2003) 3 *Marketing Theory* 79 at 84.

appropriate response to a marketing initiative of a competitor and when the costs of price reduction could be shared proportionately back up the supply chain. In other words, although the supermarket is working at the sharp end of intense competition in the retail market and must initiate responses to market conditions, it is wrong to see the supermarket as exploiting its suppliers by a price variation, because the success of the supply chain as a whole depends on the supermarket being sensitive to market competition. But the network architecture may not be complete, in the sense that the legal arrangements may not fully co-ordinate a network response to price variation. One link in the chain may be left holding the costs of the price reduction in any particular instance. The network architecture described above seems to have developed codes for adjusting the operations of the network for quantity variation and category management, but not for price variation.

So this story suggests that the legal response of holding the supermarket responsible for breach of contract may misunderstand the problem of network adjustments to external price competition. But even if this is true, it still does not follow that the law should be adjusted accordingly, for the failure of the network architecture to provide mechanisms for handling price variations (as opposed to quantity variations) may be the product of a decision to leave this aspect of network relationships to post-breach bargaining and longer-term adjustments (for example, if the supplier accepts the price cut now, the supermarket will compensate by ordering higher quantities and adjusting prices upwards on other products). Thus, the case for disturbing the traditional law of sales in order to incorporate the complexities of the network architecture is not firmly established.

V.2. External liability of networks

The problem for the victim of stock-outs concerns the external liability of networks.[24] The empty shelf signals a breakdown in the supply chain. Either the code of the software system has not generated the right responses, or someone in the supply chain has failed to comply with the code. As a result, the whole network suffers a reduction in the volume in

[24] 'External liability' here signifies that the consumer does not have a contractual relation with any participant in the network. This terminology differs from some uses where external liability concerns the ability of one participant in the network to 'pierce the contractual veil', that is to claim compensation against another participant in the network (or all participants) even in the absence of a direct contractual link: eg G Teubner, 'Piercing the Contractual Veil? The Social Responsibility of Contractual Networks' in T Wilhelmsson (ed), *Perspectives of Critical Contract Law* (Aldershot, Dartmouth, 1993) 211.

sales, and the consumer becomes the victim of stock-outs. Is it unreasonable for the consumer to seek redress against the system itself, that is, against the network as a whole?

The consumer's problem in retail supply chains is that he or she is both inside the chain for some purposes and outside it for others. The consumer lies at the heart of the chain in some respects. After all, the whole chain is designed to achieve 'efficient consumer response'. Furthermore, the consumer participates in the chain by providing a great deal of valuable information through the computerised records of purchasing patterns that are relayed down the whole network. Yet, in refusing to compensate for stock-outs, the consumer is not regarded by the participants in the supply chain as a member of the network, but as an externality. Everyone else in the chain is likely to have contractual remedies for failures in inventory control against their immediate supplier, even though the network architecture is designed to prevent such breakdowns from occurring. However, the ultimate consumer, for whom the whole system is supposedly created, is excluded from claims about inventory control because the other participants do not acknowledge that the network architecture extends to include the consumer.

Can it be argued that the network architecture could be induced to function even more efficiently if it were forced by the law to internalise the cost of this particular externality (the stock-out for the consumer)? This suggestion would lead to a successful claim by a consumer for the disappointment of not being able to obtain goods that are normally stocked by the retail outlet. Or again, should we leave the ordinary law of sales undisturbed, relying, instead, on the power of non-legal sanctions, namely, that the consumer will shop elsewhere? There can be no doubt that these non-legal sanctions are powerful, for, after all, the computerised ordering system was originally designed to overcome precisely this problem. It seems unlikely that an occasional claim for compensation brought by a disgruntled consumer would significantly alter these commercial pressures and therefore add incentives to the efficient operation of the network.

VI. CONCLUSION

A network architecture describes the links that co-ordinate and control the business entities that participate in a modern supply chain that is organised to achieve an efficient consumer response. This architecture binds together and steers the activities of the participants without using contractual links or a hierarchical organisation. This network architecture does not register on the legal radar, even though it represents a distinctive form of business organisation. It is unclear, however, whether this conclusion necessitates a normative reorientation of the law. Even if it is accepted that the law should support and protect the network architecture for the sake of protecting and enhancing its efficient properties, it remains unclear as to whether or not this policy goal requires legal interventions designed to adjust the results of conflicts within the network or to impose external liability on the network. Although it is tempting to afford legal protection to the weakest link in the network—the supermarket, in the case of price variation in response to intense competition, and the consumer who lacks any contractual claim but who still depends on the functioning of the network—in both instances, non-legal sanctions may serve sufficiently to protect the network from the disintegrative pressures which arise from opportunism, without the need for the law to reallocate liability risks.

11

The Weakest Link: Legal Aspects of Network Architecture of Supply Chains

Comment on the Chapter by Hugh Collins

STEFANOS MOUZAS*

AS A SCHOLAR interested in both 'networks' and 'contracts', but one who does not see the two as being juxtaposed, I find Collins's[1] paper both inspiring and thought-provoking. While at a general, ontological level, the paper does not reject the traditional model of chains of contracts 'in its entirety', it provides a series of critical questions with regard to the accuracy of the empirical picture and reflects on the 'potential implications' for normative re-orientation and regulation, when the alternative, intellectual lens of network architecture is adopted.

At a more specific level, the core of its significant contribution is found in two inter-related analytical propositions[2]:

- *Proposition 1*: The central distinction between 'markets' and 'hierarchies' of modern institutional economics does not help us much to capture the distinctive properties of networks.
- *Proposition 2*: The reason why a network differs from a simple chain of contracts is the existence of a co-ordination mechanism or governance structure which links each node or actor in the chain.

I will start my detailed and, hopefully, constructive critique with a discussion of (a) the accuracy of an empirical picture, and (b) the

* Senior Lecturer at Lancaster University Management School, United Kingdom.

[1] H Collins, 'The Weakest Link: Legal Implications of the Network Architecture of Supply Chains' (ch 10), in this volume.

[2] *Ibid*.

existence of a network architecture. My main objective in discussing these two general points is neither to question the accuracy of the empirical picture provided, nor to express doubts about the usefulness of adopting the alternative intellectual lens of network architecture. My aim here is a rather modest one. I will focus on the empirical observations with regard to the multiple levels of inherent connectivity and negotiation in networks, and will discuss the inherent error of assuming that companies own their networks. I will then move on to the more specific contribution of Collins's paper and comment on the inadequacy of the dichotomy between markets and hierarchies to capture dynamic processes inherent in networks of organisations. Building on the iconoclastic insight of the first proposition, I will discuss the essence of the second proposition and comment on the existence of co-ordination mechanisms among network actors as a form of continuous negotiation among actors. On this matter, I will question Collins's position 'that it remains far from clear what normative implications for legal regulations might be derived' and will proffer an argument that there is a need for the legal recognition of connected contracts. The perceptions of an extended liability throughout inter-firm networks[3] and the increasing use of umbrella agreements (framework contracts)[4] between firms, which provide a framework for future connected contracts, are phenomena that cause significant legal irritations. The law needs to recognise the methods by which contracting parties co-ordinate their aspirations and, by its own, internal, path-dependent evolutionary logic,[5] it could encourage parties' endeavours to maximise their joint gains in networks of exchange relationships, and simultaneously apply the fundamental idea of corrective justice to deal with misfortunes and restore pre-existing equilibria.

[3] The perception of an extended liability throughout networks is not a new phenomenon. In the landmark case *Donoghue v Stevenson*, the decision of the House of Lords, which dates back to 1932, states that a manufacturer of products which sells in such a form as to show that he intends them to reach the ultimate consumer in the form in which they left him, with no reasonable possibility of intermediate examination, owes a duty to the consumer to take reasonable care, although the manufacturer does not know the product to be dangerous and no contractual relation exists between him and the consumer. *Donoghue v Stevenson* [1932] AC 562, [1932] All ER Rep 1.

[4] The term 'umbrella agreement' is widely used in contemporary commercial agreements. Civil law traditions refer to such an agreement as 'framework contract'. For example, German lawyers use the term '*Rahmenvertrag*' or '*Rahmenvereinbarung*' and refer to the civil code *BGB* § 305 Abs 3, which provides that contractual parties are allowed to agree in advanced upon specified general terms and conditions for a particular set of transactions. For comments, see W Krüger, *Münchener Kommentar zum Bürgerlichen Gesetzbuch, Band 2a* (Munich, CH Beck, 2003) 1103–4.

[5] G Teubner, '*Coincidentia Oppositorum*: Hybrid Networks beyond Contract and Organisation' (ch 1), in this volume.

I. THE ACCURACY OF EMPIRICAL PICTURE

From his description of empirical findings published in international business journals, Collins derives a corollary of critical importance to the development of his theory. The corollary is that, in a manufacturer-retailer network, there is a high degree of connectivity between the actors. Hence, manufacturer-retailer networks do not correspond to the traditional economic and legal models. Instead, they comprise organisations which sell and organisations which buy for supply retail outlets. In this way, they reach a population of consumers who demand consumer goods to satisfy most of their elementary needs.[6] The core of each network is formed by major manufacturers and key retailers that represent the greatest share of turnover. These major manufacturers have a wealth of experience in the production and marketing of strong consumer brands in specific product categories such as food and drink, laundry, cleaning and tobacco products, while key retailers with their large number of selling outlets have direct contact with consumers by offering them a broad range of consumer products. The millions of consumers are not just the final stage in the manufacturer-retailer network; their buying behaviour, which is influenced by series of socio-economic and cultural trends, provides the primary stimulus of action and interaction among manufacturers and retailers. At the periphery of each network are the manufacturers, the suppliers, the transport and logistics companies, the banks, the insurance companies, and the consulting and advertising agencies. The ability of the manufacturers to supply retailers and the ability of the retailers to supply consumers does not rely entirely on their own internal assets. The relationships of manufacturers and retailers with third-party suppliers, agencies and banks can be seen as external resources that enable them to carry on their business. This is a web of interconnected exchange relationships.

In such a complex topology, Professor Collins highlights five deviations from the simple model of chain of sale of goods transactions: (a) sellers' orders, (b) marketing decisions, (c) information disclosure, (d) joint design, and (e) architectural coding. While these five deviations are useful tools in order to analyse a number of significant deviations from traditional economic and legal models, they do not fully reveal the multiple facets of how manufacturers and retailers are connected with each other. Much can be gained if we look at the interface and the process of inter-firm interactions. The interface between manufacturers and

[6] A good description of a manufacturer-retailer network which reaches consumers is provided by JM Villas-Boas and Y Zhao, 'Retailer, Manufacturers, and Individual Consumers: Modelling the Supply Side in the Ketchup Marketplace' (2005) 42 *Journal of Marketing Research* 83.

retailers is linked to their evolving organisational structures, while there is the process of inter-firm interaction with institutionalised forms of recursive practice, for example, annual negotiations between firms.

Table 1 provides an overview of a typical interface and inter-firm negotiation. At headquarters level, the historically developed interface is between the retailer's purchasing department (purchasing managers) and the manufacturer's sales department (key account managers). Purchasing and key account managers are responsible for the establishment and development of client/customer relationships, as well as for internal co-ordination, such as with marketing, finance, production, and research and development. At regional and business-centre level, the interface is between the regional key account manager or sales director, and the head of the regional/business centre or distributor. At this level, the representatives of retailers and manufacturers re-negotiate and agree on activities within the framework umbrella agreements concluded at headquarters level. The agreed activities will then be implemented at the outlet level through co-operation between the manufacturers' sales representatives and the retailers' store managers.

In discussing purchasing decisions, Professor Collins does not differentiate between the listing and the ordering process. However, this is a significant differentiation. The lack of attention to the difference between listing and ordering obscures the occurrence of an important phenomenon, namely, that manufacturers and retailers negotiate with each other and that their deals are manifested in umbrella agreements. Moreover, there is no empirical evidence that there is a role reversal in the manufacturer-retailer dyad with regard to the listing of products. Instead, a retailer's purchasing manager is still confronted with space limitation in the retail outlets, and with many different offers from various manufacturers. This requires multiple levels of interface and inter-firm negotiation (see Table 1).

Table 1: Multiple Levels of Interface and Inter-Firm Negotiation

Key Retailer	**Negotiation/ Exchange**	**Major Manufacturers**
Headquarters - Purchasing - Sales - Marketing	Umbrella Agreements: • Listing of product items • Pricing • Trade allowances • Retailer brands • Marketing decisions • Joint design • Information disclosure	Key Accounts Manager Brand Manager Logistics Manager

Key Retailer	**Negotiation/ Exchange**	**Major Manufacturers**
Regional centres/ Business centres/ Distributors	• Architectural coding • Wholesales management • Logistics management • Automated ordering	Regional Key Account Manager
Outlets Store Manager	• Stock management • Merchandising • Displays/Promotions • Contacts with consumers	Sales Director Sales representatives

In the annual negotiations that take place between September and December, manufacturers' key account managers contact the purchasing managers of key retailers and ask for the listing of brands, offering trade allowances as a fee or payment for the distribution that brands obtain.[7] Because of the critical importance of this issue, the manufacturer's key account manager is often supported by the business manager, the brand manager or the logistics manager. The outcome of the negotiations for the individual brand listings is determined by market share, trade allowances and the weight of the retailer brands inside the retailer. Key retailers with discount outlets reserve up to 80 per cent of their shelf space in specific product categories for their own retailer brands. Some retailers, such as Marks and Spencer, dedicate 100 per cent of their shelf space in the non-food business to their own retailer brand. Listing of products is just one of the key issues in the annual negotiations between manufacturers and retailers. Other major issues are pricing, trade allowances, retailer brands, programmatic initiatives activities, joint design and information disclosure. An agreement on these issues constitutes a framework that guides further contracts which may be concluded in the future. There are two important implications here: the first is that umbrella agreements between manufacturers and retailers do not predetermine future selection processes. Ordering processes, for example, may vary from region to region, and will finally be determined by the evolving consumer-demand. The second implication is that 'further contracts in the future' does not imply that these agreements are necessarily long-term contractual arrangements. It is, again, the consumer-demand and the inherent market forces, for example, competition, that will determine the duration of the business relationship.

[7] Trade allowances for new products are often called 'slotting allowances', see MW Sullivan, 'Slotting allowances and the market for new products' (1997) 40 *Journal of Law & Economics* 461.

Manufacturer-retailer networks are typified by regular rounds of price increases. Price increases are usually initiated by the leading manufacturer and followed by other manufacturers of branded products. Price increases are often presented by manufacturers to retailers as a new or revised price list. Retailers are in turn concerned with the increasing cost of goods bought, because they have to pass on higher prices to consumers. In the stagnant or slowly growing consumer goods markets, manufacturers justify the price increases as a necessary mechanism to generate funds for advertising and promotions in a process that is known as 'price up and spend back'. Manufacturer-retailer networks are not only one of the most advertising-intensive businesses in the world, they are also top in running below-the-line promotions, such as trade promotions which include 'per-case' discounts to retailers, 'buy-one-get-one-free' offers, special pack promotions, in-store promotions or co-operative advertising. The price-promotion spiral drives consumer prices up; it prompts retailers to introduce 'variable pricing' and imposes price reductions or the launch of retailer brands produced by third-party manufacturers. Retailer brands not only offer lower prices to consumers; they also offer better trade margins to retailers. Thus, retailers show resistance towards the higher prices of branded products and enthusiastically promote their own retailer brands by fostering co-operation with third-party manufacturers.

Professor Collins's analysis highlights two inter-related symptoms in the whole supply process. The first symptom is the occurrence of stock-outs, or the emergence of excess stock inventory elsewhere in the chain; and the second symptom is distorted information from one end of the supply chain to the other. Thus, the use of information technology is regarded by manufacturers and retailers as a major step towards managing the increasing data flow from the consumer's decision, up to the merchandising and production planning. It tightens the connectivity between retailers and manufacturers, and contributes to a reduction in slack and administrative costs.

II. THE NETWORK ARCHITECTURE

Reflecting on empirical observations, Professor Collins asks the plausible question of whether empirical observations justify the claim that modern supply chains have 'network architecture'. He acknowledges that the term 'network' is widely used in social sciences, albeit without a uniform meaning. Buxbaum's aphorism[8] that 'network is not a legal concept' is

[8] RM Buxbaum, 'Is "Network" a Legal Concept?' (1993) 149 *Journal of Institutional and Theoretical Economics* 698 at 704.

succinct and convincing. But what is a network? Collins proffers the cogent argument that 'networks require at least three parties, at least two exchange relationships but share one co-ordination system'. What he does not make explicit is the fact that not only is the term 'architecture' a metaphor, but so, too, is the term 'network'. The word 'network' itself connotes the connection and interdependence among organisations. As a metaphor, 'network' is anchored in the recognition of markets as networks of exchange relationships.[9] The view of markets as interconnected networks of exchange relationships allows us to operate at a higher level of aggregation than all other metaphors or approaches. It moves beyond dyadic relationships, and allows us to examine whole networks of relationships as the unit of analysis. The network view is sensitive to changes over time; it assumes that companies transform resources in order to carry out transactions which are linked by relationships, and that the cumulative effect of the developments in relationships influences both the position and the network architecture in which the company finds itself. For this reason, the use of this metaphor 'network' as an intellectual lens might lead us to a significant error in our underlying assumptions. This error is linked to the assumption that companies own their networks—an assumption that connotes the vision of a 'quasi-integration' of supply chains, and implies the existence of long-term, relational arrangements that allow for steering and tight control. Even though such inter-organisational arrangements do exist, for example, in symbiotic arrangements[10] in franchised retail operations, the brewery industry or automobile industry, a network, as a general rule, is not a property that companies can own individually. Companies operate in an interacted environment in which they are continuously involved in co-operation and competition with other companies.[11] They negotiate

[9] N Nohria and RG Eccles (eds), *Networks and Organisations: Structure, Form and Action* (Cambridge MA/Harvard, Harvard Business School Press, 1992); JC Anderson, H Håkansson and J Johanson, 'Dyadic business relationships within a business network context' (1994) 58 *Journal of Marketing* 1; T Ritter and HG Gemünden, 'Interorganizational relationships and networks: An overview' (2003) 56 *Journal of Business Research* 691.

[10] E Schanze, 'Symbiotic Arrangements' (1998) 3 *The Palgrave Dictionary of Economics and the Law* 554. Schanze describes symbiotic arrangements as 'thick contracts', which channel the hazards of input and output relationships. This distinct class of transactions requires the existence of certain conditions, such as long term-engagement, contractual documents, absence of control via equity investment, conceptual links expressed in brands or design, relationship specific investments, asymmetry of power, as well as monitoring and sanctioning of contractual behaviour.

[11] H Håkansson and ID Ford, 'How should companies interact in business networks?' (2002) 55 *Journal of Business Research* 133.

with other companies and experiment with new variations of programmes and actions within relevant time-space.[12] At this point, Professor Collins nicely introduces the notion of 'acephalous networks'—in which the co-ordinating architecture does not employ a hierarchical dimension—and emphasises that, in such acephalous networks, 'the search for hierarchy may blind us to some of the distinctive elements of these relationships'.

III. THE INADEQUACY OF MARKET-HIERARCHY DICHOTOMY

Modern institutional economists see the economy as a network of transactions, and postulate two alternative forms for conducting transactions: markets and hierarchies. The two antipodes for conducting transactions provide a simple, but strong, contingency model for investigating the governance structures under which organisations can most efficiently conduct transactions.[13] Collins's first proposition is that these two antipodes for conducting transactions do not contribute conceptually to the effort to capture the distinctive properties of networks. Transaction cost approaches have, indeed, a number of intrinsic weaknesses that make them inadequate for the purpose of researching networks. First, the transaction as a unit of analysis is not adequate for exploring the processual development of network links. Secondly, the transaction cost approach is not sufficient to explain complex inter-organisational exchanges, because it is limited to efficiency as the dominant motivation behind a firm's transactions. And thirdly, it neglects the human and socio-cultural aspects of business relationships.

The critique of transaction cost approaches is now well rehearsed.[14] What needs further investigation, however, is the role of constitutional orders and institutions in networks. The inherent connectivity among actors in networks allows for the development of new expectations. Amstutz[15] argues that 'one appropriate response is to assign these

[12] D Ertel, 'Turning Negotiations into a corporate Capability' (1999) 77 *Harvard Business Review* 55.

[13] OE Williamson, *Markets and Hierarchies: Analysis and Antitrust Implications*, (New York, Free Press, 1975). Williamson's work provided many scholars with an analytical basis to claim that most contemporary transactions are a mixture of markets and hierarchy, see JF Hennart, 'Explaining the Swollen Middle—Why most Transactions are a Mix of Market and Hierarchy' (1993) 4 *Organization Science* 529.

[14] S Ghoshal and P Moran, 'Bad for Practice: A Critique of Transaction Cost Theory' (1996) 21 *Academy of Management Review* 35; see also the response by O Williamson, 'Economic Organisation: The case for Candour' (1996) 21 *Academy of Management Review* 48–57; see P Moran and S Ghoshal, 'Theories of Economic Organization: The Case for Realism and Balance' (1996) 21 *Academy of Management Review* 58–72.

[15] M Amstutz, *'The Constitution of Contractual Network'* (2005) International Conference, Contractual Networks: Legal Issues of Multilateral Co-operation, Fribourg (Switzerland).

emergent orders of expectations to a higher-order constitution'. In a quite different way, Sabel[16] demonstrated that constitutional orders cannot be assimilated by markets or hierarchies:

> Constitutional orders consist of constituent units and superintendents. The constituent units may be market agents such as independent firms. The superintendent may be for example, a court of law, the head office of a public or private hierarchy, the elected officers of an association, a bureaucratic entity, trade associations, unions or training institutions.[17]

Contrasting the concept of constitutional orders with transaction cost approaches, Sabel argued that constitutional orders can solve co-ordination problems among organisations that neither markets, nor hierarchies, can solve. In a similar tone, North[18] draws our attention to fact that,

> [i]nstitutions are the rules of the game in a society, or more formally, the humanly devised constraints that shape human interaction. In consequence they structure incentives in human exchange, whether political, social, or economic.

Similarly, the embeddedness of manufacturer-retailer networks in institutional structures, such as the annual negotiation of umbrella agreements, the development of industry standards and software codes, or the implementation of programmatic initiatives which move beyond dyadic relationships, introduces peculiarities and distinctive properties which need to be addressed.

IV. DYNAMIC PROCESSES INHERENT IN NETWORKS

The increasing preoccupation with the distinction between markets and hierarchy also obscures the dynamic processes inherent in inter-organisational networks. I find it helpful to analyse these dynamic processes in networks as a continuous negotiation among organisations which is determined by three elementary forces:

- Domain consensus
- Goal incompatibility
- Interdependent symbiosis

16 CF Sabel, 'Constitutional Orders: Trust Building and Response to Change' in JR Hollingsworth and R Boyer (eds), *Contemporary Capitalism. The Embeddedness of Institutions* (Cambridge, Cambridge University Press, 1997).

17 CF Sabel, 'Constitutional Ordering in Historical Context' in FW Scharpf (ed), *Games in Hierarchies and Networks: Analytical and Empirical Approaches to the Study of Governance Institutions* (Frankfurt aM, Campus Verlag/Westview Press, 1993) 65 at 73.

18 D North, *Institutions, Institutional Change and Economic Performance* (Cambridge, Cambridge University Press, 1990) 3.

IV.1. Domain Consensus

Domain consensus refers to the degree of agreement over functions and roles within the network. Domains reflect the right to operate and perform within specific areas, for instance, in the production or advertisement of consumer goods, or in selling to consumers. Domain consensus is related to the definition of boundaries, and the establishment of roles and expectations within the network. Domains and boundaries are often disputed and re-defined over time. Boundary maintenance and re-definition are central elements of domain consensus. The fact that domains are often disputed and re-defined over time is vividly demonstrated in the engagement of retailers in boosting their own brands.[19] This tendency can be regarded as an attempt by the retailers to invade domains that are traditionally the preserve of manufacturers, to redefine roles and to re-draw the boundaries of the network in which both retailers and manufacturers are embedded.

IV.2. Goal Incompatibility

Goal incompatibility can generally be related to the extent of incongruities in underlying interests and premises. It can be argued that goal incompatibility is deeply rooted in the fight to capture a share of the value created in the network. It can also be argued that a quest for control is an important factor which accounts for evolution in networks. The distribution of power in a network is unevenly scattered and may change over time. At any time, this distribution may be regarded as the momentary outcome of a struggle in which actors try to increase their power, ie, their control over information, activities and resources. We can posit that the driving forces behind this struggle are human attributes such as greed, in combination with the fact that many resources are scarce. The struggle for control over information, activities and resources includes both co-operative and competitive elements in business relationships. This process generates two opposite and co-existent tendencies: one towards increasing order and consolidation of network architecture, and the other towards increasing disorder and disruption of the existing network architecture. By developing platforms of continuous negotiations within a network, organisations not only gain access to the resources of a single organisation, but they also implicitly seek control over other organisations, and through those they seek control over the business environment.

[19] Retailer brands or private labels are growing rapidly, see D Dunne and C Narasimhan, 'The New Appeal of Private Labels' (1999) 77 *Harvard Business Review* 41.

IV.3. Interdependent Symbiosis

Interdependent symbiosis reflects the need for mutuality and co-operation. Network links pre-suppose the existence of complementarity in information, resources and activities. Complementarity can lead to network links, but this has its price: mutual dependence. Cunningham[20] has argued that the dependence of *R* upon *C* is directly proportional to *R*'s motivational investment in goals mediated by *C*, and is inversely proportional to the attainability of these goals to *R* outside the *R-C* relationship. The customer's goals mediated by the supplier might include low cost, flexible credits, technical advice, etc. Again, dependence brings with it the problem of power. If firms are mutually dependent, then close co-operation will affect and develop their information exchange. Even if complementarity exists, there is always a different degree of interdependence. If firms are mutually dependent, then they may have difficulty dealing with other relationships, but should be able to manage the focal relationship reasonably well.[21]

V. THE EXISTENCE OF CO-ORDINATION MECHANISMS

At the core of Collins's second proposition lies the observation that, because of the increasing economic interdependence among organisations, the primary concern of the co-ordination system is not with the detection of deceit or betrayal, but is, instead, with the exchange of information among organisations to create joint gains and hence to improve the competitiveness of the network as a whole. He moves on to emphasize that

> communication systems are the product of deliberate design, and, once instituted regulate the multi-party relationships by their codes of operations.

What is missing from Collins's description is an answer to the question of 'why' this is happening. If communication systems are the product of deliberate design, then the codes of operations are the effect, not the cause, of the co-ordination effort.

One avenue of inquiry into this matter is to look at the logic of aspiration among actors. The logic of aspiration is concerned with the actors' indeterminate efforts to make the best use of their limited resources. It directs them to negotiate exchanges with other actors in their surrounding networks in order to create joint gains. It is the underlying

[20] MT Cunningham, 'The Power Game Paper—A Study of Power Within Supplier-Customer Relationships' (1993) 9th IMP Conference, University of Bath.
[21] G Easton, 'Industrial Networks: A Review' in B Axelsson and G Easton (eds), *Industrial Networks: a New View of Reality* (London, Routledge, 1992).

logic of aspiration that brings about any resultant exchange in the network. This, in economics, is expressed as a logic that relies on the principle of marginal utility[22] in order to make the most efficient allocation of the available resources. Not surprisingly, lawyers do not usually embrace the logic of aspiration. They prefer the logic of duty, instead.[23] Law does not condemn actors for failing to embrace the existing business opportunities, but it does condemn actors for failing to respect their duties. Thus, it may be irritating to observe that the primary concern in networks is not with the detection of deceit or betrayal, but with the exchange of information among actors, instead. The existence of the logic of aspiration among actors has one significant implication, namely, that re-negotiation[24] becomes a way of life in inter-firm networks. This is demonstrated in the institutionalised forms of annual negotiations, periodic business reviews and the sharing of information. Thus, firms retreat from the immediate conclusion of contracts, and arrange umbrella agreements to create a framework of monetary, informational and physical exchanges. This is, in fact, a framework for the conclusion of connected contracts. Such a framework may confer powers on the parties to vary their initial position, and may enable them to modify or re-negotiate some of their own duties. Thus, umbrella agreements may regulate relationships with third parties. They may also confer discretion on parties to make the best use of their capacities, such as to determine prices or stock levels, or to exercise their powers under jointly agreed criteria. Notwithstanding the increasingly significant role of institutions such as courts, the co-ordination in networks is invariably the resultant outcome, as firms relate to each other.

VI. CONCLUSIONS AND NORMATIVE IMPLICATIONS

The high degree of connectivity among organisations brings into question the accuracy of the empirical picture of modern supply chains. Manufacturer-retailer networks demonstrate distinct characteristics,

[22] Margin and Substitution are two powerful tools of economic analysis developed by A Marshal; see RH Coase, *The firm, the market and the law* (Chicago, University of Chicago Press, 1988) 33.

[23] This preference among lawyers is, however, confronted with a problem of relativity. Contract law, for example, can be seen as 'a regime of correlative right and duty'. According to Weinrib, 'the unity of the contractual relationship consists in the fact that contractual performance is the content of both the defendant's duty and the plaintiff's right', see EJ Weinrib, *The Idea of Private Law* (Cambridge MA, Harvard University Press, 1995) 136.

[24] See J Tirole, 'Procurement and renegotiation' (1986) 94 *Journal of Political Economy* 235; I Segal, 'Complexity and Renegotiation: A Foundation for Incomplete Contracts' (1999), 66 *Review of Economic Studies* 57; I Ayres, 'Valuing Modern Contract Scholarship' (2003) 112 *The Yale Law Journal* 881; see also N Cohen and E McKendrick (eds), *Comparative Remedies for Breach of Contract* (Oxford/Portland OR, Hart Publishing, 2005).

which do not correspond to the traditional economic and legal models. The need to move beyond dyadic relationships and examine the impact of these relationships on third-party relationships makes the use of the 'network' as a metaphor attractive and useful. The problem with networks, however, is that they do not have a uniform meaning and/or defined boundaries. Collins's term of 'network architecture' offers a more accurate and palpable picture than the linear depiction of 'supply chains' or the faceless topology of 'markets'. Nonetheless, the more significant contribution of Collins's paper is found in two specific and inter-related propositions. Collins's two propositions invite us to escape from the dichotomy between markets and hierarchy, and explore the dynamic negotiation processes inherent in networks. They also invite us to look at the existence of co-ordination as the product of deliberate design, as parties relate to each other. Much can be gained if we look at how firms define the basic principles of how they wish to relate to each other. It appears that parties achieve much better co-ordination when they are able to rely upon focal points of principles and rules which express a framework of mutually-perceived expectations and shared appreciation.[25] It is precisely these umbrella agreements that may contribute to the creation of such a framework. This is, in practice, a framework of monetary, informational and physical exchanges, which are facilitated by institutionalised forms of continuous negotiations. The law needs to recognize the methods by which firms co-ordinate their aspirations and, by its own evolutionary logic, it could encourage parties to maximize their joint gains in networks of exchange relationships. The three legal conditions of connected contracts suggested by Teubner[26]: (a) mutual referencing of contracts, (b) purpose (*Zweck*) and (c) co-operation, could build a starting point for a legal reconstruction of networks. A legal recognition of connected contracts does not appear to be impossible. What is far more challenging is how to deal with the problem of network externalities. How can we deal with the interests of the parties which are external to the interests of parties to the interconnected contracts? Given the fluid and, often, blurred boundaries of inter-firm networks, as well as the limited tools of private law, it is far more practicable to let the issue of externalities be dealt with by regulatory interventions such as governmental policies. All other attempts would not only be impracticable, they

[25] The importance of focal points in achieving effective co-ordination is demonstrated by TC Schelling, *The Strategy of Conflict* (Cambridge MA, Harvard University Press, 1960). For the importance and the difference between 'Principle' (*Grundsatz*) and 'Rule' (Norm), see J Esser, *Grundsatz und Norm* (Tübingen, Mohr & Siebeck, 1956).

[26] G Teubner, '*Coincidentia Oppositorum*: Hybrid Networks beyond Contract and Organisation' (ch 1), in this volume.

would also interfere with freedom of contract; and the whole essence of freedom of contract is precisely to leave parties free to negotiate their own contracts.

12

The Protection of Contractual Networks Against Interference by Third Parties

MANFRED WOLF*

I. COMBINATION OF SEVERAL CONTRACTS TO ACHIEVE A COMMON GOAL

DIVISION OF LABOUR on the one hand, and ambitious technical and economic objectives on the other, require the co-operation of several players in order to achieve their intended goals. An important means to secure such co-operation is a contractual relationship between the players. If several parties are involved, then a bundle of contracts may be necessary to achieve the goal.

The contractual co-operation of several parties can result in a partnership, or in the foundation of a company in which all the participants are parties to the same contract. But contractually-based co-operation can also take place if there are several contracts between different parties, so that it is not just one contract that forms the connecting link between the parties, but several contracts that are linked together by a common goal. The latter form of contracts is known as a chain contract or a network contract.

I.1. Chain Contracts

Contracts linked together in a transportation line from a train to a truck, to an aeroplane, and to a truck again are an example of a chain contract. Chain contracts can also be found in the transfer of money, especially in cross-border transfers from one country to another. In such transfers, several banks are involved, one after the other, starting with the bank of the debtor, with each of the intermediary banks receiving and passing on the money, like the baton change in a relay race, until it finally arrives at

* Professor of Civil Law and Procedural Law, Johann Wolfgang Goethe University, Frankfurt.

the bank of the creditor. Lease and sub-lease are also chain contracts.[1] The characteristic of such a chain contract is that one contract is put behind the other and the antecedent contract must be performed in order for the successive contract to be implemented.[2]

I.2. Net Contracts

In a net contract system, there is an organising leader that forms contracts with several other parties in order to put them together to offer the combined product to the customers.[3] Examples of such contracts can be found in the automobile industry, in which the parts of many suppliers are assembled together in order to build the car as the final product.[4] The same is true in the construction industry, where one primary contractor organises many sub-contractors in order to build a construction or a chemical plant, for example. The contracts which a tour operator concludes with a car transportation service, with an air carrier and with a hotel in order to offer a package holiday to his customers, according to § 651a *BGB*, also form a network contract in this sense.

Another kind of network contract is the franchise system, in which the franchisor, as the system leader, forms the contracts with the franchisees so that each of the franchisees may separately distribute the products or offer the services created by the franchisor, using both the franchisor's trademark and the business plan.[5]

II. PROTECTION OF SUCH CONTRACT COMBINATIONS AS A NEW APPROACH

In contrast with the problems discussed so far, I will not address the problems of damage caused by a breach of contract by one party of the

[1] See M Amstutz, *Die Verfassung von Vertragsverbindungen*, in M Amstutz (ed), Die vernetzte Wirtschaft: Netzwerke als Problem (Zürich, Schulthess 2004) 11.

[2] K Larenz and M Wolf, *Allgemeiner Teil des bürgerlichen Rechts*, 9th edn (Munich, CH Beck, 2004) § 23 para 127 *et seq*.

[3] See, eg *ibid*, § 23 para 130 *et seq*.

[4] See, eg A Merz, *Qualitätssicherungsvereinbarungen: Zulieferverträge, Vertragstypologie, Risikoverteilung, AGB-Kontrolle* (Cologne, O Schmitt, 1992); M Wellenhofer-Klein, *Zulieferverträge im Privat- und Wirtschaftsrecht* (Munich, CH Beck, 1999).

[5] See M Martinek, 'Abzahlungsgesetz und Absatzmittlungsverträge' (1986) 7 *Zeitschrift für Wirtschaftsrecht* 1440–49; G Teubner, '"Verbund", "Verband" oder "Verkehr"?—Zur Außenhaftung von Franchisingsystemen' (1990) 154 *Zeitschrift für das gesamte Handelsrecht und Wirtschafsrecht* (*ZHR*) 295 at 305 *et seq*; B Haager, 'Die Entwicklung des Franchiserechts in den Jahren 1997 und 1998' (1999) 52 *Neue Juristische Wochenschrift* (*NJW*) 2081–6, and B Haager, 'Die Entwicklung des Franchiserechts in den Jahren 1999, 2000 und 2001' (2002) 55 *NJW* 1463–75.

chain or the network contract, but will instead examine cases in which third parties damage the chain or network and thereby cause damage to all or some of the members of the chain or the network. In order to discuss the problem, some cases decided by German courts will be examined with some variations.

II.1. The Product Test Case

The Federal Court of Justice (*Bundesgerichtshof* (*BGH*)) held that the right to carry on one's business is adversely affected if a product test is falsified, be it deliberately or through negligence, and thereby causes damage to the business.[6] If the assumption is made that such a product test refers to a product distributed by the franchisor in his or her franchise system, and because of the false statements, the turnover of the franchisor and the franchisees is reduced, then the question arises as to whether the business of the franchisor and his or her franchise system alone is affected, or whether the franchisees, too, can recover the loss that has occurred because the rights of their own established and on-going business (*Recht am eingerichteten und ausgeübten Gewerbebetrieb*) is infringed, or whether the network of the franchise system is itself protected against infringements by third parties.

II.2. Intellectual Property Cases

The same question arises if the trademark provided by the franchisor for the franchise system is illegally used by a third party, or if a third party gives a false warning not to use specific intellectual property rights.[7] Can only the franchisor or can the franchisees also recover damages for their losses?

II.3. The Strike Case

Another possible case could be that an enterprise is brought to a standstill by an illegal strike. The German Federal Labour Court (*Bundesarbeitsgericht* (*BAG*)) decided that, in such a case, the right of the established and on-going business has been violated, too, and that the losses suffered can be recovered by the enterprise which has been directly

[6] See, eg BGH (1997) 50 *NJW* 2593 at 2595.
[7] See, eg BGH (1979) 38 *Entscheidungen des Bundesgerichtshofs in Zivilsachen (BGHZ)* 205 and more recently BGH (2005) 58 *NJW* 3141.

affected by the strike.[8] What if we suppose that the business affected was not a single enterprise, but a network of contracts, such as the contracts between several suppliers and the assembler, and that the strike was carried out in the assembler's enterprise or in the enterprise of a supplier which affects all other suppliers, because if one product is missing the whole production is affected? Which enterprise can recover damages, the assembler alone or all the other suppliers if they, too, have losses caused by the standstill in production? Should it make a difference if the net contracts were the contracts of a tour operator instead?

II.4. Chain Contract Cases

What are the consequences if, instead of network contracts, a system of chain contracts, such as a transportation line or a system of banks linked together in a money transfer, is affected either by an accident involving one of the transport vehicles, or if the transfer system is interrupted by a computer virus? Can only the firm which is directly affected recover its damages, or can the other members of the chain also claim for compensation?

III. PROTECTION OF ENTERPRISES UNDER GERMAN LAW

III.1. General Principles

Under German tort law, a claim for damages is only awarded in three cases:

1. If an absolute right, such as a property right, is intentionally or negligently violated (§ 823 I *BGB*), or
2. If there is a breach of a law which protects the interests of a specific person (§ 823 II *BGB*), or
3. If a person intentionally damages another person through immoral behaviour (§ 826 *BGB*).

III.2. Right of the Established and On-going Business

In order to be in a position to award damages in the cases mentioned above, an absolute right must be violated by the injuring party. In French law and in English law, in applying the general clause of tort law, judges

[8] BAG (1978) 31 *NJW* 2114; BAG (1989) 42 *NJW* 1881.

examine the behaviour of the injuring party in order to assess its illegality without having additional statutory criteria. In contrast to this, under German law, in the absence of a protective law, the violation of an absolute right is necessary to indicate that a type of behaviour is unlawful and, in the absence of any special justification, provides the grounds for the recovery of the damages. Because of this situation, the German Federal Court of Justice (*Reichsgericht* (*RG*)[9] and *Bundesgerichtshof* (*BGH*)[10]) invented the right of the established and on-going business, or, as it is also called, the right of the enterprise (*Recht am Unternehmen*), in order to have an absolute right by which to indicate the illegality of the behaviour in cases of violation thereof.

The existence of the right of the established and on-going business (*Recht am eingerichteten und ausgeübten Gewerbebetrieb*), its content and its character as an absolute right is very much discussed among German scholars.

Some of them deny such a right and claim that protection can be found only by applying the law of unfair competition (*UWG, Gesetz gegen den unlauteren Wettbewerb*), or, if the business is intentionally damaged through immoral behaviour, they apply the principles of liability for intentional immoral behaviour (§ 826 *BGB*).[11] But this protection is too weak. The law of unfair competition does not apply if the injuring party is not in competition with the injured party, and liability for intentional immoral behaviour gives no protection against behaviour which negligently violates the business activities. Thus, the right of the established and on-going business should be acknowledged by the judiciary in order to give adequate protection to its business activities.[12]

The right of the established and ongoing business poses problems in so far as its function to indicate the illegality of the behaviour is not very strong. The normal reasons to justify behaviour are not sufficient to draw a line between illegal violations of the right in an enterprise on the one hand, and on the other legal behaviour which, although it affects the business, is not unlawful, such as competition or such as the freedom of speech. Thus, when a right of an established and on-going business is accepted, it is nevertheless necessary to continue with a comprehensive weighing of interests before the respective behaviour can be determined as being unlawful. Nevertheless, it makes sense to accept a right of the enterprise because it gives a first indication that the illegality of the

[9] RG (1904) 58 *Entscheidungen des Reichsgerichts in Zivilsachen (RGZ)* 24; RG 73 *RGZ* 107.

[10] See BGH 8 *BGHZ* 142; BGH (1966) 45 *BGHZ* 296 at 307.

[11] K Larenz and C-W Canaris, *Lehrbuch des Schuldrechts*, 13th edn (Munich, CH Beck, 1994) § 81 III.

[12] A gap in the protection of enterprises is also mentioned by BGH (1966) 45 *BGHZ* 296 at 307.

underlying behaviour will be examined carefully. In this restricted function, it is, at least to German minds, better to have the right of the established and ongoing business as a first indication of illegality, rather than to have no such indication.

Other legal systems also award damages in cases similar to the German cases of the violation of the right of the enterprise, such as boycott cases, strike cases, product test cases and others. But, instead of construing a right of the enterprise as an absolute right, they directly address the unlawfulness of the injuring behaviour such as the concept of *faute* in French law.[13] The English law is somewhat confusing, in that it is not clear how far the concept of negligence can be applied to protect pure economic losses.[14] In other cases belonging to the concept of economic torts, some kind of intentional, immoral behaviour is required in order to obtain compensation for damage.[15] Taking this data as a basis, it is difficult to give an answer as to whether English or French law would award compensation if network or chain contract systems were damaged by act of negligence alone.

The German concept of the established and ongoing business raises the question of whether there is a fiduciary object (*Schutzgut*). This makes it easier to give an opinion as to whether an infringement of business activities is an unlawful act or not. It also makes it easier to decide on whether network contracts or chain contracts have a common fiduciary object (*Schutzgut*) or if there are only simple contractual relations and nothing else. Thus, it is not surprising that the Plenary Panel of the Federal Court of Justice (*Großer Zivilsenat*) only recently decided that it would adhere to the rule that a negligent false warning to use intellectual property rights is a violation of the right of the established and ongoing business.[16] The Plenary Panel of the Federal Court of Justice (*BGH*) is a common panel of all civil law panels, composed of 13 judges, and includes the President and the Vice President of the Federal Court of Justice (*BGH*), eight chairpersons of the civil law panels of the Court, and some other judges. The Plenary Panel has to decide whenever two panels express different opinions regarding certain legal questions. In this case, it was the question of whether the concept of the violation of the established and ongoing business could still be applied in the event of a false warning to use intellectual property rights. As already mentioned, the Plenary Panel sanctioned the right of the established and ongoing business.

[13] C von Bar, *Gemeineuropäisches Deliktsrecht* (Munich, CH Beck, 1996) vol I, number 38 *et seq*.

[14] See *ibid*, number 285 *et seq*.

[15] *Ibid*, number 260.

[16] BGH, 15.7.2005 *GSZ* 1/04.

In this context, it should be noted that, in Italian law, the right of free entrepreneurial initiative, which more or less corresponds to the German right of the established and ongoing business, is used to give protection in cases where several businessmen who co-operate without forming a single enterprise are exposed to a boycott.[17] From this standpoint, it seems useful to ask whether network contracts or even chain contracts possess something which forms a binding link between the members of such contractual formations, which could be assessed as a fiduciary object (*Schutzgut*) against assaults from outside.

IV. PROTECTION OF NET AND CHAIN CONTRACTS AGAINST THIRD PARTIES

IV.1. Conventional Compensation for Infringement of Net and Chain Contracts

IV.1.(a) The Product Test Case

Looking first at the franchise system, one could say that the franchisor certainly could recover his damages in the product test case, because his right of the established and ongoing business was damaged. According to general opinion, the franchisor's damages would comprise only the lost profits of his own enterprise, including any losses caused by the reduced payments by the franchisees because of a decline of their turnover. However, the franchisor could—from a general viewpoint—not recover the lost profits that the franchisees had suffered because of the decline of their turnover. Indirectly, the franchisor could recover the franchisees' losses if the franchisees themselves had damage claims against the franchisor, and the franchisor would suffer damages through the compensations he would have to pay to the franchisees. However, under German law, such damage claims exist only in so far as the franchisor wilfully or negligently breaches his contractual duties to the franchisees. In cases of an incorrect product testing, normally, no such faulty behaviour can be attributed to the franchisor. Thus, in many cases, no damage claims from the franchisees against the franchisor can occur.

IV.1.(b) The Strike Action Case

The same rules apply in cases of strikes in the franchisor's business, or if the strike occurred in the factory of an assembler or a supplier. Parties

[17] von Bar, *Gemeineuropäisches Deliktsrecht* (n 13 above) 62, number 49.

who have no contractual relationships to the person causing their damages or who are not protected by an absolute right under the present doctrine basically cannot file claims for damages. Nevertheless, the German Federal Labour Court has granted compensation to an enterprise which was affected by a strike in another enterprise.[18]

IV.1.(c) Abuse of Intellectual Property Rights

Similar questions arise in cases where a third party makes a false warning not to use specific intellectual property rights, which can cause, for example, a stoppage of production, or when a third party violates the trademark or another intellectual property right of the franchisor or the assembler, and thereby detracts profits from the franchise system or from the assembler-supplier co-operation. Is only the franchisor or the assembler in a position to recover his or her damages, or can also the franchisees and the suppliers get compensation for the damages suffered by them?

IV.1.(d) Abuse of Licensed Intellectual Property Rights

In the case of an intellectual property right being violated by a third party, the licensee has his licence violated, too, and thus may recover damages from the third party only if he has an exclusive licence, not if the licence is non-exclusive licence. The situation is somewhat different if a trademark licence is concerned. The German Trademark Law contains special provisions concerning the licensees. According to § 30(3), a licensee may recover damages from the third party regardless of whether his licence is exclusive or non-exclusive.[19] However, the licensee may bring an action against a third party only with the consent of the owner of the trademark. If the owner of the trademark has already entered into a lawsuit, the licensee may join this suit and ask for compensation for his own losses (§ 30(4)). Thus, in the franchise cases where the franchisees have a licence in the trademark of the franchisor, the franchisees are protected together with the franchisor. They can claim their own damages from the third party, and in cases where the franchisor does not give his consent to a suit against the third party they may claim damages from the franchisor. So far they need no additional protection. But if members of the network contract system have no licence in intellectual property rights, as the case may be in the co-operation of assemblers and suppliers, or if the licence is not protected against third parties, such as

[18] BAG (1989) 42 *NJW* 61.

[19] R Ingerl and C Rohnke, *Markengesetz*, 2nd edn (Munich, CH Beck, DATE) § 30, fns 8 and 73.

non-exclusive licences in intellectual property rights other than trademarks, then—according to present doctrine—the members of the network contracts can obtain no compensation for their damages.

IV.2. Search for a Subject of Protection of Network and Chain Contract Systems

The question thus arises as to how the parties of a network or a chain contract can be protected and how they can be compensated. Have network contracts or chain contracts a substance that goes beyond the mere contractual relationships which can be protected like an absolute right, and which could be attributed to the single members of the net or chain system?

Although the franchisees have per se the right of the established and ongoing business, it is doubtful whether their right would be protected in the light of the opinion of the Federal Court of Justice (*BGH*). Contractual supply relationships are not protected under the right of the established business because the business is not affected directly (*kein betriebsbezogener Eingriff*). For example, the Court decided that disruption in the delivery of electricity did not directly affect the business in question.[20]

In general, the Court holds that every business is exposed to competition and has to endure the interference that results from such competition.[21] This reasoning would certainly apply to the franchisees in cases of a false product test. The Court would certainly argue that the franchisees could exercise their business by obtaining their products from other suppliers. In addition, under the present understanding, the Court would probably hold that it is the concept, the know-how and the whole system of the franchisor, which is protected by the right of the established and ongoing business. But this right is not violated on the part of the franchisees. For the same reason, the right of the established and ongoing business can only be protected in favour of the enterprise in which the strike took place, but not in favour of other businesses, such as the businesses of the franchisees or of the suppliers that were only indirectly affected by the strike that took place in the enterprise of the franchisor or in the enterprise of the assembler. In addition, a false warning not to use intellectual property rights would only harm the franchisor or assembler that claimed to possess the intellectual property right, but would not affect the franchisees or the suppliers in their rights.

However, such reasoning does not take into consideration the fact that it is not only the franchisor and the assembler, but also the franchisees

20 BGH (1958) 29 *BGHZ* 65.
21 BGH (1980) 33 *NJW* 881 at 882.

and the suppliers that are part of the network contract system—with its constantly instituted organisation and all its ideas, trademarks, and know-how, which includes the good will to be found in the appreciation of the customers. If the business were part of the business of the franchisor or the assembler, then the courts would certainly not hesitate to grant it protection. But it would make no practical difference if the business of the franchisor or the assembler were outsourced to the franchisees or to the suppliers. The person who publishes the false product test and the workers who organise the illegal strike should not profit from the fact of the outsourcing. The substance of the whole business is affected in the same way, regardless of whether the business is a branch integrated into the enterprise of the franchisor, or whether it is outsourced into semi-autonomous businesses of the franchisees. In addition, it could be assumed that the courts would also give protection and grant damages to the whole system if the relationship between the franchisor and the franchisees were construed as an association.[22] But, again, whether the legal construction of the franchise system is an association or not makes no difference as far as the attribution of damages is concerned. The affected interest is always the same. The only difference is that, in the first case, the violated interests are part of the franchisor's business as a single enterprise, and in the second case, they are part of the business of the association, whereas, in the third case, the same interests are split among several semi-autonomous franchisees. The violated interests as the fiduciary object (*Schutzgut*) in all cases remain the same.[23]

The question of whether the social relationship of networks, such as a franchise system or a just-in-time delivery system between the assembler and his suppliers, can be assessed as a collective unit is not only relevant in connection with the liability of the members of the system against third parties,[24] but is also relevant for the protection of the system against assaults from outside. But, instead of the circumvention of legal duties by the system, which could be treated similarly to a corporate group[25] by piercing the network's veil,[26] or through a 'double'—ie, a joint—liability arising from the hybrid collective system,[27] the protection of such systems forces us to search for goods and interests which can be attributed

22 Such protection is granted by BGH (1992) 45 *NJW* 41.

23 A similar arguement is used by G Teubner, *Netzwerk als Vertragsverbund* (Baden-Baden, Nomos, 2004) 223 *et seq* in connection with the liability of the members of a network.

24 See *ibid*, 216 *et seq*.

25 *Ibid*, 220.

26 In analogy to 'piercing the corporate veil', Teubner (*ibid*, 224) uses the term piercing of the contractual veil.

27 *Ibid*, 218 *et seq*.

to all members of the system and which are worth protecting as common goods and interests against assaults from external assaults.

IV.3. Market Supply and Fixed Supply Model

The reason for German courts not to protect supply relationships against infringements by third parties certainly lies in the fact that supply relations in the market, in contrast to supply arrangements within enterprises or associations, are not continuous relationships, but are instead exposed to competition and can therefore vary over time. I will call this the 'market-supply model'. In contrast, supply arrangements within an enterprise or a corporate group are carefully organised to secure reliable and continuous delivery. I will call this the 'fixed-supply model'. Whereas a disruption in the ordinary delivery relationship between market participants in the market-supply model could, in general, easily be repaired and smoothed out by looking for another supplier in the market place, an interruption of the supply arrangement in the fixed-supply model within an enterprise or corporate group may cause severe problems because suppliers from outside could not easily adjust to the specific requirements and needs of the production process of the enterprise or the association. In addition, much effort has been employed to create such continuous supply arrangements within the business entity. This, according to the German courts, could justify a specific protection of such well-organised continuous arrangements in the form of the right of the established and ongoing business.[28] The organisational creations of the entrepreneur, which are essential to the functioning of an enterprise, should be at the core of the right of the established and ongoing business to be protected, and thus correspond to other intellectual ideas and achievements which are the substance of intellectual property rights and the supplementary protection of intellectual property in the German Unfair Competition Law (*UWG*).[29] The question, therefore, is whether network and chain contracts should be associated with the market-supply model or with the fixed-supply model. This can be evaluated only by looking at specific network or chain contracts.

[28] The business arrangement is stressed by BGH (1961) 14 *NJW* 968; BGH (1969) 22 *NJW* 1207. The functional inter-relations of the production facilities and the assets of the firm are mentioned in BGH (1983) 36 *NJW* 812 at 813.

[29] See § 4(9) *UWG* (German Unfair Competition Law).

IV.4. The Franchise System as Fixed-Supply Model

With regard to typical franchise contracts, I would assign them to the fixed-supply model. The franchisee is generally bound by the franchise contract to receive the products and services offered by the franchise system, from the franchisor or from a supplier determined by the franchisor. Thus, the franchisee is not in a position to select his or her suppliers in the market place, but has to rely on the supply system offered by the franchisor. On the other hand, the franchisor has expended much effort to establish the delivery arrangement within the franchise system. Thus, the delivery arrangement within the franchise system can be compared with the internal delivery system of an enterprise or within an association, and should, therefore, be assigned to the fixed-supply model.

There are additional grounds for associating the franchise system with the right of the established and ongoing business. For example, the franchisees make use of a trademark established by the franchisor, or they profit from the know-how of the franchisor as well as from his or her advertising in favour of the franchise system. Considering this, the franchise system could easily be compared with a business entity of a single enterprise as far as the essential elements of the right of the established and on-going business are concerned.

IV.5. The Assembler-Supplier System as Fixed-Supply Model

The same questions arise with regard to the relationship between the assembler and his suppliers. Are there such strong interconnections between the assembler and his suppliers that their system could be compared with an enterprise before the outsourcing? Does it make a difference, for example, if there is a disturbance in production through a workers' strike before the outsourcing of certain elements of the production process or after the outsourcing?

If the market- and fixed-supply test is applied again, it is important to establish whether the contractual relations provide for a fixed-supply model which ties the supplier to deliver exclusively—or at least mainly and with priority to—the assembler, on the one hand, and which binds the assembler, on the other, to obtain the equipment and accessories for his production exclusively—or at least mainly—from a certain supplier connected with him. If no such close connection exists between the supplier and the assembler, but each of them could take care to meet their own needs in the market place, then the relationship between the assembler and the supplier is not comparable to a single enterprise and should not be protected. But if there is a fixed-supply connection which comes close to the supply and production process in a single enterprise before the outsourcing of the linkage between supplier and assembler, it should be considered as one entity as far as the protection of the production process against illegal strikes is concerned.

The consequence is that a strike, for example, in the assembler's firm could affect the supplier and force him to curtail, or even stop, his production in the same way as if the production line were integrated into the enterprise of the assembler. On the other hand, a strike in the supplier's firm could damage the assembler in the same way as if it were in its own enterprise. Under these conditions, the assembler-supplier relationship should be protected as if it were one enterprise, and thus the outsourcing should be disregarded.

To give such protection, the connection of the assembler together with its suppliers should be regarded as an established and ongoing business entity, even though it is a composition of several firms and not just one single enterprise. But, in accepting the composition of several firms as the owner of the right of an established and ongoing business, the protection of this right could be granted according to the German tort law.

IV.6. Chain Contracts as Market Models

As an example of chain contracts, a bank transfer could be examined in the event that two or more banks are connected one after the other to carry out the money transfer. If one bank in the chain fails to pass on the money transfer, then the other banks in the chain are not really damaged. They can continue their whole business and all the other transfers. Damage arises only for the recipient who cannot dispose of the money, or affects the sender because he or she has to pay interest for the delay. The same is true in the transport chain. Thus, it can be stated that in these cases of chain contracts, and probably in most of them, no common fiduciary object (*Schutzgut*) exists for the chain members, and all of them can recover only their damages individually as though chain contracts did not exist.

V. LEGAL PROTECTION OF FIXED-SUPPLY MODELS

So far, two cases have been found—the franchise case and in the assembler-supplier case—where, according to German rules, a right of the established and ongoing business can exist. The question is what is the object and what are the ingredients of the established and ongoing business in these cases and to whom this right should be attributed?

V.1. Organisation of Net Contract Systems as Protected Property

The ingredients of the franchise system which constitute the right of the established and ongoing business are the same as those which are characteristic to the franchise system, ie, the trademark and other intellectual property of the franchisor which all the franchisees may use, the know-how which the franchisor makes available to the franchisees, the common name under which all the franchisees may act in the market, the goodwill which stems from the firm's name, the advertising of the franchisor, and last, but not least, the whole organisation which was built up by the franchisor. Although these ingredients of the franchise system belong primarily to the franchisor, the franchisees also suffer damage if these factors are damaged and not properly dealt with by third parties. Thus, the whole system should be considered as an all-comprising protected property.

Similar considerations could be applied to the relationship between the assembler and his suppliers. If the supply relationships between the assembler and his suppliers are so closely connected and organised as in a single enterprise, even though they are different entities and not an association, they should be protected as though they were a single firm which enjoys protection under the right of the established and ongoing business. The same principles should apply in cases of a primary contractor working together with sub-contractors and in cases of a tour operator according to § 651a *BGB*. But who is the beneficiary of this protected property?

V.2. Fractional Property for the Members of the Network Contract System

The franchise system which consists of a franchisor and many franchisees cannot be treated like a single businessman or like a legal person. Likewise, the franchise system is not an association and cannot be treated as an association, because there are no contractual relationships among the franchisees. There are also no common assets (*Gesamthandsvermögen*) which is typically connected with an association. But the German legal system offers a legal institution which could be used for the franchise system. This is the fractional property. The franchisor and each franchisee have a fractional property in the ingredients which form the franchise system, which is, in turn, protected by the right of the established and on-going business. The organisational unit between the assembler and his suppliers could also be regarded as the fractional property of all the members of the system. Similar thoughts can be applied to the relationship between a primary contractor and his or her sub-contractors or in case of a tour operator according to § 651a *BGB*.

V.3. Compensation for the Violation of the Network Contract System

As a consequence of fractional property, a single member of these systems can recover damages if the system is illegally infringed upon because of false product tests, false warnings to use intellectual property rights, illegal strikes, insulting criticism or boycotts. The same protection should be granted to the franchisees and the suppliers in the assembler-supplier system for violation of the franchisor's or assembler's trademark or other intellectual property rights. Although the franchisees or the suppliers have no licence in the trademark of the franchisor or the assembler, they are adversely affected if, because of the decline in the turnover of the franchisor or the assembler, their own turnover and their profits decrease. The third party who infringes the trademark of the franchisor or assembler has to bear the consequences and cannot profit from the fact that the franchisees or the suppliers are outsourced and are not an integrated part of the franchisor's or assembler's firm. Instead of an integrated single firm, the constantly instituted organisation of the franchise system or the assembler-supplier network contract system is the fiduciary object. These principles could again be applied respectively to the relationship between a primary contractor and his sub-contractors, or in cases of tour operators according to § 651a *BGB*.

But a member of the respective system can recover only his own damages and not the damages caused to the whole system. Thus, the franchisees can only claim compensation for the damages suffered by their own individual businesses, and the franchisor can only recover damages for the damage that he or she personally suffered, ie for example, the costs of rebuilding the franchise system and the lost profits of his or her business. Likewise, the assembler can obtain compensation only for the damages that he or she suffered and the suppliers can claim compensation for their own damages.

The objection could be raised that, by granting such a fractional right to each member of the system, and by granting compensation for the respective damages of each fractional owner, the injuring party could be excessively burdened because he or she had to pay for damages of several, or even all, members of the system. But the counter-argument against such objections is that the damages would be the same, or at least similar, if the franchise system or the assembler-supplier system were integrated in one enterprise and were not outsourced. Furthermore, the injuring party has to take care of the goods and property rights of the other people involved in the system and cannot claim that his or her illegal behaviour causes damages only to a single separate enterprise.

VI. FINAL REMARKS

The concept outlined above is certainly a progressive one and is not in conformity with the presently prevailing doctrine. But new phenomena require new solutions. Thus, the expansion and, at the same time, the revival of the right of the established and ongoing business should be a real option. Network contract systems and, possibly, also—albeit to a lesser extent—chain contract systems should be protected against interference by third parties under the right of the established and ongoing business if they are organised as fixed-supply models, ie if their internal structure is organised in a way that the members of the system are constantly tied together by their contractual relationships and are therefore dependent upon each other.

13

Fitness Clubs: Consumer Protection between Contract and Association

GRALF-PETER CALLIESS*

DURING THE LAST decade fitness has become the most popular sport in Germany and many other countries. According to a 2006 market report by IHRSA,[1] a trade association serving the industry, at the end of the year 2005 the percentage of people who were members of a commercial or public fitness club amounted to 8.1 per cent in the European Union, compared to 15.7 per cent in the United States. Front runners were The Netherlands with 15.5 per cent, Spain with 14.8 per cent and Great Britain with 12.8 per cent. With 8.5 per cent, Germany was around the average of the European countries. However, in absolute numbers, almost one million more Germans work out in fitness studios than are members of a football club. While in the United Kingdom, for instance, public and commercial providers of fitness studios share the market on an equal footing, in Germany in particular, the traditional non-profit-making sports associations have proven unable to compete with the ever more sophisticated professional services offered by commercial fitness clubs.

A 2005 study of the German market by Deloitte[2] revealed that 6.5 per cent of the population aged 15 and above were members of a commercial fitness club. Big cities like Hamburg with 10.7 per cent showed the highest penetration rates. A continuing market growth is expected, driven by a variety of factors, such as a general rise in service quality

* Professor of International Business Law, University of Bremen

[1] International Health, Racquet and Sportsclub Association in partnership with Deloitte, *The 2006 IHRSA European Market Report*, available at: http://store.ihrsastore.com/438nmd.html. A table comparing market penetration in Europe and the USA is provided at: http://cms.ihrsa.org/IHRSA/viewPage.cfm?pageId=796.

[2] See the study of Deloitte, *The German Health and Fitness Market*, 2005, available at: http://www.healthclubbenchmark.com/Content/Resources/Publications/GHFM.aspx. Key findings provided at: http://www.healthclubbenchmark.com/Content/PressRoom/Articles/20060426Germany-EN.aspx.

standards (for example, wellness), the diversification and specialisation of services (for example, family clubs, the health- and grey-markets), and the professionalisation of service providers brought about by market concentration (for example, take over and franchise). The market is highly competitive, as indicated not only by a drop in the average annual revenue per customer from 600 Euro in 2001 to 520 Euro in 2005, but also as expressed by the variety of marketed terms and conditions: While the typical contract duration, for example, lasts from six months to one year, members may also choose from an array of different options, from prepaid 'pay as you go'-plans with one-month termination periods to long-term memberships of two years or even longer.

Consistent with some general trends in modern western society—such as the drift of the economic centre of gravity from the industrialised production of goods towards the service sector, an increasing awareness of health and fitness in an aging society, and, more generally, the trend towards individualisation—sports as a functional sub-system of society seems to have become increasingly economised, as is also the case with other functional sub-systems, such as education, science, and healthcare. Today's working mothers pay for child-care services on the (black) market, while far too young-looking grandmothers buy wellness in luxurious spas. Whereas sport was traditionally organised within the public sector, with the state financing the infrastructure of public sports facilities which were run by non-profit-making sports associations that were represented by volunteers elected from and by their membership, people today willingly exchange their sovereignty as a voter, tax payer, or club member for sovereignty as a consumer of fitness services. Cuts in public spending on sports, where the state is plagued by deficit and low growth as in Germany, might be one reason for this. However, it must also be admitted that people simply prefer to receive high quality (for example, wellness) and flexible (for example, late opening hours) professional services over non-competitive public and not-for-profit services.

'Health Clubs', 'Sports Studios', or 'Fitness Gyms' usually use the term 'Membership' in their customer contracts, partly to make their customers feel more cosy and affiliated to the business, and partly to make the long-term relationship character of the contracts transparent to their customers. In legal terms, however, health clubs are not organised as associations with members. They are just ordinary businesses offering standard form contracts to individual customers, which—with the exception of stuntmen and supermodels—usually enter into the contract for a private, non-commercial purpose. It follows that the fitness studio contract qualifies as a business-to-consumer contract of adhesion, for example, under Section 310 III of the German Civil Code (*BGB*), and is thus subject to various consumer protection regulations, such as Sections 1812.80 *et seq* of the Civil Code of California,[3] or the European Unfair Contract Terms Directive.[4]

However, the underlying economic rationale of the fitness club is not met in cases where the respective contractual arrangements are treated simply like any other business-to-consumer standard form contract. In this paper, I will put forward the argument that the formal legal structure of fitness clubs, which, on the surface, consists of a multitude of parallel, but separate, bi-lateral consumer contracts, is misguiding in a similar way, as is the case with corporate groups, just-in-time networks, or franchise systems. In the former as in the latter cases, lawyers should engage in 'piercing the legal veil': when compared with other organisational forms and business models in the sports and health industry, the fitness club is specific in creating a club-like structure of mutual subsidies between its members, thus loosening the tight *'do ut des' synallagma* of the bilateral and reciprocally-binding business-to-consumer contract. In contrast to the 'privity of contract'-dogma, the very idea of the fitness club is about creating a community by means of networked contracts. After first explaining the hybrid nature of the fitness club as a third model which goes beyond the traditional alternatives of sports associations and pay-per-visit facilities (1), I shall then introduce and compare the US and European approaches to the regulation of fitness clubs (2), in order to show that both, in their aim to protect the individual consumer, tend to neglect the networked structure of the relevant contracts, although the European approach, with its inherent flexibility, could easily take the network rationale into account in the future (3).

I. CONNECTED CONSUMER CONTRACTS: THE FITNESS CLUB AS A HYBRID

'Network is not a legal concept'.[5] This statement was cited over and over again in the conference presentations which are assembled in this volume. So, is Richard Buxbaum right or wrong? In my opinion, it is the very question that Buxbaum has posed, namely, 'Is "Network" a Legal Concept?', which is wrong, or at least misleading. This is because, on the

[3] State of California, Governor A Schwarzenegger, Department of Consumer Affairs, Overview of California's Health Studio Services Contract Law, May 2003: http://www.dca.ca.gov/legal/w-10.pdf.

[4] Council Directive 93/13/EEC of 5 April 1993 on Unfair Terms in Consumer Contracts: http://europa.eu.int/comm/consumers/cons_int/safe_shop/unf_cont_terms/index_en.htm.

[5] RM Buxbaum, 'Is "Network" a Legal Concept?' (1993) 149 *Journal of Institutional and Theoretical Economics* 698 at 704.

one hand, the term network is clearly not a basic legal *concept* such as 'contract', 'tort', or 'association' are. As far as I can see, however, no one has ever promoted this idea. On the other hand, the presentations made at this conference have given ample evidence of the fact that network *is* actually used as a legal *argument*, not only in the scientific discourse, but also in adjudication. Gunther Teubner has suggested the term 'connected contracts' (*Vertragsverbund*) in order to define the precise conditions under which the socio-economic network-concept turns into a *valid* legal argument, ie, an argument which makes a difference in the process of law (for example, in contracting, legislating, or adjudicating) within a given legal system.[6] In the following, I intend to show that the term 'connected contracts' can fruitfully be applied to fitness clubs in order to integrate a socio-economic network effects-analysis into the process of judicial control of standard-term fitness contracts.

Sport for the masses is traditionally organised in the form of a club with athletes as its members or on an individual 'pay per use' basis, ie, under two different legal regimes: association or contract. Sports clubs are non-profit-making entities, in which members pay membership fees on an annual basis and, in addition, an annual fee for the right to practise a specific sport or activity. Most sports clubs do not finance their sports facilities, but are provided with free or low cost access to public sports facilities. Others, such as golf or yacht clubs, own their facilities and, in order to re-finance them, will often ask for very high entrance fees, thus selling their membership like shares. Others, again, are very attractively situated or have an exclusive membership, which they market for high fees.[7] Subsidised by the state or not, the very idea of a sports club membership is not aimed at an economic exchange of fees for the use of sports facilities. Sports clubs, like any other clubs, are also about F-connections,[8] which are so important in politics and business, about social status, meeting friends, being part of a community, about elderly people subsidising the youth, the amateurs subsidising the semi-professionals, etc. It follows, that the fairness of the rules and fee models of sports clubs cannot be judged on the economic basis of the contractual '*do ut des*' *synallagma*. In theory, all members, by virtue of their voting power, have democratically legitimised the rules and fees of a club. In practice, however, clubs are mainly governed by a small, established élite, and new members can only join on a 'take it or leave it' basis.

[6] G Teubner, *Netzwerk als Vertragsverbund* (Baden-Baden, Nomos, 2004).

[7] See H Kempf and F Moizeau, 'Conspicuous Consumption, Social Status and Clubs' (July 2000), FEEM Working Paper No 58.00: http://ssrn.com/abstract=237455.

[8] Y Ben-Porath, 'The F-Connection: Families, Friends, and Firms and the Organization of Exchange' (1980) 6 *Population and Development Review* 1–30.

In contrast to clubs, public sports facilities are run on a 'pay-per-use' basis. There is no long-term relationship between the owner of a public swimming pool or a tennis court and its users. Sports facilities open to the public may be run by the state or by a private business. I do not want to go into the details of the traditional public law relationship between state-owned facilities and their users (*öffentlich-rechtliches Anstaltsnutzungsverhältnis*)[9], since, today, most sports facilities run by the state are organised in the form of a publicly-owned limited partnership. As a result, the legal relationship between state-owned sports facilities and their users has become contractual. The state and private businesses today usually finance the facilities on credit. In order to re-finance these investments, the fees for the single use of the facilities have to be quite high. The reason for this is that there are no subsidies in this business model between frequent and rare users, customers just pay for what they get. Since individual use varies a lot over the seasons, between weekdays and weekends, between mornings and afternoons, and between early and late evenings, the hourly fees vary a lot as well, so that, for example, the same indoor tennis or squash court might be marketed at between 5 and 50 Euro per hour. The economic rationale behind this fee structure is that the owner of the facility has to earn the annual average fixed costs of the facility in the, let us say, 500 to 1000 peak hours of the year.

If we turn now to the business model of the typical fitness club, it seems to be clear that it is a kind of combination of *both* the contractual *and* the club models. The membership in an exclusive fitness club could be prestigious as well, but most users of fitness clubs do not want to socialise with other users as much as would be the case in a real sports club. At the same time, for a traditional sports club, it would be very difficult to finance the initial investments, since the modern fitness industry has turned into a high-tech business, and the usual 'wellness' add-ons are very expensive as well. A sports association, however, in itself is not credit-worthy like a business, unless its members initially contribute high amounts of money. For these reasons, fitness studios are better run by a private business. On the other hand, fitness is a sport which, when compared to other sports, should be undertaken on a very regular basis. At the same time, the users of fitness studios want to be flexible in their time schedules. This inherent structure of the fitness sport would lead to the necessity of excessive peak-hour fees, if it were organised on a 'pay-per-visit' basis. If users make a contract for longer

[9] See HJ Wolff, O Bachof and R Stober, *Verwaltungsrecht* (Vol 3), 5th edn (Munich, CH Beck, 2004) § 88 I 1 No 2, p 353.

time periods, however, the business has a much better basis for calculation, and is able to offer its services for a reasonable flat rate. For these reasons, fitness clubs mainly offer their customers long-term contracts, which they call memberships.

When compared to other industries, however, the mere fact of offering long-term contracts does not lead to a networked structure of connected consumer contracts. Annual newspaper subscriptions, for example, do not produce any specific inter-relationship among the readership. Hence, there is no relevant difference to a big retailer, offering thousands of customers the sale of goods on exactly the same standard terms and conditions. In the case of fitness clubs, the deal is somewhat different. The club does not offer its members a right to use specific training machines at a specific time of the day. Instead, the members simply have the right to use the facilities whenever and as often as they want to within the limits of the general opening hours. But this right is, in practice, limited by the same right of all other members of the fitness club. While users in a 'pay-per-use' facility are transferred an exclusive right of use within a limited period of time, and it remains the responsibility of the business to regulate the usage by means of a demand dependent fee structure, in a fitness club, this task is left to the *spontaneous self-organisation* of the membership.[10]

The fitness club somewhat resembles the German regulation of the use of motorways, where car owners just pay a flat tax, while the state regulates their use only indirectly, by transmitting traffic jam information and (with much delay) infrastructure investments at bottle-necks. Thus, shopping for a fitness club membership can be compared to buying a car. Instead of renting one only when it is actually needed, it is simply a decision on having the convenient and permanent opportunity of use within the limits set by the road use of all the other car owners. Some enjoy empty roads and high speed driving at night, others cannot avoid the daily rush hours. Thus rare users subsidise frequent drivers, but on 1 January one is usually unable to predict how many miles one will drive during the year. It is clear from the outset that one will not use the car when flying abroad for holidays, when one becomes ill, or when losing one's driving licence. But the car will be sold only when such prevention from use becomes permanent.[11]

[10] See, for a different opinion, M Wolf, in M Wolf, N Horn and WF Lindacher, *AGB-Gesetz*, 4th edn (Munich, CH Beck, 1999) § 9 F 129.

[11] Golf clubs and highways are classical examples for the so-called 'club goods' in the economic literature; see, only, JM Buchanan, 'An Economic Theory of Clubs' (1965) 32 *Economica* 1–14; and P McNutt, 'Public Goods and Club Goods' in B Bouckaert and G de Geest (eds), *Encyclopedia of Law and Economics* (vol I), *The History and Methodology of Law and Economics* (Cheltenham, Edward Elgar, 2000) Pt 0750, p 927 *et seq*, with extensive references.

It is important to understand that this nature of the club membership only works on the basis of long-term contracts. Only in the long run, ie, over a minimum period of, let us say, one or two years, is there a chance that the individual frequency of use of one member will somehow level out with the ups and downs in the use of the other members, so that, at the end of the day, an economic optimum in the average use of the infrastructure is reached, which allows the owner of the facility to ask for a reasonably low flat fee from all users (although some cross subsidies between rare and frequent users will prevail). It is precisely the *uncertainty* about the exact time and frequency of future use, combined with the regulation of these factors through spontaneous self-regulation among the membership, which—in my opinion—justifies the characterisation of fitness clubs as a hierarchic network of (inter-) connected consumer contracts, ie as a legally hybrid construct in between, or beyond, the bilateral business-to-consumer contract and the traditional sports association.

II. US AND EUROPEAN APPROACHES TO THE REGULATION OF FITNESS CLUBS

When compared to one-off or spot-market contracts, long-term contractual relationships are characterised by specific economic risks and legal problems, especially when they come with long cancellation periods or when they are entered into for a fixed time period, ie where the normal right of cancellation is excluded. From the point of view of the producer of goods or services, the risk lies in the obligation of future performance in exchange for a fixed price, where production costs could rise or money could be inflated. From the point of view of the consumer of the product, the risk lies in the contingency of his or her future personal interest in the use of the product ('*Verwendungsinteresse*'), and in a potential future decrease in his or her budget. In addition, long-term contracts involve the risk of opportunistic behaviour in so far as the producer may have an incentive to degrade the product quality over time, as the consumer's options are limited to 'voice', and 'exit' possibilities are excluded. Finally, from the point of view of economic policy, the problem with long-term contracts is that free competition is hampered when consumers are unable to switch producers.[12]

Since fitness club memberships usually qualify as consumer contracts, it is no wonder that, as a symbol for the described economisation of sports both in the United States and in Europe, they caught the attention

[12] See, eg, J Basedow in *Münchener Kommentar zum Bürgerlichen Gesetzbuch* (Vol 2 a), 4th edn (Munich, CH Beck, 2003) § 309 No 9 para 1 *et seq*.

of consumer policy and are subject to more or less specific regulations. In the United States, there is no specific regulation at federal level. However, as early as 1961, California's Health Studio Services Contract Law was enacted (Civil Code §§ 1812.80–1812.95).[13] Under these regulations, health studio services include instruction, training or assistance in physical culture, body-building, exercising, reducing, figure development and other similar skills, the use of a health studio, gym or other facilities for any of these purposes, and membership in any group formed for any of these purposes. All health studio contracts must be in writing and must state the length of the contract term in 14-point type near the place for the buyer's signature. The duration of the contract may not exceed three years, and it may not require payments that total more than US$ 1,000 over the contract term; lifetime contracts are explicitly prohibited. Furthermore, the contract must conspicuously disclose that the buyer has a three-day right to cancel after its conclusion. In addition, the contract may be cancelled at any time if the buyer becomes disabled in a way that affects his capacity to use or enjoy the club's facilities—which must be verified by a physician—or if he or she moves more than 25 miles from the facility and is unable to transfer the contract to a comparable facility belonging to the same company. In both cases, a pro-rated portion of any prepaid amount must be refunded. Any contract not complying with these regulations is void and injured buyers are entitled to triple damages.[14]

In Europe, there are no sector-specific regulations for fitness clubs, but the terms and conditions of the respective consumer contracts are subject to the European Unfair Contract Terms Directive,[15] which, in Germany, is transposed into national law by §§ 305 *et seq BGB*.[16] In the last decade, judicial control of the general business terms of fitness clubs in Germany produced a vast amount of court rulings, which often were not triggered

[13] Available at: http://www.leginfo.ca.gov/calaw.html, search 'health studio'.

[14] See again A Schwarzenegger, 'Overview of California's Health Studio Services Contract Law' (n 3 above).

[15] See n 4 above, and Basedow, *Münchener Kommentar zum Bürgerlichen Gesetzbuch* (n 12 above) before § 305 *BGB*.

[16] See, generally, Basedow, *Münchener Kommentar zum Bürgerlichen Gesetzbuch* (n 12 above) §§ 305 *et seq BGB*; to the predecessor, the German Unfair Contract Terms Act, which was integrated into the *BGB* in 2002, see Wolf, Horn and Lindacher, *AGB-Gesetz* (n 10 above).

by individual consumers, but by abstract proceedings brought by consumer pressure groups.[17] Recently, academia has started to analyse and systematise the available precedents, and, thus, a German (case) law on fitness contracts has evolved.[18]

First of all, the Federal Court of Justice (*BGH*) ruled that, irrespective of the duration of the contract, customers do have a right to extraordinary cancellation at any time, if they are permanently disabled from using the facility because of illness or because of events or circumstances which lie beyond the sphere of influence and responsibility of the customer.[19] The underlying rationale of this ruling, ie, the general principle that any long-term contractual relationship may be terminated without a cancellation period for important reasons, is today codified in § 314 *BGB*, and subsequent case law has confirmed that the right to the extraordinary cancellation of a fitness club membership also extends to customers who become pregnant, are called up for military service, or have to change location with the result that the distance to the club becomes unreasonably long.[20]

With regard to the duration of a fitness contract, ie the maximum time period for which the right of the customer to the so-called 'ordinary cancellation' of a long-term contractual relationship may be excluded, things are not that clear.[21] Under § 309 No 9 *BGB*, the term of a contract for the supply of services cannot exceed two years, and an 'automatic prolongation if not cancelled'-clause must be for a maximum period of one year. But § 309 No 9 *BGB* is not directly applicable to fitness club memberships, since they are usually categorised as mixed contracts for

[17] This is especially true for the decisions of the Federal Court of Justice (*BGH*), the most important ones being BGH (1997) 50 *NJW* 193, 195; and 739, where, in each case, a publicly-financed consumer protection association brought the proceedings.

[18] See, generally, FG von Westphalen, 'Fitneß- und Sportstudiovertrag' in von Westphalen (ed), *Vertragsrecht und AGB-Klauselwerke* (Munich, CH Beck, 2004); see, also, S Velhorst, *Fitneßcenter und Kunden. Die zivilrechtlichen Grundlagen der Rechtsbeziehungen zwischen Fitneßcentern und Kunden* (Baden-Baden, Nomos, 2000); and P Schwefer, *Die Wirksamkeit Allgemeiner Geschäftsbedingungen in Fitness-Verträgen* (Berlin, Jurawelt, 2003) (Juristische Reihe Tenea Vol 46, available at: http://www.jurawelt.com/download/dissertationen/tenea_jurawelt bd46.pdf).

[19] See BGH (1997) 50 *NJW* 193 and 195, with a very strange, if not completely misguided, dogmatic reasoning with regard to § 323 *BGB*; see also Schwefer, *Die Wirksamkeit Allgemeiner Geschäftsbedingungen in Fitness-Verträgen* (n 18 above) 131 *et seq*, who seems to be of the opinion that contrary to the clear formulations in the usual contracts and to the above described club-like nature of the fitness club the owner fulfils his obligations under the contract only, if the customer actually uses the facility.

[20] See, extensively, Schwefer, *Die Wirksamkeit Allgemeiner Geschäftsbedingungen in Fitness-Verträgen* (n 18 above) 141 *et seq*, 143 *et seq*, for the different reasons which could justify an extraordinary cancellation.

[21] See G von Westphalen, 'Fitneß- und Sportstudiovertrag' (n 18 above) at para 9; Basedow, *Münchener Kommentar zum Bürgerlichen Gesetzbuch* (n 12 above) § 309 No 9 BGB at para 8, 12 *et seq*; Schwefer, *Die Wirksamkeit Allgemeiner Geschäftsbedingungen in Fitness-Verträgen* (n 18 above) 91 *et seq*.

the supply of services and the rental of the facilities, in which the latter element is dominant. However, judicial control of these clauses can still be exercised under the so-called general clause of § 307 *BGB*. And here, on the one hand, lower courts in Germany are generally applauded by legal scholars for strictly limiting the initial duration of memberships to a maximum time period of six months,[22] sometimes even when the customer was offered a choice between different durations for different prices.[23] The Federal Court of Justice (*BGH*), on the other hand, ruled that judicial control of contract duration clauses under the general clause of § 307 *BGB* has to take into account the decision of the legislator entrenched in § 309 No 9 *BGB*, even when it is not directly applicable, thus indicating that initial fitness club membership periods could last up to two years.[24]

When comparing the Californian and the German approaches to the regulation of fitness clubs, it is striking that both—although achieved in the formal regulatory structure of prospective sector-specific legislation on the one hand, and by retrospective judicial control over the fairness of individual contract terms on the other—substantially deal with the same problems and have come up with similar solutions. This is true especially with regard to the rules concerning the regulation of the 'extraordinary cancellation' of membership for reasons of health problems or the relocation of members. However, with regard to the maximum duration of the contract, the Californian approach is much less flexible, since the time limit of three years applies, but does not necessarily fit *all* kinds of health studio services contracts covered by the regulations, not all of which imply the above described network effects on members. At the same time, the maximum price of US$ 1,000, which was amended on the last occasion in 1981, in effect, also works as a limitation on the duration of the contract, but is very inflexible with regard to the above-described differentiation of the fitness studio market. Especially high-end services can only be offered for very short fixed periods under this regime. In

[22] Graf von Westphalen, 'Fitneß- und Sportstudiovertrag' (n 18 above) at No 11; otherwise Schwefer, *Die Wirksamkeit Allgemeiner Geschäftsbedingungen in Fitness-Verträgen* (n 18 above) 106 *et seq*, if the price difference between the two options is reasonable, for example, 15% between the six-month and one- year options; generally, for choice of tariff clauses, see Basedow, *Münchener Kommentar zum Bürgerlichen Gesetzbuch* (n 12 above) § 307 *BGB* No 43.

[23] Graf von Westphalen, 'Fitneß- und Sportstudiovertrag' (n 18 above) No 10; Basedow, *Münchener Kommentar zum Bürgerlichen Gesetzbuch* (n 12 above) § 309 No 9 BGB at para 16; Schwefer, *Die Wirksamkeit Allgemeiner Geschäftsbedingungen in Fitness-Verträgen* (n 18 above) 105

[24] BGH (1997) 50 *NJW* 739 upholding a prolongation clause of six months. Consenting Wolf, 'Eingangstor fur die mittelbare Drittwerkung der Grundrechte im Privatrecht' (n 10 above) § 9 F 129; dissenting Basedow, *Münchener Kommentar zum Bürgerlichen Gesetzbuch* (n 12 above) § 309 No 9 BGB at para 16; Schwefer, *Die Wirksamkeit Allgemeiner Geschäftsbedingungen in Fitness-Verträgen* (n 18 above) 95 *et seq*, 100.

contrast, the German approach allows for very flexible, case sensitive regulation of the maximum duration of memberships, as I intend to show in the final section of this paper.

III CONNECTED CONSUMER CONTRACTS: A DIFFERENCE THAT MAKES A DIFFERENCE?

When the fairness of a standard term contract clause is challenged under the regime of the general clause of § 307 *BGB*, judges will, first of all, compare this clause with the just solution which is embodied in the so-called dispositive statutory law, from which the clause deviates (§ 307 II No 1 *BGB*). However, often the *BGB* does not contain a clear-cut rule for the problem posed by the particular standard contract clause, which could be used as a standard for a fair solution. This is especially true for non-classical contracts, which provide mixed obligations, as in the case of fitness club membership, which resemble atypical rental and service contract obligations. In these cases, the judges have to derive the standard of fairness from the 'nature of the contract' (§ 307 II No 2 *BGB*). Since it is much easier to say what is unfair, rather than to define what is fair, in practice, the judges will simply test the particular contract clause as it is by asking whether it takes the legitimate interests of both parties into account or not. What the courts actually do here is embark upon a process of weighing and balancing of the party interests.

In the case of judicial review of clauses on the duration of contracts, the courts take into consideration all circumstances of the individual case. For example, if the continuation of the contract with regard to the price constitutes a financial hardship for the consumer, or if the maintenance of a good personal relationship between the consumer and, for example, an instructor is a precondition, then the consumer has a very high interest in a short cancellation period. If, in turn, long cancellation periods are necessary or even essential for the business in question, then this interest may prevail. In case of contracts for education, the Federal Court of Justice (*BGH*), for instance, ruled that the economic and organisational interests of the school have to be taken into account. Thus, cancellation periods should be quite short in cases of individual instruction, since the necessary personal relationship with the instructor is essential, so that the instructor should bear the risk of early termination. However, in direct classroom education with limited participants, longer cancellation periods may prevail, since drop-outs in the middle of the year or term are difficult or even impossible to replace. Thus, a school class constitutes a kind of network based upon common learning progress and should not be disrupted by early cancellation as long as the duration is reasonable also in terms of education. The same is not true for distance learning contracts, where a sector-specific consumer protection regulation in Germany provides for a maximum duration of six months, in all circumstances (§ 5 *FernUSG*).[25]

When this analysis of party interests is applied to the membership of a fitness club, there is—as stated in my introduction—the danger of judging this relationship as a bilateral business-to-consumer contract only, without taking into account the network character which was described in part one of the paper. This is because long cancellation periods are seen as being in the interest of the business alone, while the consumer always seems to be interested in a contract of short duration.[26] This shortcoming is partly due to the retrospective character of judicial review of the fairness of standard contract terms under §§ 305 *et seq BGB*. This is because such judicial review is only exercised in individual cases, in which the consumer has, for some reason or another, lost his or her interest in the continuation of the membership. When the duration of the contract is judged from this *ex post* perspective—of course—the question arises as to why the consumer should continue to pay for a right which he or she does not intend to make further use of. However, the proper perspective for an analysis of the interests of the consumer is *ex ante*, ie, at the time the decision on entering into the contract was made. Thus, the question is whether it was reasonable then for the consumer to enter into the respective long-term membership.

As shown above, the business model of the fitness club is based on the uncertainty of each individual member about the exact time-table and frequency of his or her future use of the facility and the resulting cross-subsidies between the membership, some of whom later turn out to be frequent, and some to be rare, users, and a lot of whom go through individual phases of frequent and less intense training. From this perspective, it is one reasonable consumer choice among other possible choices to enter into a long-term membership, thus forming a community with other users, in the hope that one turns out to be a frequent user who will profit from the cross-subsidies by other users. If, however, members which, *ex post*, find themselves on the side of the net-payers are allowed to drop out early, either the whole business model of the fitness club will cease to work and people will have to pay higher prices which are economically consistent with shorter cancellation periods. Or—if early drop-outs through court litigation remain an exception—the fitness club

[25] See BGH (1992) 120 *BGHZ* 108 *et seq*, voiding a standard term period of 24 months in a direct classroom education contract for professional dancers with reference to the freedom of choice of occupation under Art 12 of the German Constitution (the '*Grundgesetz*'), but allowing for a binding period of one school year; see also Basedow, *Münchener Kommentar zum Bürgerlichen Gesetzbuch* (n 12 above) § 309 No 9 *BGB* at para 16 with further references.

[26] See, eg the interest analysis of Schwefer, *Die Wirksamkeit Allgemeiner Geschäftsbedingungen in Fitness-Verträgen* (n 18 above) 101 *et seq*, with further references.

model will remain successful, but consumers who, for reasons other than health problems or relocation, drop out early simply because they have changed their minds are allowed to engage in free-riding.

Let me explain this fact with an example. Amy ('*A*') shops for a fitness club. From the various offers on the market, she pre-selects club *B*, offering a one-year memberships for 60 Euro per month, and club *C*, offering a two-year membership for 40 Euro per month. If *A* chooses club *C*, and, after one year, drops out early on the basis of judicial review of the contract terms, as a result, she will have enjoyed an offer which was unavailable on the market, ie one year for 40 Euro per month. So, who pays the 20 Euro difference? Actually, the difference is paid by the membership of club *C*. This is because *A* entered the club as a frequent user, subsidised by the then rare users of the club. However, when *A* turned out to become a rare user herself, she decided to exit instead of keeping her promise to the other members, which was to subsidise them in turn. This example is even more striking when both fee models are offered within the same club, which is often the case. Fitness clubs frequently offer a rebate of up to 25 per cent for long-term contracts, for example, 400 Euro for one year and 600 Euro for two years. If *A* exits after a year, she will have had the first year for 300 Euro. Naturally, the other members do not pay the 100 Euro difference directly, since their contract terms are fixed. However, the business somehow has to, and, indeed, will, find a way to forward the loss from early drop-outs to its customers.

This is not to say that the duration of fitness club memberships should always be two years or even longer. It is just to say that a one-year, or even two-year, duration of a membership is not, in itself, unfair to consumers, when the network character of the fitness club and the related advantages to its members are taken into account. However, what is important is that the duration of the membership and—if available—the different options are transparent to the consumer, when he or she is shopping for fitness.

In addition, further consequences may result from the network character of fitness clubs. The longer the average duration of memberships in a fitness club is, the more the club becomes similar to the traditional sports association. For instance, when members cannot exit from club membership quickly, the incentive for the club owner to free-ride on the contracts by enlarging the membership to an extent that leads to over-crowding of the facility increases.[27] In theory, such over-crowding of the club would give the members the right to reduce, or even to withhold their monthly payments fully (§ 536 *BGB*). Since it is quite difficult for the individual

[27] Regarding the problem of overcrowding of clubs, see the economic analysis of P Manzini and M Mariotti, 'A Tragedy of the Clubs: Excess Entry in Exclusive Coalitions' (July 1999), FEEM Working Paper No 58.99: http://ssrn.com/abstract=200629.

member to prove this fact, clubs marketing memberships with durations over one year could be obliged, for instance, to report on the development of membership on request, so that intentional over-crowding of the club by its owner can be prevented.

14

*Regulation of Hybrid Networks at the Intersection between Governmental Administration and Economic Self-Organisation**

ANDREAS ABEGG**

I. IRRITATIONS IN LAW: CO-OPERATION BETWEEN GOVERNMENT ADMINISTRATION AND PRIVATE PERSONS IN NETWORK FORM

I.1 The Case: Swiss Federal Court Decision 109 Ib 146 (1983)

TODAY'S *increasingly co-operative relations between the state and private persons* have brought numerous new problems to the law. It may even be held that the new types of 'co-operationism' between the state and private persons has plunged the law into deep crisis. This is because by freeing the administration from the constraints which are binding by statute, on the one hand, and transferring to private entities competences hitherto incumbent on government for the upholding of public interests, on the other, the basic pillars of democracy under rule of law are called into question. This can be illustrated very clearly by the example of decision 109 Ib 146 (1983) of the Swiss Federal Court on the Agreement on the Swiss banks' code of conduct with regard to the exercise of due diligence (abbreviated as 'CDB'). But this is not all: decision 109 Ib 146 also indicates that the problem of co-operationism may be closely connected with another new sort of phenomenon which is increasingly irritating the law: the *organisational form of the network*.[1]

* Translated by Iain L Fraser.

** PD Dr iur, LL.M, attorney-at-law, Zürich/Switzerland, abegg@besbes.ch

[1] According to G Teubner, '*Coincidentia Oppositorum*: Hybrid Networks beyond Contract and Organisation' (ch 1), in this volume, a network, or combination of contracts, exists where, first, the bilateral contracts reciprocally refer to each other in the performance

Specifically, the object of the Federal Court decision 109 Ib 146 (1983) was that the Swiss National Bank, a public institution of the Confederation, had, without a specific legislative mandate, renewed, in the form of bilateral agreements, the 'Agreement on the Swiss banks' code of conduct with regard to the exercise of due diligence' with the overwhelming majority of Swiss banks.[2] The renewed CDB of 1983 contained tighter rules on the disclosure of the identity of third parties on whose behalf assets had been invested. In contrast with earlier agreements of 1977, in this version of the CDB, the range of those not required to disclose the origin of monies to be invested was reduced. The Association of Trustees (*Treuhänder-Verband*), affected by this, asked to be exempted from the identity disclosure, as the lawyers and the Chamber of Trustees and Auditors (*Treuhand- und Revisionskammer*) had been.[3] This was rejected by the National Bank in a letter to the petitioner. The Association of Trustees challenged this letter as an administrative decision in an administrative-court complaint to the Federal Court.[4]

Before briefly summarising the Federal Court's deliberations, let us mention the pre-history of the CDB. In the mid '70s, using guarantees and sureties from a major Swiss bank, and in infringement of Swiss capital influx regulations, foreign investors had transferred money amounting to over CHF 2 billion to the Texon finance company in Vaduz (Liechtenstein), which was operative in Switzerland.[5] The money invested was linked, above all, with tax evasion and money laundering, whereupon, among other things, foreign policy pressed the Swiss legislature to take corrective action.[6] The resulting scandal—which initially

programme or in contractual practice; secondly, there is reference in the content to the overall project; and thirdly, there is legally relevant close co-operation between the parties to the combination ('economic unit').

[2] For the first time in the Agreement of 9 December 1977. The Swiss Federal Court decision 109 Ib 146 was about the CDB of 1 July 1982. See the comparison of the first two versions of the CDB in P Nobel, 'Die neuen Standesregeln zur Sorgfaltspflicht der Banken' (1987) 39 *Wirtschaft und Recht* 149–66, with further references.

[3] In particular, the *Treuhänder-Verband* might have wanted to counter damage to its image. However, the overwhelming majority of the banks actually participated in the CDB, so that the limited choice of bank did amount to an economic disadvantage for the members of the *Treuhänder-Verband*.

[4] Federal Court decision 109 Ib 146 at 146 *et seq*.

[5] For a summary of the events, see the reports in the *Neue Zürcher Zeitung* (*NZZ*) 26 April 1977, p 15 and 28 April 1977, p 13; in detail, from the banks' perspective, see J Jung, *From Schweizerische Kreditanstalt to Credit Suisse Corp—The History of a Bank* (Zürich, NZZ Verlag, 2000) 245 et *seq*, especially at 257. See Federal Court decision 105 Ib 348. Specifically, there was infringement of capital-movement regulations aimed at reducing the inflow of foreign money, particularly through levies.

[6] At first, mainly Italy was affected by this capital drain of approximately CHFr 2 billion: see *NZZ* 20 April 1977, p 15, 26 April 1977, p 15, 28 April 1977, p 13 and 6 May 1977, p 17; see also Federal Court decision 105 Ib 348, especially, facts A., E. 10d) and 11; see G Müller, 'Zur Rechtsnatur der Vereinbarung über die Sorgfaltspflichten der Banken bei der Entgegennahme von Geldern und über die Handhabung des Bankgeheimnisses' (1984) *SJZ*

affected the political world, but affected the business world almost immediately afterwards—had so much impact on the image of the Swiss banking sector that, as a direct consequence, the self-restraint of the 'know-your-customer' rule was adopted, in the form of the CDB agreement in the sector. The first CDB in 1977 specifically required, in Article 4, the determination of the origins of funds.[7] Once the Texon scandal had died down, the banks agreed, in 1982, upon a new version of the CDB with the National Bank, which, while still directed against the furtherance of economic criminality by the banking industry,[8] largely formalised the duties of clarification.[9]

How, then, did the Federal Court, in decision 109 Ib 146, respond to CDB 1982 as an agreement between the National Bank and the banks, and in particular to the third-party interests of the *Treuhänder-Verband*? The Federal Court did not hear the complaint, on the grounds that the CDB was a private contract, and, accordingly, the National Bank's note to the *Treuhänder-Verband* was not an administrative (public law) decision that could be challenged. This is because the CDB was primarily aimed at taking over provisions from foreign penal law, in order to avert conflicts with foreign legal systems. However, since the actions targeted in the CDB—such as active assistance with tax offences or currency offences abroad—were not punishable in Swiss law, the interests theory did not lead to an allocation to public law.[10] And in the subordination theory, it would seem that, while the National Bank had been 'encouraged' to act by the Swiss Federal Council (ie, the Swiss Government), it was not exercising any specific legislative mandate, and the individual banks had accordingly been at liberty either to adhere to the Agreement or not. The fact that a similar arrangement could also have been created by statute was not relevant in the eyes of the court. Accordingly, the CDB was to be

349 at 350, Nobel, 'Die neuen Standesregeln zur Sorgfaltspflicht der Banken' (n 2 above) 149 et *seq*; P Nobel, *Schweizerisches Finanzmarktrecht* (Bern, Stämpfli, 2004) §6 N 6, fn 6.

[7] The main purpose of the first CDB from 1977 has remained almost unchanged to this day, Art 1 CDB 2008 (see below n 25). For an overview of the CDB's origins, see U Zulauf, 'Gläubigerschutz und Vertrauensschutz: Zur Sorgfaltspflicht der Bank im öffentlichen Recht der Schweiz' (1994) 113 *ZSR* 359 at 434 et *seq*, D Zuberbühler, 'Das Verhältnis zwischen der Bankenaufsicht, insbesondere der Überwachung der einwandfreien Geschäftstätigkeit, und der neuen Sorgfaltspflichtvereinbarung der Banken' (1987) 39 *Wirtschaft und Recht* 167, and Nobel, 'Die neuen Standesregeln zur Sorgfaltspflicht der Banken' (n 2 above). As to new developments, see W de Capitani, 'Die Aufsichtskommission VSB und das zehnte Gebot' in HCvd Crone, P Forstmoser, RH Weber and R Zäch (ed), *Aktuelle Fragen des Bank- und Finanzmarktrechts: Festschrift für Dieter Zobl zum 60. Geburtstag* (Zürich, Schulthess, 2004).

[8] Explicitly stated in the preamble to CDB 1982.

[9] Articles 2–5 CDB 1982; see the comparison with CDB 1977 in Nobel, 'Die neuen Standesregeln zur Sorgfaltspflicht der Banken' (n 2 above).

[10] 109 Ib 146 (1983) 149 et *seq*, especially E. 2.

defined as a private contract.[11] At most, a complaint to a supervisory authority might be brought against the National Bank, which

> in its private-law activities analogously [sic] has to comply with the constitutional basic rights. In particular, even as a subject of private law it must not confer rights or impose duties legally unequally or arbitrarily.[12]

Legal scholars are to date in disagreement as to the law's needful adaptations to the emerging trends to *co-operationism and privatisation* (or 'essentialisation' (*Verwesentlichung*) of the state's functions[13]): on the one hand, there are calls for the extension of public law,[14] though this certainly brings the danger of stifling the new-style co-operationist forms under restrictive regulations.[15] On the other, there are suggestions that the law should follow social changes by shifting corresponding situations from public to private law and especially the law of contract,[16] which would, however, thus be confronted with standards hitherto located in public law, and thus be irritated in the extreme, to the point of calling its own premises into question.[17]

This extremely demanding adaptation of law to increasing governmental co-operationism is however—as is evident from decision 109 Ib 146—at the same time, exposed to further irritations from equally far-reaching and novel changes in the environment: ie, the shifts from

[11] 109 Ib 146 (1983) 152 et *seq*, E. 3.

[12] 109 Ib 146 (1983) 155, E. 4.

[13] Thus, for example, G Müller, 'Wege zu einem schlanken Staat: Überprüfung der Aufgaben stete Pflicht der Staatsleitung', *NZZ*, 16 March 2005; for a wider perspective see also B Dörr, P Donges, M Künzler, A Ledergerber, M Puppis, E Schade and M Vogel, Selbstregulierung und Selbstorganisation, 'Unveröffentlichter Schlussbericht zuhanden des Bundesamtes für Kommunikation', available at: http://www.mediapolicy.unizh.ch/forschung/selbstregulierung_report.pdf (last visited 8 December 2008).

[14] Thus, for example, Richli, who criticises the Federal Court decision 109 Ib 146 for calling the CDB a private contract, but praises it for the observation that the National Bank does come under the fundamental rights: P Richli, 'Die verwaltungsrechtliche Rechtsprechung des BGer 1983: Bankengesetz' (1985) 81 *ZBJV* 428–30; see, recently, also Y Hangartner, 'Bemerkungen zu BGE 129 III 35' (2003) 6 *Aktuelle Juristische Praxis* (*AJP*) 690–93.

[15] In 129 III 35 (2003), the Federal Court responded logically to the essentialisation of state tasks being pursued politically; see M Amstutz, A Abegg and V Karavas, *Soziales Vertragsrecht* (Basel, Helbing, 2006).

[16] Thus, for example, A Marti, 'Aufgabenteilung zwischen Staat und Privaten auf dem Gebiet der Rechtsetzung—Ende des staatlichen Rechtsetzungsmonopols?' (2002) 10 *Aktuelle Juristische Praxis* (*AJP*) 1154 at 1158.

[17] For instance, in Federal Court decision 129 III 35 (2003) constitutional tasks for law of contract emerge openly: Amstutz, Abegg and Karavas, *Soziales Vertragsrecht* (n 15 above). And, in the theory of mutually absorbing systems, private law functionalized by public interests henceforth appears—to put it rather bluntly—as now just an appendage to public law.

market-related organisational structures on the one hand, and hierarchical ones on the other (reflected in law as contract and corporations) to *network-type structures*, for which the law is not prepared with categories of its own.[18]

These two new-style contextual conditions of co-operationism and network structures do not always appear as isolated contextual constraints on law, but may be so interlinked as to heighten the demands on the law's adaptability. Hitherto, such phenomena have been studied under the heading of 'self-regulation under governmental direction',[19] though this places insufficient emphasis on, first, the active role of the economy and secondly, the new-style network organisation.[20] It seems manifest to me that co-operationism between the state and private persons happening purely in individual contracts in the foreground—yet nonetheless in the background in network structures which ultimately bring about more than the sum of the individual contracts—possesses enormously explosive implications for current legal concepts such as the rule of law binding of administrations, on the one hand, or the privity of contracts, on the other.

I.2 Exploratory Movements in the Co-evolution of Politics, Economy and Law

Once the Federal Court had assigned the CDB to private law—while at the same time pointing out the National Bank's 'analogous' binding by fundamental rights—and after the ensuing criticisms by legal scholars had highlighted the inability of the Federal Court's chosen option to provide stability and had called for the CDB to be brought back under

[18] For much more on this, see G Teubner, *Netzwerk als Vertragsverbund: Virtuelle Unternehmen, Franchising, Just-in-time in sozialwissenschaftlicher und juristischer Sicht* (Baden-Baden, Nomos, 2004).

[19] Among many, Marti, 'Aufgabenteilung zwischen Staat und Privaten auf dem Gebiet der Rechtsetzung' (n 16 above), with further references; on the history of self-regulation in Switzerland, see A Mach, G Schnyder, T David and M Lüpold, 'Transformations de l'autoregulation et (re)regulation publique en matiere de gouvernement d'entreprise en Suisse (1980–2002)' (2006) 12 *Revue suisse de science politique* 1–32; Y Sancey, *Un capitalisme de Gentlemen. Emergence et consolidation de l'autorégulation bancaire en Suisse et en Angelterre (1914–1960) (Diss)* (Lausanne, unpublished thesis University of Lausanne 2004); H Bänzinger, *Die Entwicklung der Bankenaufsicht in der Schweiz seit dem 19. Jahrhundert* (Bern, Haupt, 1986).

[20] Typical of this approach is U di Fabio, 'Verwaltung und Verwaltungsrecht zwischen gesellschaftlicher Selbstregulierung und staatlicher Steuerung' in *Kontrolle der auswärtigen Gewalt: Veröffentlichungen der Vereinigung der deutschen Staatsrechtslehrer Heft 56* (Berlin, Walter de Gruyter, 1997).

public law,[21] economic and political actors responded. For the new version of the CDB in 1987, the National Bank withdrew from the Agreement, thus responding to the critics who had complained of the lack of a statutory basis for the National Bank's involvement in the CDB.[22] This change was intended to avert the danger that the CDB might, as some critics were demanding, still be brought under public law or—even more undesirably—lead to far-reaching legislation.[23] The place of the National Bank was taken by the Swiss Federal Banking Commission, which possessed the appropriate statutory powers as a supervisory authority to act in relation to the CDB, and, indeed, had even felt called upon to abrogate parts of the CDB in 1991.[24] Moreover, unlike the National Bank, the Federal Banking Commission no longer appeared as a direct contracting party with the banks, something similarly intended to avert further politicisation. Correspondingly, the network came to meet the demands from legal scholars to equip the CDB with comprehensive framework legislation on the one hand, and replace it with more or less traditional professional etiquette on the other. The position at the centre of the network, concluding the individual agreements with the banks, was now taken over by the banks' private trade association, the Swiss Bankers' Association, while the Federal Banking Commission was intended to act as supervisory authority.[25]

However, these changes could not prevent further pressure on Switzerland as a banking centre and on the CDB.[26] Attacks on Swiss banks

[21] See, especially, Müller, 'Zur Rechtsnatur der Vereinbarung über die Sorgfaltspflichten der Banken bei der Entgegennahme von Geldern und über die Handhabung des Bankgeheimnisses' (n 6 above); R Rhinow, 'Verfügung, Verwaltungsvertrag und privatrechtlicher Vertrag' in Juristische Fakultät der Universität Basel (ed), *Privatrecht—Öffentliches Recht—Strafrecht: Grenzen und Grenzüberschreitungen; Festgabe zum Schweizerischen Juristentag* (1985); R Rhinow, 'Verwaltungsrechtlicher oder privatrechtlicher Vertrag: Fiskalwirkung der Grundrechte' (1985) 4 *Recht* 57–64.

[22] Initially, the National Bank became involved because the Texon scandal not only affected the stock quotation of the Kreditanstalt, the bank involved in the scandal, but also resulted in a sharp decline of the Swiss Franc: *NZZ* 27 April 1977, p 17 and 5 May 1977, p 29.

[23] Thus also the interpretation by Zuberbühler, 'Das Verhältnis zwischen der Bankenaufsicht, insbesondere der Überwachung der einwandfreien Geschäftstätigkeit, und der neuen Sorgfaltspflichtvereinbarung der Banken' (n 7 above) 167.

[24] Specifically, this concerned the ban on Form B by the EBK circular of 25 April/1 July 1991: *Jahresbericht der EBK zum Jahr 1991* at 17 et *seq* Form B allowed trustees to declare that the party actually entitled was known, but was not being disclosed.

[25] As also in CDB 2008 of 7 April 2008, available at: http://www.swissbanking.org/20080410-vsb-cwe.pdf (last visited 6 October 2008). The EBK issues instructions as to which institutions a declaration on actual entitlement must be secured from (Art 3, N 34.4), receives notices of infringements from the audit office and the CDB supervisory commission (Arts 10 and 12(9)) and authorises amendments to the CDB (Art 14(3)).

[26] From an evolutionary-theory viewpoint, these further developments can be brought together under the concept of punctuated equilibrium: variations do not appear in a system uniformly and gradually, but are generated above all by unexpected or even scandalous events that cause the possibility of actual evolutionary jumps (in the sense of contingency),

ensued during the US 'war on drugs', and this contributed to the introduction of the penal prohibition of money laundering.[27] This penal provision stated, by way of a framework Act, that the identification duty was to be carried out with the care that was appropriate to the circumstances, something—so ran the message from the Swiss Federal Council[28]—that was fleshed out in the CDB. Numerous legal scholars immediately accused this penal framework law of infringing the principle of clarity and definiteness.[29] Renewed pressure on banking regulation, leading inter alia to further tightening of the provisions against money laundering, came after 1992, first in connection with the Italian '*Mani pulite*' campaign following bribery scandals, and more recently under the heading of terrorism.[30]

How did the Federal Court respond to these developments, ie, to the criticisms of decision 109 Ib 146 by the legal scholars and to the moves for modifications from politics and business? Two years after decision 109 Ib 146, the Federal Court again had a chance to speak on the CDB. Though the case was quite different, the Federal Court considered decision 109 Ib 146. However, it held that it would not need to examine whether the CDB was private-law or public-law in nature; and in any case, it bound the Federal Banking Commission neither to interpret the Banking Act, nor to its tasks as a supervisory body.[31] Thus, the Federal Court had not only reduced the importance of the CDB as self-regulation, but also indicated in an obiter dictum that the description of the CDB as a private contract was no longer certain. In its decision 125 IV 139 (1999), the Federal Court once again reduced the importance of the CDB and the banking sector de-regulation that it constituted. For the interpretation of the penal

thus differing from either arbitrariness or predetermination. See N Luhmann, *Das Recht der Gesellschaft* (Frankfurt aM, Suhrkamp, 1993) 243; MT Fögen, 'Rechtsgeschichte—Geschichte der Evolution eines sozialen Systems' (2002) 1 *RG Rechtsgeschichte* 14–19; M Amstutz, 'Die Verfassung von Vertragsverbindungen' in M Amstutz (ed), *Die vernetzte Wirtschaft* (Zürich, Schulthess, 2004) 55 et *seq*; Fögen has coined the appropriate expression 'sensational stories' for the jumps, and calls Gould's punctuated equilibrium an 'attractive third way the social sciences might also take': MT Fögen, *Römische Rechtsgeschichten—über Ursprung und Evolution eines sozialen Systems* (Göttingen, Vandenhoeck & Ruprecht, 2002) 16 and 18 et *seq*; Luhmann points out that, in modern society, the punctuational aspect is radicalised by the mass media, which preferentially report divergent variations: N Luhmann, *Die Gesellschaft der Gesellschaft* (Frankfurt aM, Suhrkamp, 1997) 474.

27 Art 305ter *StGB*, introduced by No I of the BG of 23 March 1990, in force since 1 August 1990 (official collection of Swiss law 1990 1077 1078; BBl 1989 II 1061).

28 BBl 1989 I 1089 f.

29 Among many: W de Capitani, 'Zum Identifikationsverfahren bei Kontoeröffnungen aus dem Ausland' (1993) 89 *SJZ* 21 at 21 et *seq*, fn 2, with further references.

30 See, eg, Art 305ter (2), introduced by the *BG* of 18 March 1994, in force since 1 August 1994 (official collection of Swiss law 1994 1614 1618; BBl 1993 III 277), and the Swiss Federal Council's message of 17 June 1996 on money laundering: BBl 1996 III 1101. On the fight against terrorism, see Art 1 of CDB 2003.

31 Federal Court decision 111 Ib 127, 127*et seq*.

provision of Article 305ter *StGB* (money laundering), the CDB was, it said, merely an aid to interpretation.[32]

This is the stage, in the intersections between the discourses of economics, politics, law and scholarship, at which the *CDB network* finds itself *today*, although it continues to be disputed whether the CDB is to be classed under private or public law.[33] Centrally, the newest version, CDB 2008, is structured as follows: the Swiss Bankers' Association concludes the agreement with the signatory banks for a period of five years in each case.[34] The governmental Federal Banking Commission checks whether the arrangement meets the requirements of the Money-laundering Act (*Geldwäschereigesetz, GwG)*.[35] The CDB sees itself as a piece of regulated professional etiquette which—in order, in accordance with Article 1, 'to uphold the reputation of the Swiss banking industry at home and abroad'—fleshes out the statutorily-regulated duties of care in the Money-laundering Act and the Criminal Code, while 'normal banking business ... [ought] not to be hampered thereby'. For the duties of care where there is a heightened risk of money-laundering, the CDB refers to

[32] Federal Court decision 125 IV 139, E. 3d, 144 *et seq*: 'While as regards the demands on verification of identity the message refers to the model role of the CDB, and the duties of care on financial intermediaries now introduced in the Money-laundering Act are in the words of the message meant to form the criterion for the care to be observed in financial transactions in accordance with Art 305ter Abs 1 *StGB*, this can of course not mean that the degree of care when receiving assets required by the penal provision is as it were absorbed into the relevant rules of the CDB. The CDB has to do with rules of professional etiquette, formulated by the Swiss Bankers' Association, to which the signatory banks submit. They are an instrument of ethical self-regulation, and serve primarily to uphold the reputation of the profession (Article 1 CDB) and thereby the interests of the banks, but are also protective as being self-protection against unclear situations that might lead to claims for damages. That they further lay claim to fleshing out 'the concept of the care required by the circumstances when receiving assets (Article 305ter *StGB*) is not binding on the criminal-court judge—for all one's recognition for self-regulatory efforts'.

[33] In favour of the classification under private law, most recently, Marti, 'Aufgabenteilung zwischen Staat und Privaten auf dem Gebiet der Rechtsetzung' (n 16 above) 1158 et *seq*, and A Marti, 'Selbstregulierung anstelle staatlicher Gesetzgebung?' (2000) 101 *ZBL* 561 at 576. For allocation to public law, see, recently, U Häfelin and G Müller, *Allgemeines Verwaltungsrecht* (Zürich, Schulthess, 2002) fn 1060. Allocation to private law while maintaining the bindingness of fundamental rights is advocated by M Schefer, 'Grundrechtliche Schutzpflichten und die Auslagerung staatlicher Aufgaben' (2002) 10 *Aktuelle Juristische Praxis* (*AJP*) 1131 at 1139 et *seq*.

[34] The most recent dating from 7 April 2008: see n 25 above.

[35] See, especially, Arts 16 and 42 *GwG*; see also J-B Zufferey and Expertengruppe Finanzmarktaufsicht, *Finanzmarktregulierung und -aufsicht in der Schweiz. Schlussbericht* (Bern, 2000) N 251, and Eidgenössische Finanzverwaltung, *Geldwäschereibekämpfung in der Schweiz* (Bern, 2003) 43, Arbeitsgruppe KYC, *Sorgfaltspflichten von Banken und Effektenhändlern bei Geldwäscherei, Terrorismusfinanzierung und Beziehungen zu politisch exponierten Personen, 2005*, available at: http://www.ebk.admin.ch/d/archiv/2002/pdf/neu090702–02d.pdf (last visited 8 December 2008) 12, and the explanations by the Bankers' Association at http://www.swissbanking.org/home/allgemein.htm (last visited 8 December 2008). On all this, see also Nobel, *Schweizerisches Finanzmarktrecht* (n 6 above) § 6 N 10, §9 N 40 et *seq*, especially N 55 et *seq* and § 11 N 27.

national law, namely, the Federal Banking Commission regulation.[36] Articles 2–8 CDB regulate the specific duties of care and define their scope. With Article 10, the signatory banks authorise a review body to monitor compliance with the CDB, and notify the CDB supervisory commission and the governmental Federal Banking Commission of infringements. The supervisory commission, set up to investigate breaches, informs the Federal Banking Commission of its decisions (Article 12, especially 12(9)). Finally, an arbitration tribunal will, upon a complaint brought by the Swiss Bankers' Association against the bank concerned, hand down a final decision as to whether there has or has not been a violation of the terms of the agreement (Article 13).

This concludes my reconstruction of the evolution of the CDB and of the social systems affected by the CDB.[37] This reconstruction of developments to date, since the emergence of the CDB in 1977, has shown the following: the Federal Court's decision 109 Ib 146, which I have commented on, had largely allocated the CDB to private law and thus given full leeway to its experimental programme. It initially sparked off vehement criticism from legal scholars, who stressed the lack of internal legal consistency in the Federal Court's ruling, especially with the concept of the democratic state under rule of law, thus showing that the decision could not bring stability. The immediately ensuing exploratory moves by the CDB network chiefly served the goal of keeping the network in the sphere of private law and thus free from political instrumentalisation, albeit without wishing to lose its link with politics.[38] However, because of repeated scandals and larger political events,[39] as well as the criticisms of the conflict with rule-of-law principles by legal scholars, this could not be maintained. Instead, the academic critique, on the one hand, and the scandals and broader events, on the other, engendered politically-led legislative impulses that reduced the CDB's importance as self-regulation, and increasingly subjected it to political structures. Even today, the economic, political and legal systems have yet to find lasting stability in their co-evolution in the area of the CDB, something which is reflected in the continuing criticisms of the doctrinal classification of the CDB as private law by legal scholars.[40]

[36] Art 1(3) CDB 2003; Regulation of the Confederal Banking Commission on the Prevention of Money-Laundering of 18 December 2002.

[37] For the dogmatic presentation of the CDB, see the relevant literature, eg, Nobel, *Schweizerisches Finanzmarktrecht* (n 6 above) § 6, with exhaustive literature references.

[38] We shall return to the link between the economy and politics in the network: III.2.

[39] Note 27 above.

[40] According to di Fabio, this finding is valid for the whole topic of self-regulation: di Fabio, 'Verwaltung und Verwaltungsrecht zwischen gesellschaftlicher Selbstregulierung und staatlicher Steuerung' (n 20 above) 275.

I shall cast an eye below over the law's neighbouring disciplines, in order to sound out the conditions for some possibilities of overcoming the crisis.[41] At the centre is the thesis that, while legal science had identified the new-style co-operationism between the state and private persons as the starting point for the continuing irritations—which are at the point of intersection of a clash of discourses of Babylonian proportions—it was unable to respond properly to these new-style irritations with the old rigid concepts, which also ignored the emergence of network-type organisations bound up with co-operationism. Consequently, it needs a theory which is able to deal with the dynamic co-evolution of the various discourses involved. I shall employ evolutionary theory for this, and, in the process, attempt to make the natural-science concept of morphogenesis bear fruit.

II. THE MORPHOGENESIS OF HYBRID NETWORKS

According to Kämper and Schmidt, the point with networks is not the harmonisation of functional systems, still less the integration of society.[42] My analysis of the co-evolutionary search-moves around the CDB network to date, however, points in precisely the opposite direction: the CDB network—and very generally, hybrid networks located between the social sub-systems of society—may constitute strategies of these social sub-systems in order to retain their own specific system nature and respond as far as necessary to contradictory irritations simultaneously.[43] What is involved here is nothing less than the *social integrative function of evolution*.[44] However, some elucidation is called for, as follows.

[41] On the call to bring the neighbour sciences into jurisprudence, see P Gauch, 'Die Fehlerwelt der Juristen' in *Festschrift für Heinz Rey* (Zürich, Schulthess, 2003) fn 19 et *seq*.

[42] E Kämper and JFK Schmidt, 'Netzwerke als strukturelle Kopplung' in J Weyer (ed), *Soziale Netzwerke: Konzepte und Methoden der sozialwissenschaftlichen Netzwerkforschung* (Munich, Oldenbourg, 2000) 227; with a different view, D Messner, 'Netzwerktheorien: Die Suche nach Ursachen und Auswegen aus der Krise staatlicher Steuerungspolitik' in E Altvater, A Brunnengräber, M Haake and H Walk (eds), *Vernetzt und verstrickt: Nicht-Regierung-Organisationen als gesellschaftliche Produktivkraft* (Münster, Westfälisches Dampfboot, 1997) 42 et *seq*.

[43] M Amstutz, *Evolutorisches Wirtschaftsrecht: Vorstudien zum Recht und seiner Methode in den Diskurskollisionen der Marktgesellschaft* (Baden-Baden, Nomos, 2001) 290 et *seq*; M Amstutz, 'Widerstreitende Götter—Zu Manfred Aschkes Rekonstruktion der systemsoziologischen Evolutiontheorie und ihrer rechtstheoretischen Bedeutung' (2003) 2 *Rechtsgeschichte* 14–24; Teubner, *Netzwerk als Vertragsuerbund* (n 18 above).

[44] On this, see Amstutz, Abegg and Karavas, *Soziales Vertragsrecht* (n 15 above).

It has more than once been pointed out that *hybrid networks are an institutional reaction to ambivalent, contradictory or paradoxical requirements*.[45] Institutionally, this response means redundancy, ie, the system reacts to particular events by repeatedly reducing the possible modes of behaviour.[46] Since the heightened demands from the environment cannot be escaped, the system at this point comes closer to the complexity of the environment.[47] This process in which the system lowers its internal consistency in one sub-area may, borrowing from the natural sciences, be called morphogenesis.[48] In fact, the CDB network is responding simultaneously—as will immediately be described in more detail—to at least three paradoxical demands from the environment, which result from the repeated banking scandals and the calls (admittedly uncomfortable for the economic system) to restrain economic logic. First, though, I wish to go into the concept of morphogenesis as further developed by the natural sciences in recent years, so as to use it as a metaphor (ie an outline solution that provides inspiration) in order to describe the function of hybrid networks in the evolution of social systems.[49]

Recent natural-science theories of morphogenesis fit almost precisely with Kauffman's concept of spontaneous order, exploited by Amstutz for legal theory. As SA Kauffman showed, not only does a system's evolution come from the selection of suitable variations, but the selection must also meet with an *internal so-called spontaneous order*, which is what makes the evolution of a system possible at all.[50] This spontaneous order keeps the system in a condition in which it is best prepared for evolutionary processes. Kauffman has shown that systems are able to respond to irritations from outside when their epistatic connectivity[51] is $K = 2$. A

[45] G Teubner, 'Das Recht hybrider Netzwerke' (2001) 165 *Zeitschrift für das gesamte Handelsrecht und Wirtschaftsrecht* 550–75; K-H Ladeur, *Das Umweltrecht der Wissensgesellschaft: von der Gefahrenabwehr zum Risikomanagement* (Berlin, Duncker & Humblot, 1995) 31 et *seq*.

[46] Luhmann, *Das Recht der Gesellschaft* (n 26 above) 355 et *seq*.

[47] Amstutz, *Evolutorisches Wirtschaftsrecht* (n 43 above) 291; see also Kämper and Schmid, 'Netzwerke als strukturelle Kopplung' (n 42 above) 229 *et seq*.

[48] For the natural sciences, see AV Spirov, 'Game of Morphogenesis: What Can We Learn from the Pattern-Form Interplay Models?' (1998) 8 *International Journal of Bifurcations and Chaos* 991–1001, with further references, and infra n 54 *et seq*. For the social sciences, see Teubner (n 45), and N Luhmann, *Soziale Systeme: Grundriss einer allgemeinen Theorie* (Frankfurt aM, Suhrkamp, 1987) 480 *et seq*, and 485 *et seq*, with further references on adoption of the concept in the social sciences.

[49] On the concept of metaphor, see Amstutz, *Evolutorisches Wirtschaftsrecht* (n 43 above) 160 *et seq*.

[50] SA Kauffman, *The origins of order: self-organisation and selection in evolution* (New York, Oxford University Press, 1993); SA Kauffman, *Investigations* (Oxford, Oxford University Press, 2000).

[51] In biology, epistatic connectivity denotes dependence between genes, *i.e.*, that one gene 'covers up' the effects of another. If, then, variant *a* leads to phenotype A and variant *b* to phenotype B, but the combination *ab* results only in phenotype A, then *a* is epistatic to *b*.

crystal with K = 1 is, in contrast, unreceptive to external irritations, while with a higher connectivity of K = N – 1, the system drifts into chaos at practically the slightest touch. Put more simply, the elements of the system must be bound loosely enough to be able to take on the irritations 'at the edge of chaos', but not too loose for the system to be unable to maintain itself as such despite the irritations.[52] The place, or *'unit of selection'*, where evolution first becomes possible along with the maintenance of intrinsic rationality is not the system in its entirety—which would be unable to effect the necessary adaptation. Instead, the system differentiates particular areas that have to accomplish this adaptation, and which are, to this end, coupled with the corresponding environment.[53]

This concept of spontaneous order has now been taken up by *recent theories of morphogenesis*: according to Harrison, morphogenesis means the emergence of a complex system from a simpler one, a process that presupposes internal spontaneous order.[54] A central place in the process of morphogenesis is taken up by the interactions between the dynamic elements of the system: on the one hand, changes in the system's relationship to its environment must be grasped quickly and precisely, and communicated within the system; on the other, change should be set in motion in the system in the other direction.[55] In the case of cells, the interplay between spontaneous order and change in form lies in a complex bio-mechanical and chemical process, in which—to put it in a nutshell—in a first step, the cell bio-mechanically 'feels' its position (form) in its environment, and thus also 'feels' the environment as such; then, this information is sent to the genome in the cell's nucleus, and finally, the genome sets off a gene cascade, in order to set off further changes on the desired path of morphogenesis. Put simply, then, morphogenic changes are set in motion, are then checked against the position aimed at in the system, and against the position relative to the system's environment, and, in a feedback loop, are checked against the changes aimed at, and then in accordance with this result and the morphogenesis

[52] Kauffman, *The origins of order* (n 50 above) 219 *et seq*, and 255 *et seq*; see Amstutz, *Evolutorisches Wirtschaftsrecht* (n 43 above) 278 *et seq*, 286 *et seq* and 290 *et seq*; see also A Watson, *The Evolution of Western Private Law* (Baltimore, John Hopkins University Press, 2001) 264 *et seq*.

[53] Luhmann, *Das Recht der Gesellschaft* (n 26 above) 281; see also Amstutz, *Evolutorisches Wirtschaftsrecht* (n 43 above) 290 *et seq*, and Watson, *The Evolution of Western Private Law* (n 52 above) 264.

[54] LG Harrison, 'Physical chemistry of biological morphogenesis' (1981) 10 *Chemical Society Reviews* 491 at 491 and 502; DJ Depew and BH Weber, *Darwinism Evolving: Systems Dynamics and the Genealogy of Natural Selection* (Cambridge MA, MIT Press, 1997) 528 *et seq*, with further references.

[55] Among many, see FW Cummings, 'Aspects of growth and form' (1994) 79 *Physica D: Nonlinear Phenomena* 146–63; Spirov, 'Game of Morphogenesis' (n 48 above).

aimed at, and the new changes in turn are set off, etc.[56] This morphogenic loop is, however, only one source of the change. Equally decisive are the aforementioned spontaneous order, and the rigid geometric constraints to which the system is subject, and along which it evolves.[57]

If this image of spontaneous order and morphogenesis is applied to the case of hybrid networks, it may be concluded that a system—in our case that of the CDB, mainly the economy, but also politics—will differentiate a particularly flexible sub-order if it has to respond to intensive and complex irritations from the environment. The system will do so by lowering its coherence, ie, bringing about a process towards a more complex form—while simultaneously maintaining its own autopoiesis. While the sub-order's specific rationality ensures a certain resistance to evolution (form), its dynamic elements will be sufficiently loosely linked to react to the irritations from the environment—but only so loosely as always to allow the sub-area's specific rationality to be maintained. The form of the hybrid network with its particularly loosely-linked elements is, then—as Teubner has shown—particularly appropriate whenever internal variations have to be formed out of contradictory or even paradoxical high-intensity irritations.[58] In effect, the point for the system is, thus, to exploit the network in order to revamp the relationship between function, performance and reflection within the system in such a way that it can react as optimally as possible to intensive, complex and even contradictory demands from the environment without endangering its intrinsic rationality.[59]

This adaptation of the system now occurs in a *morphogenic feedback loop* along the system's intrinsic constraints: at the *loci* of the structural couplings, the system 'feels' its form and its position in the environment, and, from this information, the system takes on variations within the context of the sub-system's specific rationality, which are subjected to

[56] NK Bjorklund and R Gordon, 'Nuclear state splitting: a working model for the mechanochemical coupling of differentiation waves to master genes' (1993) 24 *Russian Journal of Developmental Biology* 79–95; similarly earlier Harrison, 'Physical chemistry of biological morphogenesis' (n 54 above) 502 *et seq*, and LG Harrison, 'Kinetic Theory of Living Pattern and Form and Its Possible Relationship to Evolution' in BH Weber, DJ Depew and JD Smith (eds), *Entropy, Information, and Evolution: New Perspectives on Physical and Biological Evolution* (Cambridge MA, MIT Press, 1988) 63 and 73, referring to SA Kauffman.

[57] FW Cummings, 'The Interaction of Surface Geometry with Morphogens' (2001) 212 *Journal of Theoretical Biology* 303–13.

[58] G Teubner, *Recht als autopoietisches System* (Frankfurt aM, Suhrkamp, 1989) 75; Amstutz, *Evolutorisches Wirtschaftsrecht* (n 43 above) 290 *et seq*.

[59] There would, of course, also be much to say about the CDB network in terms of social systems, organisation and interaction. I will, however, concentrate below on the level of co-evolution of social sub-systems. On this distinction, see N Luhmann, 'Interaktion, Organisation, Gesellschaft' in *Soziologische Aufklärung 2* (Opladen, Westdeutscher Verlag, 1975).

selection (change or non-change to the previous elements and structures). The modification brought about by the selection, as well as the rejection of modification, are in turn 'felt' for their position within the system and—again with the help of structural couplings—so is the position in the environment, which can now set off new variations and selections in a further loop.

The special thing about the form of the hybrid network is that it can *simultaneously take up manifold structural couplings with various systems*. This gives more importance to the morphogenic loop, in which the results of previous selections can be squared with the internal and external demands upon the system, and, if need be, corrections can be made, until, in the long run, a punctuated equilibrium between the system and its environment is reached. In this light, the morphogenic loop is the precondition for a system's being able to take on intensive demands from its surrounding systems while at the same time maintaining its own rationality, and to aim at a punctuated equilibrium with its surrounding systems.

I wish now to use the *specific example of the CDB network* to show that, in this case, the economy responded to intensive and contradictory irritations with the form of the hybrid network, and thus differentiated a specific sub-order which created the conditions for the possibility of co-evolution for the economy with its surrounding systems through morphogenic loops. On the basis of the model of a poly-contextual society,[60] I shall further seek to draw normative conclusions from the observations derived from evolutionary theory.

Here, however, there is a need to take account of intrinsically legal constraints in the form of the *rigid compulsory connections of legal doctrine*. The institutions of organisation and contract in law build upon long traditions, whereas the forms between organisation and contract and between the state and private organisation were banished in civil law with the emergence of the police state.[61] Thus, there is no updated pool of elements that is able—without further ado—to be linked up with today's

[60] Among many, see G Teubner, 'Vertragswelten: Das Recht in der Fragmentierung von private governance regimes' (1998) 17 *Rechtshistorisches Journal* 234 at 234 *et seq*, and esp at 241 *et seq*; M Amstutz, 'Vertragskollisionen: Fragmente für eine Lehre von der Vertragsverbindung' in H Honsell, W Portmann, R Zäch and D Zobel (eds), *Aktuelle Aspekte des Schuld- und Sachenrechts: Festschrift für Heinz Rey zum 60. Geburtstag* (Zürich, Schulthess, 2003) 165 *et seq*, and, most recently, see Amstutz, Abegg and Karavas, *Soziales Vertragsrecht* (n 15 above).

[61] On this, see JHG von Justi, *Grundsätze der Polizeiwissenschaft* (Göttingen, 1782/1756), preface, and JHG von Justi, *Die Grundfeste zu der Macht und Glückseeligkeit der Staaten, oder, Ausführliche Vorstellung der gesamten Policey-Wissenschaft* (Königsberg, 1760) vol 2, § 554–5. Chiefly, since the sixteenth century, the aim was to bring the fragmented jurisdiction of church, landowners, etc, under state control as the sole kind of local government. The more this succeeded, the more the concepts of political power (as the capacity to secure

legal doctrine, from which suitable variations for the new types of phenomenon can be selected. Additionally, in today's post-modern poly-contextual society, pre-liberal solutions for a stratified society can be considered only with great caution. Thus, the locating of new phenomena, such as hybrid networks between government administration and private persons cannot be linked up with existing concepts, and the creation of a corresponding field of law *ex nihilo* is out of the question, even if only because of the internal constraints of legal doctrine. This legal doctrine watches too rigidly over the consistency of new norm variations with the existing norms. Accordingly, the new-style phenomena located between the old dichotomies of contract and organisation or of state and private organisation must be found a place in these existing dichotomies, although, of course, their 'reverse side' has to be taken account of *within* the relevant legal order.

III. THE CDB IN THE LIGHT OF EVOLUTIONARY NETWORK THEORY

III.1 Development of Paradoxical Demands: Co-operation of Competitors

The Texon scandal may definitely also be seen as one that was internal to politics. This is because Swiss policy, which profits from the banking business through taxes and levies, was afraid of falling further into disrepute and felt, accordingly, under pressure to act correctively against the banks.[62] However, for manifold reasons, such as complexity and technicality, limited means and privatisation—in addition to the globalisation of both knowledge and resources—politics had failed to regulate the dynamic economic sector of the banks authoritatively through traditional legislation.[63] Furthermore, the avoidance of political regulation that might have hampered 'normal banking business' was a primary

obedience) and legal power came to coincide in sovereignty as supreme power. To date, the field is still marked by Hobbes' theory of the state: see Luhmann, *Das Recht der Gesellschaft* (n 26 above) 407 *et seq*.

[62] See *NZZ* 6 May 1977, p 17 and *NZZ* 5 May 1977, pp 25 and 29, especially, the Federal Council's statement on the Bank scandal; Jung, *From Schweizerische Kreditanstalt to Credit Suisse Corp* (n 5 above) 261.

[63] On these factors, very widely held responsible for the increasing co-operationism of governmental administration, see, among many, TP Müller, *Verwaltungsverträge im Spannungsfeld von Recht, Politik und Wirtschaft: eine systemtheoretische Analyse von Verträgen zwischen dem Gemeinwesen und Privaten mit Hinweisen auf die rechtsdogmatischen Konsequenzen* (Basel, Helbing & Lichtenhahn, 1997)142 *et seq*; P Uebersax, 'Privatisierung der Verwaltung' (2001) 102 *ZBL* 393–422; P Zumbansen, 'Spiegelungen von "Staat und Gesellschaft":

objective of Swiss banks.[64] As a result of further scandals and major political events, this aim could not fully be achieved.[65] But the objective of not letting 'normal banking business' be 'hampered', thus averting a politically-imposed straitjacket (and let it be it noted that the sub-area's specific rationality under the sign of extreme plasticity clearly shines through), is still, to this day, formulated with noteworthy clarity in the CDB:

> This agreement lays down binding rules of good conduct in banking as a code of professional ethics. They are designed to give specific effect to certain points of due diligence governed by the Anti-Money Laundering Act (Article 3–5 of the AMLA) and the concept of 'the diligence that can be reasonably expected under the circumstances' in accepting assets (Art 305ter of the Swiss Penal Code) . . . It is not the intention to impede normal banking business.[66]

How could this objective be achieved? To avoid an inconvenient straitjacket through political regulation, politics had to be irritated by the economy in such a way as to eliminate the preconditions for politics to take regulatory action. If, however, individual economic actors had unilaterally and voluntarily taken political instructions as politico-ethical guidelines and had thus restricted their economic possibilities in the light of politics, then clearly these individual banks would have faced considerable competitive disadvantages in comparison with non-compliant competitors—without necessarily getting rid of the problem for politics. A unilateral adaptation by banks to the demands of politics was thus manifestly illusory because of the constraints immanent in the economic system.[67]

As we know, ordo-liberal theory (a German school of neo-liberalism) turned liberalism on its head by recognising that a market regime is not the consequence of, but a precondition for, the market mechanism.[68] In

Governance-Erfahrungen in der Globalisierungsdebatte' in M Anderheiden, S Huster and S Kirste (eds), *Globalisierung als Problem der Steuerungsfähigkeit des Rechts und der Gerechtigkeit, ARSP Beiheft 79* (Stuttgart, Steiner, 2001).

[64] See the leading article in the *NZZ* 7/8 May 1977 and the reports of the parliamentary debate in the *NZZ* 5 May 1977, pp 25 and 29; see, also, Mach, Schnyder, David and Lüpold, 'Transformations de l'autoregulation et (re)regulation publique en matiere de gouvernement d'entreprise en Suisse (1980–2002)' (n 19 above).

[65] See details at n 5 above; also in Section I.2.

[66] Article 1(3) CDB 2008, see also above at n 25.

[67] On the problems of business ethics, see N Luhmann, *Die Wirtschaft der Gesellschaft* (Frankfurt aM, Suhrkamp, 1989) 84 *et seq*.

[68] See the excellent presentation of the circumstances in R Wiethölter, *Rechtswissenschaft* (Franfurt aM, Fischer, 1968); and fundamentally on this, F Böhm, *Wettbewerb und Monopolkampf* (Berlin, Heymann, 1933).

the light of this ordo-liberal theory, it was up to the banks *jointly to set up a market regime* that simultaneously and equally restrained the economic possibilities of the biggest players in the banking sector and was, therefore, at least within the circle of important market participants, or the most part competitively neutral in its effects, ie, cartelised the new duties of care.[69] Joint action to this end by the competitors would, however, have brought considerable dangers. By founding a formal organisation, the competitors would have come so close together as to call the fundamental premises of the market into question, whilst, at the same time, bringing the risk of corresponding reactions from politics and law. The banks thus found themselves facing the paradoxical requirement to co-operate with each other whilst, at the same time, maintaining competition.

The *form of the network* does not—as anti-trust law[70] might suggest—resolve this paradox by suppressing one side of the organisation, but instead unfolds the paradox by using both co-operation and competition. How does this look in the CDB case? In the CDB network, regulations were formulated in which the economy, to some extent, took the environmental demands into account—specifically, in the banking area, it restricted the possibilities of business action. However, since this restriction of economic rationality in bilateral arrangements was stabilised through contract law, as, from a certain threshold of collective market power onward, the result was the above-mentioned *cartelisation*. This means that the arrangement stabilised in the contracts became competitively neutral, since one market participant no longer competed with another by underbidding the established standard. The network, *in structural coupling to the legal system* through the various bilateral, but always identical and inter-related, contractual arrangements, thus obtained control over the opportunistic conduct of its participants in a specific sub-area of competition, while the network participants continued to compete with each other in the other areas.[71]

The economy was thus able to overcome the blockade which threatened the banking sector with paradoxical demands, through a network-type organisation which was flexible enough to *unfold the paradox by*

[69] On the interplay between the legislation framework set up by the state and self-regulation of the market, see F Böhm, 'Privatrechtsgesellschaft und Marktwirtschaft' (1966) 17 *ORDO* 75–151, and E-J Mestmäcker, 'Die Wiederkehr der bürgerlichen Gesellschaft und ihres Rechts' (1991) 10 *Rechtshistorisches Journal* 177–92. On the cartellisation effect of social norms, see S Huf, 'Die sozialstaatliche Einbettung der Marktökonomie' (1999) 45 *ZfS* 221 at 227 *et seq*.

[70] The first anti-trust act to protect competition dates from 1985 (see official collection of Swiss law 1986 874).

[71] This was secured by an arbitration clause, which presupposed a private law contractual arrangement: see Article 14 CDB 1977.

introducing several levels. The network-type web of contracts was able, on the one hand, to secure the very *co-operation* that could meet the political demands, while, on the other hand, this co-operation—in the form of the conclusion of a contract between the individual bank and a neutral network centre—was so loose and so limited in content that not only was the *form of competition* maintained for the economic system, but this could correspondingly also be signalled to the other systems, especially the legal system.[72] This simultaneously minimised the target area for political or legal interventions and thus averted excessive influence by legislative policy; as the network was arranged, and, as this was also perceived by the Federal Court, it was meant to constitute only a loosely associated bundle of private contracts.

How, then, is this *re-entry of organisation into contract* to be classified legally? In the law of contract, it can be brought into the content of the contract (if need be, interpreted normatively) without problems.[73] A sober glance at *anti-trust law*, however, raises doubts as to whether the CDB ought not to be brought under the Cartel Act.[74] We may regard the CDB as a strategy of the economy for organising the sub-area of banking in such a way that it can absorb complex and intensive irritations from the environment on the basis of its internal order (in SA Kauffman's sense) and respond to them flexibly (through morphogenic loops).[75] Thus, it would, against the background of the model of a poly-contextual society, be downright fatal for the law to force the network into the traditional dichotomies of competition versus co-operation, or contract versus organisation. It would be fatal to describe it as an illicit competition agreement and thus suppress the organisation element, or else construe it as an organisation, which would fail to take the central role of the contract into account. Therefore, from this viewpoint, the so-called re-entry of the organisation into the form of the contract deserves protection—at least in so far as it allows the economy both to absorb

[72] The central function of the contract for networks is also stressed by J Sydow and A Windeler, 'Steuerung von und in Netzwerken – Perspektiven, Konzepte, vor allem aber offene Fragen' in J Sydow and A Windeler (eds), *Steuerung von Netzwerken* (Opladen, Westdeutscher Verlag, 2000) 14 *et seq*. Here, however, the point is not so much the classical contract, nor a long-term continuing contract, but a medium-term contract that gives the parties decisive freedom to adjust the contractual relationship to changing circumstances: OE Williamson, 'Comparative economic organisation: The analysis of discrete structural alternatives' in SM Lindenberg and H Schreuder (eds), *Interdisciplinary Perspectives on Organization Studies* (Oxford, Pergamon, 1991).

[73] See, for example, the forms of contract in favour of third parties (Art 112 OR). See, with further references, P Krauskopf, *Der Vertrag zugunsten Dritter (Diss.)* (Fribourg, University Press Fribourg, 2000).

[74] See also Zuflauf, 'Gläubigerschutz und Vertrauensschutz: Zur Sorgfaltspflicht der Bank im öffentlichen Recht der Schweiz' (n 7 above); see Art 5 f. *KG* (Cartel Act).

[75] See Section II.

irritations from the environment better, and correspondingly to orient its structure better to the demands of the surrounding systems.[76]

However, the network not only allows the economy to absorb intensive contradictory, or even paradoxical, demands, but it also has a socially integrative function. What this socially integrative function of the CDB network consists of, and what part the morphogenic loops mentioned play, I shall now proceed to explain.

III.2 Compatibilisation of Contradictory Rationalities

After the Texon scandal, the banking sector not only had to create a market regime while simultaneously maintaining competition, but was additionally confronted with a second contradictory demand. The banking sector had to come closer to politics while, at the same time, keeping it at arm's length: the CDB network was called into being primarily to cushion pressures from international and national politics and make them compatible with the banking sector.[77] Correspondingly, connections with this political dimension were established from the outset, first by bringing in the National Bank as the network centre, and in the second phase of the CDB, by integrating the Federal Banking Commission as the top supervisory body for the network. Nonetheless, it was always an

[76] In fact, the CDB, in which Switzerland's biggest banks were involved from the outset, clearly does eliminate competition in the area regulated: Zulauf, 'Gläubigerschutz und Vertrauensschutz: Zur Sorgfaltspflicht der Bank im öffentlichen Recht der Schweiz' (n 7 above) explicitly states this. By the political exceptional clause of Art 6(2) *KG* (Cartel Act), however, the competition arrangements, which are designated in ordinances and public announcements and concern 'particular forms of co-operation in single economic sectors, especially agreements on the rational implementation of public-law measures to protect customers and investors in the financial services area', are justified. See the Swiss Federal Council's message on auditing in BBl 1994, 564, which refers explicitly to the banking sector. In Art 6(2) *KG*, the legislator acknowledges that co-operation arrangements may also support competition or be of public (ie, primarily political) interest, as specifically the legislative reference to consumer protection in the area of financial services shows. This niche of the anti-trust system was able to bring in the more recent recognition that while competition is certainly the fundamental premise of the market economy, it may very well be compatible with that premiss for firms, for the most varied purposes and on specific points—ie, product-, project- or time-related—to change from competitors to co-operating partners: see H-J Bunte (ed), *Kommentar zum deutschen und europäischen Kartellrecht* (Neuwied, Luchterhand, 2004) § 1, fn 161; C Kirchner, 'Unternehmensorganisation und Vertragsnetz' in C Ott and H-B Schäfer (eds), *Ökonomische Analyse des Unternehmensrechts : Beiträge zum 3. Travemünder Symposium zur ökonomischen Analyse des Rechts* (Heidelberg, Physica Verlag, 1993); see also P Zurkinden, HR Trüeb and J Rutishauser, *Das neue Kartellgesetz Handkommentar* (Zürich, Schulthess, 2004), on Art 6 *KG* (Cartel Act).

[77] See above Section I.2.

intention of the CDB to keep the influence of politics as 'business-compatible' as possible, something clearly expressed in Article 1 of the CDB mentioned earlier.[78]

How, then, was the economy able to use the network to respond to the paradoxical requirement to include politics while, simultaneously keeping it at arm's length? I wish here to distinguish two dimensions: first, communication about the need for collectively binding-decisions, and second, the problem of legitimation.

II.2.(a) Communication about the Need for Collectively-binding Decisions

If the economy wishes to signal the need (or else non-need) for collectively binding-decisions to the political sphere, this communication cannot occur just anyhow and anywhere. If we take the model of the polycontextural society seriously, then, because of the unbridgeable autonomy of the various systems and of the corresponding Babylonian confusion of tongues, there is *no direct communication channel between the economy and politics* through which this information could pass without further ado. And correspondingly, even in the network the various rationalities cannot 'find each other' in such a way that, à la Savigny, they would all be within some all-embracing world-spirit.[79] From the viewpoint of systems theory and evolutionary theory, the economy is left with no alternative but to irritate politics at the locus of structural coupling by which the necessary variations are formed and selected.[80] Although the chances of success in bringing about the desired selections in a surrounding system through irritations have to be rated as poor, the CDB network did manage to install relatively effective morphogenic structures by simultaneously linking up to several structural couplings:

(i) Organisation and Collective Actor as Structural Coupling Whereas the network appears to the law primarily as a bundle of contracts, because of the network effect, it does, at the same time, present itself to politics as an *organisation,* or more precisely, as a *collective actor.* This enables the relevant sub-area of the economy to appear to legislative policy as a point of identification at which politics obtains information about the other

[78] Notes 25 and 66 above. See also T Strulik, 'Governance globalisierter Finanzmärkte: Policy-Netzwerke und Kontextsteuerung im Bankensystem' in J Sydow and A Windeler (eds), *Steuerung von Netzwerken* (Opladen, Westdeutscher Verlag, 2000) at 322, points out that something similar is true of the international level, too. However, he portrays an almost harmonious picture of the co-operation of the economy and politics in networks, something that cannot be asserted of the CDB case.

[79] FK Savigny, *System des heutigen Römischen Rechts, Band 1–4* (Berlin, Veit, 1973/1840) vol I, 22 *et seq*.

[80] A Abegg, 'Evolutorische Rechtstheorie' in S Buckel, R Christensen and A Fischer-Lescano (eds), *Neue Theorien des Rechts* (Stuttgart, Lucius und Lucius, 2006).

system, and, in particular, about the conditions for collectively-binding decisions, and communicates the possibility conditions for future collectively-binding decisions, in order to test the chances for achieving political programmes on the basis of reactions. The economy, for its part, reads this communication about planned collectively-binding decisions as a cost, and, in turn, uses the organisation to communicate the need or lack of need for collectively-binding decisions to the political sphere.[81] For the banking sector, this possibility of communicating to the political sphere a lack of need for legislative intervention about duties of due diligence is of central importance. This is because it is in this way that politics could, and, indeed, can be relatively quickly and reliably made aware of the efforts to reach a punctuated equilibrium with politics within the economy. In our case, politics, too, was pressing for a solution to the crisis (within politics) of Switzerland as a banking centre, and, from the viewpoint of the economy, the slowly grinding and (for the economy) incalculable mills of legislation should, if it all possible, not be set in motion at all.[82]

(ii) Contract as Structural Coupling While the necessary communication between the banking sector and legislative politics could not have been established through the *structural coupling of the contract* alone, the contractual incorporation of the National Bank, a political actor of great renown, as network centre, made it easier, especially at the beginning, after the influential Texon scandal, for the network to get a hearing from it. This is because, through the contract as structural coupling via which projects of various systems could, using law, be stabilised for a definite duration, the National Bank was able to bring the concerns of politics almost directly into the network.[83] Alongside this specific 'release' of a narrow range of irritations, however, the irritations at the site of the structural coupling were, at the same time, limited and an important pre-condition for the compatibilisation of the systems created by it: the network participants gave up their autonomy in two respects, so as to enable co-operation in the network. Not only did the economic actors involved in the network abstain from any actions which, while bringing them competitive advantages on the market, put co-operation in the

81 A Brodocz, 'Strukturelle Kopplung durch Verbände' (1996) 2 *Soziale Systeme* 361 at 367; G Teubner, 'Polykorporatismus: Der Staat als "Netzwerk" öffentlicher und privater Akteure' in H Brunkhorst and P Niesen (eds), *Das Recht der Republik* (Frankfurt aM, Suhrkamp, 1999) 349; N Luhmann, *Die Politik der Gesellschaft* (Frankfurt aM, Suhrkamp, 2002) 396 *et seq*.

82 See, eg, the leading article in the *NZZ* 7/8 May 1977. See, also Section I.2 above.

83 On the contract as structural coupling, see, among many, G Teubner, 'Ein Fall von struktureller Korruption? Die Familienbürgschaft in der Kollision unverträglicher Handlungslogiken (BVerfGE 89, 214 *et seq*)' (2000) 83 *KritV* 388–404; Teubner, 'Vertragswelten' (n 60 above); Amstutz, Abegg and Karavas, *Soziales Vertragsrecht* (n 15 above).

network into question, but also reduced their autonomy in mutually shaping their business relations, while the government administration involved also restricted its own possibilities of acting in the banking sector by way of the hierarchical legislative process.[84]

This *self-restraint of the systems involved presupposes their maintenance of their respective intrinsic rationalities*. Thus, the example of the early CDB shows that the network could not be stabilised with a weakly legitimated public institution—in this case the National Bank, which while it did have the necessary reputation, lacked any suitable statutory basis.[85] This is because if the network positions itself at the intersection of the economy and politics in order to influence the framework conditions of a market decisively, then it is dependent on the link to the power and legitimation resources of politics. We shall come back to this.[86]

The network thus constitutes an *institutional strategy of society's mutually estranged sub-systems* in order to have dealings with each other on condition that they maintain their own intrinsic rationalities, in search of a punctuated equilibrium. To this extent, the chameleonic network form has evolutionary importance in rendering contradictory rationalities compatible.[87] The general picture is that the economy, using the structural couplings, 'feels' its own position in relation to the demands of politics, in order to set off, on the basis of this information, changes in the sub-area of the banking sector through the structural linkage of the contract, which will, in turn, be brought to the attention of politics through the structural coupling of organisation, and checked for success, etc.

These *morphogenic processes* not only have to be respected, but also *normatively underpinned*, from the legal viewpoint; but, here, neither a reconstruction of the network solely as a disconnected bundle of contracts nor solely as an organisation will suffice; just as neither one from a purely economic nor from a purely political viewpoint will. Instead, the need is first to secure the re-entry of the organisation form into the content of the contracts in such a way that the process of squaring off between the systems of the economy and politics can take place at the site of the structural coupling of the organisation. And secondly, the various differing rationalities that come together in the network must be secured

[84] See Teubner, 'Polykorporatismus' (n 81 above) 363 with further references.

[85] This warning was already given by C Schmid, 'Die neue Vereinbarung über die Sorgfaltspflichten der Banken' (1983) 79 *SJZ* 69 at 72. Messner, 'Netzwerktheorien' (nn 42 and 52. For the question of legal statutory basis, see (n 22 above).

[86] *Passim*, Section III.2.

[87] Fundamentally on this, see Teubner, 'Das Recht hybrider Netzwerke' (n 45 above) 570; Teubner, '*Coincidentia Oppositorum*: Hybrid Networks beyond Contract and Organisation' (ch 1), in this volume 3 *et seq*.

against one another.[88] In summary, what is involved here is the institutional guaranteeing of the network in the light of its evolutionary function.

But this is only one side of the coin. The contractual form—as the Federal Court's decision 109 Ib 149 shows—also offers good protection against claims and interference by third parties: the network ought, by no means, to appear to the law as an organisation. This is why third parties can be directed to its individual nodes, which, in turn, appeal against the accusation of breach of the law to the super-ordinate political aspect of the network effect, ie, the market regime. But this opens up a legitimation problem for the network, which I shall now examine.

II.2.(b) Legitimation

II.2.(b)(i) The Problem In the case of the CDB, the banking sector could not find a solution to this crisis without any *political involvement* at all from the outset. Initially, the banks needed a neutral arbitration agency, both to overcome the competition and set co-operation in motion.[89] Thereafter, the involvement of a political actor helped the network to obtain a better hearing from politics. But this was not all: in order to implement a market regime, economic rationality needed *the political symbols of constraint and indisposability.*

But what is actually meant by this? It is already inherent in the concept of a market regime that it should apply to a whole sub-area of the economy and consequently affect a multiplicity of market participants at various levels, imposing restrictions upon their economic possibilities, and that it should, in the last instance, also be imposed coercively. If, however, law—associated with the political symbol of constraint—is used instrumentally, for instance, as in our case, to secure a particular market regime, then the question of the legitimation of this law arises. The Swiss Federal Court decision 109 Ib 146 commented upon above shows these issues clearly. What was being debated in decision 109 Ib 146 was the interests of the *Treuhänder-Verband* and its members. They had undergone a considerable competitive disadvantage from the new CDB arrangement, and yet were unable to influence the CDB—which had primarily been set up by the banks—in any way. Moreover, the reactions to the case clearly showed that purely private-law legitimation—legitimising the legal stabilisation of bilateral differentials by the free will of the participants, and the exclusion of third-party interests by the

[88] Thus, also, the interpretation by Messner, 'Netzwerktheorien' (n 42 above) 50 *et seq* and 57.

[89] In fact, the National Bank took on a leading role in the coming to terms with the Texon-scandal: see *NZZ* 27 April 1977, p 17 and 28 April 1977, p 13.

mechanism of the self-regulating market—was too weak to establish a permanent stabilisation, for the CDB network amounted to more than just a bundle of contracts.[90] Instead, the intended network effect, by combining overwhelming market power and incorporating politics, attained something which exceeded the sum of the individual contracts, namely, a comprehensive market regime—and did so in a key market of central political importance. Today, these issues are already signalled in law by the fact that the Cartel Act is inapplicable simply because of political exceptional clauses.[91] The legitimation issues were accordingly not resolved by the traditional legitimation mechanisms of private law, but, in their stead, *recourse had to be had to political legitimation mechanisms.*[92]

To obtain legitimation, it has to be admitted, the economy cannot copy the sort of ramified participatory procedures that serve to produce legitimacy for the democratic rule of law without denying its own rationality, which relies on lowering transaction costs.[93] In this respect, it is subject to the constraints intrinsic to its system. *Accordingly, the economy must find another way of obtaining the political symbolism of constraint and, above all, of legitimation for its self-regulation.*

In the CDB case, this was initially done by bringing a political actor into the network by contract. While the law enabled the rationalities involved in the contract to clothe their project in the form of law and thus link to the *rule-of-law* legitimation mechanisms, the involvement of politics was meant to convey the *democratic* aspects of legitimation.[94] However, the co-operationist solution with the National Bank as network centre proved incapable of stabilisation, as the critique of the Federal Court decision 109 Ib 146 from legal scholars shows: the National Bank already lacked a statutory basis for becoming involved in this area at all. Thus, despite its great political prestige, it could not adequately convey the democratic symbolism, thus creating the danger of the very political interventions that were to be averted. Correspondingly, structural changes were initiated in the network, in order to oppose this danger. The National Bank was replaced in the network by the politically better underpinned Federal Banking Commission.

[90] On legitimation, see R Brownsword, 'Network Contracts Revisited' (ch 2) in this volume.

[91] See n 76 above.

[92] On this distinction, see Weber, *Wirtschaft und Gesellschaft* (Tübingen, Mohr & Siebeck, 1980/1921–1925) 123.

[93] On legitimation in democracy under rule of law, see Luhmann, *Das Recht der Gesellschaft* (n 26 above) 416 *et seq*.

[94] This is also indicated by Müller, when he calls the involvement of the National Bank the 'official veneer' for the CDB: Müller, 'Zur Rechtsnatur der Vereinbarung über die Sorgfaltspflichten der Banken bei der Entgegennahme von Geldern und über die Handhabung des Bankgeheimnisses' (n 6 above) 350 *et seq*.

But even with the legislative mandate that the Federal Banking Commission possesses, a co-operationist combination of the economy and politics by contract would have been hard to stabilise. This is because *the contractual combination between politics and the economy even threatens to break up the existing legitimation mechanisms of the democratic state under rule of law*: if government administration is to be able to have dealings with other areas of society in co-operationist fashion, it must have the corresponding freedom to negotiate the ends and the means of this selfsame co-operation. Here, the administration determines not just the way to the political goal, but increasingly also the goal itself, thus calling into question the administration's formal and material legality as (i) (central for the economy) the guarantor of the rule-of-law restraints on social happenings and (ii) (for society in general) the intermediary of democratic legitimation in the form of a developed participatory procedure.[95] Correspondingly, in the CDB network, the contractual connections between politics and the economy were loosened. The political actor was replaced at the network centre by the banks' own trade organisation, while politics repositioned itself at the periphery of the network and took on the role of overall governmental supervision.[96] In this way, the network arrangement was, on the one hand, brought closer to an unproblematical private-law code of professional ethics, and, on the other, subjected to a public-law political framework system.[97] These structural adjustments to the network justified the criticisms of the legal scholars who had sought to resolve the legitimation problem by *extending the political demands and suppressing the contradictory demands of conflicting spheres of action*.[98]

With the *partial retreat into the traditional dichotomies* of public and private spheres, the network partially managed, through its withdrawal

[95] J Habermas, *Faktizität und Geltung: Beiträge zur Diskurstheorie des Rechts und des demokratischen Rechtsstaats* (Frankfurt aM, Suhrkamp, 1992) 519 *et seq*; E Schmidt-Assmann, 'Das Recht der Verwaltungsverträge zwischen gesetzlicher Bindung und administrativer Gestaltung' in W Drenseck (ed), *Festschrift für Heinrich Wilhelm Kruse zum 70. Geburtstag* (Cologne, O Schmidt, 2001).

[96] For the relationship between the CDB-supervision and the Federal Banking Commission, see de Capitani, 'Die Aufsichtskommission VSB und das zehnte Gebot' (n 7 above), and Zuberbühler, 'Das Verhältnis zwischen der Bankenaufsicht, insbesondere der Überwachung der einwandfreien Geschäftstätigkeit, und der neuen Sorgfaltspflichtvereinbarung der Banken' (n 7 above).

[97] Section I.2 above.

[98] See, especially, Müller, 'Zur Rechtsnatur der Vereinbarung über die Sorgfaltspflichten der Banken bei der Entgegennahme von Geldern und über die Handhabung des Bankgeheimnisses' (n 6 above) and Rhinow, 'Verfügung, Verwaltungsvertrag und privatrechtlicher Vertrag' (n 21 above); with a similar opinion, Marti, 'Selbstregulierung anstelle staatlicher Gesetzgebung?' (n 33 above) 576, fn 81; and for another, differentiated one, Schefer, 'Grundrechtliche Schutzpflichten und die Auslagerung staatlicher Aufgaben' (n 33 above) 1139 *et seq*.

into more traditional self-regulation, to lessen the danger of politicisation through direct legislative intervention or through a judicial classification as public law, which would inevitably have seen the politicised 'public interests' alienating the network from economic rationality. However, the CDB also lost a significant part of its capacity to adapt to the contradictory demands of conflicting rationalities: the economy's direct link to the symbiosis of law and politics to secure the symbol of legitimation through a contractual connection with politics was largely severed, and the possibility of morphogenesis was thus restricted. Admittedly, the morphogenic structures remained, in so far as the economy and politics could continue to perform exchanges (or, more precisely, to irritate each other) about the need for collective decisions at the locus of the structural coupling of organisation. And with the Federal Banking Commission, politics could continue to benefit from the banks' specific technical knowledge of how a functioning market regime is to be constituted, and, at the same time, let its demands flow into the network—albeit no longer in the existing differentiated co-operationist fashion, but only in the sense of an *ordre public*.[99] Politics thus lost influence over the details of the arrangement, and the economy now had no way of pushing the morphogenesis far enough for the political demands to be able to flow into the CDB directly via the structural coupling of the contract. Thus, today's numerous legal provisions in this connection are also pointers to the *failures of the CDB as an experimental programme,* at least, in its original radicality.[100] And even if a sizeable core of self-regulation has been left, we nonetheless have to state that today's self-regulation—as the Federal Court decision 125 IV 139 shows—cannot lead much further than a traditional code of professional ethics.[101]

From the *viewpoint of an evolutionary theory* taking the model of a polycontextural society as its basis, this development of the CDB is regrettable. This is because the original CDB network with its morphogenic structures had proved to be a promising strategy for opening up contradictory, and even paradoxical, demands at the intersection of conflicting social systems. Thus an important contribution to the co-evolution and integration of mutually estranged social systems was

[99] For a description of reflexive regulation of the banking sector, see Strulik, 'Governance globalisierter Finanzmärkte' (n 78 above) 308 *et seq*.

[100] See, only, the now copious regulations in the Federal Act of 10 October 1997 to combat money-laundering in the financial sector (Money-laundering Act) and the corresponding EBK order of 18 December 2002 on the prevention of money-laundering (EBK money-laundering order).

[101] See n 32 above.

performed—while simultaneously maintaining each of their own intrinsic rationalities.[102] This does not mean that one should forget the difficulties that the CDB network raised for politics. Certainly, in my view, the withdrawal into the traditional dichotomy of private and public came far too early. This is because there definitely are possibilities for reconciling a network structure, especially one based on the structural coupling of the contract for the integration of the mutually estranged systems, with the need for legitimation. I shall briefly outline these approaches to solutions.

II.2.(b)(ii) Rule-of-Law Legitimation Mechanisms When it comes to rule-of-law legitimation mechanisms, very basically and in the framework of the traditional application of fundamental rights, the *effect of political communication on the economic side of the network* can be tested against the fundamental rights:

(A) Freedom of the Private Person and Freedom of Thought To the extent that the administration grants private persons the possibility, through their entry into a co-operative relationship directly with the administration, of preventing a command-type procedure being commenced, the *freedom of the private person* is not a pre-requisite. It is only once the private person is faced with the option between 'contract or command' that the decision in favour of freedom—pre-formed by the administration—can be taken, in the light of the conduct demanded by it. The freedom traditionally pre-supposed in private law (as freedom to do something or not) is here conferred by the administration. Åkerstrøm Andersen has persuasively pointed out that before this conferred freedom as a premise, all that remains is bare 'freedom of thought' (*Gewissensfreiheit*). This freedom of thought constitutes the very residue of the traditionally presupposed freedom without preconditions that is due to human beings by virtue of their being human.[103] The freedom conferred by the administration is thus far removed from the Kantian freedom, which has no prior cause, which is, transcendentally, a value in itself, and, as such, is, in principle, not dependent on sensuous or social needs, either.[104] Here, the legitimating function of private law's delegation of self-organisation is almost completely absent, so that the co-operationist relationship between private persons and government administration is to be allocated to public law and its legitimation mechanisms, which are

[102] See Messner, 'Netzwerktheorien' (n 42 above) 58 *et seq*.
[103] N Åkerstrøm Andersen, 'The Contractualisation of the Citizen—on the transformation of obligation into freedom' (2004) 10 *Soziale Systeme* 273–91.
[104] I Kant, *Kritik der reinen Vernunft* (Hamburg, pub house, 1993/1787) 561 *et seq*; I Kant, *Kritik der praktischen Vernunft* (Hamburg, Felix Meiner, 1993/1788) 60 *et seq*; I Kant, 'Metaphysische Anfangsgründe der Rechtslehre' in *Rechtslehre: Schriften zur Rechtsphilosophie* (Berlin, Akademie Verlag, 1988/1797) 27 *et seq*.

traditionally concerned with securing society's areas of freedom against the state, as well as with the legitimation of the interventions that restrict freedom through the concept of the democratic rule of law.[105] In the case of the CDB, the prospect of market regulation by legislative policy was not so immediate that the banks' freedom in the decision of whether and how to build self-regulation would have to be regarded as mediated by the state. Instead, the proactive conduct of the banks in the course of the evolution of the CDB shows that the decisive thrusts towards self-regulation always came from the private side.[106]

- Even if a case of self-regulation is—particularly on the criterion of freedom of decision—assigned to private law, we must first ask whether the *governmental pressure for self-regulation or the pressure to co-operate* infringes fundamental rights. Since free assent is constitutive for private self-regulation, a self-regulation imposed by governmental administrative units potentially constitutes an infringement of fundamental rights, which correspondingly has to be justified. Here we must also bear in mind the gradual evolution of the selfsame co-operation and self-regulations which may very well start within the framework of the fundamental rights, but which may later cross the threshold to infringe fundamental rights. Or, in other words, a gradual increase in duties of co-operation and self-regulation cannot justify an infringement of fundamental rights without further ado.[107] For instance, the Federal Banking Commission ban on a CDB form upon which trustees could declare that the economic beneficiary, while known, would not be disclosed should correspondingly have been checked for compliance with fundamental rights.[108]
- It should then be a principle that politics is not to be freed of its ensuring liability[109], whenever it is involved in a regulation or influences it. Accordingly, in a mixed hybrid network, the political

[105] See, also, the neo-liberal position of W Zöllner, 'Regelungsspielräume im Schuldvertragsrecht' (1996) 196 *Archiv für die civilistische Praxis* 1 at 26 *et seq* and 35 *et seq*.

[106] Müller 'Zur Rechtsnatur der Vereinbarung über die Sorgfaltspflichten der Banken bei der Entgegennahme von Geldern und über die Handhabung des Bankgeheimnisses' (n 6 above) 350 *et seq*, argues in the opposite direction, but then calls the National Bank's involvement the 'official veneer' for the CDB.

[107] Di Fabio, 'Verwaltung und Verwaltungsrecht zwischen gesellschaftlicher Selbstregulierung und staatlicher Steuerung' (n 20 above) 256 *et seq*.

[108] See n 24 above.

[109] The concept of the ensuring state emphasises on a continuing state responsibility for the common good and rejects the idea that changes in statehood reduce state responsibility. See, eg, G F Schuppert, 'Der Gewährleistungsstaat—modisches Label oder Leitbild sich wandelnder Staatlichkeit?' in Schuppert (ed), *Der Gewährleistungsstaat—ein Leitbild auf dem Prüfstand* (Baden-Baden, Nomos, 2005) 11–52. See also Art 16, 86 Abs 2 of the treaty establishing the European Community, OJ C 325, 24 December 2002.

> communications of the public-law network nodes must be challengeable as a decision, so that higher priority ought also to be attributed to the justification of the administrative decision.[110] Clearly, this does not mean that every corresponding court decision would have direct repercussions on the network and on the private-law contracts: in so far as the network is to be described as a bundle of private contracts, any infringement of the private-law rationality which, in principle, stabilises the bipolarity of the contracting parties and excludes third-party interests would require special justification.[111] However, alongside the possibility of demanding damages from the political actors, an appropriate judgment ought also to impose upon political actors a duty to act upon the network.[112]

As an extension of this sort of mono-causal application of the fundamental rights against politics, the law has to call on the systems involved for a new way of applying them: *a polycontextural application of the fundamental rights*. This is because if politics can no longer be trusted with, nor be expected to handle, the constitutional shaping of the total polycontextural society, then the consequence is that *each social sub-system* has to be called on for a corresponding self-restraint, with—as its object—the legal liberation and, at the same time, the curbing of the system's specific rationality vis-à-vis internal spontaneous order and vis-à-vis other social sectors.[113] This demand may be placed on the CDB network in various ways. In particular, the Federal Banking Commission, as the regulatory body, ought to call for this self-restraint when granting authorisation to the CDB in connection with the general clause of the Banking Act, which prescribes the ensuring of proper business conduct. And the courts should call for this sort of self-restraint of economic rationality when—as in the Federal Court decision 109 Ib 146—dealing with relevant cases. This sort of substantive self-restraint by the economy is often discussed under the heading of democratic legitimation mechanisms. I should like—again sketchily—to show how democratic legitimation mechanisms might be recast for these issues.

[110] N Luhmann, *Legitimation durch Verfahren* (Frankfurt aM, Suhrkamp, 1983/1969) 215 *et seq*.

[111] In detail, see P Gauch, 'Zuschlag und Verfügung—Ein Beitrag zum öffentlichen Vergaberecht' in *Mensch und Staat, Festgabe für Thomas Fleiner* (Freiburg iUe, édition universitaires, 2003).

[112] See also di Fabio, 'Verwaltung und Verwaltungsrecht zwischen gesellschaftlicher Selbstregulierung und staatlicher Steuerung' (n 20 above) 270 *et seq*.

[113] G Teubner, 'Globale Zivilverfassungen: Alternativen zur staatszentrierten Verfassungstheorie' (2003) 63 *Zeitschrift für ausländisches öffentliches Recht und Völkerrecht* 1–28; Messner, 'Netzwerktheorien' (n 42 above).

II.2.(b)(iii) Democratic Legitimation Mechanisms According to such authors as Habermas or Grimm, new types of administrative conduct, detached from the traditional structures of the democratic rule of law, can secure legitimation, above all, by supplementing recourse to normative grounds by a process of internal democratisation. This so-called internal democratisation can, according to area—with the exception of the legal protection to be adapted to the new forms—result from participation in administration, ie institutionalisation of ombudsforms within the administration, court-like procedures, hearings and publications, involvement in decisions of those affected or their representatives, etc.[114] As with the concept of the social state, the point is for the individuals, or the addressees of the administrative action, to be put into a position to able to cultivate and protect their interests and bring them to bear on decision-making processes.

From the viewpoint of an evolutionary theory based upon systems theory, caution is, of course, in order here, since the polycontextural aspects of today's society, ie, the differentiation of society into various sub-systems, each functioning on a different intrinsic logic, have to be taken as the basis for the model of today's society, as achievements of modernity. Whether society's differentiation already contains—as in Teubner—a normative principle,[115] or whether the observer has to take this differentiation as the basis for his model of society if he is to secure an adequate picture which he can orient himself by, need not be gone into here. This is because acknowledging the polycontextural society as a society of law can already point at the dangers, such as those described under the heading of Teubner's regulatory trilemma, which threaten if Habermas's proposals are implemented.[116] Thus, in the light of evolutionary theory, we must be warned against any too direct interference with the complex, evolutionarily-grown structures of other subsystems.[117] The point must instead be—from the viewpoint of evolutionary theory—to support the system's internal reorientation of function, performance and reflection through law, in such a way that the system

[114] Habermas, *Faktizität und Geltung* (n 95 above) 527 *et seq*; similarly, D Grimm, *Die Zukunft der Verfassung* (Frankfurt aM, Suhrkamp, 1991) 414.

[115] Teubner, 'Ein Fall von struktureller Korruption?' (n 83 above); here di Fabio agrees with Teubner: di Fabio, 'Verwaltung und Verwaltungsrecht zwischen gesellschaftlicher Selbstregulierung und staatlicher Steuerung' (n 20 above) 262.

[116] G Teubner, 'Das regulatorische Trilemma: Zur Diskussion um post-instrumentale Rechtsmodelle' (1984) 13 *Quaderni Fiorentini per la Storia del Pensiero Giuridico Moderno* 109–49.

[117] In this sense, Schneider also warns against over-direct politicization of policy networks. Instead, he calls for a strengthening of the traditional democratic legislative processes: V Schneider, 'Möglichkeiten und Grenzen der Demokratisierung von Netzwerken in der Politik' in J Sydow and A Windeler (eds), *Steuerung von Netzwerken* (Opladen, Westdeutscher Verlag, 2000) 342 *et seq*.

can react optimally to intensive, complex and even contradictory environmental demands without endangering its own rationality.[118] We shall come back to this.

However, we certainly should follow Habermas in his finding that numerous forms of co-operation between the state and private persons, as in our case of the early CDB network, cannot meet the demands of politics for legitimate regulation. Although the economy does link up with politics, it still either fails to achieve, within the concrete co-operation, the re-entry of the political sphere, or succeeds only insufficiently. Today, too, the continual demands from many legal scholars for a more strongly reinforced return of the network into public law indicate that the CDB still lacks legitimation, so that the banking sector has not yet met the political demands with regard to a punctuated equilibrium. How, then, can these demands of politics on the economy be supported by a polycontextural application of the fundamental rights?

II.2.(b)(iv) Evolutionary-Procedural Legitimation Mechanisms The *statements so far* have identified the morphogenic structures[119] of co-operationist and, in particular, network-type arrangements as an evolutionary strategy for adapting to the polycontextural society. This sort of morphogenic structure, supported by law, thus makes it easier for the various social systems to enter into dealings with each other, whereby the rationalities rebounding from each other within these structures have to be secured against each other by reconfigured fundamental rights.

The difficult constitutional question now is how the different systems can be brought—by law—to take into account the differentiation of their surrounding systems and their most important demands, in order to obtain a punctuated equilibrium. To apply this to the CDB case, how, on the one hand, can politics be induced, despite a political programme that has to be implemented and despite continuing ensuring liability, to respect economic freedom even within self-regulation (as the re-entry of the economy into politics)? And how, on the other hand, can the economy be induced to enter into the political demands for a legitimate CDB network (as re-entry of politics into the rationality of the economy)—especially if legislative interventions by politics are to be avoided on grounds of the legislator's being overburdened for the specific object,

[118] On the triad of function, performance and reflection, see Luhmann (n 59 above).

[119] What is meant are particularly the feedback loops between the structural couplings and the selection within the system that repositions it within its environment: Section II above.

while, at the same time, the law in a polycontextural society has neither the knowledge nor the possibility of implanting specific, effective regulations into the economy?[120]

We can be helped over this uncertainty as to the right law by a *procedural approach*, as described by Wiethölter. He—much as Habermas has done—calls for the continual renewal of the integration of the society of law through the involvement of society in the production and justification of law, thus simultaneously creating a new type of legitimation.[121]

In a procedural method, the courts, in particular, need to have more dealings than before with the differentiated polycontextural society. The job of finding socially-adequate norms must no longer be delegated *solely* through private autonomy to the economy and through legislation to politics. In the difficult task of finding the legal needs of the polycontextural society, the courts are, of course, supported by *the law's neighbouring sciences*: law is structurally coupled with these (for example, legal sociology, legal philosophy, legal history, legal psychology, etc), first, via legal theory as the reflective mechanism of law, and secondly, in a narrowly limited normative fashion, through (mainly politically) inserted general clauses as well as norm references. The systems in conflict, such as the economy, the family or politics, are, however, just as far from science—be it economic, family or political science—as from the law.

If, then, as stated above, the need is to promote possibilities for the mutually-estranged sub-systems of society to observe each other and respond to the various demands of the surrounding systems, then attention must be directed not just to the structural couplings—which, as we have seen, enable systems to perceive themselves as the environment for the other systems in each case—but also to the structures on the basis of which systems respond to demands from their environment while taking account of their own intrinsic rationality. If these morphogenic structures are so threatened by one system that other systems can no longer adapt their operations and structures to the changing environment, the law should protect them. This could be done by, for example, a judicially-established obligation to contract. In particular, such a obligation to contract could be applied in cases like the Federal Court decision 109 Ib 146, when the political legitimation demands on a market regime established by the economy are not covered because of structural shortcomings. This, however, calls for some further explanation, as follows.

[120] This is sometimes forgotten when the by now familiar concepts of a procedural or reflexive law are being talked about: see, eg, Strulik, 'Governance globalisierter Finanzmärkte: Policy-Netzwerke und Kontextsteuerung im Bankensystem' (n 78 above) 322 *et seq*, with an interesting perspective on the reflexive regulation of the international banking sector.

[121] Fundamentally, R Wiethölter, 'Materialization and Proceduralization in Modern Law' in G Teubner (ed), *Dilemmas of Law in the Welfare State* (Berlin, de Gruyter, 1982).

From the viewpoint of legal doctrine, decisions intended to promote a balancing of the relationship between function, performance and reflection within the system—in the CDB case to demand re-entry of the political demands into economic rationality—can be located in so-called *niches*[122]: First, possible niches in which variations with contents capable of compatibilisation may be formed should be sought in the legal sub-system coupled with the observed rationality, in our case, law of contract. For the most part, such niches can be found in the form of reservation norms, which act as signal norms pointing to the issues in conflict. Such *conflict norms* are, as a rule, couched openly, in order to be able to grasp the evolutionary dimension of the co-existence of systems. Traditionally, in Swiss law of contract, the general clauses on public morals (Article 19 f *OR*, Article 27 f *CC*), good faith (Article 2 *CC*) and the application of the law (Article 1 *CC*) take on this role.[123] Corresponding niches, through which the CDB network could be brought to render political demands compatible with the rationality of the economic sub-system are, however, also present in anti-trust law.[124] If the niche and the conflict norm have been set up, the need is then to identify the *specific legal sub-rationality that produces consistency within the sub-systems*. Only in this way can the reason for the conflict, on the one hand, and the external form of the evolutionary capacity, on the other, be recognised. This specific legal sub-rationality is to be gathered from the relevant precedents (empirically), because it is not already laid down fixedly from the outset, but is constructed through the applicable cases.[125]

Such a decision ought not only to protect the morphogenic structure in the case before judgment, but, simply because of its coarse structure, should also set off a complex process of 'social' law-making in an interplay of law, scholarship and the systems involved in the conflict. These systems are led by the judicial considerations to generate new variations, which are, in turn, checked by legal scholars for doctrinal consistency, and then, if need be, are presented to the courts for selection,

[122] This model was developed for economic law: Amstutz, *Evolutorisches Wirtschaftsrecht* (n 43 above) 326 *et seq*.

[123] Swiss Civil Code *CC* (SR 210); Swiss Code of Obligations *CO* (SR 220). See, most recently, the methodological observations of P Gauch, 'Der Schätzer und die Dritten' in *Norm und Wirkung: Festschrift für Wolfgang Wiegand zum 65. Geburtstag* (Bern, Stämpfli, 2005).

[124] By Art 7 *KG*, abuse of a position of market domination is impermissible. Clearly, the *Treuhänder-Verband* as consumer of the service could probably not have based its claim on antitrust law, since by Art 12 KG claims arise under anti-trust law only for those who are 'hampered in the initiation or exercise of competition by an impermissible restraint of trade'; see also J Ensthaler and D Gesmann-Nuissl, 'Virtuelle Unternehmen in der Praxis—eine Herausforderung für das Zivil-, Gesellschafts- und Kartellrecht' (2000) 55 *Betriebs-Berater* 2265 at 2270.

[125] On all this: Amstutz, *Evolutorisches Wirtschaftsrecht* (n 43 above) 326 *et seq*; Abegg, 'Evolutorische Rechtstheorie' (n 80 above).

perhaps sent back again, etc,—until a selection capable of stabilisation has been found.[126] In short, the point is to refer the conflict back to the systems involved—with, of course, an indication of the solution to be sought.

In the 109 Ib 146 case, the problem was essentially that the legitimation for the market regime produced ought to have been brought about by politics and the law through the structural coupling of the contract. The specific shape of the CDB at the locus of the structural coupling of the contract suffered from the fact that no contractual partner adequately legitimated by political mechanisms was included in the network, so that the two systems of the economy and politics were brought together in a structurally unsatisfactory fashion. Accordingly, the network nodes ought to have been forced into contracting with the third parties concerned, until the network had linked its market regime with a sufficiently legitimated political body or established some other adequate source of legitimation, which would subsequently have led to a situation-specific re-entry of the political legitimation demands into the CDB's economic rationality and thus to a step in the direction of a punctuated equilibrium. This is because normative protection of the structural coupling of the economy and (legislative) politics also guarantees the possibility of co-evolution of the systems, allowing both of them to irritate each other with their respective demands. In the case of decision 109 Ib 146, the banks involved in the network would then have been obliged to treat the members of the *Treuhänder-Verband* on an equal footing with the privileged lawyers and members of the Chamber of Trustees and Auditors ('*Treuhand- und Revisionskammer*') in relation to the disclosure duty.[127] Thus, a simple 'not that way' and relatively vague demands on the legal doctrine in the light of the above-stated normative demand ought to initiate a process whereby—utilising evolutionary structures in a procedural way—empirically underpinned solutions are sought. These solutions need to obey the strict normative requirements of the law, and, at the same time, have to respect and follow the selfsame rationalities that brought the conflict before the law.

Finally, it should be pointed out that, through this procedural approach, the various systems involved in the conflict are squared off with each other, along with the law, in evolutionary fashion *at the locus of structural couplings*, and, thus, a co-evolution of the systems is ensured, which reciprocally promotes the differentiation of the conflicting systems—in a direction towards constitutionalising the respective systems in relation to the systems in their environment, making them

[126] See Amstutz, Abegg and Karavas, *Soziales Vertragsrecht* (n 15 above).
[127] See n 4 above.

compatible.[128] This procedural extension of law, set in motion by court decisions, is appropriate to new types of problems that arise in today's polycontextural society; it finds its normativity in formal respects by utilising the structural couplings of law and other social systems, and it moves in strikingly parallel fashion to the law's stated function of protecting the morphogenic structures between the systems involved, so that the systems, in our case, politics and the economy, can observe each other and guarantee each other in their differentiation. Or, to put it another way, the substantive normative demand for protection for morphogenic structures and structural couplings between the conflicting social sub-systems, in order to guarantee the capacity for evolution (or as Wiethölter puts it: developmental dynamics), can be secured in the form of the procedural and evolutionary method of adjudication described, at the sites of the structural couplings between the law and the various social sub-systems.[129] In this sense, the law—as called for by democratic legitimation theories—both involves the society of law in finding the law, and protects the differentiated society—as with rule-of-law legitimation theories—while at the same time preserving the central rule-of-law function of the courts.

[128] Similarly, R Wiethölter, 'Recht-Fertigungen eines Gesellschafts-Rechts' in C Joerges and G Teubner (eds), *Rechtsverfassungsrecht: Recht-Fertigung zwischen Privatrechtsdogmatik und Gesellschaftstheorie* (Baden-Baden, Nomos, 2003).

[129] See also Wiethölter, 'Recht-Fertigungen eines Gesellschafts-Rechts' (n 128 above).

15

Mixed Public-Private Networks as Vehicles for Regulatory Policy

Comments on the Chapter by Andreas Abegg

TERENCE DAINTITH*

I. INTRODUCTION: THE ISSUES

THE AIM OF this paper is to examine—briefly—the same phenomena as those analysed by Andreas Abegg, but from the standpoint of regulatory policy analysis, rather than that of evolutionary systems theory. My use here of the word 'regulatory' will be broad enough to encompass rules and other ordering devices which are designed to achieve the purposes of private as well as state actors.[1] In this acceptation, sometimes now referred to as a 'de-centred' view of regulation,[2] the state, while it remains at all times a highly important actor, is not necessarily at the origin, or even at the centre, of the regulatory enterprise. As Abegg notes, this phenomenon is not simply one of the state's using the self-regulatory capacities of economic organisations to advance its own policies.[3] The state may also co-operate with private actors, using different legal and organisational devices, in order to advance compatible state and private policy goals. Abegg calls this 'co-operationism', or 'co-operative relations between state and private

* Professor of Law, University of Western Australia.

[1] See T Daintith, 'Regulation' in R Buxbaum and F Madl (eds), *International Encyclopedia of Comparative Law*, vol XVII (Tübingen, Mohr & Siebeck, 1997) ch 10.

[2] J Black, 'Critical Reflections on Regulation' (2002) 27 *Australian Journal of Legal Philosophy* 1.

[3] 'Self-regulation under governmental direction': Abegg, 'Regulation of Hybrid Networks at the Intersection between Governmental Administration and Economic Self-Organisation' (ch 14), 259. This is often referred to in 'official' regulation literature as 'co-regulation': see, eg, Better Regulation Task Force (UK), *Imaginative Thinking for Better Regulation* (London, Better Regulation Task Force, 2003) 45–6.

persons', and argues that it 'has plunged the law into deep crisis'[4] by reason of the inability of the law's existing categories to offer characterisations for these relationships which would submit them to adequate democratic and legal controls while at the same time preserving their essential functional advantages.

The response proposed by Abegg in his complex and closely-argued paper is to use systems theory to identify the elements in such relationships which represent effective structural couplings between the political and economic systems that they exist to link; to propose appropriate legal rules to protect and reinforce such couplings; and thereby to provide the conditions for a process of co-evolution of the relevant systems, so that public interest demands can be satisfactorily harmonised with commercial imperatives over extended periods of time. This may involve using the kinds of contractual networks that are the main concern of this volume to frame these relationships and provide these couplings. For him, the early versions (1977 and 1982) of the Agreement on the Swiss Banks' Code of Conduct with regard to the Exercise of Due Diligence ('CDB') offer an example of such a network which, but for one important flaw—the absence of a sufficiently legitimated public actor—could have efficiently coupled the banks' interests in their market, international reputation, and competitive position inter se, with those of the Swiss state in maintaining Switzerland's reputation for financial probity, and in being seen to co-operate actively in international attempts to control money-laundering and the varied and nefarious activities that it facilitates. Legal challenges to the propriety of the early CDB, both in academic writing and in the courts, led, in Abegg's view, to a process of change in its legal shape and environment—the replacement of the Swiss National Bank, as the banks' contractual partner, with the Swiss Bankers' Association, and the subordination of the Agreement to public law rules about money-laundering—the result of which has been to reduce it to 'a piece of regulated professional etiquette' which does no more than to flesh out some broad statutory duties of care which have been superimposed upon it.[5] For him, this reassertion of the traditional public-private law dichotomy damages the structural coupling achieved by the early arrangements, which could have been preserved and strengthened, at the right moment, by appropriate judicial use of contractual remedies.

For a student of regulation with a public law background, this is a challenging and stimulating argument, a challenge which is increased by the relative lack of interest displayed by legal systems such as that of the

[4] Abegg, 'Regulation of Hybrid Networks at the Intersection between Governmental Administration and Economic Self-Organisation' (ch 14), 255.

[5] Abegg, 'Regulation of Hybrid Networks at the Intersection between Governmental Administration and Economic Self-Organisation' (ch 14), 262.

United Kingdom,[6] for example, in issues of legal classification. I stress the term 'relative', because it is necessary to distinguish public and private law issues for certain purposes, such as the choice of the appropriate litigation procedure. Such distinctions, however, are viewed as pragmatic necessities, and are certainly not felt as fundamental to the point where it would be conceivable to talk of a challenge to these categories throwing the law 'into deep crisis'.[7]

From this standpoint, the CDB assumes a rather different appearance from that perceived by Abegg. What, for him, is a contractual network with a high capacity for structurally-coupling different social systems (politics and economics) with positive results, looks to me like an ingenious, though essentially artificial, use of contract as a formal vehicle for command-and-control regulation,[8] under a scheme whose lack of legitimacy could not be cured without depriving the structure of the very advantages which Abegg attributes to it.[9] The interest of this disagreement for the general topic of this volume is the light which it may throw on whether contractual networks can function as a stable and effective regulatory device in the service of both public *and* private policy aims, where these overlap sufficiently. Abegg's praise for the CDB in its original form implies a positive response to this general question.[10] In my opinion, however, the CDB—though located within an informal network of relationships between the Swiss banks, the Swiss National Bank, the Swiss Bankers' Association, the Federal Banking Commission and other bodies—does not exhibit key characteristics attributed in this volume to contractual networks, and such networks are, in general, unlikely to have regulatory potential. My argument towards this conclusion discusses first, the nature of the CDB arrangements, and second, the general relationship between contractual networks and regulation.

[6] The distinct systems of English and Scots law, in fact, display little difference in this respect.

[7] Abegg, 'Regulation of Hybrid Networks at the Intersection between Governmental Administration and Economic Self-Organisation' (ch 14), 255; on the traditional attitude to the public-private distinction in the United Kingdom, see T Weir, 'The Common Law System' in R David (ed), *International Encyclopedia of Comparative Law*, vol II (Tübingen, Mohr & Siebeck, 1974) ch 2, paras 2–115 to 2–134.

[8] By this, I mean regulation by way of a set of rules which identifies particular conduct and seeks to control it, and limit its risks, by means of a system of prohibitions and consents, which may be general or individualised in operation, or both.

[9] The paper asserts the advantages of structures which allow 'co-evolution through morphogenesis', but makes no attempt at any empirical demonstration.

[10] Abegg, 'Regulation of Hybrid Networks at the Intersection between Governmental Administration and Economic Self-Organisation' (ch 14), 269–73.

II. A REGULATORY ANALYSIS OF THE CDB

In its original (1977) form, the CDB described itself as

> an agreement between the banks domiciled in Switzerland and the Swiss Bankers' Association, on the one hand, and the Swiss National Bank, on the other hand.[11]

The eligible individual banks were invited by the Swiss Bankers' Association to adhere to the agreement. The agreement's preamble made it clear that it converted good practice in the acceptance of funds and the practice of banking secrecy into binding obligations, and the bulk of the agreement was composed of a series of obligations and prohibitions imposed on the banks and designed to ensure that clients were fully identified and that bank accounts were not used for a variety of unacceptable purposes. The normal operation of these rules did not require the intervention of either the Swiss Bankers' Association or the Swiss National Bank. The principal involvement of these bodies was in the enforcement procedure, under which an Arbitration Committee, composed of two representatives of each body, under the chairmanship of a federal judge unanimously appointed by them, could impose a 'conventional fine' of up to CHFr 10 million on a bank which it found to have breached the agreement.[12] The National Bank provided the secretariat for this Committee. Information relating to breaches was provided to the Committee (and to the Federal Banking Commission) through the auditing procedure for banks established under Swiss banking law, adhesion to the agreement being taken as authorisation by the bank to the relevant agency to communicate this information.[13] The only other involvement of the Bankers' Association was that its board of directors was authorised by the signatory banks, under Article 15(4),

> in co-operation with the Swiss National Bank, to make further definitions or any modifications to the agreement that may prove necessary on the strength of the experience gained.

The extensive literature on regulatory practice which is today disseminated by regulatory review bodies within national governments,[14] as

[11] Quotations are from the official English translations of the CDB, as promulgated from time to time.

[12] CDB (1977) Art 14.

[13] CDB (1977) Art 13(1).

[14] For example, for Australia, the Office for Regulatory Reform of the Australian Productivity Commission, see Commonwealth Office of Regulation Review, *A Guide to Regulation*, 2nd edn (Canberra, Office of Regulation Review, 1998), available at: http://www.pc.gov.au/orr/reports/guide/reguide2/index.html, especially Sections B3 and E2, or the Victoria Department of Treasury and Finance, see *Victorian Guide to Regulation* (Melbourne, Department of Treasury and Finance, State of Victoria, 2005), available at:

well as by bodies such as the European Commission[15] and the Organisation for Economic Co-operation and Development,[16] lays heavy emphasis on avoiding automatic resort to command-and-control regulation as a first response to every problem. When, however, one is faced with the need to control practices which facilitate possibly criminal conduct, and it is possible to frame, for this purpose, rules which are clear and precise enough to be the subject of judicial enquiry and are backed up, where appropriate, by specific penalties, even those who favour the consideration of a broad range of regulatory possibilities (including exhortation, self-regulation, taxes, contracts and so on) are likely to conclude that command-and-control regulation is what is needed.

In this case, however, formal regulation by a public authority, based upon a legislative mandate, did not follow the major banking scandals of the 1970s. Here, I have no difficulty in following Abegg's suggestion that an important factor was the strong desire of the banking industry to avoid subjection to formal regulation in the interests of not hampering 'normal banking business'—a risk which might be perceived to flow from intervention by possibly ill-informed and inflexible public regulators.[17] Likewise, I can see how a possible lack of mutual trust among Swiss banks might lead to difficulty in embracing either unilateral acceptance by each bank of an official, but voluntary, code of conduct,[18] or, indeed, of a 'self-regulatory' solution sustained solely by the prestige of the Swiss Bankers' Association. But such approaches are unlikely to have been seen as adequate by the public authorities, either. It appears that the shape of the scheme owed most to the National Bank, which largely drafted the agreement, persuaded the big banks to sign up, and then used the Swiss Bankers' Association as the means to get smaller banks to do likewise.[19]

The result—in which strict rules and sanctions were combined with a choice (albeit doubtless heavily constrained in practical terms) as to whether to sign up or not, and with the formal guarantee, for the Swiss Bankers' Association, of being involved in any modification or development of the CDB—offered much both to the public authorities and to

www.vcec.vic.gov.au, Appendix B; for the UK, Better Regulation Task Force, *Imaginative Thinking for Better Regulation* (London, Better Regulation Task Force, 2003).

[15] See, eg, *Final report of Mandelkern Group on Better Regulation* (Brussels, Commission of the European Communiities, 2001), available at: http://www.cabinetoffice.gov.uk/regulation/europe/documents/pdf/mandfinrep.pdf, Section 2.2.2.2.

[16] See OECD, *Regulatory Polices in OECD Countries: From Interventionism to Regulatory Governance* (Paris, OECD, 2002) Annex II.

[17] Abegg, 'Regulation of Hybrid Networks at the Intersection between Governmental Administration and Economic Self-Organisation' (ch 14), 269.

[18] *Ibid*, 270.

[19] Correspondence to the author from A Abegg, 25 October 2005.

banking interests. In particular, the central role to be played by the Swiss National Bank, as an active participant in the banking industry which might be expected to be both knowledgeable about, and sympathetic to, established banking practice, must have appealed to the banks. Indeed, the absence of statutory authority in the National Bank to exercise formal powers in the area, which proved to be the Achilles' heel of the original design of the CDB after the 1983 Federal Court decision,[20] may originally have been seen by the industry as providing a comforting barrier to political accountability.

The formal legal device through these different interests and pressures were reconciled in 1977 was, of course, that of contract. The 1977 CDB, as already noted, announced itself as

> an agreement between the banks domiciled in Switzerland and the Swiss Bankers' Association, on the one hand, and the Swiss National Bank, on the other hand;

and the 2003 agreement as

> an agreement on the Swiss banks code of conduct with regard to the exercise of due diligence (CDB 03) between the Swiss Bankers' Association on the one hand and the signatory banks ... on the other hand.[21]

Doubtless both agreements are formally effective in Swiss law as contracts, and the 1977 agreement was, of course, categorised as a 'private contract' by the Federal Court.[22]

With regard to the substance, one is entitled to be a little more sceptical. The CDB, whether in its 1977 or later versions, neither sets up nor reflects any kind of economic relationship between the banks and the institution—the National Bank or the Bankers' Association—with whom they contract. The benefit to the banks of subjecting themselves to the set of obligations owed to those institutions is to be found elsewhere: in the maintenance of reputation, and latterly—since the introduction of the criminal prohibition of money-laundering in 1990—in avoiding more direct and detailed public regulation on that basis.[23] For larger banks that are influential within the Association, a further benefit is the ability to exercise a powerful influence on the development of the scheme. For the Association, the absence of any particular interest in the performance of

[20] Abegg, 'Regulation of Hybrid Networks at the Intersection between Governmental Administration and Economic Self-Organisation' (ch 14), 257–8.

[21] www.swissbanking.org/1116_e.pdf (visited 11 November 2005). This was the version in force when this chapter was prepared. The latest version, in force since July 2008, and available at www.swissbanking.org/en/20080410-vsb-cwb.pdf, represents a developed and reinforced version of the 2003 structure.

[22] Federal Court decision 109 Ib 146, and discussion referred to at n 20 above.

[23] See Abegg, 'Regulation of Hybrid Networks at the Intersection between Governmental Administration and Economic Self-Organisation' (ch 14), 263.

the agreement by any given contractual partner (as opposed to a general interest in the maintenance of good banking practice) is demonstrated by the fact that it could appear with equal comfort on either side of the contract: on that of the banks in 1977, on the other side in 2003. In 1977, its key role was to appoint members of the Arbitration Committee; otherwise, it assumed no duties and enjoyed no powers, save that of amending the agreement in conjunction with the National Bank. Since 2003, investigatory and enforcement functions have resided wholly in the Association, though these are to be performed essentially by appointing investigators, and a Supervisory Board of 'independent experts', for five-year terms.[24] The Association retains a power to amend the Agreement without reference to the banks as its contractual partners, but now only on the initiative, or with the consent, of the Federal Banking Commission.[25]

It seems reasonable to regard the CDB, in its earliest as well as its latest manifestations, as a privately-enforced scheme of command-and-control regulation operating under a degree of public patronage (by the National Bank under the 1977 and 1982 Agreements) or of public surveillance (by the Federal Banking Commission under the 1987 and later Agreements). The public bodies involved, and the articulation of their involvement, have changed, but it is difficult, from the point of view of regulatory analysis, to see the change as being as profound or as disturbing as Abegg suggests. In particular, there seems to be no reason why the mechanisms for the transmission of information between the public and private actors involved in the scheme—the Association, the banks, bank auditors, the National Bank, the Federal Banking Commission—should function any less effectively under the 2003 dispensation than under that of 1977.

One reason for this is that, contrary to what Abegg suggests in his various references to 'structural coupling',[26] the original contract between a signatory bank and the National Bank had no communicative potential whatsoever. Far from maintaining the kind of individualised relationship that is typical of contractual ordering (even under standard-form contracts, the two parties are still concerned with supplying the specific needs of one by deploying the specific capacities of the other), the CDB sought to avoid it. Under the contract, the two parties would at no time even be in contact, except in the case where a bank was believed to have breached the agreement and this information was brought to the

[24] CDB (2003) Art 12. See also Art 13 (arbitration procedure: this now functions as an appeal from the decisions of the Supervisory Board).

[25] CDB (2003) Art 14 (3).

[26] See Abegg, 'Regulation of Hybrid Networks at the Intersection between Governmental Administration and Economic Self-Organisation' (ch 14), at 274–5 and *passim*, in this volume.

notice of the Arbitration Committee, presumably through the CDB secretariat, provided by the National Bank. Thus, no bank party to the CDB had any means, *in its capacity as such a party*, of influencing either the interpretation of the contract or its development. Only by arguments in its defence before the Arbitration Committee would a party be able to express any views about interpretation. These communication possibilities are normally associated more with the world of criminal procedure than that of consensual agreement.

I find it hard, therefore, to accept that, with the removal of the National Bank from the CDB arrangements in 1987, 'the CDB lost a significant part of its capacity to adapt to the contradictory demands of conflicting rationalities', or that 'political demands [could no longer] flow into the CDB relatively directly via the structural coupling of the contract'.[27] The scope for public participation in the development of the CDB, through its amendment in the course of its fixed five-year term, was, in legal terms, increased by the 1987 reform, which granted the Federal Banking Commission the power to initiate changes where the National Bank only had power to agree to changes proposed by the Swiss Bankers' Association. In fact, the contractual obligations binding the banks themselves have at all times been quite irrelevant to the process of communication between the banking sector and the public authorities. Those obligations do not permit or organise the communication process: they merely embody its results. The real locus of any structural coupling between economics and politics was, in 1977, and doubtless remains today, the close and informal consultative relationships which the Swiss Bankers' Association, and the larger banks within it on their own account, have always maintained with the National Bank and other public authorities. It will have been this relationship, rather than the sterile terms of the CDB itself, which originally enabled the CDB to evolve from its 1977 to its 1982 version.

III. NETWORK CONTRACTS AND REGULATION IN GENERAL

III.1. Issues of Definition

So far, I have not discussed the 'network' attributes that Abegg finds in the CDB and that, in his view, both complicate the task of its legal characterisation, and add specific risks to its operation. If, as seems to be the consensus among authors in this volume, 'network' is not a legal

[27] See *ibid* at 280.

concept,[28] the decision to describe any given cluster of contracts as a network is essentially one of intellectual taste and not worth extended argument. But it is relevant to point out that the contracts which adopted the CDB were, and remain, very different in nature and purpose from those usually treated under the heading of 'contractual networks'. In these networks—exemplified by such phenomena as franchise agreements, just-in-time manufacturing schemes, complex building projects, or money transmission schemes—the participants share a common business goal involving co-ordinated activity. The contracts that link them, whether or not strictly synallagmatic in character, require of all parties some active contribution to the realisation of the collective project, whether in terms of funds, advice, representation, services or goods. This notion of co-ordinated business activity underpins the definitions of 'network' used in this study. One may quote Sydow's

> modes of organising economic activities that bind formally independent firms which are more or less economically dependent upon one another through stable relationships and a complex reciprocity that is more co-operative than competitive in form[29];

or Teubner's 2004 definition,[30] cited by Abegg,

> a network, or combination of contracts, exists where, first, the bilateral contracts reciprocally refer to each other in the performance programme or in contractual practice; second, there is reference in the content to the overall project; and third, there is legally relevant close cooperation between the parties to the combination ('economic unit').[31]

III.2. Network Interdependencies

As just noted, it is certainly a strain to accommodate, within these conceptions of contractual networks, the CDB contracts, which aim not at framing any kind of co-ordinated business project, but at imposing restrictions on business behaviour by firms (banks) which otherwise can operate quite independently in the relevant phase (recruitment of clients)

[28] Citing RM Buxbaum, 'Is "Network" a legal concept?' (1993) 149 *Journal of Institutional and Theoretical Economics* 698.

[29] J Sydow, *Strategische Netzwerke: Evolution und Organisation* (Wiesbaden, Gabler, 1992) 82 *et seq*.

[30] Teubner, '*Coincidentia Oppositorum*: Hybrid Networks beyond Contract and Organisation' (ch 1), in this volume eschews any specific definition of Networks.

[31] Abegg, 'Regulation of Hybrid Networks at the Intersection between Governmental Administration and Economic Self-Organisation' (ch 14), in this volume, fn 1.

of their business. There may, however, exist some more general difficulties in accommodating public actors within contractual networks, at least, if these actors are acting with any kind of regulatory purpose. Although Teubner at one point seems to say that these networks are necessarily intersystemic, 'in that they link autonomous units from different social systems with one another',[32] he specifically recognises a place for public actors only in innovation networks which aim to 'create design and production technologies and facilitate common research and development'.[33] These, he says,

> are not confined to a process of business co-operation, but rather, in addition to fulfilling normal economic functions, are also subject to political priorities, undertake long-term scientific research without regard for immediate economic advantages and must also be able to secure their own social acceptance. As a consequence, political bodies, scientific institutions and other social network actors bring their non-market perspectives to bear within the network; a process that gives rise to novel type co-ordination problems within such inter-systemic networks.[34]

At the same time, Teubner treats as 'peripheral' to discussion of contractual networks what he calls 'technical networks', where 'certain goods and services can no longer be produced within the market, but only within a technically intertwined infrastructure',[35] as with transport, energy and telecommunications networks. Because these networks often result from processes of privatisation of what were once monopolistic publicly-owned enterprises, public regulatory actors may frequently be found at their centre (where network operators function under a system of concessions granted by the public authority), or at their margins, in a supervisory position (where the network service depends upon, or is facilitated by, contractual exchanges between network operators, as with electricity pools), or in both places. While the sub-set of technical networks that produce so-called 'network effects'[36] may be distinctive, in general it seems hard to draw a dividing line as clear as the one perceived by Teubner between technologically-determined technical networks on the one hand, and technology-dependent contractual networks (like just-in-time systems) on the other. Moreover, such technical networks need not necessarily result from public initiatives such as privatisation. Privately-owned companies in a relevant sector, such as electricity

[32] Teubner, *Networks as Connected Contracts* (Frankfurt 2005), ch. 1, text above n. 57.
[33] *Ibid.*, text above n. 82.
[34] *Ibid*, and see further Teubner, '*Coincidentia Oppositorum*: Hybrid Networks beyond Contract and Organisation' (ch 1), in this volume.
[35] Teubner, *Networks as Connected Contracts* (Frankfurt 2005), ch. 1.
[36] On this, see MA Lemley and D McGowan, 'Legal Implications of Economic Network Effects' (1998) 86 *California Law Review* 479.

supply, might voluntarily contract to associate in a network: for example, by agreeing arrangements (including quantities and prices) for 'wheeling' electricity across each other's supply and distribution systems.

The question here is whether the public regulatory supervision of a 'technical' network, or the existence of a detailed legislative framework to govern its operation, provides an effective substitute for the general legal rules governing contractual network relationships, and hence renders such rules inapplicable. Here, I suspect that the stronger categorising tendencies in civil law countries may make a general response more attractive, whereas scholars from common law jurisdictions which economise on classifications would be more likely to favour a case-by-case approach, in which the mixture of public (legislative) and private (contractual) elements in the legal architecture of a network, coupled with the specific nature of the problem that has arisen within it, would determine whether contractual rules should apply. Taking such an approach in the United Kingdom, it would be possible to identify a number of cases in which contract-network scholarship might profitably be brought to bear on public-private 'technical networks'.[37]

If we examine other clusters of contracts which link public and private sector actors, we rarely find the combination of the two factors which seem to shape the special problem-set of contractual networks: the co-ordination of business activity; and the economic interdependence between network actors (including those not directly linked by the bilateral contracts constituting the network) which may follow as a consequence. What the CDB so interestingly demonstrates is a kind of interdependence between the banks that are party to the CDB, which is *not* a consequence of any co-ordinated operation. Instead, it derives from the competitive disadvantage for economic actors that flows from the acceptance by them of restrictive rules of conduct when their competitors are not subject to the same rules. What the banks in question wanted from the CDB was a system that could provide strong assurances that those who accepted such rules would be effectively bound to abide by them, on pain of substantial sanctions. This need is, however, in no way different from that of any economic actor concerned about the market behaviour of competitors, but reluctant to emulate it, and its gratification may, as often as not, result in formal public regulation. An example is offered by the reaction of the (then) two airlines competing for the

[37] For example, the passenger rail service now operating under the Railways Act 2005, provided by private companies acting as franchisees of the Department for Transport (formerly the Strategic Rail Authority), whose franchises require them to reach agreement with one another on such matters as through-ticketing arrangements. Continental legal systems would be likely to characterise this as a concession with its own specific and well-established set of legal rules ('*concession de service public*', '*Konzessionsvertrag*', etc).

domestic Australian market, when confronted with growing demands from an important part of their clientele for the elimination of smoking on their aircraft. Neither company was prepared to risk the unilateral introduction of non-smoking flights, for fear that the other would exploit the smokers' market. Eventually, they jointly requested the government to ban smoking on aircraft in pursuance of its regulatory powers.[38] An entire school of regulatory theory has, indeed, been based on the assumption that this desire for protection from competition through product differentiation is the main driving force for the production of public regulation.[39]

Formal public regulation, therefore, may well produce the same kinds of problem deriving from interdependencies between its subjects as do contractual networks. The classical public law answer is, of course, the application of principles of non-discrimination and proportionality in order to ensure that common rules *do* bear down fairly on the activity of different subjects. In considering how far, or with what effect, non-discrimination principles should be applied within contractual networks,[40] the flexibility of their application in such regulatory contexts should be kept in mind.

The CDB, as a privately-enforced scheme of command-and-control regulation, appears to apply these principles with considerable strictness, admitting diversity of treatment according to circumstances only in relation to the size of the fine to be imposed on any offending bank.[41] Other contractually-based command-and-control schemes may exploit the opportunities offered by contract so as to produce individually-negotiated obligations for each party. An example is offered by the so-called 'Climate Change Agreements' in the United Kingdom. Under the Finance Act 2000, the Department of Environment is empowered to enter into such agreements with companies in a number of selected industries that are heavy energy users. Companies which undertake, as a matter of contractual obligation, to reduce their energy consumption by a certain amount can obtain an 80 per cent reduction in the energy-use tax that they would otherwise have to pay under the Act.[42] While the

[38] M Colebatch, 'The concept of regulation in the analysis of an organised world' (1989) 11 *Law and Policy* 71.

[39] The primary source here is G Stigler, 'The Theory of Economic Regulation' (1971) 2 *Bell Journal of Economics and Management Science* 3.

[40] See M Wellenhofer, 'Third Party Effects of Bilateral Contracts within the Network' (ch 7), in this volume.

[41] CDB 1977, Art 14(2); 1982, Art 13(3); 2003, Art 11(1).

[42] Finance Act 2000 s :30 and Sch 6, whose Part IV provides a detailed framework for such agreements. Detailed information on the working of the scheme in practice will be found at: http://www.defra.gov.uk/environment/ccl/index.htm.

technical parameters of the contracts for each industry, such as measurement methods and bases, are negotiated collectively with industry-representative bodies, each company's target is a matter of individual negotiation and agreement. This process of individualisation does not, however, go beyond what could be accomplished under the individualised consent arrangements (for example, for emission and discharge of pollutants), familiar under orthodox command-and-control regulation and accepted—in principle at least—as compatible with non-discrimination principles. While the network characteristics of this scheme are suggested by legislative recognition of the 'combinations of contracts' required for its operation,[43] these contracts still function as a regulatory instrument, tightly structured by legislation and sustained not by a common business purpose but by the desire of participants to avoid the alternative regulatory instrument—the imposition of a burdensome tax.

III.3. Legitimation Defects and Their Remedies

Public authorities more commonly conclude large clusters of similar contracts that do not create any significant economic interdependencies between their contracting partners. Examples include the agreements through which specific agricultural or industrial subsidies are granted and regulated. A single public policy purpose inspires the subsidy scheme, but there are no legal or economic links between the individual subsidy agreements: the utility of one agreement does not depend on the existence of others, nor on the way others are performed. This remains true with more complex contractual arrangements, such as those through which the state disposes of natural resources under its ownership or sovereignty, such as offshore oil and gas resources.[44] In contrast to my earlier examples, this is a case where, as between the state and the oil company to which it grants an exploration or production contract for a given area, there does exist something in the nature of a common business venture: both parties are aiming at the discovery and production of oil—the company, for the profits this will bring, and the state, in order that it may enjoy the associated royalties or taxes, as well as the benefits of enhanced economic development and energy security. While these objectives are common to all exploration and production contracts,

[43] Finance Act 2000 Sch 6, Pt IV, para 48.

[44] There are a few states, including Germany and Australia, that effect this disposition by purely administrative means: see T Daintith, 'A Critical Evaluation of the Petroleum (Submerged Lands) Act as a Regulatory Regime', *AMPLA Yearbook* (AMPLA, Melbourne, 2000) 91.

these contracts are in no way legally linked.[45] Interdependencies can later develop between different contract-holders as pipeline networks develop to bring oil and gas to shore, but tend to be dealt with outside the framework of the original state-company bilateral contracts, under a mixture of contractual and regulatory arrangements that can be assimilated to the public-private 'technical networks' discussed above.[46]

Public contracts are, of course, not necessarily primarily regulatory in purpose: they may simply be concluded to obtain for government the goods and services it needs. A public authority may thus appear in the 'client' position in contractual networks, such as those associated with large building contracts, or other forms of complex procurement, such as military aircraft.[47] Jurisdictions that do not have a specialised and comprehensive law of public procurement may find it appropriate to rely for the resolution of issues in this area on concepts developed in the sphere of private contractual networks. Such economically-driven public-private contract networks may, in principle, also be pressed into regulatory service, by incorporating into building, services or supply contracts ancillary obligations which advance other public policies, such as securing the payment of minimum wages, avoiding employment discrimination, favouring domestic industries, and so on. The extension of these obligations, through the contract network, to sub-contractors and to sub-sub-contractors, may permit an extensive application of such policies. A successful example of this utilisation of existing networks for regulatory ends is offered by the operation in the United Kingdom, from 1891 to 1983, of the so-called Fair Wages Resolution, a House of Commons Resolution requiring government contracts to contain a clause ensuring that the workers under such contracts were paid not less than the going rate in the relevant industries.[48]

While we see here a genuine example of the successful exploitation of commercial networks for public policy ends, the special circumstances that assured this success were always rare and are becoming steadily rarer. The reason for this, which is clearly illustrated by the fate of the

[45] A special exception deals with the case where holders of neighbouring acreage find that a single oil field underlies both areas. The contracts will contain provision to avoid competitive (and wasteful) drilling wherever such a field could best be exploited as a single unit.

[46] For comparative discussion of these issues of access to specialised infrastructure, see T Daintith, *Discretion in the Administration of Offshore Oil and Gas: A Comparative Study* (AMPLA, Melbourne, forthcoming) paras 6301–12.

[47] Public authorities may of course also appear (though much less frequently than was once the case) in the role of commercial suppliers. Public banks, for example, might figure as suppliers in banking networks.

[48] See B Bercusson, *Fair Wages Resolutions* (London, Mansell, 1978). The Resolution was rescinded for political reasons in 1983 after the government denounced ILO Convention No 94 on Labour Clauses (Public Contracts).

original version of the CDB, lies in the need for proper legitimation of public policy measures. Where such measures adversely affect only those who explicitly agree to them—such as those who sign up to contractually-supported schemes of regulation—it may be argued that this agreement in itself provides sufficient legitimation, though important qualifications to this argument (for example, was the consent unforced?) are developed by Abegg,[49] and it may also be relevant to ask whether such measures respect other values like protection of public revenue. But when persons who are *not* parties to such agreements may also be adversely affected by the regulatory scheme, a much starker legitimation problem appears: how to justify the production of adverse effects on persons who have been denied both the opportunity to opt out by refusing consent, and the opportunity to participate in a democratically-grounded formal regulatory process.

This was the situation which arose when the UK government attempted, for the purpose of restraining inflation, to add a further general clause to procurement contracts in 1977, forbidding the payment of wage increases greater than a government-approved average figure.[50] Whereas the Fair Wages Resolution, while not formal law, had been legitimated by a resolution of the democratically-elected lower house of Parliament,[51] and third parties (workers and their unions) drew only benefit from it, its counter-inflation counterpart of 1977 was clearly the result of the inability of the government to secure the passage of legislation in the same sense, and operated to the detriment of those same third parties, who had had no say in its making. Its short life-span—it operated effectively only for about a year—should come as no surprise. Other types of procurement-related public policies have likewise come to an end, though usually in less spectacular fashion. Clauses requiring that contractors' own procurement be domestically sourced once provoked little fuss, because the adversely affected parties—foreign competitors in the supply of goods and services—were non-persons so far as domestic political participation was concerned. That situation has been radically changed by the non-discrimination obligations of a new

[49] See Abegg (ch. 14), Section III.2.(b), and especially para (ii) therein.

[50] T Daintith, 'Regulation by Contract: The New Prerogative?' (1979) 32 *Current Legal Problems* 41.

[51] Public procurement in the United Kingdom was in 1891 almost entirely unregulated by legislation, and, with the exception of the application of European Union rules, the situation is not very different today.

generation of free trade agreements, and by the transfer of competences within ever-broadening trade frameworks like that of the European Union.[52]

It was this same issue of legitimation that, despite the *imprimatur* of the Federal Court, brought down the original structure of the CDB in the mid-1980s. While the immediate cause was the apparent discrimination in not extending to the members of the *Treuhänder-Verband* the same advantages in maintaining client anonymity as were explicitly granted to a rival organisation in the 1982 revision, the general legitimacy of the CDB appeared dubious from the outset, by reason of its indirect imposition of burdensome self-identification requirements on bank clients, without formal regulatory process. This doubt about legitimacy does not derive from any characterisation of the CDB as a contract network, but simply from the scope that *any* public use of contract—or, for that matter, of the pressures commonly referred to as 'moral suasion', without the support of binding contracts—offers for the public control of private behaviour without resort to such processes.[53] The presence of a contractual network through which these control impulses may be transmitted may certainly reinforce their efficacy, but equally clearly, is not a precondition for it, as some of the foregoing examples should show.

In addition, the presence or otherwise of a commercial contract network should surely be irrelevant to the question of how the law may provide appropriate remedies for the adversely affected non-participants in the contractual scheme. What remedies are available, and which of them is best, will naturally depend on the content of particular national (or supra-national) legal systems. One may speculate on whether, had an appropriate cartel regulation been in force in Switzerland in 1983, a claim by the *Treuhänder-Verband* based on such a regulation might not have enjoyed more success than did its complaint founded in administrative law.[54] The fact that the common front of the banks towards the *Treuhänder-Verband* derived from contracts with a public body acting

[52] Thus the acceptance of national procurement obligations disappeared as a condition of UK petroleum production licences in 1983 and of equivalent Norwegian licences after Norway joined the European Economic Area (thereby accepting the substance of a number of EU obligations) in 1994.

[53] See generally Daintith, 'Regulation' (n 1 above).

[54] See, on this point, Abegg, 'Regulation of Hybrid Networks at the Intersection between Governmental Administration and Economic Self-Organisation' (ch 14) fns 70, 74 (with accompanying text), and 124. *Quaere* whether 'the *Treuhänder-Verband* as consumer of the service could probably not have based its claim on antitrust law, since by Article 12 KG claims arise under antitrust law only for those who are "hampered in the initiation or exercise of competition by an impermissible restraint of trade"' (*ibid*); it was surely the members of the *Treuhänder-Verband* who were the consumers of banking services. The *Treuhänder-Verband* might have been in the position of a competitor with other bodies for the affiliation of those members.

without specific legal competence appears an unconvincing justification in the eyes of cartel law. The alternative remedy of an action for unjustified refusal to contract might well, as Abegg suggests, have operated with greater refinement in a jurisdiction like Switzerland[55]—but would have been unavailable in common law systems. In some jurisdictions, such as the United Kingdom's, the lack of a deep-rooted distinction between public and private law would almost certainly have permitted a court to do what the Federal Court in 1983 could not, or would not do, that is, to isolate the element of public power in the CDB arrangements—specifically, the ability of the National Bank to concur in the design and amendment of the CDB—and subject the lawfulness of its exercise to control by the administrative law technique of judicial review.[56]

IV. CONCLUSION

Whether we are talking about 'co-operationist' arrangements or the narrower category of 'co-regulation', it seems to me that we are considering mechanisms for linking public and private (or 'political' and 'economic') interests and actors that largely exist alongside, rather than substantially overlapping with, the terrain occupied by contractual networks. If it is profitable to think of these mechanisms in network terms, it must (save in the unusual cases where contractual networks do function in this way) be for reasons other than that of understanding the awkward transformations of contract law. Regardless, however, of their qualification as networks, these co-operationist or co-regulatory mechanisms remain of interest to this study because they may produce some of the same problems—notably for less powerful participants within these mechanisms, and for external actors who have dealings with them—that flow from contractual networks themselves. How far we may generalise any analysis of these problems across different legal systems is, however, uncertain. The issue is not simply one of the varying availability of legal remedies in different systems, as indicated above. It also operates at the deeper level of the understanding of basic legal concepts in those systems. Differences here may contribute to contrasting readings of problems in the operation of networks, or of regulation: the more cynical view of the contractual aspects of the CDB taken here may owe something to a more demanding conception of contract in Anglo-American

[55] Abegg, 'Regulation of Hybrid Networks at the Intersection between Governmental Administration and Economic Self-Organisation' (ch 14), 288.

[56] *R v Panel on Takeovers and Mergers, ex parte Datafin plc* [1987] QB 815 (Court of Appeal).

law than in Swiss law.[57] They may even determine whether a problem is perceived at all. What appears as a 'crisis' in a legal system which has invested heavily in 'the rigid compulsory connections of legal doctrine'[58] may register as no more than a minor irritation in one where categorisation is seen as a child of practice, rather than as a master of thought.

[57] See H Beale, A Hartkamp, H Kötz and D Tallon (eds), *Cases, Materials and Text on Contract Law* (Oxford, Hart Publishing, 2002) 12–17 and 129–54.

[58] Abegg, 'Regulation of Hybrid Networks at the Intersection between Governmental Administration and Economic Self-Organisation' (ch 14), 268.

16

The Constitution of Contractual Networks

MARC AMSTUTZ*

ANYONE TACKLING CONTRACTUAL networks will quickly find that this phenomenon cannot be grasped using traditional doctrine. The deeper reason for this lies in an emergent phenomenon: contractual networks allow new orders of expectations to arise from bilateral contracts, linking several, sometimes many, actors, who selectively interact with each other (as, for instance, in franchising or in inter-bank payment systems). Traditional law of contract is blind to these new expectations. One appropriate response is to assign these emergent orders of expectations to a *higher-order constitution*. By 'higher-order constitution' I mean that a new (and thus also emergent) *legal* order is developed from the rules of contract law that apply to the individual contracts that constitute the contractual network. The design of this sort of 'constitution' can succeed only in so far as the findings of sociological theory are brought into civil-law doctrine—specifically because, with contractual networks, one is concerned not with classical legal normativity, but with normativity which, nonetheless, is sometimes legally relevant. I shall first discuss below how modern contract law may open itself to sociological theory (Section I.). Building on this, I shall look specifically at contractual networks and their special features in the light of the recent Swiss case law (Section II.). Finally, in a concluding section, I ask how the aforementioned higher-order constitution may be designed on the basis of general principles of contract law (Section III.).

* Professor of Commercial Law and Legal Theory, University of Freiburg i.Ue.

I. THE *'MONDES INTÉRIEURS'* OF SOCIETY AND THE LAW

I.1. Law's Closure

The predominant style of civil-law studies in the twentieth century was marked by a strict focus on the legal and institutional 'superstructure' of life. The law thereby detached itself in its operations from its social environment (in a radicalisation of the Romans' *'quod non est in actis non est in mundo'*), and left out the *'mondes intérieurs'* of society. A high degree of autonomy of law is the consequence of this closure, in line with the functional differentiation of modern society that has been exhaustively studied for decades.[1]

In this historical configuration, the operational closure of law is not something dysfunctional. When differentiated social systems such as the economy, sport, art or religion come up against the limits to what they can do in coping with their internal conflicts and therefore turn to the law, it would be awkward for the law to seek to decide the dispute to be settled according to the specific logic of the social system from which it emerged. For this is the very logic that, in the specific case in question, has demonstrated its inability to settle the dispute. Something else is expected from the law, namely, to approach the conflict entrusted to it 'with quite different eyes'. It is asked to *'alienate'* the dispute that emerged from a particular social system.[2] This creates the opportunity for this particular social system that has been blocked by the dispute to secure a hitherto unavailable approach to the situation and to unblock it. The dispute is thus given a new 'meaning', so that there can be a restoration of the social system under discussion's hampered capacity to function. It is only its high degree of autonomy that allows the law this kind of creation of social meaning.[3]

[1] On the functional differentiation of society, see Section III.2.(a).

[2] Perhaps this is the explanation for the blindfold on the Lady of Justice. She is supposed not to see the intrinsic rationality of the systems involved—so as to be able to see better (ie, only in the light of the law's own rationality).

[3] See G Teubner and P Zumbansen, 'Rechtsentfremdungen: Zum gesellschaftlichen Mehrwert des zwölften Kamels' (2000) 63 *Zeitschrift für Rechtssoziologie* 189; see, also, G Teubner, 'Zur Eigenständigkeit des Rechts in der Weltgesellschaft: Eine Problemskizze' in RJ Schweizer (ed), *Festschrift für Jean Nicolas Druey* (Zurich, Schulthess, 2002) 149; M Amstutz, 'Das Gesetz' in P Gauch and P Pichonnaz (eds), *Rechtsfiguren: K(l)eine Festschrift für Pierre Tercier* (Zurich, Schulthess, 2003) 155 at 160 *et seq*.

I.2. Law's Reflection

Why, then, the surprise at the continually recurring relative dissatisfaction with the law on the part of the public, documented in numerous works ranging from Roscoe Pound's well-known article,[4] to Christie's provocative thesis,[5] and to recent opinion surveys.[6] If social systems overstrained by internal disputes are begging the law for a 'different' view of things, how does it then come about that legal decisions are sometimes accepted and sometimes rejected?[7] Evidently, it is insufficient merely to 'alienate' the *social* conflict and transform it into a *legal* conflict.[8] This process seems to be tied to certain conditions, on compliance with which its success—ie, the creation of new social meaning—depends. But what are the conditions involved?

In this context, one should continue to bear in mind the consequences for law of the differentiation of society, albeit, this time, from the converse perspective, looking not at the conversion of a social conflict into law, but at the *response* to a legal decision in the social system concerned. In this respect, the law is at the mercy of the internal operations of the social system from within which the conflict now legally decided emerged. For it is these alone that decide whether one can speak of a 'successful' legal intervention. Thus, the creation of the conditions mentioned is not within the law's own power: the law is—like the physician with his patient—dependent on the autological forces of the disrupted social system. Whether an intervention 'succeeds' qua law is thus determined by the very system in which there has been the legal intervention. Does this finding compel the conclusion that the law's aforementioned dependency must be its inevitable fate?

If it is true that the law can operate only through the operations of the disrupted social system, then the insight just gained has to be interpreted

[4] R Pound, 'The Causes of Popular Dissatisfaction with the Administration of Justice' (1906) 40 *American Law Review* 729 *et seq*.

[5] N Christie, 'Conflict as Property' in CE Reasons and RM Rich (eds), *The Sociology of Law: A Conflict Perspective* (Toronto, Buttersworth, 1978) 295.

[6] See, eg, T Raiser, *Das lebende Recht: Rechtssoziologie in Deutschland* (Baden-Baden, Nomos, 1999) 352 *et seq*.

[7] On the social consequences of faulty legal decisions, see R Nobles and D Schiff, *Understanding Miscarriages of Justice: Law, the Media, and the Inevitability of Crisis* (Oxford, Oxford University Press, 2000).

[8] See N Luhmann, *Das Recht der Gesellschaft* (Frankfurt aM, Suhrkamp, 1993) 39: 'The concept of positiveness suggests an explanation through the concept of decision. Positive law is seen as having force *qua* decision. This leads to the accusation of 'decisionism' in the sense of an arbitrary possibility of decision, dependent only on the power of enforcement. *This however leads up a blind alley, since ultimately everybody knows that in law it is never at all possible to decide arbitrarily*' (my emphasis).

using a *second-order logic*.[9] The point has to be for the legal resolution of the conflict to sensitise the conflict-laden system to its 'blind spots', ie, to support the system in recognising its misperceptions in its observation of its own environment and in drawing conclusions from this selfsame recognition, in order to bring about conduct which is more appropriate to that very environment. The law's task would then be (1) for example, in relation to the economy, to 'trump' the obsession with profit maximisation and promote empathy for alternative social interests (employees, consumers, the public, etc); (2) for example, in relation to science, to quieten the blinding euphoria over progress and intensify concern about nature, future generations and the like; and (3) for example, in relation to sport, to halt the spiral of demand for increasingly unnatural records and bring the physical, mental and social living conditions of athletes to the awareness of the public (especially in the sports industry), etc. This calls, however, for a 'pan-social' view of law, and therefore calls for the law to make voyages of discovery into society's *'mondes intérieurs'*. Only if the law approaches society 'from within' can opportunities for it to help other social systems locate their 'blind spots' arise at all.

How, though, is the law to make such voyages of discovery? In a functionally differentiated society, this is a question of the legal system's *reflection*: through reflection, the law learns to see itself as part of its environment, which, at the same time, compels it to develop the conceptions of its environment that enable and support its task—namely, constructions of reality.[10] Reflection presupposes within each social system the creation of a 'reflexion apparatus', and in law this comes about through the development of legal theory (in the singular).[11] Luhmann has pointed out that

> a 'theory' can be conceived of as a mechanism of structural linkage, linking the reflecting legal system … with the knowledge system.[12]

Here, then, lie the opportunities—but also the risks—of the law's access to society's *'mondes intérieurs'*: the opportunities, since it is in this way that the law obtains observational instruments which enable it to grasp

[9] See, eg, H von Foerster, *Wissen und Gewissen: Versuch einer Brücke* (Frankfurt aM, Suhrkamp, 1993) 236 *et seq*.

[10] See, eg, M Wehr, 'Die Inseln der Propheten: Emergenz kognitiver Repräsentationen' in T Wägenbaur (ed), *Blinde Emergenz? Interdisziplinäre Beiträge zu Fragen kultureller Evolution* (Heidelberg, Synchron, 2000) 65.

[11] See M Amstutz, 'Historizismus im Wirtschaftsrecht: Überlegungen zu einer evolutorischen Rechtsmethodik' in RJ Schweizer (ed), *Festschrift für Jean Nicolas Druey* (Zurich: Schulthess, 2002) 9 at 21 *et seq*; D Wielsch, *Freiheit und Funktion: Zur Struktur- und Theoriegeschichte des Rechts der Wirtschaftsgesellschaft* (Baden-Baden, Nomos, 2001) 23 *et seq*.

[12] Luhmann, *Das Recht der Gesellschaft* (n 8 above) 564.

the relationships and processes in its environment better. These instruments are what Foucault calls *'épistémés'*,[13] which allow legal theory to interpret reality in a particular way. But—and here come the risks—they allow it only in one particular way (an 'overall view' is not available). Since a host of *'épistémés'* is offered in the social sciences, the law has to make a choice which is underpinned by nothing—and thus runs the risk of failing to grasp society. It is the pressure of this selection that explains the burgeoning number of competing legal theories (this time in the plural), all of which claim to be *the* legal theory (as 'reflexion apparatus' of law): natural-law theories of the most diverse types, positivisms of every kind, Law & Economics of every hue, discourse and argumentation theories, feminisms, Critical Theories, etc (ad infinitum).

I.3. Evolutionary Semantics

One way around the dilemma of this, fundamentally impossible, but nonetheless necessary, choice might lie in having the law's self-description and operations do without the causality or teleology patterns which are more or less markedly inherent in the legal theories just mentioned, and consistently switch to an *'evolutionary semantics'* in their place.[14] Heinz von Foerster has indicated with exemplary sobriety where the strengths of such semantics are to be seen:

> What is ontologically inexplicable may prove to be an ontogenic necessity. The navel is an ontological joke, a whimsical ornament, a grotesque riddle, on one's own belly. Ontogenetically, however, we could not exist without it. Evolutionists and creationists are in similar fashion seeking an ontogenic explanation for an otherwise inexplicable phenomenon: we are here![15]

It is no doubt here that the reason for the renaissance of evolutionary theory, recently under way in the social sciences, and sometimes interpreted as an 'interdisciplinary paradigm shift', is to be found.[16]

[13] M Foucault, *Die Ordnung der Dinge: Eine Archäologie der Humanwissenschaften* (Frankfurt aM, Suhrkamp, 1974).

[14] M Heilmann, 'Angepasste Selbstbeschreibung: Zu Niklas Luhmann "Evolution der Evolution"' in RJ Schweizer (ed), *Festschrift für Jean Nicolas Druey* (Zurich, Schulthess, 2002) 145.

[15] Von Foerster, *Wissen und Gewissen* (n 9 above) 370.

[16] DG Shaw, 'An Interdisciplinary Paradigm Shift' in P Pomper and DG Shaw (eds), *The Return of Science: Evolution, History, and Theory* (Lanham, Rowman & Littlefield, 2002) 1; MT Fögen, *Römische Rechtsgeschichten: Über Ursprung und Evolution eines sozialen Systems* (Göttingen, Vandenhoeck & Ruprecht, 2002) 14 et *seq*; R Moser, 'Evolutionismus in den Kulturwissenschaften' in A Dieckmann and R Moser (eds), *Evolution in den Natur-, Sozial- und Geisteswissenschaften: Referate einer Vorlesungsreihe des Collegium generale der Universität Bern im Sommersemester 2000* (Bern, Haupt, 2003) 217.

If, as here, we are on a search for a possibly more 'realistic' approach by the law to society's *'mondes intérieurs'*, then, this epistemological manoeuvre may, at first, be surprising, since, in comparison with current epistemologies, it is associated with a withdrawal of the claim to 'explain the world'. But this sort of freely chosen withdrawal may also offer new opportunities. Precisely what sort of heuristic withdrawal is meant here can probably best be explained in terms of the history of science. For a long time, the social sciences were oriented to the 'mechanistic' (deterministic) ideal of the natural sciences, particularly associated with Cartesian and Newtonian conceptions of reality.[17] At the centre was the assumption that, in all areas of life, something comparable to *unalterable truths* actually existed, and in them was to be seen the possibility of the predictability of social (historical, economic, sociological, legal, etc) processes. These dreams were gradually dispelled, because of the most varied experiences: Gödel's logical discoveries[18]; the recurrent, ineradicable paradoxes in science and life[19]; the realisation of the lack of universal validity of physical laws[20] etc. Gradually, indeterminacy crept into the imaging of reality and the reality images of science, but in the very specific form of *'evolutionary uncertainty'*, as McNeill has aptly called it.[21] It was recognised that neither the elements of a system of knowledge nor the regularities deduced from them are limited in number, but *re vera*

[17] Perhaps the most impressive analysis of these references (on the example of the relation between economics and physics) is given by N Georgescu-Roegen, *The Entropy Law and the Economic Process* (Cambridge MA & London, Harvard University Press, 1971); see also for the example of law and economics: M Amstutz, *Kollektive Marktbeherrschung im europäischen Wettbewerbsrecht: Eine evolutorische Perspektive* (Tübingen, Mohr & Siebeck, 1999); see, recently, the excellent, concise survey of the epistemological interactions between the natural and social sciences in: WH McNeill, 'History and the Scientific Worldview' in P Pomper and DG Shaw (eds), *The Return of Science: Evolution, History, and Theory* (Lanham, Rowman & Littlefield, 2002) 13.

[18] See eg, N Luhmann, *Die Wissenschaft der Gesellschaft* (Frankfurt aM, Suhrkamp, 1990) 506 *et seq*.

[19] See WV Quine, *The Ways of Paradox* (Cambridge MA & London, Harvard University Press, 1976); DG Hofstadter, *Gödel, Escher, Bach: An Eternal Golden Braid* (New York, Basic Books, 1979).

[20] See, eg, H Atlan, *La fin du 'tout génétique': Vers de nouveaux paradigms en biologie* (Paris, INRA, 1999) 11 *et seq*.

[21] McNeill, 'History and the Scientific Worldview' (n 17 above) 23. It should be clarified that where reference is made to 'evolutionary uncertainty' this is in no way connected with the evolutionary theory of knowledge (see, eg, KR Popper, *Objekzive Erkenntnis: Ein evolutionärer Versuch* (Hamburg, Hoffmann & Campe, 1984). An example from McNeill (*ibid*) makes the concept clearer than a long, abstract explanation: 'Whatever its start, the regime that prevails among the complex molecules now constituting earth's biomass soon imposed new balances on the earth's physico-chemical system. Forests, for example, altered rainfall patterns on land, while decaying organic matter laid down strata of limestone under the sea. On a global scale, plants eventually transformed the earth's atmosphere by releasing oxygen, making the earth hospitable to animals, who ate the plants and one another, establishing a series of ecological equilibria across geological time, each of which gave way to its successor in bursts of change whose precise provocation remain unclear'.

infinite.[22] The possibility of generalised explanations vanished, and it was realised that everything that can be 'known' can only be so situationally, piecemeal, in relation to time and context.

For the social sciences in general, and legal science in particular, this 'discovery' meant something quite specific, perhaps expressed most precisely by Meleghy recently. This author points out that evolutionary theory contains no universal law, of whatever nature. Instead, it indicates a mechanism (or algorithm) that

> is able, in principle, to imitate the goal-directed rational actions of a human being just as much as the goal-directed planned action of a creator.[23]

What originally, then (in the scientific world of the nineteenth century), counted as the great drawback of evolutionary theory[24]—namely, its inability to make predictions and its limitation to the description of contingent processes of change[25]—is in these circumstances perhaps its secret strength. For knowledge, then, is no longer dependent on the premise of a universal law (something that particularly in the social sphere can never be found):

> [F]rom the ruins of the old cosmos of essence with its subdivision into genera and species the Darwinian theory emerged, able to show that one could do without a plan of creation and still explain why non-arbitrary relations prevail in the world of living things, on the basis of selection processes.[26]

[22] See, eg, I Prigogine, *Les lois du chaos* (Paris, Flammarion, 1994) 16 *et seq*.

[23] T Meleghy, 'Methodologische Grundlagen einer evolutionären Soziologie' in T Meleghy and HJ Niedenzu (eds), *Soziale Evolution: Die Evolutionstheorie und die Sozialwissenschaften* (Wiesbaden, Westdeutscher Verlag, 2003) 132: 'Darwin showed us that the mechanism of natural selection can, in principle, imitate the purposeful, planned activity of a creator, and similarly also rational, purpose- or objective-oriented human actions'; see also A Diekmann and R Moser, 'Vorwort' in Diekmann and Moser (eds), *Evolution in den Natur-, Sozial- und Geisteswissenschaften: Referate einer Vorlesungsreihe des Collegium generale der Universität Bern im Sommersemester 2000* (Bern, Haupt, 2003) VI.

[24] See McNeill, 'History and the Scientific Worldview' (n 17 above) 15; see, with comprehensive disquisitions on the status of the theory of evolution, B Feltz, 'Auto-organisation, selection et émergence dans les théories de l'évolution' in B Feltz et al (ed), *Auto-organisation et émergence dans les sciences de la vie* (Brussels, Ousia, 1999) 483.

[25] Well described in Heilmann, 'Angepasste Selbstbeschreibung' (n 14 above) 143 *et seq* (with quotations from N Luhmann, *Die Gesellschaft der Gesellschaft* (Frankfurt aM, Suhrkamp, 1997)): 'Evolution seeks no change-bearing structures, in order to bring about structural change; it happens without reason, nor does it happen as history. It builds not on enabling over time, but on chance opportunities … Its time has "the form of a historical present happening but once"… And it is only when something is observed as an entity (different from other ones) and "lined up" in time … that questions of reasons and genesis, of common features in what was only now different, arise—questions evolution knows not of'.

[26] N Luhmann, *Die Politik der Gesellschaft* (Frankfurt aM, Suhrkamp, 2000) 408.

For law, the opportunities of an evolutionary epistemology lay in finally working through its shock experience of disenchantment in the nineteenth and twentieth centuries, which consists of the insight that law is not bound to anything fixed, whether in heaven or on earth (for example, 'God', 'reason', 'justice').[27] Despite the impossibility of 'planning society' through law—an impossibility still barely disputed only by legal positivism, which in order to veil this fact makes use of all sorts of fictions (such as 'the legislator', 'the legislative will', or 'the purpose of the Act')—an evolutionary epistemology could be a way of settling one old debt of legal science: the demonstration that, in its action on society, law cannot proceed arbitrarily, but is bound by *certain regularities (or 'conditions')*—be it only because there must be an evolutionary equilibrium between law and society, a 'reciprocally produced homeostasis'.

But how can the law observe its objects 'in terms of evolutionary theory' in the sense just described?

II. IN SEARCH OF THE *'MONDES INTÉRIEURS'* OF CONTRACTUAL NETWORKS

II.1. Analytical Framework

Ultimately, this is a question of choosing one of the numerous theoretical designs that are available in evolutionary theory today.[28] In the social sciences, for some time now, the Darwinist model of *Variation–Selection–Retention* seems to have imposed itself.[29] If one proceeds according to this model, the challenge is to locate within society itself the mechanisms for producing new social forms (Variation), for choosing among these offered forms (Selection), and for fixing on them lastingly in social practice (Retention).[30] This gives one an understanding of the *non-arbitrary* nature of society, *without* its forms having to be brought into

[27] The modern paradoxologists have also taught us why this is so: because the law cannot apply its prime distinction, between (legally) right and wrong, to that distinction itself; see G Teubner, 'Der Umgang mit Rechtsparadoxien: Derrida, Luhmann, Wiethölter' in C Joerges and G Teubner (eds), *Rechtsverfassungsrecht: Recht-Fertigung zwischen Privatrechtsdogmatik und Gesellschaftstheorie* (Baden-Baden, Nomos, 2003) 25.

[28] An overview from a social-science viewpoint can be found in T Meleghy and HJ Niedenzu, 'Einleitung: Die Evolutionstheorie und die Sozialwissenschaften' in Meleghy and Niedenzu (eds), *Soziale Evolution: Die Evolutionstheorie und die Sozialwissenschaften* (Wiesbaden, Westdeutscher Verlag, 2003) 11.

[29] On this model, see, eg, M Neves, *Zwischen Themis und Leviathan: Eine schwierige Beziehung. Eine Rekonstruktion des demokratischen Rechtsstaates in Auseinandersetzung mit Luhmann und Habermas* (Baden-Baden, Nomos, 2000) 13 *et seq*.

[30] Done in exemplary fashion for the legal system in the study by Fögen, *Römische Rechtsgeschichten* (n 16 above).

connection with *ontological* necessities or *intentional* plans of an all-knowing entity. And, above all—this is central with regard to the interaction of law and society—it gives one an understanding of social phenomena that is not dependent on some universal law which determines the way that these phenomena function.

The explanatory focus of this approach is very helpful. Yet, the *Variation–Selection–Retention* framework falls short by not indicating any theory-led criterion for choosing from among several possible evolutionary explanations for living or social reality.[31] Such a criterion is, however, indispensable, because—as Gould and Lewontin have shown—an analysis using the *Variation / Selection / Retention* framework often allows for several plausible theoretical evolutionary hypotheses.[32] Accordingly, a more comprehensive analytical pattern will have to be sought, which, as Gould and Lewontin say, will enable the definition of 'criteria to identify proper explanations among the substantial set of plausible pathways to any modern result'.[33] Now Gould, in his opus magnum *The Structure of Evolutionary Theory*[34] (in which, shortly before his death, he presented all the findings from his fruitful research work in evolutionary theory), has developed an analytical framework which enables such criteria to be identified. These criteria could be useful for the social sciences (especially, legal science), too. Gould's model builds on three points—termed 'Agency', 'Efficacy' and 'Scope'[35]—on which he makes the convincingness of an evolutionary explanation depend:

1. *Agency*: Where is the 'place' where the evolutionary forces develop their effect? Evolution needs a 'locus of action',[36] or a 'unit of selection'. In biology, Darwin consistently took it that this 'locus' is the individual organism. Recent work has begun to discover that other 'units of selection' at lower or higher levels (genes, cells, organs, or else groups, species, etc) exist at the same time, ie, that, as well as *micro-evolutionary* phenomena, there are also *macro-evolutionary* phenomena.[37] The social sciences, and in particular

[31] See, in detail on this, M Amstutz, 'Rechtsgeschichte als Evolutionstheorie: Anmerkungen zum Theorierahmen von Marie Theres Fögens Forschungsprogramm' (2002) 1 *Rechtsgeschichte* 26.

[32] SJ Gould and RC Lewontin, 'The spandrels of San Marco and the Panglossian paradigm: a critique of the adaptionist programme' (1979) 205 *Proceedings of the Royal Society B: Biological Science* 581 at 588.

[33] *Ibid*, 588.

[34] SJ Gould, *The Structure of Evolutionary Theory* (Cambridge MA/London, Belknap, 2002).

[35] This schema marks the structure of the whole book; it is briefly explained by Gould, *ibid*, 14 *et seq*.

[36] *Ibid*, 14.

[37] The assumption of a multiplicity and hierarchy of levels of selection is based particularly on the fact that there are selections that remain invisible at the classically

legal science, should take inspiration from this hierarchical theory of selection: in the area of social evolution, too, a narrowing of the view of the evolutionary forces to one sole level of action, say that of 'communication' or the 'social system', must be avoided.

2. *Efficacy*: Alongside the mechanism of natural selection, are additional explanatory factors required in order to understand the evolutionary process? Classical Darwinism denies this with the argument that, with sufficient variation, a slow and steady (gradualist) elimination of individual organisms which are not adapted to their environment is sufficient to guarantee the production of new life-forms that are fitter for survival.[38] By contrast, modern evolutionary biology emphasises the importance of so-called *'constraints'*: Darwinism's 'external' perspective is certainly true, but remains incomplete since organisms possess 'internal' developmental constraints that play an important part in the evolutionary process (put crudely, an elephant will not turn into a cat even after millions of years of variation and selection; as Darwin said, its 'unity of type'[39] rules that out).[40] Evidently, there are similar 'constraints' in social evolution, too: historical or structural reasons occasionally channel the selective forces at work in society in an unexpected direction.[41]

Darwinian level of the organism; see DJ Depew and BH Weber, *Darwinism Evolving: Systems dynamics and the Geneology of Natural Selection* (Cambridge MA, MIT, 1996) 381 at 381: '[T]here can … be some sort of higher-order selection … in which the spatiotemporally individuated species of the modern synthesis are said to stand to the overall direction in whole clades (branching phylogenetic lineages, from Greek for 'branch') as variation among individual organisms stands to the adaptedness in populations … In this event, direction in a clade will be the result of a sorting process in which characteristics of the clade itself have the statistical edge. These might include higher speciation rates, lower extinction rates, or other traits that cannot be reduced to the adaptive prowess of individual members of the component species of a lineage'. It thus becomes evident that the selections coming about at the different levels can sometimes 'contradict' each other; see DS Wilson, 'Group Selection' in EF Keller and EA Lloyd (eds), *Keywords in Evolutionary Biology* (Cambridge MA/London, Harvard University Press, 1992) 145: 'Because adaptations can occur at a variety of levels … what is adaptive at one level may be maladaptive at another. It is adaptive for predators to capture prey, but if they are too successful the predator population can overexploit its prey and itself go extinct. It is adaptive for a group of monkeys to post sentries to watch for predators, but maladaptive for the individual sentry who must watch while its fellows eat'. This hierarchical view thus makes more complex patterns of the effects of selective forces perceptible; see on all this also M Lenzen, *Evolutionstheorien in den Natur- und Sozialwissenschaften* (Frankfurt aM/New York, Campus, 2003) 79 *et seq*.

[38] See SJ Gould, 'Darwinism and the Expansion of Evolutionary Theory' (1982) 216 *Science* 380 at 381.

[39] C Darwin, *The Origin of Species by Means of Natural Selection or the Preservation of favoured Racies in the Struggle for Life* (London, John Murray, 1859) 206.

[40] See in detail on this, M Amstutz, *Evolutorisches Wirtschaftsrecht: Vorstudien zum Recht und seiner Methode in den Diskurskollisionen der Marktgesellschaft* (Baden-Baden, Nomos, 2001) 266 *et seq*.

[41] For law, see, eg, JB Ruhl, 'The Fitness of Law: Using Complexity Theory to Describe the Evolution of Law and Society and Its practical Meaning for Democracy' (1996) 49

Perhaps it is here that we should look for the reason for the increased interest of the social sciences in phenomena of path dependency.[42]

3. *Scope*: Can the diversity of nature be explained by Darwinism's micro-evolutionary mechanisms alone? Does one not additionally need to take into account 'non-evolutionary' (ie, non-algorithmic) phenomena (such as climatic changes, or the impact of large meteorites or of volcanic eruptions)? This brings up the controversy between uniformitarians and catastrophists: while the former embrace strict Darwinism and see natural selection as the exclusive cause of ecological diversity, the latter take the view that this diversity can only be explained by bringing other causes into account.[43] In current evolutionary theory, it is the catastrophist viewpoint that is recognised, and a theory of social evolution should also be open to it: it is precisely because social systems are structurally linked, ie, they reciprocally rely on their structures (for instance, the economy relies on the existence of the legal contract, or politics on the state's having a constitution), that 'jumps' in one particular system (for example, the invention of writing, money, the printing press or the Internet) may have massive evolutionary consequences for other systems.[44]

I wish, in a first stage, to employ this pattern of evolutionary analysis to help explore the network phenomena in society (ie, 'outside' of law). These phenomena are (one may assume at least this much) very closely connected with the emergence of contractual networks in law (ie, 'within' law).[45] In a second stage, we must go on to look at how the internal structures of law actually ought to respond to these phenomena. To this

Vanderbilt Law Review 1428; for economics, see, eg, V Vanberg, 'Institutional Evolution Within Constraints' (1996) 152 *The Journal of Institutional and Theoretical Economics* 690.

42 See, eg, OA Hathaway, 'Path Dependancy in the Law: The Course and Pattern of Legal Change in a Common Law System' (2001) 86 *Iowa law Review* 601.

43 See, for a clear historical summary of the uniformitarian/catastrophist controversy, Depew and Weber, *Darwinism Evolving* (n 37 above) 95 *et seq*.

44 Usually, in order to grasp this phenomenon attempts are made to identify rules of co-evolution; see, for example, Fögen, *Römische Rechtsgeschichten* (n 16 above) 18. To date, however, social co-evolution remains a riddle. At least part of the problem can convincingly be approached using Gould's 'Scope'.

45 In the main, we shall not explicitly go into the connection between network phenomena at social level and contractual networks at legal level; instead we shall assume, on the basis of Teubner's work, that both phenomena are 'forcibly linked'; see in detail, G Teubner, 'Verbund, Verband oder Verkehr? Zur Aussenhaftung von Francising-Systemen' (1990) 159 *Zeitschrift für das gesamte Handelsrecht und Wirtschaftsrech* 295; G Teubner, 'Den Schleier des Vertrags zerreissen? Zur rechtlichen Verantwortung ökonomisch "effizienter" Vertragsnetzwerke' (1993) 90 *Kritische Vierteljahresschrift für Gesetzgebung und Rechtswissenschaft* 367; G Teubner, 'Das Recht hybrider Netzwerke' (2001) 165 *Zeitschrift für das gesamte Handelsrecht und Wirtschaftsrecht* 550.

end, I shall begin by looking at social practices in connection with contractual networks in the light of the recent case law.[46]

II.2 Observing Social Practice I: Agency

II.2.(a) Multi-Level Evolution

We must first look at a number of judgments that make it clear that, in the institutional sphere, variations are not produced at one level only. Just as, in nature, things do not happen solely at the level of the organism, so, in the social sphere, private autonomous systems (contracts, companies, etc) may have effects at higher levels[47] that produce emergent systems, but nonetheless remain invisible if Gould's 'agency' is not taken into account.[48] This aspect is expressed in exemplary fashion in the description of the network of the tenancy and sub-tenancy relationship given by the Federal Court in BGE 120 II 112 ff. It is worthwhile quoting the relevant passage in full:

> Sub-letting is marked by two linked tenancy contracts on the same property. The principle of contractual privity, while it makes it easy to see the legal autonomy of the two contractual relationships, cannot conceal the fact that they are nonetheless linked with each other . . . for the main tenancy limits the sub-tenant's legal power . . . *and the resulting economic combination of the two or more contracts also requires legal solutions that are able to do justice to conflicts of interest which involve no longer only two people* ... It has, therefore, rightly been pointed out that, between the main lessor and the sub-tenant, a special legal relationship, even if not a direct contractual relationship, obtains ... Here, it should also be noted that the lessor is no longer free to permit sub-lets or not (Art. 262 Abs. 2 CO); and is therefore legally obliged to enter into *specifically constituted relations with a third user*.[49] (emphasis added)

It can be seen from these statements that, while the tenancy relationship consists exclusively of bipolar legal relationships, these relationships are functionally correlated and must, in legal transactions, 'stand the test' of

[46] The focus on recent Swiss case law is aimed solely at limiting the volume of the material to be analysed; it is by no means intended to imply that older case law in this context is unimportant. Concurrent references to note are accordingly: BGE 25 II 473; 63 II 414; 94 II 161; 94 II 355; 97 II 390; AGVE 1981, 38 ss; LGVE 1986 I, Nr 35, 57 ss; ZGGVP 1991/92, 163 ss; PKG 1991, Nr 61, 203 ss; PKG 1992, Nr 63, 230 ss; PKG 1994, Nr 50, 160 ss; see also BGE 116 II 634; BGE 26 September 2001, Nr 4C.161/2001; BGE 9 July 2003, Nr 4C.163/2002.

[47] And perhaps also at lower levels.

[48] The 'agency' criterion is thus one possible technique for making 'derived' variation and selection visible. It is not intended to imply that there are no other techniques that could do something similar.

[49] BGE 120 II 115.

that correlation.[50] In terms of evolutionary theory, this finding can be expressed by saying that not just the primary level of the individual agreements, but also the secondary one of the system derived from the linking of the agreements (ie, the contractual network as such), is exposed to selective environmental forces.

II.2.(b) Law's Selective Force

This second-order level also clearly emerges in a Geneva judgment of 2 December 1998[51] concerning Article 254 Code of Obligations ('CO') which forbids the tying of the tenancy contract to another contract if: (1) the tying is a condition sine qua non for the conclusion of the tenancy contract; and (2) the tied contract has no direct link to the use of the rented premises.[52] The case was as follows: On 5 September 1994 *A* and *X* agreed to transfer ownership of the whole stock (furniture, equipment, signs, etc) of the bar located in *A*'s building to *X*. By separate contract of 8 November 1994, *A* then rented the premises in which the bar had been installed to *X* for a period of five years. In connection with court proceedings over this tenancy agreement, with the object of dissolving the same for breach of contract by *X*, the latter alleged, inter alia, the nullity of the transfer agreement of 5 September 1994 for infringement of Article 254 CO. In the specific case, while *A* had met the first constituent element of the statutory definition by making the conclusion of the tenancy contract dependent upon the transfer of the stock, the Court took the view that the 'direct connection' between the transfer contract and 'the use of the rented property', required by Article 254 CO for the admissibility of the tied transaction, was actually present, since this contract,

> clearly constitutes an obligation linked to the use of the rented premises. The transfer agreement of 5 September 1994, hence, does not fulfil the second condition set forth in Article 254 CO.[53]

[50] The prevailing view in the literature, that in combined legal transactions the principle of mutual independence of the contracts applies (see, eg, R Cerutti, *Der Untervertrag* (Freiburg i Ue, Universitätsverlag, 1990) 54 *et seq*), has the result of disputing such a multilevel consideration.

[51] 1ère Cour civile de Genève, 2 December 1998, SJ 1999 I 167; see also the references to the recent case law in R Weber, 'Art. 254' in H Honsell (ed), *Basler Kommentar zum Schweizerischen Privatrecht: Obligationenrecht I (Art. 1–529 OR)* (Basel, Helbing & Lichtenhahn, 2003) 1303 N 4.

[52] Art 254 CO reads as follows: 'A transaction tied with a rental agreement for residential or business premises is null and void if the conclusion or the continuation of the rental agreement is dependent thereon, and if the lessee assumes an obligation towards the lessor or a third party which is not directly connected with the use of the rental object'.

[53] 1ère Cour civile de Genève (n 51 above) at 169.

The Court was helped in arriving at this conclusion by a comparison with the legal position applying to the takeover of a business pursuant to Article 181 CO[54] along with the assignment of the tenancy of the business premises.[55] In this case, which is—in the Court's view—analogous, there could be no notion of a tying being barred by Article 254 CO, and therefore the same decision should be taken in the case in hand.[56]

It was undoubtedly not a coincidence that, in this case, two separate contracts—and not a single agreement—had been concluded. For the parties intended neither a tenancy agreement linked with an incidental assignment transaction, nor a purchase contract more or less coincidentally accompanied by a transfer transaction, but rather a *partial assignment of a business*: X was to take over business 'assets' (the bar's stock) and could, economically speaking, amortise them during the five-year duration of the tenancy. A mixed contract with tenancy and purchase elements could not have met this intention (or only with great difficulty), since it would have 'conveyed' the social-law safeguards of Articles 253–274g CO (tenancy law), in a way that the parties could hardly predict, into the sales-law dimension of the transaction. The special way that the parties had chosen of maintaining the business connection between the shop premises fitted out as a bar and the installations especially fitted to that bar[57] could hardly have been brought about except by concluding two connected contracts.[58] And it is in this connection that one can find the reason why the Court rightly preferred not to consider the agreements as having been concluded in isolation.[59] In so

[54] Art 181 CO reads as follows: '(1) Whoever assumes assets and liabilities, or an enterprise with assets and liabilities, becomes automatically liable to the obligees for the liabilities connected therewith, as soon as the assumption has been notified to the obligees by the assuming party or is published in the press. (2) The previous obligor is jointly and severally liable, however, together with the assuming one for two more years, which start running for claims due from the notification or publication date, and for claims becoming due subsequently from the due date. (3) Otherwise, this assumption has the same effect as the assuption of an individual obligation'.

[55] The Court referred in this connection specifically to P Higi, 'Art. 253–265 OR' in P Gauch (ed), *Kommentar zum Schweizerischen Zivilgesetzbuch: Obligationenrecht, Teilbd V/2b: Die Miete* (Zurich, Schulthess, 1994) 126 N 16.

[56] 1ère Cour civile de Genève (n 51 above) at 169.

[57] Presumably a sale of the bar's stock to a third party not simultaneously renting the shop premises and thus needing to use it elsewhere would have meant a considerable reduction in the selling price.

[58] This view has recently been challenged by L Thévenoz, 'Intro. Art. 184–529' in L Thévenoz and F Werro (eds), *Commentaire Romand: Code des obligations I* (Code des obligations art. 1–529; Loi sur le crédit à la consommation, Loi sur les voyages à forfait) (Geneva, Helbing & Lichtenhahn, 2003) 978 *et seq* N 14 *et seq*.

[59] One should here further mention the fact that the tenor of Art 3 *VMWG*, which specifies Art 254 CO, could have suggested a contrary finding (were one to suppose that the bar's stock consisted mainly of furniture, something, to be sure, not specified in the judgment reproduced [1ère Cour civile de Genève (n 51 above) at 167f]): 'Within the meaning of Article 254 of the Code of Obligations especially an obligation on the tenant to

doing, it unmistakably measured the case by the connection between these agreements and thus by the system emerging from them. *The law, correspondingly, operated not at the level of the individual agreements, but at that of the contractual network. In terms of evolutionary theory, this can only mean that the law's selective force acted not at the former ('lower') level, but at the latter ('higher') level.*

II.2.(c) 'Overall System' View v 'Single Contract' View

The same direction was taken by BGE 115 II 452, which concerned two contracts between the operating company of Clinic *Y* and physician *X*. On 6 May 1983. the parties had concluded a so-called co-operation contract, regulating *X*'s activity as the clinic's official physician. The agreement was entered into for an indefinite period, upon six months' notice of termination (Article 5 of the contract). Less than one year later, on 1 April 1984, the same parties concluded a tenancy agreement over rooms in the clinic building for *X* to run a private medical practice there. This contract, too, was for an indefinite period. Its termination arrangements were laid down by reference to the corresponding provision in the co-operation contract, whereby 'the period agreed in Article 5 of the co-operation agreement of 06.05.83' was to apply. On 3 January 1989, *Y* terminated the co-operation contract and called on *X* to vacate his medical offices in the clinic by 7 July 1989. On the basis of Article 272 CO,[60] *X* requested an extension of the tenancy until the end of 1990, which was rejected by both the first[61] and the second instance courts. The Federal Court followed the lower courts in the substance, but not in the *rationes decidendi*.

The lower courts had assumed not two separate contracts, but a single (mixed) agreement, which enabled them to circumvent the application of

buy … *furniture* … shall be treated as a tied transaction'. That the court does not keep strictly to the wording of this provision is justified on the grounds given in the text.

[60] Art 272 CO reads as follows: '(1) The lessee may request the extension of a limited or unlimited rental relationship if the termination of the rental would result in a hardship for him or his family not justifiable by the interests of the lessor. (2) In weighing the interests, the competent authority shall particularly take into account:
a) the circumstances of the conclusion of the agreement and the contents of the agreement; b) the duration of the rental relationship; c) the personal, family and economic condition of the parties and their behaviour; d) a possible need for personal use by the lessor for himself or close relatives or in-laws, as well as the urgency of such need; e) the local market conditions for residental and business premisses. (3) If the lessee requests a second extension, the authority shall also take into consideration whether he did all that could reasonably be expected of him to avoid the hardship'.

[61] The facts of the case state here that the first instance denied 'in principle an entitlement of the plaintiff under Art. [272] CO … but nonetheless [extended] the tenancy until 31 October 1989' (BGE 115 II 453). More detailed information on the justification for this decision is unavailable.

Article 272 CO on the basis that the co-operation law elements of the agreement were dominant, and 'absorbed' and rendered inapplicable the statutory rules applicable on the 'admixed' tenancy law elements.[62] In contrast, the Federal Court started from 'a plurality of contracts', namely, two separate agreements, based on the consideration that there was no single act of consent-formation between the parties.[63] It began by remarking that

> the question of whether room utilisation arrangements based not on a pure tenancy agreement, but . . . on a complex of contracts in which a tenancy agreement is linked with other contracts are also eligible for extension . . . has not been answered in general by the legislator.[64]

It then sought a doctrinal answer. But in vain, since here there are statements only about the mixed contract, the extendability of which is made

> dependent, on the one hand, on whether the tenancy-law elements are dominant in the mixed contract . . . on the other, on a balancing of interests in the individual case.[65]

Having reached this point, the grounds of judgment take a spectacular turn. Without actual justification, they assert that, for a contractual network, 'the like [must] . . . hold'. Verbatim, they read:

> Here, too, extension of the tenancy is excluded, if the linked contract strongly marks the legal relations between the parties and the tenancy appears merely as a subordinate agreement. In each individual case, one must accordingly analyse what importance the parties attached to the linked individual contracts *as regards the pattern of the overall legal relations between them* and what dependency relation these contracts stand in to each other in their legal and economic importance.[66] (emphasis added)

Here, again, the law's action—as a selective force in the environment of the autonomous system of co-operation that *X* and *Y* have set up on the basis of two contracts—comes at the level of the overall system, ie, the contractual network as such. Each contract is not looked at separately, but rather the contractual network, as such, is the focus. This is so, even though positive law actually presses for a 'single-contract' view of the matter. This is because Article 272 CO is a mandatory (not an optional)

[62] BGE 115 II 453.

[63] This is nowhere explicitly stated in the grounds. In explaining the special features of a compound contract, however, the Court mentions that one has to be presumed inter alia 'failing a single act of consent formation' (BGE 115 II 454).

[64] *Ibid.*

[65] *Ibid.*

[66] *Ibid.*

rule[67] that is applicable as soon as the defined elements of the rental of the domestic or business premises are met. Since these elements were unquestionably present, the written law in itself would have suggested that the tenancy agreement of 1 April 1984 be brought into specific, isolated consideration. Instead, the Federal Court did not even consider the relevance of Article 272 CO, and made it clear, by its focus on the 'overall position', that the case in point concerned solely the level of the contractual network (not that of the individual contracts), and that anything else would have amounted to a 'sundering' of a meaningful system.

II.3. Observing Social Practice II: Efficacy

II.3.(a) Constraints in Evolution

If we now change viewpoint and look at BGE 115 II 452 no longer using Gould's criterion of 'agency', but that of 'efficacy', we are able to uncover another crucial aspect of the contractual network. The judgment makes it clear that the contractual network has 'constraints' which (entirely in Gould's sense) channel the selective effect of the law in a particular direction. The contractual network resists 'atomisation' into individual contracts and, as it were, blocks off classical contract law, which naturally aims to split complex factual situations into individual, bipolar contractual units. The result of this is that the 'network' logic wins out, or, in other words, the contractual network forces itself on the law as a separate institution (and not as a compilation capable of dissection). It is precisely these 'constraints', inherent in contractual networks, that highlight the fact that practice and theory so desperately seek to grasp the familiar terms of approximation: 'inner linkage' or 'internal connection' of unitary contracts;[68] a 'final nexus' at the level of the contractual network[69]; *'identité d'objet'* or *'communauté de cause'*[70]; 'multilateral synallagma',[71] etc. But what exactly is this aspect that these admittedly suggestive, though

[67] See Higi, 'Art. 253–265 OR' (n 55 above) 167, N 12 *et seq.*

[68] J Gernhuber, 'Austausch und Kredit im rechtsgeschäftlichen Verbund: Zur Lehre von den Vertragsverbindungen' in G Paulus (ed), *Festschrift für Karl Larenz zum 70. Geburtstag* (Munich, CH Beck, 1973) 472; in this direction, see also E Kramer, 'Art. 19–22 OR' in A Meier-Hayoz (ed), *Berner Kommentar: das Obligationenrecht, Bd. VI/1.Abt./2. Teilbd./ Unterteilbd. 1a: Inhalt des Vertrags* (Bern, Stämpfli, 1991) 33, N 64; Cerutti, *Der Untervertrag* (n 50 above) 6 *et seq.*

[69] Gernhuber, 'Austausch und Kredit im rechtsgeschäftlichen Verbund' (n 68 above) 469 *et seq*; similarly, J Gernhuber, *Das Schuldverhältnis: Begründung und Änderung, Pflichten und Strukturen, Drittwirkungen* (Tübingen, Mohr & Siebeck, 1989) 710 *et seq.*

[70] B Teyssié, *Les groupes de contrats* (Paris, LGDJ, 1975) 295; F Chaix, *Le contrat de sous-traitance en droit Suisse: Limites du principe de la relativité des conventions* (Basel, Helbing & Lichtenhahn, 1995) 47 *et seq.*

ultimately imprecise, locutions denote? A confrontation of two more recent Supreme Court judgments, of 21 May 2001[72] and 16 January 2002,[73] takes us further in this respect:

II.3.(b) Network Logic and 'Overall Project'

In the first of these decisions, the parties had concluded two separate agreements, namely, a tenancy agreement and a lease contract. These continuous obligations had, as their object, a bar with furniture and fixtures, and were linked in so far as the tenants/lessees (a husband and wife) could continue the operation only on condition that all the obligations entered into in the two contracts were furnished in parallel and simultaneously by the landlord/lessor.[74] With regard to the question of whether the tenants/lessees could properly terminate the lease contract without rescinding the tenancy agreement, the Federal Court found that, although two separate contracts were entered into, they formed in the mind of the parties *one legal complex entity which cannot be split*: 'In such a situation, neither of the two contracts may be terminated separately'.[75] The reasons given are scant: reference is made, on the one hand, to the *Panic v Fleury* case (which takes us no further in the theory of contractual networks)[76] and, on the other, to a scholarly opinion from Engel, who, however, at the place cited, does not directly address the question of terminating linked contracts.[77]

The second decision mentioned above involved the scrutinising of a contract between *H* (the customer) and *W* (the contractor) concerning the building of 56 detached houses. Over time, this contract for construction services had become irksome to *H*, who sought to get out of it. To this end, he claimed that the contract had been linked to the conclusion of a sales contract (actually never concluded) whereby *W* would have undertaken to buy one of the 56 houses. The fact that the intended sales contract was never concluded had—*H* went on—the consequence of nullifying the main contract, since both contracts affected each other as

[71] PW Heermann, *Drittfinanzierte Erwerbsgeschäfte: Entwicklung der Rechtsfigur des trilateralen Synallagmas auf der Grundlage deutscher und U.S.-amerikanische Rechtsentwicklungen* (Tübingen, Mohr & Siebeck, 1998) 138 *et seq*; PW Heermann, 'Ringtausch, Tauschringe und multilaterals Bartering' (1999) 54 *Juristenzeitung* 183; see also PW Heermann, 'Verbundene Geschäfte im Sinne des § 9 Abs. 1 VerbrKrG' (2000) 200 *Archiv für die civilistische Praxis* 19.

[72] BGE 21 Mai 2001, Nr 4C.43/2000.

[73] BGE 21 Mai 2001, Nr 4C.43/2000.

[74] *Ibid*, E. 2.d.

[75] *Ibid*, E. 2.d.

[76] BGE 107 II 144 E. 2.

[77] P Engel, *Contrats de droit Suisse: Traité des contrats de la partie spéciale du Code des obligations, de la vente au contrat de société simple, articles 184 à 551 CO, ainsi que quelques contrats innommés* (Bern, Stämpfli, 2000) 741 *et seq*.

connected contracts, in the sense of a condition of validity. Although it was undisputed that the parties had seriously contemplated the sales contract mentioned, the Federal Court rejected *H*'s argument. Here, too, it will be helpful to provide further analysis in order to provide the tenor of the grounds of judgment:

> According to the findings of the court below, the parties first agreed on the conclusion of the contract for construction services, and were concordantly of the view that the plaintiff would later buy one of the houses still to be built, plus parking space, at an established price. Why, in these circumstances, there was supposed to be a connected contract is not stated in the judgment challenged. It is thus also questionable what the exchange relationship between the reciprocal obligations from the two contracts is supposed to be. As follows . . . from the judgment [in the first instance], evidently, the fee for the work was set in the light of the selling price in the sales contract to be concluded later. This is, however, not sufficient . . . for connected contracts. Instead, the case shows that the price calculation is made in the expectation that a certain compensation will result from the future transaction. An exchange relationship between the reciprocal obligations under the services and sales contracts does not, however, result therefrom.[78]

Basically, in the second judgment, the Federal Court supplied the justification for the first one: While the considerations in the bar case can also be interpreted as meaning that whether a contractual network is present depends on the parties' will ('*dans l'idée des parties*'), the considerations in the housing development case make it clear that *the consensus of the parties cannot be decisive for the question of linkage.*[79] Accordingly, an unspecified consensus of the parties that the agreements concluded are somehow connected (for example, because—as was the case with the second judgment—the intention was to establish the price calculations in the services and sales contracts on an overall basis) cannot suffice to detach the law of obligations from its particularistic perspective. Instead, it is the Supreme Court's view that there must be a connection between the various agreements, as it were, 'in substance'; in other words, there is a connection which arises out of the circumstances of the conclusion of the

[78] BGE 21 Mai 2001, Nr 4C.43/2000, E. 2.

[79] This clarification is important: by contrast with a tendency in doctrine (see, recently, W Schluep, 'Zusammengesetzte Verträge: Vertragsverbindung oder Vertragsverwirrung?' in H Honsell et al (eds), *Aktuelle Aspekte des Schuld- und Sachenrechts: Festschrift für Heinz Rey zum 60. Geburtstag* (Zurich, Schulthess, 2003) 288 at 304 *et seq*) to make a contractual network depend on a 'linkage agreement', the Federal Court's statements show not just that such an agreement is not necessarily required in order to justify applying the doctrine of the contractual network. The two judgments compared in the text must further be seen as implying that the parties' will plays only a subordinate role in establishing a contractual network—'subordinate' in the sense that while there cannot be contracts reached without being supported on the parties' assent, the connecting of these contracts always depends on circumstances the parties need not necessarily have thought about.

contract (or contracts). But what does the nature of this connection have to be? The Federal Court's answer seems clear to me: *only in so far as the 'overall project' based on several bilateral undertakings is of such a nature that its realisation requires the fulfilment of all the undertakings as a sine qua non can a departure from 'linear' contractual thought in favour of a 'networked' version be justified.* This allows us to see why the highest court has, in the judgments in question, come to diametrically-opposed findings in each case, although, in both cases, elements of the parties' will which pointed to a linkage of the agreements were present. In the first case, the operation of the bar depended categorically on the fulfilment of both the tenancy and the lease contract; not so in the second, where the 56 detached houses could very well have been produced even without the sales contract contemplated between *H* and *W*. From these observations, important conclusions for the ontogenesis of the combination of contracts follow.

II.3.(c) Constraints v Selection

It is only where both the will of the parties and the circumstances are combined in such a way that, among several contracts, the formation of a connection of the nature described comes about, that 'constraints' in the multi-contract formation come into existence. These constraints oppose the selective factors in the environment of this selfsame formation, and change or even remove the effects of these factors. These 'constraints' are the product of the contribution—required from each contract that makes up a component of the transactional network—to the stabilisation of the whole (which in the final analysis is extremely unstable, being marked by the several contradictory views of the individual agreements[80]). The individual contracts are thus not (as is otherwise the case in contractual situations) aimed at bringing about a self-coherent order closed within this coherence, but at contributing to the formation of a consistent higher order that has, as its object, an 'overall project' which goes beyond the various 'projects' of the linked contracts. These 'stabilisation contributions' are evolutionary forces which, in the sense of Gould's 'constraints', operate alongside Darwinian natural selection and place the contractual network into the competition which takes place among the various forms of institutional arrangements (contract, association, corporation, etc) as an *institutional form* in its own right.

[80] See V Lemieux, *Les réseaux d' acteurs sociaux* (Paris, PUF, 1999) 17 *et seq.*

II.4. Observing Social Practice III: Scope

II.4.(a) 'Heterarchicalisation'

It remains questionable as to whether the contractual network is now adequately clarified in terms of evolutionary theory. Gould's third criterion of 'scope' points out that, in the process of evolution, non-evolutionary phenomena (such as catastrophes, of whatever kind) can sometimes exert decisive influence on the forms of life. And it is just such events that have to be brought into consideration to round off the ontogenetic picture of the contractual network. The slogan here is *network revolution*.[81] Everywhere in society, for some time now, heterarchical phenomena have been recorded, and contract law has not been spared from this. On the contrary, the 'heterarchicalisation' of the social world seems, in certain areas of life, to be drastically encouraging the contractual network as a new organisational form, indeed sometimes to be imposing it as inevitable and making it permanent.

II.4.(b) Emergence of Judicial Rules

Evidence for this comes from the much-noted and highly controversial decision in BGE 121 III 310.[82] In this judgment, the Federal Court had to

[81] See, eg, M Fassler, *Netzwerke: Einführung in die Netzstrukturen, Netzkulturen und verteilte Gesellschaftlichkeit* (Munich, W Fink, 2001) 119 *et seq*; A-L Barabaási, *Linked: How Everything is Connected to Everything Else and What it Means for Business, Science, and Everyday Life* (New York, Plume, 2003); T Stonier, 'The Wealth of Information and the Emerging Global Community' in H Eichmann et al (eds), *Netzwerke: Kooperation in Arbeit, Wirtschaft und Verwaltung* (Vienna, Falter, 2000) 13 *et seq*; an informative survey of various network theories in the sociological and economic area can be found in S Dinter, *Netzwerke: Eine Organisationsform moderner Gesellschaften?* (Marburg, Tectum, 2001); A Brand, *Funktion und Auftreten von Unternehmensnetzwerken aus der Sicht der Neuen Institutionenökonomie und soziologische Ansätze: Welche Rolle spielt die Informationstechnik?* (Stuttgart, Ibidem, 2002).

[82] See W Fellmann and J Schwarz, 'Geldüberweisung mit Hilfe des Bankenclearingsystems; vertraglicher Direktanspruch des Überweisenden gegen die sich weisungswidrig verhaltende Empfängerbank (Art 32, 112, 127, 398 Abs 3 OR): Bundesgericht, I Zivilabteilung, 27.6.1995, T. c. Bank X, Berufung (= BGE/ATF 121 III 310)' (1996) 5 *Aktuelle Juristische Praxis* 97; M Hess, 'Bargeldlose Überweisung mit Hilfe von Interbankzahlungssystemen—Vertrauenshaftung im Zahlungsverkehr? BGE 121 III 310' (1996) 14 *Recht* 144; W Wiegand, 'Die privatrechtliche Rechtsprechung des Bundesgerichts im Jahre 1995' (1997) 133 *Zeitschrift des bernischen Juristenvereins* 123; H Dietzi, 'Zahlungsverkehr' in W Wiegand (ed), *Rechtliche Probleme des Zahlungsverkehrs: Berner Bankrechtstag* (Bern, Stämpfli, 2000) 161; S Bettschart, *Virement en chaîne et assignation bancaire: Droit suisse des obligations et contexte international* (Zurich, Schulthess, 2000) 284 *et seq*; HP Walter, 'Vertrauenshaftung im Umfeld des Vertrages' (1996) 132 *Zeitschrift des bernischen Juristenvereins* 274; T Ackermann, 'Verjähren die Ansprüche von nicht am Vertrag beteiligten Dritten nach Delikts- oder Vertragsrecht? Oder: Die verpasste Chancen für den Vertrag mit Schutzwirkung zugunsten Dritter: Bundesgericht, I. Zivilabteilung, 9.6,1997, A.X. c. Privatklinik Y AG (4C.422/1996), BGE 123 III 204, Berufung' (1997) 6 *Aktuelle Juristische Praxis* 1555; X Favre-Bulle, *Les paiements transfrontières dans un espace financier européen* (Basel *et al*, Helbing & Lichtenhahn, 1998) 381 *et seq*; M Moser, *Die Haftung*

deal with a money transfer made using the Swiss banks' clearing system (Swiss Interbank Clearing (SIC)).[83] *T* had held out the prospect of a loan of CHF 300,000 to *B*, declaring his willingness to transfer the sum immediately (ie, even before conclusion of the loan contract) to an escrow account with Bank *Y* (the recipient bank). *T* commissioned the transfer from Bank *Z* (the sending bank), which acted in conformity with the contract and described the beneficiaries to the recipient bank with the formula '*B* & *T* escrow account'. Subsequently, the conclusion of the loan contract between *T* and *B* fell through. Nonetheless, *B* freed the 'blocked' amount without any collaboration from *T*; the recipient bank performed this operation, even though, within the bank, the account was entitled the '*B* & *T* escrow account'.[84] *T* asserted a *contractual* claim against the recipient bank for compensation, and received protection from the Federal Court.

The academic response to this decision was unanimous.[85] Representatively, Fellmann and Schwarz say:

> The judgment ... is certainly correct in the upshot. The justification is unconvincing, however ... The impression is that the decisive factor for the decision was not rational considerations, but a more or less definite 'sense of the law'.[86]

'Irrationality' of the argument, 'sense of the law' as the grounds of the decision, or even 'right result' *v* 'wrong reasons'[87]—all this arouses one's curiosity, and from the viewpoint not just of law but also of legal sociology. Let us start, however, by dwelling a bit on this seemingly so wrong ground of judgment. The Federal Court begins by observing that the SIC is

> a giro system in the service of multi-membered transfer transactions... [enabling] a centrally controlled and therefore rapid accomplishment of chain transfers, the reason for which is the recipient's not having an account at the same branch as the transferor.[88]

gegenüber vertragsfremden Dritten: Ein Beispiel zur Lehre von der Vertragshaftung gezeigt am Beispiel des Wirtschaftsprüfers (Bern, Stämpfli, 1998) 86 and 147 *et seq*; H Honsell, *Schweizerisches Obligationenrecht: Besonderer Teil* (Bern, Stämpfli, 2003) 313.

[83] See, on Swiss Interbank Clearing Bettschart, *Virement en chaîne et assignation bancaire* (n 82 above) 35 *et seq*.

[84] See BGE 121 III 310 s.

[85] See references n 81 above.

[86] Fellmann and Schwarz, 'Geldüberweisung mit Hilfe des Bankenclearingsystems' (n 82 above) 97.

[87] Hess, 'Bargeldlose Überweisung mit Hilfe von Interbankzahlungssystemen (n 82 above) 155.

[88] BGE 121 III 312 E. 3.

It, then, analyses the contractual organisation of an inter-bank payment system in two steps. First comes a general description of the legal relations obtaining between those involved:

> In multi-membered transfer transactions, the interposed banks act in their own name but on another's account, and thus as indirect representatives. A transfer made in this way comes about through several chain-linked contracts in which various parties are involved, and the principal of privity governing contractual relations has to be borne in mind. Thus, between the transferor and the first bank, there is a giro contract, to which the rules of law of mandate apply. The payment order coming about in this context is an instruction ... to the first bank ... The banks involved are then linked with each other through separate giro contracts, to which the rules of law of mandate similarly apply. It follows from all this that, between the transferor and the recipient bank, in principle, no direct contractual relations exist.[89]

The Court goes on to describe the triangular relationship between the transferor (*T*), the sending bank (Bank *Z*) and the recipient bank (Bank *Y*), seeing, within this, an authorised substitution within the meaning of Article 398(3) CO[90]:

> The first bank [Bank Z] received from the plaintiff [T] the mandate to transfer Fr. 300,000 to the beneficiaries 'B & T' in an escrow account with Bank Y. The plaintiff could in accordance with the principle of trust expect the making of the credit entry in the 'escrow account' also to form part of the content of the contract. The first bank was accordingly obliged *vis-à-vis* the plaintiff not only to indicate to the recipient bank its willingness to pay, but also to cause the credit to be made to the account indicated. For legal reasons, it could not itself effect the credit, but had to mandate the recipient bank keeping the account to do so; and thus, to achieve the object of the contract and fulfil part of the contract, in the customer's interest, call in a third party not involved in the contract. Under these circumstances, the recipient bank is to be regarded as a substitute within the meaning of the law of mandate.[91]

Having thus cleared the ground, the Court went on to test the really interesting question: Is *T* entitled to a damages claim *ex contractu* against Bank *Y*?[92] The structure of the argument does not, as Wiegand, in particular, notes,[93] follow the usual mode, something which, as will be

[89] BGE 121 III 312 s. E. 3.

[90] Art 398(3) CO reads as follows: 'He [the mandatary] shall personally perform his obligations unless he is duly authorised, or compelled by circumstances, to entrust a third person with their performance, or if the right of substitution is considered permitted customarily'.

[91] BGE 121 III 324 E. 4; this view is not undisputed; see the overview in Dietzi, 'Zahlungsverkehr' (n 82 above) 161.

[92] This question arises mainly because a tort claim—accepted by the lower court in principle—was statute-barred, see BGE 121 III 312.

[93] Wiegand, 'Die privatrechtliche Rechtsprechung des Bundesgerichts im Jahre 1995' (n 82 above) 126.

explained in more detail below, is of special importance in the present case. Because a substitution relationship exists in the law of mandate, the Court's starting point is the question of whether *T* is entitled to a damages claim under Article 399(3) CO that would give the principal mandator a direct claim against the substitute. However, according to the wording of Article 399(3) CO, such a claim substantively covers only the claims to which the *mandatary* is entitled against the substitute. In the case in point, this is manifestly no further help, since the loss *T* wishes to claim against Bank *Y* arose only for him and not from the mandatary (Bank *Z*).[94] A dead end? By no means: the Federal Court finds that doctrine 'without exception' advocates accepting the mandator's direct claim against the substitute, irrespective of whether the latter has harmed the mandatary by his conduct.[95] Clearly, only a minority derive this direct claim from Article 399(3) CO.[96] The majority see the legal basis of the claim in the contractual relationship between the mandatary and the substitute, on the grounds that this relationship is to be described either as a contract in favour of a third party (*'Vertrag zugunsten eines Dritten'* (Article 112 CO[97]))[98] or as a contract with protective effect for third parties (*'Vertrag mit Schutzwirkung für Dritte'*).[99] After comparative law considerations which show that, in neighbouring countries, a direct claim by the principal mandator against the substitute is recognised especially

[94] See, eg, F Werro, 'Art. 399 CO' in L Thévenoz and F Werro (eds), *Comentaire Romand: Code des obligations I (Code des obligations art 1–529); Loi sur le crédit à la consommation, Loi sur les voyages à forfait* (Geneva, Helbing & Lichtenhahn, 2003) 2061, fn 6; R Bühler, 'Art. 399 OR' in JK Kostkiewicz et al (eds), *OR: Handkommentar zum Schweizerischen Obligationenrecht* (Zurich, Orell Füssli, 2002) 500, fn 4; mainly, this point is no longer separately established in the literature, it being held, following BGE 121 III 310, that the principal mandator's claim pursuant to Art 399(3) CO also covers his own damage; see, eg, RH Weber, 'Art. 399 OR' in H Honsell et al (eds), *Basler Kommentar zum Schweizerischen Obligationenrecht I (Art. 1–529 OR)* (Basel, Helbing & Lichtenhahn, 2003) 2189, fn 6, with references. As matters stand, then, this claim seems scarcely at dispute any longer; only the dogmatic basis is still being searched for; see, however, Section II.4.(c), as well as Sections III.2.(c) and III.3.(c).

[95] BGE 121 III 315 E. 4.a).

[96] BGE 121 III 315 E. 4.a); today this view is hardly taken any longer in Swiss law.

[97] Art 112 CO reads as follows: '(1) If a party acting in his own name has been promises performance to and in favour of a third person, he shall be entitled to ask that the performance be effected in favor of such third person. (2) The third person or his successor in title is entitled in his own right to require performance in his favour if this was the intention of the two contracting parties, or if this is customary. (3) In such case, the original obligee can no longer release the obligor from the time such third person has declared to the latter that he claims his right'.

[98] BGE 121 III 315 E. 4.a); see P Tercier, *Les contrats spéciaux* (Zurich, Schulthess, 2003) 672; for a criticism of this construction (with convincing arguments) see Fellmann and Schwarz, 'Geldüberweisung mit Hilfe des Bankenclearingsystems' (n 82 above) 98.

[99] BGE 121 III 315 E. 4.a); this construction has met with a positive response in the literature; see Fellmann and Schwarz, 'Geldüberweisung mit Hilfe des Bankenclearingsystems' (n 82 above) 99; Wiegand, 'Die privatrechtliche Rechtsprechung des Bundesgerichts im Jahre 1995' (n 82 above) 127.

for multi-membered bank transfers,[100] one could have expected the Supreme Court to plump for one of the three possible legal constructions. It did not—which is presumably the extraordinary aspect of BGE 121 III 310 that has to be understood. In the end, the Federal Court affirmed the questionable direct claim *without* any doctrinal construction, but with a reference to the *de facto needs of legal relations* (hence also the widespread impression that this decision grew out of a 'sense of the law'—whatever that means). Such references to factual aspects are anything but commonplace in Supreme Court judgments, especially if, as in the judgment at issue here, they act as *rationes decidendi.* The decisive passage runs:

> It should be noted … that the acknowledgement of a direct claim imposes itself … on the basis of … considerations which, irrespective of the question of the applicability of Art. 399(3) CO, focus directly on the legal evaluation of the interests of the parties involved in the transfer relation. The starting-point is the fact that the indirect representation relations in multi-membered transfer transactions as a rule are apparent, since neither of the banks involved may presume the other is acting exclusively on its own account. Third-party interest is inherent in giro transactions within banks and everywhere recognisable, as is the need for transferors to be protected against mistakes by the banks. The giro transactions within the banks are at the service of the parties to the transfer and should facilitate processing of business among the banks. The risks of mistakes associated with this facilitation must, however, properly be borne by the banks, not the parties to the transfer. These ought not to be unprotected merely because of the interposition of a further bank, though the preconditions for a breach of duty as such are present. The point is ultimately to prevent purely technical aspects of payment or organisational happenstance from voiding claims or nullifying duties that 'really', ie, apart from the damaged party's position as contractual creditor, exist.[101]

II.4.(c) 'Catastrophism' in Law

It is easy to see that, in these statements, the claim which the judges allow remains vague from the standpoint of legal doctrine. Whether, in this respect, a viable foundation can be found is a question of the law's internal viewpoint, which comes up for discussion only in the next section.[102] What matters here is the fact that the Federal Court evidently felt that the solution was to be sought not at the classical single-contract level, but directly at the emergent level of the contractual network. From an evolutionary perspective, this may be interpreted as follows: *The alternative to treating the case on the basis of traditional law-of-obligation considerations did not, in the final analysis, exist at all; it was 'destroyed' by the*

[100] BGE 121 III 315 ss E. 4.b).
[101] BGE 121 III 317 E. 4.c).
[102] See Section III.

institutionalisation of the SIC (as a 'catastrophic' event). The Federal Court's refusal to base the outcome that it advocated on traditional legal constructions can therefore be interpreted as meaning that it took the view that the thoroughly 'bipolar' policy strategies pursued by customary contract law would not 'fit' the emergent order of the multi-membered bank transfer.[103] BGE 121 III 310 thus teaches us that the appearance of contractual networks in the economy may be not only the outcome of selectively operating environmental forces and 'constraints', but also the consequence of radical changes in the life-world. Thus, 'Catastrophism' also plays a part in the evolution of institutional arrangements.

III. DESIGNING A CONSTITUTION FOR CONTRACTUAL NETWORKS

III.1. The Shortcomings of Law of Contracts

Looking at institutional arrangements built on a plurality of connected contracts through the looking-glass of evolutionary theory, using Gould's analytical framework of *Agency–Efficacy–Scope*, has shown three things: (1) Emergent orders may arise out of the linking of contracts, and differ from the 'bipolar' orders of the individual contracts and operate according to a logic of their own (a 'network' logic).[104] (2) These arrangements are then (inter alia) exposed to the selective forces of the law of contract, which tend to approach contractual networks not in their linkage, but as 'autonomous' units. If, however, connected contracts in their mutual references reach such an organisational density that the real meaning of agreements among the parties is located no longer at the level of the declarations of intent exchanged in each case, but at that of their linkage—we might even say at the level of their *'symbiosis' as a contractual network*—then, they form 'constraints', which very effectively counteract the contract law reflex mentioned above. This formation of 'constraints' occurs notably where the contracts in the linking of legal transactions are so amalgamated that achieving the 'project' that is 'common' to all of them[105] inevitably presupposes fulfilling all the performance obligations

[103] A detailed discussion of this point—specifically the deficits of the classical law-of-obligations models in coping with defaults in performance extending beyond a contract—can be found in M Rohe, *Netzverträge: Rechtsprobleme komplexer Vertragsverbindungen* (Tübingen, Mohr & Siebeck, 1998) 65 *et seq*.

[104] See Section II.2.

[105] The term 'common' is in no way meant to imply that the parties are pursuing a common purpose (in the company-law sense). This very feature is alien to contractual networks, since they are formed from bipolar contracts. In short, *the 'common' project referred to in the text is one structurally upheld by the contracts, not by all the parties.*

undertaken.[106] (3) In some areas of life today, socio-economic or technological changes have attained such importance that the choice between a single-contract or contractual-network-based view is no longer open. In such 'catastrophist' cases, the individual contracts that are the components of the combination of legal transactions have 'lost' their autonomy. The autonomisation of the system which is derived from the aggregate of bipolar agreements appears particularly clearly here,[107] and one wonders how the law ought to respond.

This is the question to which this section is devoted. In approaching it, two steps have to be taken: (1) First, we must recall the reasons why classical law of contract had such difficulty in grasping the case of the contractual network with current legal constructions. Undoubtedly, we know the problem lies in its (historically conditioned) inclination to reduce institutional arrangements interpretively to individual legal transactions. But this remains an external viewpoint of the law of obligations, which was adopted in the previous section. The present point is to illuminate the law of obligations 'from within'. This means the question now becomes: Why does law of contract seem so confused in its internal operations when confronted with contractual networks? What is the reason why it must, as the analysis of BGE 121 III 310 has, in particular, shown, reach for approaches to solutions that it cannot manage to justify by the criteria of traditional legal doctrine? (2) We must then ask how the insights derived from looking at connected contracts in terms of evolutionary theory, as we have done, can be 'brought into' the law of contract, and, above all, what constructions compatible with legal doctrine these insights suggest.

III.2. Social Multi-Dimensionality of the Contract

III.2.(a) Functional Differentiation of Society

With regard to the first point mentioned, I start from the thesis that contractual networks are directly connected with the phenomenon of the functional differentiation of society, and that this connection is just what overstrains the law of contract.[108] This thesis manifestly presupposes that (even if only summarily) the concept of societal differentiation is dealt

[106] See Section II.3.

[107] See Section II.4.

[108] See in detail, M Amstutz, 'Vertragskollisionen: Fragmente für eine Lehre der Vertragsverbindung' in H Honsell et al (eds), *Aktuelle Aspekte des Schuld- und Sachenrechts: Festschrift für Heinz Rey zum 60. Geburtstag* (Zurich, Schulthess, 2003) 165; see also N Luhmann, *Organisation und Entscheidung* (Opladen/Wiesbaden, Westdeutscher Verlag, 2000) 411.

with first. It means—quite classically—the sort of social formation that seems largely to be making headway in modern times, leading to a polycentric structure of society, or, in other words, to a society with no top and no centre.[109] This form of society is marked by the absence of a central body with the competence for integrating the whole.[110] This obviously raises the question of what nonetheless holds this society together.[111] Modern sociology assumes that social integration today comes about primarily through phenomena of structural coupling *(strukturelle Kopplung)* of social sub-systems and the reflections that these enable. The term structural coupling refers to

> observational schemas [within the system] … suitable for endowing events in the environment [of the system] with informational value and making them the occasion for further operations of the system.[112]

Thanks to these schemas, the system can take account of the operational closure of its co-systems by learning to understand itself as a system-in-an-environment-of-other-systems—and permanently so.[113] It does so by tracing its internal information-processing processes back to certain problems connected with its co-systems, the solution to which it then uses for its self-description. In this way, the system's capacity to identify and orientate itself is called reflection *('Reflexion')*. This capacity is integrative in so far as 'the system has to monitor its effects on the environment by the repercussions on itself'.[114]

What, then, do the social differentiation and integration processes that it has sparked off have to do with law of contract? To explain this, we must unveil the differentiation theory dimension of the contract. From a systems theory point of view, the contract is not a consensual act among several actors, but a structural coupling among the functional systems of society (the economy, law, science, etc).[115] What this says is basically that

[109] N Luhmann, *Politische Theorie im Wohlfahrtsstaat* (Munich, Olzog, 1981) 22.

[110] See, eg, U Schimank, *Theorien gesellschaftlicher Differenzierung* (Opladen, Leske & Budrich, 2000) 189.

[111] See, eg, M Aschke, *Kommunikation, Koordination und soziales System: Theoretische Grundlagen für die Erklärung der Evolution von Kultur und Gesellschaft* (Stuttgart, Lucius & Lucius, 2002) 1.

[112] *Ibid*, 78.

[113] See N Luhmann, *Ausdifferenzierung des Rechts* (Frankfurt aM, Suhrkamp, 1981) 440: 'A sub-system's identity can then be founded only upon a special function the system performs for society as a whole'.

[114] N Luhmann, *Soziale Systeme: Grundriss einer allgemeinen Theorie* (Frankfurt aM, Suhrkamp, 1984) 642.

[115] See, eg, Luhmann, *Das Recht der Gesellschaft* (n 8 above) 440 *et seq*; G-P Calliess, 'Das Tetralemma des Rechts: Zur Möglichkeit der Selbstbeschränkung des Kommunikationssystem Recht' (2000) 21 *Zeitschrift für Rechtssoziologie* 296; Wielsch, *Freiheit und Funktion* (n 11 above) 56 and 59 *et seq*; P Zumbansen, *Ordnungsmuster im modernen Wohlfahrtsstaat: Lernerfahrungen zwischen Staat, Gesellschaft, Vertrag* (Baden-Baden, Nomos, 2000) 206; T

contract enables the systems involved to describe and observe each other.[116] This is accomplished because the contract (as a form of structural coupling) stores a certain number of possibilities that the systems involved can use as information. Luhmann emphasises this from this viewpoint:

> [S]tructural coupling has on the one hand an exclusion effect—in this area the system is indifferent—and on the other brings about a channelling of causalities that the system can use.[117]

This raises the question of how, precisely, the information derived from the contract is used in the systems involved. In this connection, it has rightly been pointed out that this information is

> constitutive for a social system in so far as ... [it] converts latent expectations into actual obligations, mere projections into operational ties.[118]

Put another way, this information produces the structures of a sub-system that 'press for fulfilment of the contract's purpose' in the functional system concerned.[119] Here, then, the fragmentation of the contract in the context of social differentiation becomes fully visible: for it is through this institution that *autonomous discourses* occur in the systems involved, which, according to the intrinsic logic of the area concerned, assume different forms. The contract leads, for example: (1) in the economy, to an economic *transaction* as an organised procedure of resources allocation[120]; (2) in the law, to a *normative discourse* in the context of the contract as a 'governance structure'[121]; and (3) in other functional systems (science, art, medicine, education etc), to a *project*, which, in its communicative implementation, alters the production process in the system (gaining knowledge, aesthetic value, improving health, enhancing socialization and skills, etc).[122] And all of this occurs *simultaneously*!

Lieckweg, *Das Recht der Weltgesellschaft: Systemtheoretische Perspektiven auf die Globalsierung des Rechts am Beispiel der lex mercatoria* (Stuttgart, Lucius & Lucius, 2003) 45 *et seq*.

116 Zumbansen, *Ordnungsmuster im modernen Wohlfahrtsstaat* (n 115 above) 206; Lieckweg, *Das Recht der Weltgesellschaft* (n 115 above) 46 *et seq*.

117 N Luhmann, *Einführung in die Systemtheorie* (Heidelberg, Carl-Auer-Systeme, 2002) 121.

118 G Teubner, 'Vertragswelten: Das Recht in der Fragmentierung von *Private Governance Regimes*' (1998) 17 *Rechtsgeschichte* 249.

119 *Ibid*, 249.

120 Lieckweg, *Das Recht der Weltgesellschaft* (n 115 above) 46.

121 O Williamson, 'Transaction Cost Economics and Organization Theory' in N J Smelser and R Swedberg (eds), *The Handbook of Economic Sociology* (Princeton/New York, Princeton University Press/Russell Sage, 1994) 77.

122 See G Teubner, 'Im blinden Fleck der Systeme: Die Hybridisierung des Vertrages' (1997) 3 *Soziale Systeme*, at 313; a good example is given by Teubner, 'Vertragswelten' (n 118 above) 249 *et seq*: 'When a medical operation is to be done, a technical project carried out or

III.2.(b) The Problem of Looped Reflexive Operations

Bringing in this 'social multi-dimensionality of the single contract'[123] makes it possible to reconstruct the specific problems that contractual networks cause in contract law doctrine. This is because it can then be seen that, in the functional systems of society, the contract contributes to the emergence of discourses that do not remain blocked at the level of simple interaction,[124] but sometimes reach a complexity that compels them to develop the capacity for reflection, ie, it consolidates them into reflexive (sub-) systems.[125] This is conceivable particularly in case of long-term contracts (franchise, just-in-time, joint venture, etc), in which the relationship between the parties is no longer marked by the boundedness and short-term nature of the spot transaction; these relationships then reveal more of the nature of close co-operation relationships. The (sub-) systems that derive from the structural coupling 'contract' then start to observe, or reflect, their environment, which means, in particular, that they anticipate the possible conflicts between themselves and the systems-in-their-environment. These conflicts are assessed in the relevant (sub-) system through reflection, with an eye to their consequences, and evaluated for possible internal steering corrections in response. If, now, several contracts each set off—within the functional systems through which they are linked—discourses that build up reflexive complexity, then it may come about that these discourses observe and reflexively take account of each other. In other words, different discourses become looped together, and these very discursive loops confront traditional contract law with hard, indeed, in part insoluble, problems. These problems may be described as follows.

On the legal system's internal screens, these reflexive loops appear not as such, but as something that has first to be 'translated' into the language of law. The analysis that we have performed on the recent case law on contractual networks has shown that the law reconstructs the reciprocal reflections that take place in other social systems, between discourses which were all initiated by *different* contracts, as a *contractual network* (and thus not as looped reflexive operations—which means something only to legal sociologists, not to lawyers). However, this reconstruction, which—in line with systems theory's basic rule—is an 'internal' reconstruction of the legal system, falls short in the sense that

a complex service provided, the contractual relation actualizes this potential and converts it into the mandatory structure of a social system, an obligatory discourse and the real performance of a social dynamic'.

[123] Teubner, 'Im blinden Fleck der Systeme' (n 122 above) 314.

[124] On this concept, see H Willke, *Systemtheorie I: Grundlagen* (Stuttgart, Lucius & Lucius, 2000) 68 *et seq.*

[125] See *ibid*, 96 *et seq.*

the legal system cannot grasp the reality of the operations that it observes in other systems: it does not know to which of the discourses involved in a contractual network it should assign a conflict arising within this network. This is because the participating discourses each observe the conflict from their own viewpoint, and bring it into their own *calculus*. Thus, the conflict is, as it were, 'present' in each of the discourses involved, something which, in the legal system, produces unintelligibility—law cannot see with the requisite precision whether the conflict belongs in the context of contract A, contract B or contract C, etc. It then diagnoses a 'contractual network', but without achieving any more than a labelling of the problem through this finding.

III.2.(c) The Paradoxes of Case Law

This can be shown from the example of BGE 121 III 310 presented above. It was unclear from a legal viewpoint whether the conflict (sparked off by the unfreezing, contrary to instructions, of the escrow account by Bank *Y* (recipient bank)) belonged in the context of the contract between Bank *Z* (sending bank) and Bank *Y*, or of the contract between *T* (principal mandator) and Bank *Z*. Ultimately, the answer was paradoxical: in neither, but in both! And this paradox can only be overcome by deploying it on a 'higher' level, namely, that of the linkage of legal transactions (which the Federal Court then did). The same picture is presented by BGE 115 II 452: The linkage of the agreements made it seem uncertain whether the termination of cession of premises in the clinic building to *X* was to be judged according to the co-operation contract or the tenancy agreement. This uncertainty is additionally underlined by the fact that *in casu* it could be argued that, in all cases, it was 'its own' rules that applied to the tenancy agreement (ie, Article 253 *et seq* CO), since the relevant Article 272 CO has a *mandatory* nature and prevents the parties from opting out. In the eyes of the Supreme Court, the 'attractive force' (the 'network' logic) of the co-operation contract was strong enough to rule out the application of mandatory tenancy law and hand the conflict over to the rules of the co-operation contract.[126]

III.3. 'Constitutionalising' Contractual Networks

III.3.(a) The Absence of Legal Rules

Can, then, the figure of the contractual network, derived from considerations of evolutionary theory, offer some help here? The decisive thing in

[126] See Amstutz, 'Vertragskollisionen' (n 108 above) 170.

this connection is to see that the network of contracts possesses 'constraints' that shift the 'meaning' of the overall picture onto an emergent level—the level of the system formed by the symbiosis of the contracts. Correspondingly, conflicts arising in this network should be approached at this 'higher' level, not at the level of the individual contracts, the relevance of each of which is, as we have said, *unclear* from the point of view of the law. But it is here that the problem lies: the overall picture has no order de jure, possesses no *legal* constitution that would enable a *legal* resolution of the conflict, which takes account of 'network' logic, to be found. The question thus arises as to how the combination of legal transactions can be assigned to some overall order.

Some advocate a consensus-based solution and assume a 'net contract' ('*Netzvertrag*') to exist behind the contracts in the network, pulling all the threads together, which all the 'network participants' have joined, through an (implicit) declaration of intent.[127] Others seek to apply company law or even group-of-companies law rules by analogy to the contractual network.[128] To date, the most differentiated and convincing attempt to handle combinations of contracts in legal terms aims at doing justice to the specificities of this arrangement by developing a special technique of attribution by:

1. designing enhanced loyalty duties to the network;
2. developing contractual patterns of liability among non-contract-partners, with the object of taking account legally of the differentiation into areas of competition and co-operation within the contractual network; and
3. selective double attribution of network acts to individual contractual partners and to the network as a whole ('network share liability'), so as to identify legal consequences appropriate to the network.[129]

The picture of the contractual network obtained here points to a different way of designing a 'network constitution'. This way is based on the same regularities (algorithms!) which, in the economy, determine the evolutionary formation of contractual networks.

[127] Rohe, 'Netzverträge' (n 103 above); W Möschel, 'Dogmatische Strukturen des bargeldlosen Zahlungsverkehrs' (1987) 186 *Archiv für die civilistische Praxis* 211.

[128] See the survey in G Teubner, *Netzwerk als Vertragsverbund: Virtuelle Unternehmen, Franchising, Just-in-Time in sozialwissenscaftlicher und juristischer Sicht* (Baden-Baden, Nomos, 2004) ch 2.

[129] *Ibid*, chs 3–6.

III.3.(b) Conflict of Laws Method

If it is true that the contractual network leads to a new, emergent order of expectations, to a 'higher' order which comes under 'network' logic, then we have to ask ourselves whether the rules which applied *ex lege* to the individual contracts in the combination have the potential to be 'extrapolated' to the whole network. The emergence of a 'higher' order of expectations would then correspond to the emergence of a 'higher' legal order, on the basis of the legal rules which apply to the individual contracts in the network. Specifically, the point would then be to derive an emergent legal order for the contractual network from the rules of classical law of contract. Instead of building a new constitution of the network from the ground up, using doctrinal elements hitherto unknown to the law of obligations, the norms 'incorporating' the individual contracts of the network would serve as the building blocks for a legal constitution for the whole complex.[130] The only question, then, is from which viewpoints this sort of network-oriented 'extrapolation' of classical contract law is to be undertaken. My suggestion, in a nutshell, is that subsuming 'network conflicts' under rules that 'incorporate' the individual contracts of the network means giving these rules a *second (emergent) dimension*. For them to reach this 'second' dimension, their applicability need not be governed by the usual criteria meant for bipolar contracts, but by a *new criterion of application*. One legal technique suited to providing such a criterion is the *conflict of laws method*.[131]

To explain this suggestion, I shall start with a comparison of the basic issues of the contractual network with those of conflict of laws. Clearly, with contractual networks, it is not a multinational but a *'multi-contract'* situation that is obtained. However, in both cases, we ultimately have to deal with the same type of legal problem: *by what 'governing law'* (in conflict of laws, which national legal system; in the case of connected contracts, which contract in the network) is the conflict at hand to be judged? For the contractual network, this problem can be reduced to the question of how conflicts which arise in the network can be assigned to one of the individual contracts which form the network by the criteria of 'network logic'. If such criteria could be developed, then, the norms

[130] This process of the constitution (in the active sense of the term: the activity of constituing) of the contractual network came about in this case on a pattern described by G Teubner, 'Globale Zivilverfassungen: Alternativen zur staatszentrierten Verfassungstheorie' (2003) 63 *Zeitschrift für ausländisches öffentliches Recht und Völkerrecht* 18: 'Constitution always starts as the linking of two real processes: from the viewpoint of law it is the production of legal norms intimately interwoven with basic structures of the social system; from the viewpoint of the constituted social system it is the production of basic structures of the social order, which at the same time inform the law and are in turn normed by the law'.

[131] For more detail on this, see Amstutz, 'Vertragskollisionen' (n 108 above) 170 *et seq*.

which apply at the level of individual contracts would be 'raised' to the 'higher' level of the contractual network and there—qua rule of conflict of laws—packaged into a legal constitution of the whole. One possible way of doing this would be to take inspiration from Schnitzer's doctrine of functional connection:

> What is decisive for classifying [a legal relation is] the *function* of this legal relation in society . . . since a legal relation orders rights and duties between people that have a functional meaning [ie, these rights and duties perform a function in a certain social context].[132] (emphasis added)

With regard to the contractual network, one would deduce from these considerations that, in order to assign a conflict to a particular contract building part of the network, the viewpoint of the *function* that this contract performs in the network has to be the guide. To put it another way, the sought after 'proper' criterion for articulating the conflict of laws rule would have to be the *capacity of the contractual network to accomplish its role (function) in the economy or society.* Correspondingly, this rule could be formulated to the effect that *conflicts in a contractual network come under the contract the rules of which, in the specific case, ensure the functionality of the network as such.*

III.3.(c) Network-Functional Criteria

Does this sort of rule shine through in the Federal Court's judgments? Should we seek to explain the doctrinally rather vague constructions in BGE 115 II 452 and 121 III 310 on this basis? In short, are these decisions the embryo of a new 'network' doctrine in the law of obligations? *Ex facto ius oritur?* One thing, at least, is certain: in the end, in BGE 115 II 452, the issue of termination of the tenancy was adjudicated by the rules which govern the co-operation contract. And in BGE 121 III 310, T's damage claim was deemed to be of *contractual* nature. This can only mean that the dispute that had arisen was settled according to the rule of either the main mandate (T / Bank Z) or the substitution mandate (Bank Z / Bank Y), so that, at least, one *conflict-of-laws* referral was made (even if it is not clear from reading the court's motivations which contract was specifically meant).

If one is prepared to follow this thesis and 'constitutionalise' contractual networks by using a functional conflict-of-laws rule in the sense described, then, admittedly, one has to ask what is, in practice, meant by 'functionality of the contractual network'. This is undoubtedly a question

[132] AF Schnitzer, 'Die funktionelle Anknüpfung im internationalen Vertragsrecht' in Rechts-, wirtschafts-, sozialwissenschaftliche Fakultät der Universität Freiburg (ed), *Festgabe für Wilhelm Schönenberger* (Freiburg i Ue, Universitätsverlag, 1969) 397.

to which no generalised answer is possible; presumably, reality has enormous numbers of types of contractual networks which function in different ways.[133] A phenomenological study of all these manifestations cannot be performed here. One can, however, show that, for individual combinations of contracts, the written law uses *network-functional criteria* to solve questions of the sort discussed here, and thus provide contractual networks with a constitution under the law of obligations.[134]

III.4.'Network-Functional' Calculus in Statutary Law of Contracts

This finding is interesting because it shows that the solution developed here fits flawlessly into the architecture of Swiss law of contract.[135] Yet, we cannot go into all the norms of Swiss law here. We shall take up only Article 262(3)[136] and Article 399(3) CO, which enable two different techniques for 'constitutionalising' the network, based on the conflict of laws mechanism described, to function. By Article 262(3) CO, the main lessor can hold not only the under-lessor (ie, his own tenant) but also the *sub-tenant* (not linked to him by any contract) directly to a use of the rented property in line with the *main tenancy contract*.[137] By Article 399(3) CO, again, in connection with mandate, in cases of substitution, the mandator can assert the claims, which the mandatary is entitled to

[133] See, for example, P Hessinger, Vernetzte Wirtschaft und ökonomische Entwicklung: Organisatorischer Wandel, institutionelle Einbettung, zivilgesellschaftliche Perspektive (Wiesbaden, Westdeutscher Verlag, 2001) 196 *et seq*.

[134] See Art 262(3), Art 268(2), Art 291(3), Art 299c, Art 399(3) CO and Art 21 KKG.

[135] In particular, the solution advocated here is not in contradiction with private autonomy. This point cannot of course be gone deeply into here, but let us say only: traditional legal theory bases the principle of the mutual independence of contracts in a contractual network on the principle of privity (for a nearly paradigmatic example see Cerutti, *Der Untervertrag* (n 50 above) 54 *et seq*, fn 214 *et seq*). In a very precise study of the subcontractor contract, Chaix, *Le contrat de sous-traitance en droit Suisse* (n 70 above) 91 *et seq*, has shown that this principle leads, in many cases, to unsatisfactory solutions, unacceptable in modern private law. If one also follows the thesis put forward here that the differentiation of society faces contract law with network constructions for which classical patterns in law of obligations no longer suffice, then this law must develop new answers. For these network constructions meet real needs in the life-world that the legal system has to do justice to (see, eg, W Schluep, 'Innominatverträge' in F Vischer (ed), Schweizerisches Privatrecht: Bd. VII/2: Obligationenrecht: Besondere Vertragsverhältnisse (Basel & Stuttgart, Helbing & Lichtenhahn), 1979) 798).

[136] Article 262(3) CO reads as follows: 'The lessee is responsible to the lessor for the sublessee not using the object differently from the use allowed to the lessee. The lessor may directly require this from the sublessee'.

[137] See Higi, 'Art. 253–265 OR' (n 55 above) 664, fn 27; D Lachat, 'Art. 262' in L Thévenoz and F Werro (eds), *Code des obligations I (Code des obligations art. 1–529; Loi sur le credit à la consummation, Loi sur les voyages à forfeit)* (Geneva, Helbing & Lichtenhahn, 2003) 1371, fn 7.

against the substitute, directly against the latter (with whom he has, of course, concluded no agreement).[138] Cerutti stresses out that these norms have the *common peculiarity* in

> that they grant the initial contracting party [the first link in the chain formed by the main contract and sub-contract] only those privileges regarded by the legislator as necessary for the given sub-contract.[139]

This raises the question of precisely what is 'necessary', or what the decisive *criterion* is for allocating rights and duties to positions within the network of contracts.

Looking first at Article 262(3) CO more closely, one is struck by the fact that the lessor is allowed to call on the sub-tenant to comply directly with end-use clauses in the main tenancy agreement, but is, at the same time, denied the right to require payment of the (sub-) rent.[140] Bringing in the *duty of care* makes the *network-functional* reason for this rule manifest. The tenancy network cannot, from its very design, have, as a consequence, the financial interests involved being placed in common. Its functionality, however, depends on the *suitability* of the rented property *for transfer*, which (in line with the still prevailing basic principle of the market society) is secured by the person who has the ownership of it, ie, the (main) lessor. Therefore, Article 262(3) CO serves to *spread the incentive to preserve the substance of the object transferred* network-wide, by letting the 'motor' of that incentive—property—'operate' in all the ramifications of the network.

A different 'network' logic runs through Article 399(3) CO[141]: the mandate is typified with regard to the mandatary's performance programme by *high indeterminacy*.[142] This is a corrolary of the fact that the mandatary is, as a rule, a highly specialised expert (patent lawyer, heart surgeon, etc), so that the mandator de facto often cannot, for lack of

[138] See W Fellmann, 'Art. 394–406 OR' in H Hausheer (ed), *Berner Kommentar: Das Obligationenrecht, Bd. VI/2. Abt./4 Teilbd.: Der einfache Auftrag* (Bern, Stämpfli, 1992) 537 *et seq*, fn 610 *et seq*, 577 *et seq*, fn 92 *et seq*, with references.

[139] Cerutti, *Der Untervertrag* (n 50 above) 39. It might further be stated that in both cases a 'linkage agreement' (see n 79 above) is lacking.

[140] Cerutti, *Der Untervertrag* (n 50 above) 39; Chaix, *Le contrat de sous-traitance en droit Suisse* (n 70 above) 205 *et seq*.

[141] As Chaix, *Le contrat de sous-traitance en droit Suisse* (n 70 above) 234 *et seq*, shows, the question of the purpose of Article 399(3) CO is still insufficiently illuminated in the Swiss literature; see Fellmann, (n 138 above) 577 N 93; Cerutti, *Der Untervertrag* (n 50 above) 45; P Derendinger, *Die Nicht- und die nicht richtige Erfüllung des einfachen Auftrages* (Freiburg i Ue, Universitätsverlag, 1988) 146 *et seq*; J Hofstetter, 'Der Auftrag und die Geschäftsführung ohne Auftrag' in W Wiegand (ed), *Schweizerisches Privatrecht: Bd. VII/6 Obligationenrecht—Besondere Vertragsverhältnisse* (Basel, Helbing & Lichtenhahn, 2000) 98.

[142] See F Werro, *Le mandat et ses effets: Une étude sur le contrat d'activité indèpendante selon le Code suisse des obligations: Analyse critique et comparative* (Freburg i Ue, Universitätsverlag, 1993) 192 *et seq*.

relevant knowledge, give that person substantive instructions. This shortfall in specificity is bridged by orienting the duties of performance for the contract to the mandator's interests. In substitution relationships, the indeterminacy described is intensified, in so far as the substitute's performance programme is not directly tied to the *mandator's interests.*[143] Article 399(3) CO remedies this by installing a *network-wide feedback mechanism*[144]: by giving the mandator direct access to the substitute, in order to enforce the obligations posited by the substitution contract (ie, 'sub-contract'), it places the *'incentives'* for those involved in the *network of successive mandates* in such a way that the substitute's performance programme is, as far as possible, oriented to the mandator's interests.[145]

The disclosure of the 'network-functional' calculus on which Article 262(3) and Article 399(3) CO are based opens up the possibility of understanding these provisions as norms of a network constitution. From the considerations presented, it follows in particular that both Article 262(3) and Article 399(3) CO build on the viewpoint of the *functionality of the contractual network*, whereas the concretisation of this feature occurs *differently* according to the specific functional mode of the 'network' concerned. While Article 262(3) CO is concerned with extending the main lessor's ownership position in the tenancy network, by 'locating' it in the main tenancy agreement, Article 399(3) CO aims at tying the substitute's performance programme 'located' in the sub-contract to the mandator's interests. And the respective constitutions of the tenancy or mandate network are structured differently accordingly: *Article 262(3) CO subordinates the debtor's position* (the sub-tenant's position) *to a contract* (the main tenancy agreement) *in which the debtor formally has no standing as a party. By contrast, Article 399(3) CO subordinates the creditor's position* (the mandator's position) *to a contract* (the substitution contract) *in which the creditor formally has no standing.*[146] This puts the judge, in every case, in a position in which, through the specific application of the network-oriented functionality criterion to the legal question to be assessed (eg for Article 262(3) CO, the utilisation of the sub-let property; and for Article

[143] To the point here is Werro, *ibid*, 191 N 558.

[144] Fellmann, 'Art. 394–406 OR' (n 138 above) 540 *et seq*, N 618 *et seq*, seems to argue in the same sense.

[145] In the same sense, Chaix, *Le contrat de sous-traitance en droit Suisse* (n 70 above) 237; this purpose orientation becomes clearly recognizable in the Federal Court's (correct) view in BGE 110 II 186 s. that the claims under Art 399(3) CO also embrace the right of recall pursuant to Art 404 CO; see Chaix, *Le contrat de sous-traitance en droit Suisse* (n 70 above) 209; Tercier, *Les contrats spéciaux* (n 98 above) 672, fn 4661; rejected in Fellmann, 'Art. 394–406 OR' (n 138 above) 580 N 103; Cerutti, *Der Untervertrag* (n 50 above) 40 and 119 *et seq*.

[146] Chaix, *Le contrat de sous-traitance en droit Suisse* (n 70 above) 185 *et seq* differentiates, as here, between 'effets négatifs du contrat' and 'effets positifs du contrat'.

399(3) CO, the carrying out of the substitute's performance programme), he or she can link up with the 'proper' contract (eg for Article 262(3) CO: the *main contract*; and for Article 399(3) CO: the *sub-contract*), and thus design an appropriate network constitution in law of contract.

Index

www.ingramcontent.com/pod-product-compliance
Ingram Content Group UK Ltd.
Pitfield, Milton Keynes, MK11 3LW, UK
UKHW020234290926
15470UKWH00002B/532

9 781841 139456